A Yankee Scholar in
Coastal South Carolina

A Yankee Scholar in Coastal South Carolina

William Francis Allen's Civil War Journals

Edited by James Robert Hester

The University of South Carolina Press

© 2015 University of South Carolina

Published by the University of South Carolina Press
Columbia, South Carolina 29208

www.sc.edu/uscpress

Manufactured in the United States of America

24 23 22 21 20 19 18 17 16 15   10 9 8 7 6 5 4 3 2 1

Library of Congress Cataloging-in-Publication Data can be found
at http://catalog.loc.gov/.

ISBN: 978-1-61117-496-0 (cloth)
ISBN: 978-1-61117-497-7 (ebook)

This book was printed on recycled paper with 30 percent
postconsumer waste content.

Contents

Illustrations

Preface

At 9:45 A.M., November 5, 1863, aboard the steamer *Arago* somewhere off Maryland's eastern shore, New Englander William Francis Allen set pen to paper, beginning the first of three journals that would cover his time in the South. Allen, his wife, Mary, and her cousin Caty Noyes were en route to St. Helena Island, South Carolina, to teach 150 contraband slaves from three plantations. These freedmen were part of approximately ten thousand who had been left behind on the Sea Islands after their masters fled in the wake of the Battle of Port Royal two years before.[1] Allen, who was from the Boston area, spent eight months (November 1863–July 1864) as a teacher on St. Helena, and, after the Civil War, he spent three months (April–July 1865) as acting superintendent of schools in Charleston. Between those assignments, he served five months (September 1864–February 1865) at Helena, Arkansas, as an agent of the Red Cross-like Western Sanitary Commission and superintendent of the freedmen's and refugees' schools.

Allen is best known today as the lead editor of the 1867 anthology *Slave Songs of the United States*.[2] He contributed about 30 of the 136 songs in the collection, and he wrote the introduction, which is largely devoted to a discussion of the music and language of the former slaves he encountered on St. Helena. My interest in Allen's writings began in the fall of 2009, when I began research on the origin of six songs in *Slave Songs* attributed to Augusta, Georgia, for which he was credited.[3] During the course of my research, I accumulated Allen's southern journals, his 1864–67 diaries, and a number of personal letters he wrote to family members in 1865–67. I was fortunate to have Dr. Lee Ann Caldwell, director of the Center for the Study of Georgia History at Georgia Regents University, as principal reader of my research paper. Dr. Caldwell continued to provide advice and encouragement as I prepared transcriptions of Allen's journals and diaries, which eventually led to this book.

Allen's writings from the South have attracted relatively little notice by scholars. The musicologist Dena Epstein cited musical examples from all three of his journals in *Sinful Tunes and Spirituals*, and the historian Willie Lee Rose drew on his St. Helena journal in discussing the 1864 land sale crisis in *Rehearsal for Reconstruction.* In addition, the education historian Gerald Robbins wrote a short 1965 article in the *History of Education Quarterly* chronicling Allen's experiences as a teacher on St. Helena.[4]

This book provides annotated transcriptions of Allen's St. Helena and Charleston journals, of which the most interesting aspect is his description of people he encountered. He named and described 188 former slaves of all ages who he came to know on St. Helena. He described a host of Northerners he met at both St. Helena and Charleston, ranging from fellow teachers to missionaries and abolitionists and military men—privates to generals—as well as officials of all stripes, including plantation superintendents and tax commissioners.

Allen's Charleston journal also recounted interviews with native Southerners, such as the Reverend Anthony Toomer Porter, an Episcopal cleric and ardent secessionist; Roswell T. Logan, associate editor of the *Charleston Daily News*; First Lieutenant Edmund Mazyck of the Confederate Army; and George Alfred Trenholm, the Confederacy's treasury secretary. In each case, Allen probed these men's thoughts about secession and slavery and their views about the South's prospects for rejoining the Union.

Some of what Allen wrote in his journals was mundane. He described the flora of St. Helena, and he wrote about gardening and repairs he made to the Captain John Big House, where he lived. But he was a trained historian, able to understand the changes going on around him, and he brought that training to bear in discussing the attitudes and habits of the freedmen and their potential for education and employment in a free labor economy. He wrote about military and government policies and their effects, positive and negative. He was especially interested in labor arrangements and the distribution of confiscated lands. And he recorded firsthand evaluations of the South's prospects for Reconstruction.

Above all, Allen was a scholar. His scholarly qualities were clearly displayed in a series of essays he wrote over the course of the war for the *Christian Examiner* and in a series of letters he wrote at war's end for the newly inaugurated magazine the *Nation*. These essays and letters demonstrate the reach of his scholarship. He often buttressed his arguments with examples from classical history and observations from his journals. His treatment of these materials shows that his journals were more than quaint travelogues.

Possibly because of his tight, academic reasoning, Allen's published writings have a modern feel. He had biases. He was a New Englander, and he had a New Englander's faith in the Yankee work ethic and the virtues of free labor. He was a moderate in his stances on black suffrage and reconstruction. These perspectives undoubtedly colored his writings, just as the perspectives of modern historians color theirs. He had the "disadvantage" of living the events he chronicled, without the "advantage" of hindsight. Still, one senses that his reasoning came off well, even when he projected the outcome of complex events, such as the struggle for equal rights for blacks. When compared with present-day conclusions, such as those of Eric Foner's *Reconstruction*,[5] Allen's forecasts fare well.

Allen's life was briefly summarized in an entry in the 1911 edition of the *Encyclopedia Britannica*:

> ALLEN, WILLIAM FRANCIS (1830–1889), American classical scholar, was born at Northborough, Massachusetts, on the 5th of September 1830. He graduated at Harvard College in 1851 and subsequently devoted himself almost entirely to literary work and teaching. In 1867 he became professor of ancient languages and history (afterwards Latin language and Roman history) in the University of Wisconsin. He died in December 1889. His contributions to classical literature chiefly consist of schoolbooks published in the Allen (his brother) and Greenough series. The *Collection of Slave Songs* (1867), of which he was joint-editor, was the first work of the kind ever published.

The scholarly bent of mind that Allen brought to his work in South Carolina is the focus here. The pursuit of knowledge characterized his life from the time, as a boy, he began to explore history books in his father's library through his tenure as a professor at the University of Wisconsin.[6] He was an unpretentious man who wrote out his thoughts in an unpresuming, scholarly way. Even his informal journals evidence humane thoughtfulness. A marble tablet in Allen's honor at the First Unitarian Church of Madison, Wisconsin, portrays his spirit:

> A man of varied, exact, and broad scholarship.
> A teacher of creative power and original methods.
> A wise, sincere, and generous friend.
> A citizen, active and efficient in all movements for
> Education, Reform, and Philanthropy.
> A Lover of Flowers, Poetry, and Music.

A Note on the
Transcriptions and Sources

The Wisconsin Historical Society (WHS) holds many of William Allen's writings in a collection titled William F. Allen Family Papers. The interest here is Allen's writings during two stays in South Carolina: on St. Helena Island and in Charleston. The St. Helena writings consist of a typescript journal and his 1864 manuscript diary. (It is likely that Allen's daughter or his wife typed his journal.) The Charleston writings consist of a manuscript journal and his 1865 manuscript diary.[1]

Allen wrote his journals, a few sheets at a time, as letters to be circulated among family and friends. They consist of descriptions of people, places, and events, which he mailed home to West Newton, Massachusetts. His 1864 and 1865 diaries were written in pocket-size books having 3½- by 5½-inch leaves. Each page contained three dated blocks in which he jotted down items of interest, including the weather, where he went, whom he saw, letters he sent and received, and incidental reminders. Frequently he made note of things he read.

Allen's St. Helena journal begins on November 5, 1863, the day after he departed New York Harbor for the Sea Islands. It concludes on July 15, 1864, when he recorded his landing in New York the previous day. The typescript consists of 8½- by 11-inch sheets. The first page is unnumbered, and subsequent pages are numbered 2 through 231, with a partial page numbered 62a, a page numbered 94A, and two pages numbered 155, making 234 pages total. The double-spaced text has the appearance of having been produced on a vintage typewriter. Sheets up to page 140 are annotated with handwritten marginal comments (possibly by Allen's daughter or his wife). Twenty sheets, scattered through the document, contain music staves with hand-drawn music symbols and (mostly) handwritten lyrics. Two songs contain typewritten lyrics, and one contains mixed hand- and typewritten lyrics. There are occasional notations, both hand- and typewritten, indicating where maps or illustrations were to be inserted.

The St. Helena journal transcription presented here omits three features of the typescript: (1) marginal notes and page numbers; (2) music symbols, although lyrics are retained; and (3) the hand-drawn maps. Where map directions help clarify the text, location numbers referring to the enclosed Port Royal (P.R.) Map and Key are provided.[2] For example, the route from the John Fripp Big House to Coffin Point is No. 8 to No. 12 on the map.

Allen's Charleston journal begins on April 14, 1865, the day of the flag-raising ceremony at Fort Sumter, and it concludes on July 14 as he contemplated returning north. It consists of sixty-four 4¾- by 7½-inch handwritten pages. The first page is unnumbered, with subsequent pages numbered 2 through 64. Allen's handwriting is usually legible. One leaf contains a map of Charleston, with handwritten inscriptions, and one contains the song "Nobody Knows the Trouble I See" with handwritten lyrics and musical notation.

Neither line breaks nor spatial arrangements in either journal are retained here, except approximate spatial arrangements of song lyrics in the St. Helena journal. Foreign words are rendered in italics. Allen's nonstandard grammar is retained. For example, he uses the word "class" in a distributive sense ("the class are"). This also applies to his use of adverbial forms in place of adjectival forms ("He is quite miserably"). His frequent use of hyphenated words ("to-day") has been retained, as has his use of semicolons where commas would perhaps be indicated.

The St. Helena text has been lightly edited to eliminate obvious typographical errors. Strikethroughs and underlines have been eliminated in both journals. And both have been paragraphed freely to enhance readability. Allen often used a dash before a sentence, instead of beginning a new paragraph. In these cases, especially, paragraphs have been supplied.

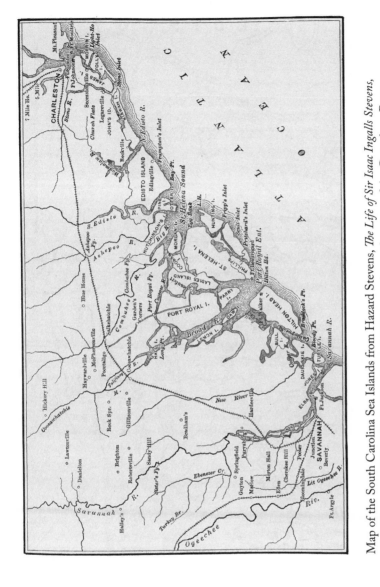

Map of the South Carolina Sea Islands from Hazard Stevens, *The Life of Sir Isaac Ingalls Stevens*, vol. 2 (Boston and New York: Houghton, Mifflin, 1900), 352. Courtesy of the Gutenberg Press.

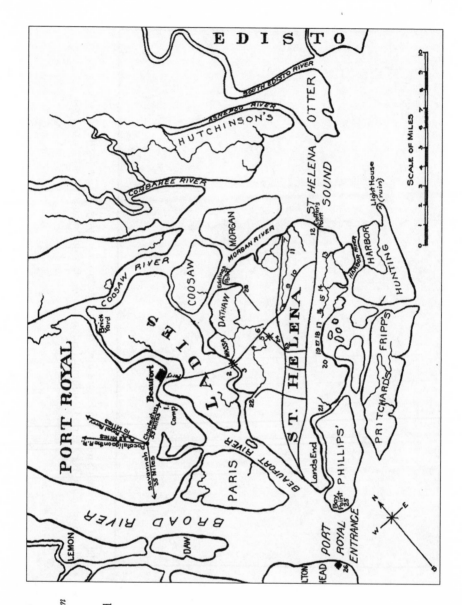

Port Royal Map and Key adapted from Elizabeth Ware Pearson, *Letters from Port Royal.* According to local lore, the "R.'s" designation for the Reverend Robert Fuller Place (No. 4) refers to (T. Edwin) Ruggles, its Gideonite superintendent.

Plantation Names and Owners	Number
Cherry Hill (T. A. Coffin)	16
Coffin's Point (T. A. Coffin)	12
Corner (J. B. Fripp)	5
Eustis	2
Edgar Fripp [(Seaside Place)]	20
Hamilton Fripp	10
Capt. John Fripp (Homestead) [(Big House)]	8
Capt. Oliver Fripp	22
Thomas B. Fripp [(Cedar Grove)]	9
Fripp Point [(William Fripp)]	11
Frogmore (T. A. Coffin)	19
Rev. Robert Fuller ("R.'s")	4
Hope Place (Alvirah Fripp)	18
Dr. Jenkins	21
Mary Jenkins	28

Plantation Names and Owners	Number
Martha E. McTureous	14
James McTureous	15
Mulberry Hill (John Fripp)	17
The Oaks (Pope)	3
Oakland	6
Pine Grove ([William] Fripp)	13
Smith	1
Dr. White [(Woodlands)]	27
Other Sites	
Brick Church (Baptist)	24
White Church (Episcopal)	23
St. Helena Village [and nearby T. J. Fripp Place]	7
Fort Walker	26
Fort Beauregard	25
Camp of the 1st S.C. Volunteers (Colonel Higginson)	1

Abbreviations

Acronym	Organization	Headquarters
ABMU	American Baptist Missionary Union	Boston
AMA	American Missionary Association	New York
NEFAS	New England Freedmen's Aid Society	Boston
NFRA	National Freedman's Relief Association	New York City
PRRC	Port Royal Relief Committee	Philadelphia
USCT	United States Colored Troops	

Introduction

I have never, in Johns Hopkins or elsewhere, seen his equal as a scholar.

Ray Allen Billington, *Frederick Jackson Turner: Historian, Scholar, Teacher*

The year 1830 was a time of expansive optimism in peaceful New England. As Thomas Nichols put it, "Every boy knew that . . . there was nothing to hinder him from being President; all he had to do was to learn."[1] That year, four hundred miles to the southwest, in Washington, D.C., President Andrew Jackson was in the middle of his first term. Cotton was king, and the "darkies" were at work in the fields of St. Helena Island, South Carolina, singing their "peculiar" songs in the quarters. And yet, the Nat Turner Rebellion was only a year away, and South Carolina, led by Vice President John C. Calhoun, was chafing under the hated tariff that would prompt the Nullification Crisis two years later. In the North, abolition sentiments were beginning to coalesce around Boston; Garrison's antislavery *Liberator* was only months from its first issue, and the abolition leader Wendell Phillips was a student at Harvard Law School. Far in the west, steamboats loaded with cotton, rice, timber, tobacco, and molasses plied the Mississippi around Natchez and Vicksburg, Mississippi, and Helena, Arkansas. Throughout the country, the Second Great Awakening was in flower; temperance was the cause of the day, and Emerson's "Nature," the clarion call of transcendentalists, was six years away.[2]

William Francis Allen was born September 5, 1830, thirty-five miles west of Boston in Northborough, Massachusetts, where his father was minister of the Unitarian church.[3] He was the youngest in a close family of three sisters and four brothers. His parents, Joseph Allen and Lucy Clarke Ware, were from families whose roots in Massachusetts went back two hundred years. Allen demonstrated interests in music, literature, history, and politics from a young age. According to his sister, singing came as naturally to him at age three as speaking. He wrote a play, a tragedy with a fully developed plot, at age six. As a child, he made lists of kings and dates and battles. "His interest in politics," wrote his sister "was awakened during the famous Harrison campaign [the 1840 presidential campaign of William Henry Harrison], when he was ten years old, and it grew with his love of History. He wrote a political song to be sung at a Log Cabin meeting that year."[4]

Allen was educated until age fourteen in the parsonage school maintained by his parents. That schooling, plus a year at the Roxbury Latin School,[5] prepared him for college. In 1847 he entered Harvard College, where he studied philology and the classics, graduating in 1851. He was elected to the Harvard Alpha Chapter of Phi Beta Kappa in 1858. By the time he finished college, he had become proficient at sight singing and at playing flute and piano, skills he used to preserve slave songs he was to hear in the South. While at Harvard, he taught school in Lancaster and Fitchburg, Massachusetts, during the winter months. After Harvard, he taught privately for three years in the home of Martha Brooks Waller in New York City.[6] While in New York, he indulged his passion for the arts, often attending galleries, operas, and concerts.

Like many others of his time and place, Allen was drawn to the precepts of transcendentalism. It does not stretch credulity to believe Allen was influenced by Ralph Waldo Emerson's "The American Scholar," which espoused the belief that modern scholars should reject old concepts and think for themselves—becoming not mere thinkers but "Men Thinking."[7] Emerson's notion of drawing ideas from nature and the world would have been especially appealing to him. Allen had briefly thought of entering the Unitarian ministry, but his transcendentalist sympathies and his admiration of Theodore Parker,[8] toward whom the Unitarian clergy was hostile, may have dissuaded him. Instead, he set his sights on the life of a scholar, and he determined to further his education in Europe. In deciding on such a course, he may have been following the spirit of the transcendentalist William Henry Channing's "My Symphony," which doubtless would have appealed to him: "To live content with small means; to seek elegance rather than luxury, and refinement rather than fashion; to be worthy, not respectable, and wealthy, not rich; to listen to stars and birds, babes and sages, with open heart; to study hard; to think quietly, act frankly, talk gently, await occasions, hurry never; in a word, to let the spiritual, unbidden and unconscious, grow up through the common—this is my symphony."[9]

Allen embarked for Europe two days after his twenty-fourth birthday, on September 7, 1854. His travels took him to England, Germany, Italy, Greece, and France. He attended the Universities of Berlin and Göttingen. At Göttingen, he absorbed Professor Arnold Heeren's approach to the study of ancient history.[10] Allen continued to refine and develop Heeren's ideas throughout his life. In late October 1855, Allen left Göttingen for Rome, where he remained through mid-February 1856, imagining the city as it had been under the

Caesars. After excursions to Greece and France and a visit to London, he returned home in mid-June 1856.

Arriving in Massachusetts, Allen moved to the village of West Newton, eleven miles west of Boston, where he became associate principal of the West Newton English and Classical School, which his cousin Nathaniel Allen had founded in 1854.[11] It was at the School that he met student Mary Lambert,[12] whom he married on July 2, 1862. He remained at West Newton for seven years, teaching, studying, and refining the principles of historical research he had learned in Germany. In his biography of Allen, Owen Stearns noted that "Allen was busy in the years 1856–63 reading, reviewing, and writing about contemporary scholarship. . . . He read widely and well in these years, giving focus to his knowledge with . . . critical and often exhaustive reviews."[13]

In the meantime, the clouds of war had gathered and broken in the South, and more and more Northern men were called to the fray. It is likely that Allen would have remained in West Newton except for the Military Draft Act passed by Congress on March 3, 1863. Shortly thereafter, he arranged for an appointment as a teacher of the freedmen on St. Helena Island, South Carolina. He later told the freedmen there "how I was drafted myself." If nothing else, the timing of Allen's decision to go to the South points to his having received a draft notice.[14]

St. Helena is one of the Sea Islands located below Charleston. (See map of the South Carolina Sea Islands.) The Islands, with their plantations and slaves, had fallen into Union hands in November 1861 following the Battle of Port Royal.[15] The sudden capture of the islands and the equally sudden departure of the former landowners left behind about ten thousand slaves, who presented an immediate humanitarian and logistical problem for the occupying military commanders. In Washington, the joint problem of abandoned lands and abandoned slaves was construed as an issue of unpaid taxes on the part of absentee landowners. As a tax issue, it was turned over to Treasury Secretary Salmon P. Chase. Chase's first action was to dispatch cotton agents to Port Royal to dispose of the bumper crop of cotton left behind on wharves and in warehouses by the departing Southerners. Subsequently, Chase launched an ambitious program, called the Port Royal Experiment, with the dual aims of restoring cotton production on the Sea Islands and raising the condition of the freed slaves.[16] With the eager assistance of antislavery and religious organizations from Boston, New York, and Philadelphia, the effort developed rapidly, and the first group of fifty-three plantation superintendents, teachers, and missionaries departed for the Port Royal Islands aboard the *Atlantic* on March 3, 1862.

Allen's trip to St. Helena twenty months later was sponsored by the New England Freedmen's Aid Society (NEFAS), one of several aid organizations that sent representatives to the South.[17] Collectively, the members of this relatively small number of teachers, plantation managers, and missionaries were called "Gideonites," after Gideon's band of three hundred in the Bible.[18] Although older than most Gideonites, Allen was, nevertheless, a prime example of the Boston branch of the band—well educated and drawn from a solid antislavery background. By training and temperament, Allen would prove to be an apt observer of the former slaves, among whom he would spend eight months. He was interested in their music, language, and culture and in their relationships with one another as well as with outsiders. He also contemplated their prospects for joining a free workforce and eventually becoming citizens and voters.

William and Mary Allen left New York for St. Helena, with Mary's cousin Caty Noyes,[19] on November 4, 1863. Allen's first cousins, Charley and Harriet Ware,[20] lived at Coffin Point on the island, about three miles from the John Fripp Big House, where he was to live. (See Port Royal Map and Key [Nos. 12 and 8].) Charley was the plantation superintendent at Coffin Point, and Harriet taught school there. They had come to St. Helena a year and a half before Allen arrived, and they had already absorbed a good deal of the slave culture, especially slave songs. (Charley eventually contributed about half of the songs in *Slave Songs of the United States*.)[21] Doubtless, the Allens and the Wares shared many enjoyable evenings among themselves and with others, discussing the music they found so fascinating and recounting experiences of their day among the freedmen.

Although Allen came south under the auspices of the New England Freedmen's Aid Society, he was in the direct employ of Edward Philbrick. Philbrick, a successful Boston engineer and architect with strong antislavery credentials, was one of the original Gideonites who came down on the *Atlantic*. After the 1862 cotton season, in which cotton production had failed for a host of reasons, Philbrick determined to try a different approach during the 1863 season. His idea was to produce cotton using nonslave, paid labor on plantations in the hands of private owners. Accordingly, in March 1863, he purchased about eight thousand acres on St. Helena and neighboring islands with the intent of placing them into cotton production.[22] Besides hiring superintendents to oversee the agricultural work, Philbrick hired teachers to attend to the education of the former slaves in his charge and their children. The Allens were perhaps the last teachers to join Philbrick's enterprise.

Besides teaching, Allen came to St. Helena with a variety of interests, including the freedmen themselves.[23] He had read newspapers and periodicals, many of which had covered the "contraband," as slaves under Union protection were called, intensely. It is also likely that he had had communication about the freedmen from his cousins Charley and Harriet Ware, who preceded him. Although he had notions about the contraband before he arrived on St. Helena, given his temperament it is unlikely that his preconceptions were of a sentimental sort or that they were inflexibly held. On the voyage, he took walks on deck, engaging in the first of many discussions with Edward Philbrick to get a sense of affairs on the island and the condition of the freedmen there.[24]

Allen got his first close look at a former slave on Lady's Island on November 9, 1863, when "there appeared a rickety old covered buggy with the top down" driven by a "comical little darkey" taking his party to Coffin Point on St. Helena. He recorded his first impression of the freedmen on the evening of November 10 in the cozy confines of the Coffin Point plantation house he shared temporarily with his cousins. Writing with no hint of surprise or irony, he found the freedmen to be "human beings, neither more nor less." He amended his assessment of the freedmen about halfway through his stay on St. Helena, when he wrote, "here I find the people so much less degraded that I expected, and the barbarities [of slavery] so much greater than I supposed, that I have been led to place more stress upon them than I ever did before."[25]

Those first days on St. Helena were spent meeting fellow Gideonites,[26] exploring the plantations in the vicinity, and getting a feel for how things had been run under their former owners. Allen first went to the fields at Coffin Point on November 11, 1863, to learn about the work of growing cotton. It was then he began to form an opinion about the freedmen's capacity to compete in a free labor market and their readiness to farm their own lands. On November 15, the first Sunday after arriving, Allen spent the morning in his usual pastime, reading. About midday, he, Mary, Caty, and Rufus Winsor, Philbrick's clerk, went to the praise house in the quarters, where he heard slave singing for the first time. He had read about slave songs the previous summer, but nothing had prepared him for the actual sound of the singing.[27]

Allen spent about a week unpacking and repairing the rundown John Fripp Big House where he, Mary, and Caty lived and held school. During that time, he also made forays on horseback into the neighborhood to become familiar with the island. In those early weeks, he had a chance to see how the freedmen handled money in Philbrick's store. The Allens moved into the Big House on November 23, 1863, and a few days later they celebrated their first holiday on the island. That Thanksgiving was a happy one for the extended group of Gideonites who gathered at Coffin Point for fellowship and dinner. Among those in attendance was Captain Edward W. Hooper, who was "practically the head of the Freedmen's department," from whom Allen was to learn much about the island and its inhabitants.[28]

Once, Allen met a woman in the "long pasture." After recounting their exchange, which he struggled to follow, he concluded, "I've only picked up a few expressions and idioms so far, but hope to study their grammar and vocabulary more closely—it is really worthwhile as a study in linguistics."[29] Much of his journal over the following eight months would be taken up with descriptions of the freedmen's language (Gullah) and their songs. Here, in an unexpected place, Allen's scholarship, linguistic skills, and musical training came fully into play. They served him—and posterity—well.

Allen's school got "under weigh," as he termed it, about the first of December 1863. The Allens were to teach children and adults from three of Philbrick's plantations: John Fripp, Mulberry Hill, and Cherry Hill, but children from Hope Place came so often that they were included as well. They soon settled into a more or less routine schedule, punctuated by Christmas celebrations, periodic scares due to soldiers looking for men to draft, and turmoil over land sales.[30] Through it all they had to deal with the constant problem of erratic attendance by adults and children alike.

In the seven months he taught on St. Helena, Allen was able to impart to the freedmen in his charge a sparse ability to read, a few multiplication tables, and a little geography. Measured in these terms, his stay on St. Helena might be deemed a failure, but the scholar in Allen was also at work. In anthropological terms, he had been, in effect, collecting field data for study. As Frankenburger noted, "Here was an opportunity for the historian to note the decay of the old order of things and the rise of the new."[31] He also maintained an energetic reading regimen during this time, perusing everything from newspapers to volumes on Roman history.[32] On January 1, 1864, Allen began studying William Grant Sewell's book on free labor in the West Indies, thus beginning preparation for his essay "The Freedmen and Free Labor in the South," for the *Christian Examiner.*[33] Comparing references in the essay shows that about half of Allen's readings from January through mid March were devoted to research for the essay.

During this time, Allen continued to hone his assessment of the freedmen. On June 3, 1864, he noted that the freedmen "are learning habits of independence a great deal faster, at any rate, than there is any notion of at the North." This observation may have been prompted by an exchange he had two days earlier with some of the men, who were dissatisfied with their pay and chafing at not being permitted to lay claim to the land they worked. When Allen reminded them that the land belonged to Mr. Philbrick, one shot back, "Man! Don't talk 'bout Mr. Philbrick lan'. Mr. Philbrick no right to de lan'."[34] The freedmen were, indeed, learning independence, and they were nurturing expectations that, for the most part, were to be disappointed.

Allen remained on St. Helena Island through June 1864, teaching, observing, and absorbing impressions. He interacted often with the island inhabitants, with fellow Gideonites, and with outsiders, civilian and military. Mary and Caty left the island for the North aboard the steam transport *Fulton* on May 30. Allen followed them on the propeller ship *Dudley Buck* on July 9. Before leaving, however, he recorded his impressions of the freedmen once again:

It seems evident that a slave population has been turned into a free peasantry very rapidly and completely. The community is entirely self-supporting and prosperous, and has advanced in the path of independence much more rapidly and further than is generally supposed at the North. I think they have outgrown the admirable system (admirable for a temporary one) which has been in operation here, and that another year it will be much better—probably unavoidable, at any rate—to give up this transitional, quasi-dependent relation, and establish things on a more permanent basis, and on the principle of rendering labor wholly independent of capital. Probably by another year the homesteads, at least, will be secured to all the people. Peasantry is the proper word to apply to these people in their present condition. Their industry is independent, and they are wholly free, but still morally dependent and very ignorant and degraded. It will be a delicate question how fast and in what way to raise them from the condition of peasants to full citizenship, and some of the tendencies and influences at work are not of a healthy and promising character. There is too much sentimentality and theorizing at head-quarters, and a desire to push things, which will make it hard to secure steady and conservative progress.[35]

Allen's St. Helena journal ended eight months and ten days after he departed from New York, when he noted, on July 15, 1864, his arrival there the previous day. He had left St. Helena probably not knowing that Mary was pregnant. Exactly when he realized that fact was not reflected in his diary, probably because of his settled conviction that "A diary is for facts, and not for sentiment."[36]

Back home in West Newton, Allen spent the next month reading, writing, and visiting with family and friends. On July 25, 1864, he went into Boston to see Dr. William Greenleaf Eliot, commissioner of the Western Sanitary Commission. Then, on August 12, he received a telegram from James Yeatman, president of the Commission, inviting him to come to St. Louis for a job.[37] Allen telegraphed Yeatman, accepting the job, the following day. On September 8, Allen's father drove him to his boyhood home of Northborough, where he spent three days visiting family and friends. He traveled thence by train to Troy, New York, by way of South Acton, Massachusetts, and Keene, New Hampshire. And, on September 13, he took the train to Detroit, Chicago, and St. Louis, arriving at his destination about midnight September 14.

At St. Louis, Yeatman assigned Allen to the Mississippi River port town of Helena, Arkansas. The city had fallen into Union hands early in the war and beginning in July 1862 was used as a supply center. Health conditions there were deplorable. When Allen arrived it was, in Stearns's words, "a malarial pest-hole teeming with hundreds of freedmen and disease-ridden 'white trash'."[38] Allen spent the next four and a half months distributing clothing, foodstuffs, and other necessities in refugee and military camps and hospitals. In addition to humanitarian duties, Colonel John Eaton[39] appointed Allen Superintendent of the Colored Schools effective October 28, 1864. Thereafter, he had the oversight of four schools for children, and he opened a night school for adults, more than half of whom were soldiers. On January 18, 1865, he wrote a report summarizing his work for Colonel Eaton and prepared for his return to Massachusetts. He left Helena on January 28, returning by way of Memphis, Cincinnati, Cleveland, Buffalo, and Albany.

Allen reached West Newton on February 4, 1865, where he enjoyed family and friends. Mary safely delivered a daughter, Katharine, on February 17, but her condition soon deteriorated. Her health ebbed for a month, and she died on March 23. Allen spent the days after Mary's death with family, writing letters and attending to her things. After his wife's death, he soon returned to writing for publication. He prepared an essay, "Free Labor in Louisiana," for the *Christian Examiner*.[40] This essay was a short (sixteen versus thirty-one pages) update of his previous essay, "The Freedmen and Free Labor in the South." Unlike in the May 1864 piece he did for the *Examiner*, there was no correlation between his readings and the essay. Instead, it was based on his knowledge of changing events during the intervening year and his experiences in Arkansas.

Although there was no indication in his diary, Allen had probably determined to accept a job in South Carolina before Katharine was born. He had visited NEFAS secretary Hannah Stevenson[41] in Boston on February 13, 1865, and again on March 6, at which time the position of assistant superintendent of schools in Charleston was probably offered to him. He exchanged several letters with Miss Stevenson, and he called on her again on March 28, five days after Mary's death. That afternoon he went to Dorchester for a nurse, presumably for Katharine, and the following day he visited Miss Stevenson once again, this time with his seventeen-year-old niece, Gertrude,[42] who accompanied him to Charleston. Apparently, Allen left Katharine in the care of the nurse at Mary's parents' home.[43] He and Gertrude departed New York Harbor on April 7 aboard the *Creole*. Also in Allen's care was a bevy of NEFAS teachers bound for Hilton Head and Charleston.

Allen arrived in Charleston via Hilton Head on April 13, 1865, in time for the large influx of people who had come for the flag-raising ceremony at Fort Sumter the following day. He resumed his journal the next day, explaining that he had forgone the ceremony to avoid the crowds. Unknown to Allen, President Lincoln was shot that evening. On April 19, he wrote, "We received the terrible news today of Mr. Lincoln's assassination, and it has thrown a gloom over the city—for if any rejoice, it must be in secret."[44]

Allen soon settled into his duties as assistant superintendent of schools under Superintendent James Redpath.[45] Because Redpath was preoccupied with other matters, the management of the schools fell almost wholly to Allen. Under him were eight public schools, four night schools, and a normal (teacher training) school. All totaled, there were ninety teachers and four thousand students in the school system.[46] Allen's days in Charleston were a whirr of activity, visiting schools, making arrangements for classrooms, and attending to scores of other details. In the evenings, he and Gertrude often visited around town. He also attended Unitarian meetings, and on occasions he drilled with a colored Home Guard in which he had been appointed first lieutenant. And, of course, he read widely and wrote letters. Tragically, on June 3, 1865, Gertrude became ill with a fever, and on Saturday, June 10, she died. On the Monday following Gertrude's death, Allen resumed his busy schedule. He wrote letters that week to his brother Prentiss, Gertrude's father, and to other family members, but otherwise he kept up a normal routine.

Allen's experiences in Charleston were radically different from those he had had on St. Helena Island. The war was over, and amid the postwar bustle he came into contact with a wider range of people.[47] There were teachers and students, Freedmen's Bureau agents and high-ranking military officers, church leaders and demagogues, freedmen and freemen, Unionists and former Confederates. The Confederates, however, most arrested his attention. At the end of his stay, Allen was weighing the possibility of returning to Charleston in the fall, and he delayed his return to the North for more than a month to form a better assessment of Southern opinion. He had met a few disagreeable former Confederates at a "Reconstruction" meeting at Hibernian Hall on May 11, 1865, but he had a pleasant meeting with the Reverend Toomer Porter, "a strong secessionist," on June 30. It seems that the Reverend Porter took the initiative to call on Allen, but what prompted the call Allen did not say; their exchange was cordial, however. He came in contact with more former Confederates and was able to glimpse the interior of South Carolina during an extended trip to Columbia over the Fourth of July.[48] On the train from Charleston to Orangeburg, he engaged in an extended conversation with First Lieutenant Edmund Mazyck of Goose Creek, South Carolina, and two other Confederate officers who had recently been released from imprisonment at Fort Delaware.

On the overland trip between Orangeburg and Columbia, his party stayed over in the home of Walter and Mary Cupp, whom the war had driven from their home in northern Virginia; they were later caught up in Sherman's march through South Carolina. At the Cupps' home Allen was encouraged to see bands of homeward-bound Confederate soldiers pass by occupying Union troops as peacefully as if the war had never occurred. He met numerous blacks at the Independence Day celebration in Columbia, where he got a firsthand look at the devastation wreaked by Sherman. He spent the night there with a Mr. Taylor, a former slave whose master had left him a house.[49]

On his return from Columbia, Allen paused at Orangeburg on July 9, 1865, to meet Captain Charles Soule and Major Calvin Montague, the Freedmen's Bureau agents who administered labor contracts in the midstate region. Allen's interest in the contract system stemmed not simply from an academic interest in free labor but from personal interest. He wrote his sister shortly after to tell her that "I have been waiting quietly here [West Newton] for matters to be decided in the Freedmen's Bureau &c., so as to know what I shall do myself."[50] Apparently, Allen had applied for a job with the Freedmen's Bureau, perhaps through General Alfred Hartwell, a fellow Harvard graduate. Although no job offer came about, the possibility explains his interest in labor contracts and the attitudes of South Carolinians.

On the train from Orangeburg to Charleston, Allen shared a car with George Trenholm, the treasury secretary of the Confederacy, with whom he spoke about slavery, the rebellion, and reconstruction. Trenholm and Allen engaged in a free discussion, with which Allen was pleased. On the subject of slavery, for instance, he wrote of Trenholm: "As to slavery, altho' he believed it a divinely ordained institution, he not only acquiesces in its overthrow, but would oppose any attempt to revive or prolong it. He had for years never expected any other termination of the question—'it was a religious faith with us, and it was the same with you; and it could not be settled except by the sword.' And now it is settled once for all."[51]

Allen recounted his experiences during his trip to Columbia in correspondence to the recently inaugurated biweekly magazine the *Nation*. The first issue of the magazine came out on July 6, 1865. The fourth issue, on July 27, contained a set of three letters by Allen, writing under the pen name Marcel. The set of letters was fittingly titled "A Trip in South Carolina." The first one covered his trip from Charleston to Columbia. In it he remarked on how quickly tranquility had settled over the countryside after Sherman's march through it. He praised the blacks of Columbia for the decorum with which their Fourth of July celebration had been carried off. The second letter, written during his layover in Orangeburg on the return trip, recounted the progress South Carolinians had seemingly made in renouncing slavery and secession—especially in interior towns such as Abbeville, which had issued a "manifesto" professing loyalty and requesting the restoration of local civil authority. While Allen applauded this development, he pointed out that much of the change of heart was the result of the presence of Union occupation forces in locales such as Newberry, Orangeburg, and Columbia. In the third letter, written from Charleston after his return, Allen contrasted postwar conditions in the upper and middle districts of the South Carolina with those in the low country. He believed that the prospects for early recovery were better in the upstate, which had been less dependent on slavery, than in the low country with its impotent slavocracy, bereft of its accustomed labor force.[52]

In the short time before he departed Charleston for the North, Allen availed himself of two occasions that provided him with fodder for other letters to the *Nation*. On July 16 he met with a group of native South Carolinians, including Roswell T. Logan, associate editor of the *Charleston Daily News*. Over tea, he engaged the group in a wide-ranging discussion about the attitude of Carolinians in the aftermath of the war. They discussed the readiness of the state to return to the Union and to give up the notion of reviving slavery. They touched on free labor and the prospects for blacks under such a system. They explored the shift in agricultural practice from large plantations to small farms. They discussed the "safety" of a too-rapid return to civil governance and whether such a return would prolong the disenfranchisement of the freedmen. Logan was adamant in opposing governance by outsiders.

The second occasion of which Allen availed himself took place on July 18, 1865, when he made a foray aboard a "steam flat" to James and Johns Islands to inquire about the progress of blacks, who were farming the land under General Sherman's Special Field Orders, No. 15. He chose these islands because of their proximity to Charleston and because they, along with Edisto and Wadmalaw Islands, had been specifically set aside for the freedmen's use. Allen visited two plantations, and he found the results there encouraging. He contrasted the situation on these islands with that on the mainland, especially along the Cooper River, where things were in a state of disorder, punctuated by violence.

On July 21, 1865, the day before he left for the North, Allen wrote letter to the *Nation* titled "The State of Things in South Carolina." This letter provided his assessment of two questions: was the "spirit" of slavery truly dead in South Carolina, and were blacks able to take care of themselves? On the basis of his interview with Logan and his companions, he deemed an affirmative answer to the first question doubtful. He was encouraged by the candid exchange he had with the Carolinians, but he feared that they would succumb to the temptation to reestablish the old order if civil government was restored too quickly. As to the second question, on the basis of his observations of black progress on James and Johns Islands, Allen believed that the freedmen were indeed capable of fending for themselves.[53]

Allen departed Charleston aboard the *Granada* on July 22, 1865, never to return to the South. He arrived in West Newton in time for breakfast on July 26. He wasted no time in sitting down to write another letter to the *Nation*, this one titled "Feeling of the South Carolinians." This letter was an extended account of Allen's exchange with a certain "Mr. O.," who was in fact Roswell T. Logan, with whom he had had tea only a few days before. Besides outlining Mr. O.'s sentiments, Allen closed by summarizing the July 9 contract discussions he had had with Captain Soule and Major Montague at Orangeburg.[54]

Apparently, Allen had considerable pent-up energy for writing because he returned to a more rigorous medium two days later, writing a twenty-six-page essay for the *Christian Examiner*—his first in more than a year. His diary of July 28, 1865, noted, "Wrote art. on S.C."[55] He returned to lighter writing on August 10 when he wrote a letter to the *Nation* titled "The Southern Whites."[56] In this letter, he drew on his experiences in Arkansas and South Carolina to distinguish three classes of Southerners: (1) poor, degraded "white trash"; (2) small planters and farmers; and (3) aristocrats. After musing on the lingering effects of slavery on white Southern society, he concluded with his oft-expressed conviction that "In order to make these people trustworthy citizens, they must be brought to the conviction that slavery and rebellion are *hopelessly* at an end. So long as there exists in their minds the least shadow of hope that the institution will be revived they cannot be trusted.... If they should once get the notion that by intriguing with the Democrat party they could get the institution restored, even under another name, I do not doubt that they would be ready to do it.... But the idea, sometimes thrown out, of withdrawing our troops, seems to me nothing short of madness."

Allen also addressed the fear among Southerners that blacks would "rise" in violent rebellion as being absurd—that is, unless an attempt were made to re-enslave them.

On August 29, Allen wrote a letter titled "The Basis of Suffrage"[57] to the *Nation*, critiquing a number of proposals for extending suffrage to blacks. A joint proposal by Dr. Francis Lieber, Senator Charles Sumner, and General Robert Schenck called for a constitutional amendment that would base the number of representatives for each state on the number of voters, rather than the total inhabitants. Another proposal, advanced in the August 24 issue of the *Nation* by a writer using the pseudonym "T. F.," involved reinterpreting the Constitution so that Congress would assume authority over elections. After rejecting the possibility of leaving voting rights to each state "as at present," Allen advanced his own proposal, which involved two constitutional amendments. The first would give Congress authority over federal elections only, leaving state elections in the hands of the states. The second amendment, which Wendell Phillips had proposed in 1863, would have prohibited any discrimination on the basis of race or color. Allen saw the first of these amendments as a way to bridge the gap until the second gained popular support. He repeated his oft-expressed conviction that voting rights should not be granted to uneducated voters, white or black.

In December 1865, Allen wrote the last letter to the *Nation* that should be considered among his South Carolina writings. In a letter titled "The Negro Dialect," he wrote about the dialect that had so arrested his attention on St. Helena Island.[58] In this piece, he described the black dialect recognized today as Gullah. He also sketched out the lyrics of a number of songs that were later included in *Slave Songs,* anticipating that work by two years.

Allen wrote five essays for the *Christian Examiner*[59] over the course of the Civil War. The last three of these were touched on lightly earlier, but they deserve more detailed attention in order to understand the man, because in these essays his scholarly qualities come most clearly to light. As a group, the five essays form a natural progression. Early on, when things were going badly for the North, Allen wrote pieces defending the war. Later, when the tide of war shifted in favor of the North, he wrote on the postwar topics of free labor and reconstruction.

The first two *Examiner* essays predated Allen's coming to South Carolina. The first, titled "The War Policy, and the Future of the South" and written in 1862, was a defense of President Lincoln's timing of the Emancipation Proclamation. The second, titled "Democracy on Trial," written in early 1863, was a refutation of an "I-told-you-so" article by the British politician (Lord) Robert Cecil in which the author maintained that American democracy had led to the death of the Union. Allen's biographer Owen Stearns ably discussed these early essays, and they are not discussed here.[60]

The third *Examiner* essay—Allen's first from the South—was titled "The Freedmen and Free Labor in the South."[61] Like many Northerners, Allen saw slavery as an economically inefficient system and a drag on the progress of the nation. The essay dealt with the four free labor systems that had been implemented in the South: Port Royal, South Carolina; the Mississippi Valley in the vicinity of Vicksburg; lower Louisiana; and Fortress Monroe, Virginia. This essay is interesting from a number of perspectives, but especially for what it reveals about Allen's activities on St. Helena and his writing process. His journal and diary show that, besides teaching and mundane pursuits such as gardening, he spent a considerable amount of time researching the article. Allen read constantly, and from January 1 through mid-March 1864 at least half of his reading was directly related to this essay.

The essay begins with a general statement of the problem of suddenly releasing more than three million freedmen into the severely weakened economic and social systems of the South. The problem for the nation, as he saw it, was to reorganize the industry of the freedmen (i.e., set up and enforce free labor systems); feed them; educate them for a time, until local provisions could be made; and "make men of them" (i.e., help the freedmen raise themselves from slavery). Although he declared each of these challenges to be a problem, he devoted the bulk of his essay to the first one, namely free labor. Before launching a discussion of free labor, however, Allen quoted, in scholarly fashion, from John Stuart Mill's *Considerations on Representative Government* on theoretical policies for raising a people out of slavery.[62] From there, he entered into a review and critique of the four large-scale free labor systems in existence at the time. He found the Port Royal Experiment to be a success, especially from the standpoint of promoting the welfare of the freedmen. He found deficiencies in the Mississippi Valley and the Louisiana systems, particularly their provisions for wages based on time spent rather than on tasks performed, as at Port Royal. He objected strongly to the Louisiana system because it provided for the partial payment of wages in goods, such as food and clothing, a practice he considered prone to abuse. Last, he touched lightly, with approval, on the Fortress Monroe system.

Allen considered any plan that involved simply leaving the freedmen to themselves after the war to be untenable. He was primarily concerned about blacks who remained on plantations. He believed that leaving plantation workers in the hands of the southern states would be to consign them to "prædial servitude"[63] or perhaps even lead to the revival of some form of slavery under state laws. He saw the renewal of "state rights" as the chief evil that would lead to such an outcome. His favored remedy to prevent this was Wendell Phillips's recommendation that Congress pass constitutional amendments (1) abolishing slavery nationwide and (2) prohibiting discrimination based on race or color in state laws.[64] Alternatively, he believed that Congress should exercise its authority to require the repeal of discriminatory laws by the states as a condition of their readmission to the Union.

Subsequent to provisions to ensure the legal equality of the races, Allen looked forward to the creation of a Freedmen's Bureau, which would appoint superintendents, inspectors, and commissioners under a superintendent-general and take charge of the freedmen and the reorganization of their labor system. He foresaw the need for permanent regulations governing conditions of service, rate of wages, and arrangements for land distribution, which would protect landholders and laborers alike.[65] Allen laid out specifics of contract provisions based on his experience at Port Royal, recommendations for the Freedmen's Inquiry Commission, and suggestions set forth by James Yeatman, president of the Western Sanitary Commission.[66]

Allen assumed that cotton and sugar, the "great staples," would continue to be grown on large plantations even as small farms worked by freedmen, poor whites, and immigrants increased in number. Still, the prospect that landowners might replace the slavocracy with a landed aristocracy raised concerns in some quarters. Allen dismissed these concerns, however, noting that the destruction of slavery had destroyed the aristocracy itself. He went on to buttress this argument with examples of free labor outcomes in the West Indies.[67] Far from a dominant aristocracy, he foresaw a coming scarcity of labor, giving workers the upper hand.

Allen consistently urged caution on two controversial issues: the distribution of confiscated lands and the granting of suffrage. He thought that the wholesale confiscation of lands would have been vindictive in the first place and that the awarding of confiscated lands to the freedmen as a gift would be deleterious to the interests of the nation as a whole and of the freedmen themselves. He argued that awarding land free of charge would reward the lazy along with the industrious and would encourage the freedmen to congregate in segregated districts. He believed the sale of lands should be structured to bring the races together rather than separating them. Doing so would break down class distinctions and bring the freedmen into contact with whites, who could materially assist them in their rise from slavery. As to suffrage, he advocated that it be granted to the educated only, black or white. He touched briefly on education, which he saw as the key that would ultimately lift the freedmen from the residual shackles of slavery. Allen concluded by saying: "A good organization of their industry, and adequate political guarantees for its security, will be the best education for them. For their faults and defects are for the most part those that slavery produces, and liberty will cure. Freedom alone can make freemen. Nothing will so surely weed out the base growths of servitude as the protection of equal laws and the free competition of free society. Already even the hard experiences of their imperfect and insecure freedom has begun to make men of them. . . . At any rate, a good beginning has been made; and we who knew that it was as champions of freedom and civilization that we took up the gage on the 12th of April, 1861, feel now that we did well then, and that the issue is justifying our hopes."[68]

Allen's fourth essay for the *Examiner* appeared in the May 1865 issue under the title "Free Labor in Louisiana."[69] It was written in West Newton days after Mary's death as an update of his third essay a year earlier. He probably sketched it out on March 30, when he noted in his diary, "Wrote a good deal. . . . In eve. Jos. [his brother Joseph's home] Read papers aloud." The papers he and Joseph read that evening were probably the February 11, 1865, issue of the *National Anti-Slavery Standard* and the February 24, March 8, and March 17 issues of the *Liberator*, all of which were cited in the essay. (He had read Colonel John Eaton's report, which he also cited, on January 31.)[70] Likely, Allen and his brother, who was editor of the *Examiner*, discussed the piece that evening. The following day, March 31, Allen noted in his diary, "Wrote art. on La Labor System. At 4 to W.N. In eve. wrote." Apparently, he remained at Joseph's overnight, continued writing the following morning, and finished the essay that evening in West Newton. He met Joseph in Boston on April 3, where he likely turned over the essay for publication.

Allen devoted the first two-thirds of the fourth essay to a review of results obtained in Louisiana under General Nathaniel Banks's labor regulations promulgated in 1864. (Banks's plan had also been adopted in the upper Mississippi Valley in 1864, superseding James Yeatman's plan.) Allen's review was prompted by what he considered unwarranted criticism of Banks from various quarters, including Wendell Phillips, who had led the charge.[71] Allen found fault with Banks's system because it permitted partial payment of wages in food and clothing, which invited fraud, and because wages were based on time spent and not jobs completed. In the end, however, he found that "The result of our inquiries is, that the Louisiana Labor System, without being all that could be desired, is not in itself unfair or oppressive. It is open to criticism, not on the ground of injustice, but for errors of judgment in certain features. Where it has been carried out with energy and good faith, it has worked tolerably well. Where it has met with obstructions, or has been managed badly, it has failed. It is a system, however, which we do not conceive to be capable of the highest and truest success, because it allows no scope to that personal ambition of the laboring man, which is the only stimulus to rise. Under this system, it is not made to appear for his interest to do his utmost, but to spare himself all he can; and it is not peculiar to the freedmen of the South, that they need the incitement of a definite personal advantage in order to work with all their might."[72]

The last third of Allen's Louisiana essay speculated on the future of the freedmen. His conjectures fell into two categories having to do with (1) the character and capacity of the colored race and (2) the relation of capital to labor (i.e., employers to employees).

Allen's experience in the South, on St. Helena Island and in Arkansas, led him to conclude that the freedmen were misunderstood by friend and foe alike. Detractors saw blacks as a worthless race, which must eventually return to some form of slavery, while would-be friends were prone to overlook unfavorable traits and set impossible standards, leaving supporters destined to be disappointed. He found that the freedmen were what slavery had made them: lazy, dishonest, and licentious. "It is impossible" he wrote, "that slavery should exist, and not corrupt all with whom it comes in contact. . . . Treated like beasts, they became beasts." But, he also asserted that, "In all parts of the South, we find encouraging indications that they have not lost the power of rising again from their degradation. From the children especially we have everything to hope, through the admirable schools that have been established; and we need not despair of the adults."

As to the relation of capital to labor, profits from agricultural ventures in the South were looked on with the suspicion that, as Allen put it, "Whatever profit is made by the owner of the plantation, is thought to be so much filched from the earnings of the laborers." He cited Edward Philbrick's letter defending profits,[73] and he dismissed arguments against profitability thus: "This great mass of needy freedmen must either be supported by charity, or work must be found for them. . . . The fact remains,—Northern capitalists will not assume the enormous risks from brigandage, overflow, and the uncertainties attendant upon a new branch of business, unless a chance of profit is made commensurate with the risk."[74]

Allen closed the Louisiana free labor essay by reiterating his opposition to granting free land to the freedmen, insisting that to do so would be against the interests of the freedmen themselves and that it would reward unworthy recipients. He clarified his position by stating: "We are very far from desiring, in the unfavorable judgment we have expressed, to underrate the capacities of the race, or the actual attainments of some members of it. The colored people themselves are not responsible for their present condition, and we need not be in any degree discouraged by it. That slavery has reduced the mass of them, as the fact tells in their favor, that such men as Robert Smalls and Prince Rivers have risen, in spite of all obstacles, to attest to the powers of the race. And they are not rare exceptions."[75]

The fifth, and final, Civil War essay Allen penned for the *Examiner* appeared in the September 1865 issue under the title "South Carolina, one of the United States."[76] In true "Allenian" fashion, he launched the essay with the question "What constitutes a State?" Then he traced the etymology of the term through history from Roman times. He extended the notion of statehood to the concept of nationality, reasoning that neither states nor nations could be constructed of disparate peoples. He contended that South Carolina, far from being ready to rejoin the Union, was not yet a state, in the proper sense, because it was disorganized, being composed of disparate peoples. He cataloged "hostile" elements, consisting of repentant Confederates and Unionists versus as yet unrepentant Confederates and the "incorrigible," all of whom had to be reconciled before the state would be ready to rejoin the nation.

Allen's development of the notion of "nationality" reflected an ongoing debate in the North. Questions about nationality had been framed by the publicist Orestes Brownson's *The American Republic*,[77] and it was precisely such questions that Allen addressed in the fifth essay. In practical terms, he thought that military rule would be necessary for many years, not a matter of months as South Carolinians desired, before the state would be ready to take its place among the free states. In view of how Reconstruction actually played out, Allen was close to the mark.

Allen devoted the following two sections of the essay to an extended refutation of discourses advocating universal suffrage and confiscation of

Confederate lands by Henry Ward Beecher and Wendell Phillips, respectively.[78] Allen repeated his opposition to extending suffrage to all freedmen, not because they were black but because they were ignorant. He feared that the votes of ignorant blacks would be coopted by demagogues, contrary even to their own interests. He favored universal educational standards, such as minimal reading and writing proficiency, as a condition for voting. The confiscation of Confederate lands as advocated by Phillips, Allen believed, would complicate and prolong South Carolina's "path back to allegiance." He bemoaned the "revengeful spirit manifested in the North since the close of the war," insisting that "It is not merely to promote good feeling, that we urge a lenient and conciliatory policy in civil matters towards the South, but because we are convinced that there is an element here which will be of real value in the State."

After speculating about measures needed along the road to reconstructing South Carolina, such as establishing healthy local governments, Allen ended the essay on a hopeful note:

> Through much toil and suffering, through the most fearful ravages of war, and the wholesale impoverishment of her citizens, with diminished population, diminished wealth, and in the humiliation of an insufferable pride, South Carolina commences her new career as one of the United States. She has learned a bitter lesson. She has been forced to recant her favorite doctrine of State rights, and to surrender her favorite institution of slavery, and to return to the sisterhood that she once spurned. We believe she will take the lesson to heart, and will act in good faith; so that a heartier Union than has ever existed heretofore will spring out of these dissensions. If there was any one sentiment that at first spurred her on to war, it was contempt for the Yankees. That is all over now,—forgotten in a gallant contest for four years; and a friendly intercourse is going on such as has never taken place before. We have great faith in the healing power of Time, and look to see this intercourse continue and increase, until we have once again the cordial feeling that existed when South Carolina gave her vote for John Adams, and Massachusetts hers for Charles Cotesworth Pinckney.[79]

Allen shared this essay with family members as he wrote it. He began the piece in West Newton on July 28, 1865, two days after returning from Charleston. He put it aside for a few days; then, on August 1, he noted in his diary, "Wrote on article. To Prentiss' to tea—father there. In eve. to Geo's w. them. ... Read article afterwards to father & Prentiss."[80] He wrote on August 2 and 3, and then, on August 5, he and Joseph went to the "printing office." On August 7, he noted "revised Ms.," meaning, perhaps, he had corrected the printer's proof.

This essay closed Allen's writings on South Carolina until the introduction to *Slave Songs* two years later.

Allen was a perceptive observer of culture and events in South Carolina during and immediately after the Civil War. Of his qualifications as a cultural observer, the musicologist Dena Epstein said of him, "In addition to his musical abilities, he brought to the Sea Islands the perspective of a trained historian who understood the changes going on around him, and the interest of a philologist for the strange Gullah dialect of the coastal Negroes. . . . A man of such broad interests, training, and understanding was surely as qualified as anyone of his day to collect slave songs and study their dialect."[81] He was known to his associates as a dispassionate political observer. Wendell Garrison, literary editor of the *Nation* from 1865 to 1906, said of him, "His interest in national affairs never abated; he was a dispassionate observer and true independent."[82] His colleagues in the academic community viewed him as discriminating in his approach to history. "No historical fact is of any value," he was known to say, "except so far as it helps us to understand human nature and the working of historic forces."[83] His biographer Owen Stearns well expressed the effect Allen's Civil War experiences had on him personally: "Allen had learned the lesson of man's relations with man: understanding, not pity; realism, not sentimentality; education, not demagoguery."[84] The eminent historian Frederick Jackson Turner paid Allen the highest compliment when he said of him, "I have never, in Johns Hopkins or elsewhere, seen his equal as a scholar."[85] Always the scholar, Allen saw things through the eyes of a scholar.

St. Helena Journal

—⊗⊗⊗—

William Allen, his wife, Mary, and her cousin Caty Noyes left New York for St. Helena Island, South Carolina, at 1:20 P.M. on November 4, 1863.

Steamer Arago,[1] Nov. 5, 1863, 9¾ A.M.

Head wind, clouds and rising sea—some white caps. Storm threatening, but it doesn't seem to grow worse rapidly. However, we are promised a hard blow off Hatteras tonight, which name has always had an ill boding sound to me, from some sailors' jingle I remember hearing or reading years ago—

> If the Bermudas you should pass
> Keep good look-out for Hatteras.[2]

It was a perfectly beautiful day when we sailed yesterday at twenty minutes past one, and we went at good speed through the beautiful harbor, passing the Russian fleet which lay at anchor near the Battery.[3] When we went through the Narrows we were at dinner, and on going on deck afterwards, we saw Sandy Hook stretching before us with the fine Nevisink Hills rising over it—the last high land on the coast to one going south,—behind us the noble form of Staten Island and the characterless expanse of Long Island, and to the east the open sea. Then we changed course, skirting along the Jersey coast as near as possible, and then standing south, so that in the evening the North Star was nearly astern. We have a very pleasant company. For some time after we came onboard we didn't see any familiar faces, altho' we made acquaintance thro' father,[4] of Mr. Davis,[5] the chaplain of the 54th. Soon we saw Seymour Severance's[6] pleasant face, and shortly Mr. Philbrick's;[7] Mr. P. introduced us to Mr. Ruggles[8] and Mr. Folsom,[9] two of his superintendents, with the latter of whom we are to live, and gradually we made other acquaintances.

There is a large number of officers on board, mostly fine looking gentlemanly men. The highest in rank is Gen. Terry, one of Gillmore's best division commanders—a tall straight slender man, with a very engaging face, and a goatee beard.[10] As senior officer, he assumed command of the troops on board—there are a large number of soldiers forward, some two dozen of them deserters. In the evening some twenty of these came aft to make some complaint to the general—which they did in rather an improper manner. He left them for a moment—I don't know why—and then came back and ordered them forward. They obeyed reluctantly and slowly, and one of them was so noisy and profane that the general seized him and threw him down upon a bench, ordering him to sit there while he sent the others forward. But presently the fellow started and undertook to run off, the general and two or three others after him, who brought him back and he was marched off under guard to confinement. It was quite an exciting interruption of my quiet walk on deck with Mr. P., who was giving me a good deal of information about affairs at Port Royal.

We have our regular seats at table, assigned by the purser. Mary, Katy[11] and I sit next each other, and at our left, at another table, Mr. P. and another gentleman of our acquaintance. Opposite us are three very pleasant gentlemen with whom we are beginning to get acquainted. Mr. Martindale[12] is a stout farmer like man from Cleveland, who introduced himself to me, thinking that he recognized my face. He is going south on some civil service and looks like a very competent person. Next to him sits Capt. Robinson[13] of the 9th Maine, a middle aged man of a somewhat severe countenance, and taciturn habits, but I made him talk this morning, and found him very agreeable. Then Lieutenant Benjamin, of the [1]57th New York, a very pleasant seeming young fellow, large and well built, modest and quiet.[14] At our right are some Germans, very noisy and impolite. We have also just made the acquaintance of Mrs. Peck and her two daughters. Her husband, Dr. P., who is also on board, was one of the pioneers in this educational movement, a Baptist clergyman, established, I believe, at Beaufort. They seem pleasant people.[15]

Nov. 5 and 6, 7½ P.M.

Creeping creaking along at about seven knots an hour, against the wind. We could go faster, but have a schooner in tow loaded with cattle, and the captain says if we went faster we should pull them under water. The wind is rising, and it will probably blow pretty hard in the morning. Molly [Allen's nickname for Mary] has been pretty sick all day, has not been at any meals, but has eaten a few crackers. Katy was sick too, but is better to-night. Almost all our party have been more or less uncomfortable—I least, as I have not felt the least qualm until now as I sit here writing with a very slight sensation of discomfort. I have employed the day in walking on deck, writing and reading "Idées Napoléoni-ennes,"[16] also read the second part of the New Gospel of Peace[17] aloud to Mary, thus beguiling her sickness a little.

Nov. 6, 8¾ p.m.

It rained this morning with considerable wind and sea, but cleared up about noon, when the sea-sick ones began to make their appearance upon deck one by one. It has been a lovely afternoon, so warm that I put on a thinner coat. We passed Hatteras Light, I believe, this evening, so our voyage is more than half done, and we are now making eight knots. I have been reading Romola[18] to-day and like it much—better I think than Adam Bede.[19] Still, as an historical novel, it lacks a little in distinctness—it has so complicated historical events and such a large number of characters.

There is a good deal of snobbishness and exclusiveness among some of the officers, who seem to conceive that their shoulder straps set them up above other men. Mr. Davis, the colored chaplain of the 57th,[20] has to sleep on a sofa in the companion way and eat with the servants. I think it is an affront to the commonwealth, and if the captain[21] were a different sort of man I had a notion of asking him why it is so. But he is the biggest of snobs, very polite to ladies and to the high officers on board, but high and mighty towards the rest of the passengers. I never sailed with a captain before who didn't take pride in making his ship equally comfortable to all. Part of the distance on the part of some of the officers arises no doubt from the feeling that civilians have no business on board, and are in the way. There is some ground for this, because it is true that some officers were crowded out by the number of civilians, among others Capt. Saxton,[22] brother of the general. But it all depends upon the military authorities themselves. If they choose to arrange matters so loosely that important officers can be kept out, they have nobody to blame but themselves. And besides, the real abuse is that persons who have no right to them get passes. There is room enough for officers and for bona fide teachers, but there is a lot of officer's wives, who are not wanted, but who get appointments as teachers, without any inten-tion of teaching, that they may join their husbands. But the officials in New York refused to let me take on board that box I packed in Keene [N.H.], and I had to leave it to come by express. This was a mere piece of malice because I was a civilian. I saw on board several boxes with officers' names on them, which were quite as little personal baggage as mine. That it was mere piggishness is clear from this, and from the fact that the box would have come on by express in this very steamer, if I had delivered it in season.

Sunday, Nov. 8, 10½ A.M.

We have just passed Charleston harbor, stopping twice to receive dispatches and land passengers. We stopped outside the bar, and boats came off from the Wabash[23] and other vessels. We saw Charleston quite distinctly, and Fort Sumter standing defiantly in the middle of the harbor. The top is all knocked to pieces, and there was still going on a slow bombardment from Battery Gregg.[24] We would see a column of smoke arising from Gregg; then casting our eyes to Sumter we would shortly see a puff of white smoke denoting the bursting of a shell, or a dark spot on the side wall where the ball struck and knocked up a cloud of dust and debris. Gradually this would disappear, and by that time we would hear the report. Morris Island we saw very distinctly, white with tents, and its shore lined with vessels. We could make out the ironsides and several monitors. Then Folly Island, with less tents, but with a high tower to serve as an observing station. We are now making good headway, and there are to be services soon.

Yesterday was a delightful day, passed as usual in reading, walking and talking. I talked a little with Lt. Col. Strong,[25] of the 1st S.C. (Higginson's),[26] a middle aged man who seems to be genuine, earnest and brave. Before breakfast we were passed by the famous Peterhof,[27] now bought and put in commission by Uncle Sam. Then there were the other variations of a sea voyage—porpoises, heaving the log,[28] and an attempt at a dance,—not very satisfactory, because there were only three ladies and a fat colonel had to take the place of the fourth.

Hilton Head, Nov. 8, 8 P.M.

We reached here about 5½ this afternoon—just about one hundred hours from New York—and here we are lying at the foot of the pier in the bright starlight, with the water all around reflecting the lights of the numerous vessels that lie at anchor on both sides the harbor. It is very beautiful. A steamboat is to carry us up to Beaufort in the morning, and so we have another night on the steamer. The day has passed about as usual except for the holding of services at 11, and the excitement of approaching land. Mr. Strout,[29] chaplain of the 9th Me., conducted services; but Dr. Peck made the address, and Mr. Martindale and Mr. Davis made prayers. We had a circuitous route to enter the harbor, as the channel runs far to the south, and we had to pass quite by before we turned to come in. The harbor is quite broad (Port Royal Entrance) and runs straight back under the name of Broad River so far that we can see no land beyond it.

Hilton Head is, you know, the southern side of the Entrance, and Bay Point the northern. The first landing made by our troops was, I suppose by accident, at Hilton Head, so this has continued to be ever since the chief army-station, head quarters of the department of the South, altho' less healthy, less pleasant, and a less secure harbor than Bay Point, which is occupied by the vessels of the navy department. There is quite a settlement at Hilton Head, and the forest of masts on both sides give the bay the appearance of a great emporium. It seems to me it must be so in future, for it has the best harbor between Norfolk and Pensacola.

Seymour Severance stood by our side as we came up to the pier (1/4 mile long) pointing out the various buildings on shore, and the town had a decidedly oriental look with its broad-topped pines, tents and low buildings (only two in the place having two stories) So our voyage is ended—very pleasant to me, but very unpleasant to Molly, who has been very sick nearly all the time. We had to find our chief enjoyment by ourselves, for the passengers were not very social. Those I have mentioned, and one or two others, were very affable and met us half way; but most were very distant, and ill-disposed to make acquaintance, so I soon gave up the attempt and made myself comfortable with books and the few persons I knew.

Our special party is a very pleasant one. Mr. Philbrick is short, with sandy hair, and full sandy beard, a full forehead and good eyes; he is one of those who is full of ready information and practical good sense on all subjects. Ruggles is tall and well-built, very handsome, with full brown beard, and manly, weighty face; no great talker, but genial, companionable and self-reliant. Folsom is very tall and slender, with hair as light as mine, and boyish sunburnt face; full of fun and with a good deal of ready wit. He looks very young, but Mr. P. says he has a great deal of tact and practical sagacity. Dyer,[30] Ruggles' companion, is about my height, slender, light-complexioned, with whiskers and a somewhat reserved look, altho' I find him sociable enough. Socially he seems the least valuable of the company, but he has a good tenor voice, and will be quite an acquisition in that way. I should think he had a good deal in him, but it isn't so easily got at as in the others. Then there is Winsor,[31] Mr. P's clerk, a handsome young fellow, whom I have not talked with at all. Capt. Hooper,[32] Gen. Saxton's aid, has just been in, and we had a few words with him. The steamer was signaled to Beaufort, and he and some others came down in a steamboat to get the mail, and Folsom and Ruggles have gone back with him. Capt. H. is practically the head of the Freedmen's department, and a very competent and efficient person, from all accounts. He is very much beloved and admired. He is of middle height, with beard about his mouth, of dignified bearing, and one of those faces that is habitually without a smile, altho' his smile is a very pleasant one. He brought news to a Mrs. Murray[33] of Newport that her sister at "the Oaks"[34] is at the point of death; and she and her mother also went to Beaufort with him.

Coffin's Point,[35] Nov. 10, 1 P.M.

We had an early breakfast yesterday morning, and then Mr. P. and I went on shore to get our passes to Beaufort. At about ten a small steamboat was ready for use to us, and we steamed up the Beaufort River, which branches from Broad River directly opposite Hilton Head, having Parris Island on our left and Bay Point (Phillips Island) and St. Helena Island on our right. There was a large number of ships lying in this fine harbor, among them two monitors. We went very near one of them, a queer flat raft with the "cheese box," smoke pipe, railing, pilot house and several human beings rising from about the level of the water. Of the other, the smoke pipe was quite riddled with balls. Here at Land's End (the end of St. Helena) is the proper place for a great city and here are already foundries, dock-yards etc. going up. It was a pleasant sail up the river, novel to us, but with little variety; and we talked on the quarter desk with Mr. P., Mr. Hammond,[36] the superintendent of Parris Island, and others. Soon we came to Port Royal Island on the left, and Cat, Cane and Ladies' on the right. Beaufort is a charming looking place from the water, and indeed is quite pleasant in itself. The houses are large and airy, and it is well shaded.

Capt. Hooper met us at the pier and took us to his office, while Mr. P. saw to getting the baggage to the ferry. We mailed several letters here—one I mailed for home with two sheets of my journal, for fear I might miss the mail if I waited. You will probably receive this by the same mail. Our baggage went across in a flat boat, while we were rowed by four lusty negroes, with a white coxswain. The ferry, as well as the steamboat from Hilton Head, are government affairs, and charge no fare. [See Port Royal Map and Key for Allen's route from Beaufort: to the "R.'s" (No. 4), past the John Fripp (No. 8) and Thomas B. Fripp (No. 9) Places, past Pine Grove (No. 13), and ending at Coffin Point (No. 12).]

We were now on Ladies' Island (Beaufort is on Port Royal Island), and walked up the road a few rods to a negro's quarters, where we sat on some logs until fate should get us further along. Mr. Philbrick borrowed a horse and rode on to Ruggles'; Winsor went on with Ruggles' team, which had come for his luggage, and took some of our lighter pieces, while Molly, Katy and I sat down and waited. It was now about 12½. There was a hedge of prickly pears on the other side of the road,—a cactus with fierce thorny leaves, and I picked one of its handsome purple pears, in so doing, getting my fingers full of minute thorns or prickles, which it took some time to get out; one of them broke out and my finger is quite sore now with it. Then I opened the concern, taking good care not to touch it with my fingers, and dug out a little of the rich red pulp, but found it not worth eating, altho' in hot summer weather it may be refreshing. We hadn't provided ourselves with anything but two or three apples, and by half past one we waxed hungry, and knowing that we shouldn't reach Coffin's Point before evening, I laid in with a negro woman to bake some sweet potatoes. Then Katy bought some nice roasted ground nuts, which we were soon munching, while we listened to a couple of negroes bargaining for a pig.

Before the potatoes were done, at about two o'clock, there appeared a rickety old covered buggy with the top down, drawn by two horses, one with a saddle and one without, the harness patched together with ropes, and with a single pair of reins (the horses mouths being connected by a transverse strap). A comical little darkey was driving this establishment, who pulled his cap violently, and handed me a letter addressed to either Mr. Philbrick, Winsor or myself, from which I learned that the team was Mr. Gannett's,[37] which he had sent at once on learning of our arrival. A raw-boned horse was fastened behind, and there was an excellent McClellan saddle in the buggy, I was to ride. As soon as the potatoes were done we piled them in the bottom of the buggy, I mounted Buckskin, Mary and Katy took their seats and "Daniel Sar" perched on the floor at their feet—the dasher[38] being fortunately broken—and off we started. The road was very sandy and we went slowly—at first, too, the sweet potatoes delayed us.

The roadsides are very beautiful, a tangle of trees and shrubs, the great live oaks hanging heavily with long gray moss, and the bright scarlet casina berries and white tufts of mocking-bird flower making the way-side bright.[39] Presently we came to a marsh and narrow creek which we crossed by a bridge, and then we were on Saint Helena. A few rods further we turned up a lane to the right and came to Ruggles' house,[40] where we found him, Dyer, Winsor and Mr. P., with a fine carryall from Coffin's Point, which Harriet[41] had sent along as soon as she heard of our arrival. We were delayed here some time by the harness being out of order, and Ruggles' boy had gone off with the key to the carriage house. First they shifted a horse from the buggy to the carryall, but they hadn't been introduced to each other and a furious kicking ensued. That wouldn't do, so a collar was changed from one horse to another, but it was too big, and a still different change had to be made.

Finally we were all ready, Mr. P. mounted a little horse of his own, Daniel rode Buckskin; I drove Mary in the buggy, while Winsor, Katy and our traps went in the carriage. I think this Island is less beautiful than Ladies', but it seems more under cultivation—cotton, corn, sweet potatoes, beans, and in one place rice. The cotton is a less dignified plant than, I supposed, two or three feet high, with thin straggling branches covered with yellow blossoms and pods in all stages—some empty, some just bursting with its white tuft. It was mostly pretty well grown up with weeds until we came to Mr. P.s' plantations. Sometimes the road was quite hard, sometimes very sandy and heavy. At intervals there are gates across the road, which young Demas, who rode on a perch behind the carriage, got down and opened. The roadsides are not fenced, and this method is necessary to keep the cattle of one plantation from straying into another.

Presently a road branched off to Land's End, and then another to Helena Village, and soon after we came to our future home, the Capt. John Fripp "Big House." It is a plantation of a thousand acres and the large house stood back an eighth of a mile from the road, with a long avenue of cypress and ailanthus leading to it. We met quite a number of the people here, who seemed very glad to see Mr. P., and who all saluted us very respectfully, with a "Huddy" (How do?)—as all the blacks we have met have done. One nice looking girl (a good way back) said very smilingly "Mas'r William huddy," but we were at a loss to guess whether she confounded me with Mr. Gannett, William Hall, or a Mr. Williams who is near here.[42] Leaving this plantation, we came to the Thomas B. Fripp, which does not belong to Mr. P., and then to Pine Grove, where Mr. Gannett is superintendent. At the branching of the road Mary and I changed places with Mr. Winsor, who was to spend the night with Gannett, while we drove a couple of miles here [Coffin Point] where we arrived in the dark, and were greeted by Harriet, Wm, Mr. Soule (Mr. P's agent), and Lt. Wood of the 55th, who is here for his health—an old pupil of ours in Newton.[43] Charley is off on business and has not yet returned.[44]

Coffin's Point, Nov. 10, 1863, 8¾ P.M.

I sent a letter this afternoon, closed rather hurriedly, to go by the Arago on Thursday, and will write a few lines to-day, to bring matters down to to-night while they are fresh in my mind. Charley and Mr. P. are sitting at the table, talking over accounts; Mr. Soule is reading the paper, Wm. Hall looking over "War Songs," Molly reading a novel, while Lieut. Wood and Katy are sitting in their chairs doing nothing, and Harriet is upstairs about some household matters. It is a large high-studded room, a fine wood fire is blazing in the fire place, the clock is ticking on the mantle-piece, and a large kerosene lamp is burning in the middle of the round mahogany table.[45] Except for lack of carpet, the room is furnished as well as at the north; for the furniture found here was very solid and handsome, and a great many little things have leaked down here from the North in driblets—pictures on the walls, vases, and really a large number of books. Just now there is quite a panic, however, for all the personal property found on the estates,—furniture, horses, cows, wagons etc., is ordered to be sold by the Treasury Department, and all this handsome furniture, the pride of Coffin's Point, all the lean horses and broken-down go-carts, must be "toted" to Beaufort to be knocked down to the highest bidder. We newcomers at the Big House, with our ten chairs, three wash-stands, and cracked dining table, will be really better provided than most of our neighbors.

It has been a cold day, with a fresh north wind, which will bring Mr. P.'s schooner on in good time, and except in the sunshine it has been quite uncomfortable. We haven't done much to-day. We breakfasted late, and about the middle of the forenoon Mary and I strolled on the beach which runs within a few rods of the house the path to it leading thro' a grove of lemon trees hanging with fruit. Then I went into William Hall's school for a short time—the school for beginners—and then wrote to get my letters ready for Mr. Winsor to take to Beaufort. After dinner we took a walk to the negro quarters—Mary and Katy sitting in the open buggy, while Harriet and I walked. The quarters make a broad straight street, with two or three trees—fig and Pride of Asia[46]—standing in the middle, the little wooden cabins lining the two sides, most of them for two families. About half way along is the mill, where a man and girl were grinding corn; the upper millstone turned by means of a pole fixed in a beam above, and fitting in a hole near the edge of the stone. All the people came very promptly to greet Mr. P., whom they seemed very glad to see. Many of they were demonstrative and gleeful, but most were quiet and sober, although with very pleasant smiles on their faces when they spoke. They nearly all came to shake hands with us and say "huddy," and presently they began to bring eggs as a mark of good will, so that by the time we had made our rounds Mary and Katy had eleven in their laps.

I was urged by a "Conservative" to give free scope to first impressions, as being more likely to be true than any reasoning upon them; and here they are.[47] I find the people I meet seem much, very much, less degraded than I expected. That is to say, they seem human beings, neither more nor less. There is as great a difference in their faces as in the faces of whites. They are not handsome, but some of them, especially of the men, are very noble, fine-looking fellows—much superior to the average of whites. In their manners they are very respectful and often obsequious; less obsequious, Mr. P. says, than formerly. They are said to be very dirty, but it is very hard to distinguish dirt upon them, and I can only say that their dress is slovenly, altho' nothing like so bad—at least, I have seen nothing so bad—as among the Irish children in the North. In William's school the children seemed as bright as white children of the same age; but then I have never had much experience in the abc's. It seems trite and common-place to say so, but I must say that the wickedness of slavery never seemed so clear as when I saw these people (about 240 on this plantation), so entirely human as they appear, and considered how they have been treated, and how little reason there is that they should be selected from all mankind for this awful abuse. I only write here first impressions; but I am struck with the fact that Mr. P., Charley and the others speak of the negroes just as they would of whites. This one is stupid, this one lazy, this one tricky, this one industrious, this one honest, this one intelligent. Exactly as we talk of Yankees or Irish.

Nov. 11, 9½ P.M.

This morning after breakfast I walked out with Charley and Mr. P. over the lands. First we went down to the wharf, on the creek about a mile from here, as Charley wanted to examine the heaps of sedge that the women had hoed up. It is coarse and dry, and is carted by the men to a place where it can soak in salt water, and is then used for manure—the sea-island cotton[48] requiring this salt manure. A man with an ox team was at work carting it, using a long-handled garden fork which Mr. P. brought from the North last Spring. Asking him how it worked, he answered that it was very good—"better dan a hoe;" a comparison which rather entertained me, but they have always used hoes for everything—great heavy affairs. I gathered some beautiful grass on the marsh. Mr. P's wharf he built last year of palmetto logs which are very durable in water, with live oak planks laid over them.

Returning to the house, we set out for Gannett's plantation, where we meant to dine. We soon turned off from the main road (the sea-side road it is called) to the left, thro' patches of sweet potato, corn, etc. cultivated by the negroes. There are two kinds of sweet potato, the red, which is early and has a plain leaf and white meat; and the yellow with deeply lobed leaves, which is much better. There is also the Georgia yam (not a true yam) with large plain leaves, deep yellow and very excellent. They plant seed early in the season, and in July set slips for a late crop; these they have not yet dug. There were also some patches of benny,[49] a curious plant, which they use the seeds of to eat. Soon we came into the "back field," containing about a hundred acres of cotton and a hundred and thirty of corn. The people were picking the cotton in aprons hanging like bags before them, piling it then in sheets which they carried to be weighed—each pile is kept separate. About three quarters of the cotton is picked now. This brought us to the marsh towards the sea, and soon we crossed a brook into the Pine Grove plantation, under Gannett's charge, where we dined with him, Miss Rice[50] and Folsom, and then walked home. I give a map of the northern end of St. Helena Island.[51] [See Port Royal Map and Key (Nos. 8–19).]

The Coffin's Point plantation is under Charley's care; Gannett has Pine Grove and Fripp Point, and Miss Rice teaches and keeps house. At present

Folsom lives with them he has care of Capt. John Fripp's "Big House," Cherry Hill and Mulberry Hill; and it is these plantations I am to teach. The other plantations on the plan belong to government, Mr. P's other plantations being in other parts of St. Helena and Ladies' Islands.[52] Ruggles lives about three miles from Capt. John's, beyond Indian Hill; Capt. John's is about three miles from Pine Grove, and five miles from here. Everybody is full just now of a new order of Gen. Saxton's, ordering certain plantations to be sold to the negroes in lots of twenty acres, reserving in some cases "school farms" of 160 acres. Thus the Hamilton Fripp plantation is to be sold outright, but the Thos. B. Fripp and McTureous lands with the reservation. The object is an excellent one, but there are certain very serious objections to the method pursued. In the first place, a clear title cannot be given yet, because the lands were sold for taxes, and the time of redemption has not expired yet.[53] Then the new order gives the right to "squat" and "preempt," practices which have certain advantages in the west where they originated, but are very unsuitable to be introduced here. Besides this, the negroes find it hard to understand it. They have very strong local attachments, and they thought they were going to be required to buy land away from their old homes—some of them thought it was as bad as to be sold. I give this latter consideration as it strikes Mr. P. and others. It remains to be seen how it will work practically, but at present it seems as if there were serious difficulties in the way, and as if the plan, which is very good in its outline, had not been sufficiently matured in its details.

I believe I haven't described our new friends. Mr. Soule is a middle-aged man, rather short, with a fine, kindly, intellectual face, something like Uncle William's. Mr. Gannett is middle height, with full round face, handsome dark blue eyes, and black hair and beard. He speaks in a very low and quiet voice, as if he was very diffident. Miss Rice is quite tall, about thirty, with a very efficient look and manner, and wears glasses. She used to be a school teacher in Cambridgeport, and came here thro' John Ware's[54] means.

Nov. 12, 8 p.m.

Mary had a sick headache to-day, and I left her lying on the bed at about ten, being determined to go to our new house, even if I had to walk. But Mr. Soule, finding that I was starting, offered me his mare "Black Mink," which he assured me he didn't mean to use to-day. It was a warm sunny day, but with a few clouds, which before night nearly overspread the sky. Black Mink is easy and a free goer, but I didn't care to hurry, and let her walk whenever the road was at all heavy. There is a gate to pass from the yard into the first field, and in a few rods I passed a grove which is the negro burial place on the left, and on the right a group of plantation houses—the cotton house, corn house, etc., and further from the road the "Nigger House."[55] Half a mile further on, through a gate into the great field, a mile and a quarter long, with a wooded brook running across the road. There are a hundred and twenty acres of cotton in this field.

At the end of this field [there is] another gate into the Pine Grove lands, where I met Winsor on a horse, waiting for Folsom and Gannett, who were walking through the fields. We waited some time, and then rode along a foot-path by which we expected them, thro' fennel some of it higher than our heads. When we came back to the road, we found G. and F. there, and Folsom mounted Winsor's horse and rode alone with me, thro' a gate which a black man was mending, into the narrow strip of the McTureous lands, which belongs to the Coffin's Point estate and is cultivated by Mr. Philbrick. Then into the Hamilton Fripp plantation, which has lain uncultivated for a good many years—the owner, a worthless fellow, living on a little island near the Port Royal Ferry. Then the Tom B. Fripp plantation, of which a Mr. Harrison[56] is superintendent, living in a pleasant looking cottage on the creek.

A couple more gates—brought us to the Capt. John Fripp place, and a handsome avenue led from the road to the house. The avenue is of cypress and "Pride of Asia" trees, a tree like the ailanthus, and I think of the same family; now hanging very full with yellow berries as large as small cherries. A gate opens into the yard, and the road winds round a circular plot, on both sides, full of trees and shrubs. The house is of two stories in front, only one behind, raised on brick pillars to keep it from the dampness of the earth. The creek comes to within three or four rods of the house, behind, and beyond are salt marshes. There are some handsome oaks along the creek, and the various out-houses are on both sides of the house. Capt. John Fripp was the owner of about 300 negroes and 3000 acres of land three different plantations I believe—and was one of the richest men on the island. His house was about in the style of a second-rate New England farm house, of course very dilapidated now after two years of negro occupancy, but shabby and thriftless at best. Folsom has had the floors cleaned and the walls white-washed, and is going to paint some of the woodwork, put on new locks and door-handles etc. There are four rooms below and three above; making parlor, school-house, kitchen, three bed-rooms for us, and guest chamber. I will send a plan when we are fairly established. Then we went out into the out-houses and the garden. The garden was one of the best on the island, and I gathered a handsome bunch of rosebuds to carry home. Then mounted and trotted off. At the first gate met Charley on his way to St. Helena Village, not expecting to be back to-night. A pleasant ride, arriving at home to dinner.

Nov. 14, 9 p.m.

Very little incident these two days. Until the house is ready for us, we are to stay here, and particularly we can do nothing until the schooner arrives—a great event in our little community; everybody waiting impatiently for something that is to come in the schooner. Harriet is out of flour and sugar, the shops are empty, Mr. Folsom has no trunk, and we no furniture—that blessed schooner is to supply all our needs. And to-night, Harriet, Mary, Katy and Mr. Soule returning from Pine Grove, where Gannett is sick with chills and fever, report that the schooner is really in, lying in the creek at Ruggles'. So next week will be a busy one.

Yesterday and to-day I have been busy cabinet making. I have a chair fashioned out of a barrel, but it cannot be covered until the schooner disgorges its store of calico. I have the uprights of two towel stands (Winsor helped me materially in these—it is Rufus Winsor, who was hurt so badly at Mrs. Fay's), and the cross pieces are to be of bamboo, from a fine patch of this plant at the Capt. John Fripp place. I have also manufactured a couple of cribbage boards, one for Coffin's Point, which William Hall and Winsor are now using. Book case, clothes horse etc. I shall probably go to work on in the intervals of unloading and fitting up the house; but my nice tools are all in the schooner. It has been like summer weather to-day, so that I put on my thinner clothes—I wear my straw hat all the time. Smart showers at intervals, and a brilliant sunset.

Sunday, Nov. 15, 8 p.m.

A little cooler to-day, I have spent most of the day in reading, and at 12½ we—Molly, Katy, Winsor and I—went to the Praise House in the Quarters. They had already begun, but a man came out and invited us in. We preferred to stand outside in the shade, however, as the room was full, and we should only make a disturbance, so he brought, us chairs from a house, and we sat down there. They were just beginning a hymn, which the preacher (a stranger), deaconed out, two lines at a time. The tune was evidently Old Hundred,[57] which was maintained throughout by one voice or another, but curiously varied at every note, so as to form an intricate intertwining of harmonious sounds. It was something very different from anything I ever heard, and no description I have read conveys any notion of it. There were no parts properly speaking, only now and then a hint of a base or tenor, and the modulation seemed to be just the inspiration of the moment—no effort at regularity, only that one or two voices kept up the air—but their ears are so good, and the time is so perfectly kept (marked often by stamping and clapping the hands) that there was very seldom a discordant note. It might be compared to the notes of an organ or orchestra, where all harmony is poured out in accompaniment of the air; except that here there was no base [bass].[58] (Mary says I draw it too strong. I tried to describe the character of the music, and think I have—I haven't said that it was beautiful, and I must hear it again to form a fair judgment. She noticed more discord than I did.)[59] Exhortation, prayer, another hymn, benediction, and then a "shouting song" I believe they call them, beginning "Good morning,"[60] at which all began to shake hands and move about the room in measure. The chorus was "Hallelujah," but the words were very hard to catch.

Charley has come in to-night with the word that the schooner is still at Beaufort, and will go to Ruggles' to-morrow. He says also that Gen. Gillmore has issued an order forbidding all sales of land for the present, and also all exportation of cotton. As for the latter, probably Gen. G. is going beyond his powers; in the sale of land, it is mortifying that our authorities are so at cross-purposes, but perhaps it is as well to have the sale deferred. Charley was "off on commission" yesterday (as justice of the peace) and spent the night at the "Edgar Fripp" place, (next beyond Frogmoor),[61] going to church to-day, where he met Mr. Philbrick and others. The church is about west of Frogmoor, and will be about three miles from us in our new house—about eight miles from here. It is under the charge of Mr. Phillips,[62] a Baptist minister from the North.

Nov. 17, 8½ P.M.

These two days have passed quietly enough, in cabinet making and upholstering for the most part. I have finished the towel-stands, all but the cross-pieces, which I am to get at our new home, and the putting together, and the chair is now ready to be covered. Mary and Katy have been making a cushion for a sofa, which was found in pieces in the garret here, and put together by Harriet. The cushion is stuffed with the grey moss, which has to be boiled first and dried. My chair is stuffed with corn-shucks and moss, but Mary will make a movable cushion.

Yesterday morning we had a little excitement, enough to diversify our monotony. You know that we are at the extreme end of the island, and can easily see the shores of Secessia[63] across the sound. The gunboat Kingfisher lies opposite the house near the other shore, and Capt. Dutch (from Worcester) has been here several times to call. He is a very active officer, and keeps the rebels pretty busy with his expeditions. Yesterday morning we heard several shots from the Kingfisher, and Charley and I went on the roof, while Molly and Katy went on the beach to see what was going on. We could see the shots from the gunboat ricocheting over the water, and a small boat in the quarter they were firing, pulling towards the ship, and rapid signaling from a high tower on the main, or rather on Otter Island. We could imagine all sorts of things, but the likeliest was that they were firing at a mark. We hear more or less firing nearly every day—sometimes from Charleston, sometimes from the direction of Port Royal Ferry, sometimes more South.

In the afternoon I went down to the beach and practiced with my pistol, using the ruins of the overseer's house for a mark. I also gathered some palmetto leaves to use in making my chair. This morning, being desirous to know what news there was from the schooner, I mounted the grey mare Nelly, and rode with Charley to Pine Grove. We found Miss Rice at home—Folsom and Gannett had gone to Ruggles' to see about the schooner. After a short call I rode over to Fripp Point, to see the land, and then home. It was a pleasant road enough, thro' belts of wood and broad fields of cotton and corn; and we found the negroes hard at work digging their "slip potatoes."[64]

Coffin's Point, Nov. 18, 1863, 9½ P.M.

Coffin's Point still, and still no letters, altho' we hear that the Fulton[65] is in, and were told that Mr. Philbrick and Soule would be here to-night. We learn that our furniture is safely arrived at Capt. John Fripp's, and that Mr. Folsom is to sleep there to-night: to-morrow I shall go there and help get things in order. I have been engaged to-day in putting a lock, or rather a latch-catch, on one of the doors here, and in making certain fixtures for our house. At about eleven I started and walked nearly to Pine Grove, to learn about our house and the mail, but met Mr. Gannett and Miss Rice in the elegant vehicle which I described in a former letter, on their way to Coffin's Point, so turned and walked back.

Shall I describe the approach to Coffin's Point minutely, so as to give a notion of one of these largest plantations? On passing thro' the gate from the Big Pasture, about three quarters of a mile from the house, we see the house surrounded with trees directly in front, a straight, sandy road leading to it, thro' a bare, level, forlorn-looking pasture. This was planted with cotton last year, and will be next; this year it lies fallow and is fed upon by two dozen or more cattle; but what they find to eat I can't imagine, for nothing grows there but fennel, vermifuge (a coarse, strong-smelling herb), and a low scrubby grass, armed with the most troublesome, sharpest and most catching burrs I have ever met.[66] On each side of the road, this field extends for a quarter of a mile or so to a belt of timber. Directly in front of you, at the left of the road is a group of buildings—the cotton house, corn-house etc., and beyond them to the left down a slight slope towards the creek, the negro quarters. A little beyond the yard, on the other side of the road, is the grove which I mentioned before as the negro burial ground. As you approach the yard, you will perhaps stir up half a dozen pigs, sunning themselves in the sand, and you will probably see a small horde of black children who will shout out their "Good morning, Sar." To-day I met a man driving an ox cart to the field, who touched his hat, as they all do, with a polite "good morning." After passing the yard, the bare pasture continues, and beyond it to the left you see the water of the sound, with Morgan Island and the coast of rebeldom beyond. This is, I believe, the largest plantation on the island, and the only one which has a superintendent to itself. The house too is very much the best and most commodious, and so is occupied by Mr. Soule, and will be this winter by Mr. Philbrick and Mr. Winsor, besides Harriet, Charley and William.

President Lincoln delivered his iconic Gettysburg Address on November 19, 1863, yet Allen took no notice of it in the days to come, probably an indication of how little regarded the speech was at the time.

Nov. 20, 9½ P.M.

Both yesterday and to-day I have been to the house, painting and unpacking goods and doing various other jobs. Both the large chambers are painted of a very ugly red, and in our room this is shabby, smoked and defaced so that we are painting it over a sort of cream color. Yesterday I went on Nelly, to-day on Charley's horse, Rob Roy, the best saddle-horse in the establishment. While I was at work in my shirt sleeves, I heard voices in the yard, and looking out of the window, saw Mr. Gannett and Miss Rice, who had come, thinking we had moved in, bringing a nice piece of roast beef—a great luxury—to us here. Folsom and I made a good dinner off it. I gave them some apples and a bunch of rose-buds. The apples, by the way, came in very good condition, but the paper in which they were wrapped was completely saturated with moisture. Nothing of our articles is broken, so far as I have unpacked. Mary and Katy haven't been into the house yet at all, and probably will not until we move in,—probably Monday.

The road from here to Pine Grove is very uninteresting, such as I described, but beyond there is very pleasant; first thro' beautiful woods on the Hamilton Fripp plantation, then thro' the T.B. Fripp (Cedar Grove, it is called), which lies very pleasantly on the creek. The woods are mostly of pine, live oak, magnolia and sweet gum. The live oak is a handsome tree, particularly when it grows in masses and is obliged to run up to some height; but when standing by itself it spreads too much for its height, and is shaped very much like an apple tree—I often take a small one in a pasture for an apple tree. The magnolia is a very handsome, shapely tree, with large, glossy leaves. The sweet gum is a good deal like the maple, with star-shaped leaves, which are almost the only leaves here that turn handsomely. They are generally a very rich deep red. Then there are the sumac and sassafras leaves—these are small, by the roadside. The palmetto grows by itself in pastures and marshes, and is a very ugly tree, with a straight round trunk, and a round head like a cabbage. Its wood is valuable, as resisting decay, but very hard to cut—you have to pick out the chips with your fingers. It is curious that South Carolina should have taken as her type a tree which is not ornamental, but useful; its unsocial dignity on a very small capital appears to be the point of resemblance.

As I was coming home yesterday, I overtook a negro riding in a cart and talked with him. He used to belong to William Fripp of Pine Grove; Good William Fripp he was called, as being a good Baptist, not as being a good man, for he was less liked than his brother, Capt. John Fripp. William died about two years ago, but John is still living, a very hale old man. William had four sons, one of whom died in a drunken frolic a few months ago; the others are in the rebel army, altho' two of them were probably Union. Washington, he told me, was forced into the army. Clarence is a doctor, and from all accounts the most of a man of any about here. "His father couldn't make him drive the colored people"—it was too much like driving cattle. He is now a surgeon in the rebel army. Alvira, the fourth brother, was a very cruel master.

Mr. Soule came in last night with the mail, but nothing for either Mary, Katy or me. Either you haven't the run of the steamers yet, or there is some mistake at Beaufort. The schooner went round from Ruggles' last night, and will be expected here to-morrow. Our things however landed at Ruggles', which is two miles nearer us than this place is.

Nov. 22, 3 P.M.

It has threatened rain for three or four days, and is now half drizzling. The weather has been perfectly lovely most of the time since we have been here— like our finest September weather. I have worn my summer woolen suit and straw hat, and there has been no rain except a little one day about like to-day.

Yesterday I went to the Big House again, in the gig with Nelly. It is rather inconvenient to drive because there are so many gates—about six or eight between here and there. On horseback I can open and shut them without getting off—Rob Roy particularly has a way of putting his head down and making at the smallest opening in a gate that is quite fascinating. But it requires a careful calculation of time to jump from the gig while it is going, open the gate just in time for the horse to walk thro', shut it and then climb up behind—some acrobatic skill too, for the gig tottles fearfully.

I spent all my time yesterday in painting, and our room now looks quite respectably. The parlor is really quite a pretty room. This morning Mr. Gannett, Mr. Folsom and Miss Rice came in; Mr. Philbrick and Mr. Winsor came yesterday in the schooner, so being all together—twelve of us—we initiated the Sunday services that we mean to have this winter. William Hall conducted them, reading Mr. Frothingham's[67] Springfield sermon, and one of Mr. Parker's[68] prayers; and we sang Brattle Street and Boylston ("Teach me my God and King"). We shall probably continue to have them here [Coffin Point], as this is the central one of our establishments. Pine Grove, to be sure, is half way between ours and Coffin's; but there are six here, and only four at our house, and then this family seems to be a sort of patriarch to the rest of us.

Mr. Gannett brought word that my Keene box has arrived at Pine Grove. One of the negroes, Limus, a very capable fellow, runs a boat from Pine Grove to Hilton Head, and I sent by him for the box. Curiously enough, there was no charge on it, for they go on the principle of prepayment—the express company—and I had sent the city express in New York to get the box and leave it with Adams' Express;[69] so between them the charge was overlooked. I feel quite relieved, for I didn't feel sanguine as to ever seeing the box again.

The schooner was in sight off the bar yesterday morning, but as it turns out was stuck on the shoals. The pilot, Dan, from Fripp Point, insisted that there was a clear channel where the chart indicated shoal water, so ran the schooner high and dry, where she had to wait for the tide. Then Mr. P. and Winsor undertook to come ashore in a little sail-boat which Charley had sent for; but the wind and tide were such that they didn't get in until noon. The schooner remained stuck till four o' clock, when she was lifted by the tide and came merrily up to the wharf, where she lies now.

I am beginning to understand what the negroes say, but it is much harder to understand the women than the men—it often sounds entirely foreign. The other day I met a woman in the long pasture, and after passing with a "good morning," she stopped and called out—"What side you stay in sar?" I shouldn't have made it out at all, if I hadn't heard the day before that the negroes never use "when" or "where"—for when they say "what time," and for where, "what side." It is curious too how they use the pronouns. When I told this woman I was "Miss Harriet's cousin," she said something about my "come down see we"—meaning, I suppose my visit to the quarters; and a little boy the other day, speaking of his sister, always said "him"—"him go to school" and "him min' chile"—With the infinitive they generally use "for"—they go out "for dig tater." I've only picked up a few expressions and idioms so far, but hope to study their grammar and vocabulary more closely—it is really worthwhile as a study in linguistics.[70]

Big House, Nov. 23, 7 P.M.

In at last, and comfortably settled; a jolly wood fire burning on a pair of huge iron dogs, so preposterously ugly as to be really elegant—adorned too, with medallions of Washington, and the cabalistic figure 1.[71] Our pretty brass and-irons have been assigned to our bedroom, as being too small for the sitting room. All of us are busy writing. We came this morning from Coffin's, in a gig with Nelly, Mary and Katy in the mule cart, driven by a fine stalwart negro named Rodwell. It was a busy scene when we left. They were hard at work unloading the schooner, and a constant stream of ox and mule carts was going to and from the wharf, empty or laden. Gannett had ridden over to see his goods, and his carts too were coming and going. Charley stood in the yard, checking off the goods as they arrived, William Hall and Harriet stood at the top of the steps to bid us good bye, and just as we passed out of the gate a stranger met us gallop-ing up on a grey horse. We have got very comfortable here, altho' we are far from being completely arranged yet; our beds are up, our pictures hung, our barrels and boxes unpacked, and our furniture mostly in place.

To-morrow will see us quite regular. It has been pretty busy here too all day, for Folsom has got his goods in, and has begun to sell them; so the shop in the yard has been thronged all day with purchasers. You know Mr. Philbrick has six superintendents, and each one has a shop to supply his people with goods. Gannett, Ruggles, Folsom and Ware are right on the road to Beaufort. Wells is off the road towards Morgan River, about four miles from here: Hull is on Ladies' Island near Beaufort—it was here I thought of going at first.[72] Folsom has on his three plantations—Big Place [John Fripp Place], Mulberry Hill and Cherry Hill—about 150 people; and to-day he took $257.70, mostly for dry goods. A good many articles haven't been offered for sale yet. Some of them spent from twenty to thirty dollars. There was one old man, Limus, over fifty, who for ten years before his freedom had been excused from cutting marsh grass, because it is the hardest work on the plantation, and only the youngest and strongest men were set at it. Well to-day, Limus came with twenty five dollars in his pocket—all earned by cutting marsh grass. At the rate the goods went to-day, Mr. Philbrick will have to send another schooner before long.

Mr. P. and his "concern" are making money by the enterprise, and they deserve to if anybody ever did. He was one of the original and largest subscrib-ers to the Educational Commission,[73] and not content with that threw himself into the work personally; was one of the first company sent out—as were also Gannett and Ruggles. The first year, while it was an experiment, he constantly advanced from his own purse to pay the workmen, as government was very dilatory in payments, and bought goods from the north which he sold to the negroes at less than cost. One year being past, he determined to try the experiment of free labor on a large scale, and so obtained from a number of gentlemen subscriptions for the purchase of plantations—warning them not to give more than they were willing to lose outright, he himself subscribing some ten or twenty thousand dollars. With this he bought thirteen plantations,[74] which are owned in shares by these subscribers, and worked in the best style under the direction of these six superintendents, who also receive as pay a proportion of the profit. The purchase money of the land, pay to the workmen, cost of the cargo etc., all included, he has paid out about fifty thousand dollars this year, so that the sale of the cotton is expected to cover this and leave a profit.

The crop this year is about as large as in old times: the price of sea-island about double the old price, so that the profit will probably be very handsome. Instead of subscribing to the Educational Commission this year, he undertakes to supply teachers himself to his plantations; and William Hall, Miss Rice, Miss Wells,[75] Mr. Dyer and myself (perhaps others) are paid out of the profits of the crop. He undertakes too furnish the houses with all necessary furniture; whatever hardware etc. we need we shall get out of his stores, and they will remain, of course, property of the concern. Of course the living expenses—hire of servants, provisions etc.,—will come upon us. Horse flesh—a very essential thing in these latitudes—is at present as found on the plantations. All these horses—the cows, oxen and sheep as well—really belong to government, and will be sold before long.[76] Meanwhile each gentleman has a horse for his use, and Nelly has been assigned to me, together with an excellent new saddle. Nelly is by no means a model steed, but I find that her powers surpass her inclinations. She is very thin now, as her colt, Tilly, has been with her until now, artho' she ought to have been weaned long ago. As I said before, she has a very comfortable jog-trot; but her fast trot or canter shakes you to pieces. However, if neither handsome nor fleet, I have learned to respect her powers. The other horses at Coffin's have evidently respected her and stood in fear of her—as one of the negroes told us she used to be a fine horse, "one of the big bugs."

Yesterday all the horses were browsing about in the yard, and Charley brought some pumpkins and threw to them. It was good fun to see them champing the pieces, and the ducks waddling round to pick out the seeds. For a while there was enough for all, but when it was nearly all gone, the character of the horses came out, and it soon was manifested that Nelly was mistress of the field. An aggressive thrusting forward of her head, with a flattening of her ears and a wicked look in her eyes would send them all flying. At last one choice bit of pumpkin remained undevoured. Black Mink drove Rob Roy away from it, but up came Nelly, and B.M. made tracks, whereupon Nelly gracefully restored the tidbit to the injured Rob Roy, with whom she appeared to be very good friends. It was very amusing to see. Tilly, who doesn't appreciate pumpkins yet, look gravely on at the busy scene before her, and every now and then marching round her mother, bumping against her nose, and interrupting the feast.

Nov. 24, 8½ P.M.

It has been a pretty busy day. We had breakfast in reasonable season, and after breakfast I got the dining table supine upon its back and spliced on that broken piece. Just as I got it finished Mr. Gannett's carts came with a lot of Dutch ovens and kettles, and, to our joy, our long-lost Keene box. Folsom being away, I opened the shop and saw the goods into their places, and then went at my box. The cover came off in quick time, and the first sight that greeted our eyes was a luxuriant bed of verdure—the turnips had sprouted and were getting along at a fine rate. The paper they were wrapped in was wet, but only one turnip was moulded so as to be thrown away. Under the turnips we had thoughtlessly put two or three books and some papers—which were all damp and the books somewhat injured. Then the bag of beans, the toasting iron, the bottle of whiskey, a jar of apple-sauce, and various other packages in good preservation. Presently a soft, odorous, reeking mass was discovered to be the *disjecta membra* [scattered fragments] of a smashed bottle of Oude sauce; and a similar one, but hard, another—that was not smashed, but had leaked half away. It was the smallest that was broken, and the other two were in good preservation. I feel quite proud that this was the only article of my packing that was broken, while of a barrel of some four dozen bottles of ale that came for Mr. Philbrick, only 27 arrived safely. The Doctor's cathartic pills, however, were melted into mass resembling printer's ink hardened.

Having emptied the box, I put it in a corner of the entry to serve as a wood-box, and proceeded to my work. Katy had a large nice box, and by fastening the parts of the cover together with cleets and putting it on with hinges, I rendered it a convenient chest. Then I put up pegs in the closets, and by this time dinner was ready. One of the women, Lucy, had brought us some oysters which are very plenty here, and we had just sat down to our repast of, oysters, hominy, sweet potatoes, mashed potatoes, crackers and cheese, tea, and a wee bit of tongue, when Dick announced a gentleman riding up. It turned out to be Mr. Lowe[77] of Somerville, who came down with the conscripts, and is going back in the Arago, Saturday. He knew Folsom, and called on his way to Coffin's Point. He sat down with us, and after dinner went with us into the Cotton house, Gin house and then rode off.

By this time, my scholars had assembled in great numbers. I had directed them to come, so that I might take their names, and see what books were needed. Four had come this morning from Cherry Hill—Gilead, Reddington, Menia, and Linda; forty this afternoon, from this place and Mulberry Hill. I find they will fall into four classes; the highest consists of a very nice set of fellows from sixteen to twenty Tony, Taffy, London, Paris, Bristol, Wake, Robert, Billy and Dick. Mr. Folsom has taught a little, and there has been a school this summer, kept by a colored man from across the creek, named Tim. They paid him quarter of a dollar a month. When these were dismissed, it was about five, by a new clock, Mr. Folsom has just brought from Ruggles; and I went out to cut some bamboo to finish my towel-stands. I also picked a few roses, leaving the buds to grace Harriet's table. By the time I had cut the bamboo into proper lengths, it was too dark to do anything more so I came in, and we soon had tea. Since then, Euchre and writing. It is now nine. I don't like to read by the flickering light of candles, and we have no kerosene yet, so I think I shall work awhile on my towel-stands.

I forgot to say that Mr. Folsom brought home the report at noon that the rebels made a raid yesterday on Morgan's Island, which belongs to Mr. P.—and carried off the cattle-driver. We have been fearful of some movement there: it is outside our lines, and there must be a great temptation to come and burn the cotton. Mr. Ruggles and others have been busy to-day in getting it away.

Nov. 25

I have been busy all day, but have very little to show for it. This puttering work takes up a good deal of time. First, I finished my towel-stands, which are pronounced quite a success, altho' another time I should avoid some mistakes. Besides this, I put up a rack for my tools: mended the handle to a table-drawer; filed down a brad-awl which I had broken, to a sharp point; worked on my curtain-fixtures; sorted some papers, and did some other little jobs. Mr. Lowe lunched here on his way back to Beaufort, and just as we were ready to sit down to dinner, Mr. Philbrick drove up, on his way from Beaufort, bringing letters for Mary and Katy, but none for me. I have not heard a word since I sailed, and have no doubt there is a pile of letters at Beaufort.

About five o-clock we took a walk down to the quarters. They are a good deal nearer the house than at Coffin's Point, and the houses are more scattered, not being in a single straight street as there. The first house we came to was of Moses, the foreman, and his wife Joan. They have a lot of children and grandchildren—London, Paris, Tony, Gabriel etc.,—and she went with us to her sister's house—Peg. It seems to be a large family circle. Peg's daughter Eliza came up on crutches—a married woman—and the first words were a request for a spelling-book. Several have asked me for testaments, and several gave in their names as scholars—making about fifty in all. Further on, we came to the

house where Justina lives—sister of our wash-woman, Ann. It was quite entertaining here to shake hands with a little boy, whom his mother was teaching
to be polite. "Shake hands" said she, and he held out a flabby paw; "pull foot,"
and a polite scrape of the foot followed, as the little fellow stared fixedly into
our faces. In a little enclosure by the side of the house were some conical heaps
of earth, which it seems contain potatoes. They cover them with corn-stalks,
and heap the earth over them. A little further on, an old woman came out of a
house and almost threw her arms round our necks, exclaiming "Got a missus
again?" We learned afterwards that she was crazy. Her daughter was a pitiable
object, covered with sores. While we stood here, a very pretty girl named Jane
came up, and soon after, Paris, who is a very wide-awake, showy fellow. He and
Jane began chaffing together, and we thought it was a flourishing flirtation;
but afterwards learned that Jane was married[78]—I believe to Paris' brother. The
cabin of William, the carpenter, was the neatest that we visited, and William
seems a very intelligent man, altho' I understand that he is a little "crooked."

There are about a hundred people on this "plan'shun," almost all of them
born on it. It was not the custom on these islands to sell the negroes, altho'
there was considerable cruelty in other ways. The consequence is that there is
a very strong feeling of locality, and jealousy of strangers. Phoebe, our cook—
Ann's mother—was bought about twenty years ago, but her family is regarded
as "interlopers" to this day. It would have been very easy to change slavery here
into prædial serfdom. It may lead to some embarrassment in transactions of
land hereafter, that the negroes feel that they have a sort of right to live upon
their own plantations. It was curiously illustrated the other day when one of
the superintendents was explaining to a negro—one of the most intelligent and
trusty—that he could buy land on another plantation. He seemed inclined to
be suspicious of it, as if they were going to be made to buy, and thought it was
as bad as slavery if they had to leave their old homes. This feeling gives a new
hold to the superintendents, however, over bad hands; that they can threaten
to send a person from the plantation if he doesn't work or behave well, or can
advise him to buy twenty acres at the government sale.[79]

I think I will draw a plan of our plantation, and another time I will send a
plan of the house. In the pasture you must imagine a dozen cows and oxen and
eight or ten sheep—the only ones on the island—grazing. Next year this will be
cultivated, and the part that is now cotton land will be pasture. Both fields are
flat and bare; the land is better than at Coffin's Point, and the road less sandy.
The avenue that leads up to the house is about an eighth of a mile, and very
beautiful—it must be exceedingly beautiful in the spring, when the Asia-berry
trees and the vines are leaved out, and the yucca in full blossom. To-morrow is
Thanksgiving, when we all dine at Coffin's Point, and I shall probably give the
letter to Capt. Hooper to mail.

St. Helena, Nov. 28, 1863, 7 P.M.

Raining hard, with thunder and lightning. We are sitting at our square table—Mary writing, Katy reading Eleanor's Victory, and Mr. Folsom my little Burns [Robert Burns] which has been to Germany, and has now accompanied me to the seat of war. It is so warm that we let the fire go out this morning, and haven't lit it again. But it is astonishing how damp everything gets. We left our trunks two or three days at Coffin's Point, and when we opened them everything was sticky and musty. And this is the dry season—altho' this week has been a wet one compared with the last. I have been hard at work these two days, yesterday painting the sashes of the sitting-room windows ,with a mucilage brush; to-day glazing. Thirty six panes of glass had to be set in our house, and we expected to have to do it after the schooner arrived with the glass. But before we came here, Mr. Gannett, who is always doing something for other people, got the glass at Mr. Hunn's[80] store, and set all the windows. But he hadn't putty enough, and had to leave about twenty of them merely stuck in with tacks or those triangular bits of tin. So I got some more putty yesterday, and to-day have been at it nearly all the time. I can't say that my work looks like Mr. Valentine's[81] but it will probably answer, to keep the glass from falling out.

This morning I tinkered for a while on an old rusty fender, and managed to get it a little into shape. When it is scrubbed up and polished, I shall go at it again, and I think it can be made quite presentable. Taffy has been at work all day stripping corn-shucks for a bed for our spare chamber, and the result is a barrel-full of very nice ones. Charley spent last night with us, and this afternoon he and Folsom worked on our stove-pipe till they got it in fair working condition. It came with a funnel too small for it, and they had to cut it at various points and stretch it, so that it would fit. The kettles etc. were all left at Ruggles', and couldn't be found; but to-day they were discovered and brought home in triumph.

I have another job on my hands now, which I shall undertake on Monday. Nelly has a sore back, and it won't do to ride her, so I sent up to Coffin's to-day for a double sulky which Mr. Philbrick fabricated last winter out of a pair of wheels and an axle. A couple of stout shafts and a box for a body were added, but there is no seat, I think I can make it work with a chair, but shall undertake a regular seat if I feel equal to it. I have also added blacksmithing to my other professions. I found a piece of the handle of an iron kettle-cover the other day, and hammered it into shape for a door scraper—using a brick for an anvil (there are no stones in this region), on the hearth, while Mary was toasting bread for breakfast. I think of applying for the Rumford Professorship[82] of the application of science to the useful arts. I must mention, however, that one of my contrivances failed ignominiously this morning. Miss Rice gave Mary a great bag of bitter oranges, with directions for converting them into some toothsome sweetmeat. But they must be scraped, and our establishment boasts not a grater. Forthwith I offered to manufacture one, by driving tacks thro' a bit of board, but when finished, the teeth were too fine, and too far apart. Then I tried it with the heads, but that was no better. Brads I was sure would work and was about to try them, but just then Phoebe appeared with a huge potato-grater, and my invention was no longer needed.

Thanksgiving day has been long looked forward to by the dwellers on this part of St. Helena, as there was to be a real turkey and plum pudding at Coffin's Point. Soon after breakfast Rodwell appeared with our trunks in its mule-cart, and a note from Harriet begging for our plates, cups and saucers etc., as the perfidious schooner had left the expected treasures at Ruggles', together with all the parts of her new stove except the shell. Legs, covers, funnel—all were minus, and they were obliged to have recourse to an old range that had once cooked for the Coffin household. Henry, a very intelligent mulatto from Cherry Hill, who used to be the trusted slave of the Coffins, was to cook the dinner, and performed his work to perfection—except that he put in too much pepper.

Well, I packed up our crockery in a bushel basket—you must know that Mr. Philbrick's mother was buying a new dinner-set, and he persuaded her to donate the old for educational purposes; so he spent all one afternoon in barreling it up, and we have the most of it, Harriet a part. The dozen and half stone-china dinner-plates, and an equal number of soup-plates form a large proportion of our goods in that line. After dressing and locking up, Mary and I ran to the garden and gathered a great bunch of roses, and off we started. Nelly was tied behind, because her back was a little sore, and I wanted to spare her—I knew I should have to ride her home at night. The mules went slowly, and we had to go out of our way to Pine Grove (half a mile from the road), so that we were more than two hours on the road, and found most of the guests already there. There were our four families—Coffin's Point, Pine Grove, our house and Ruggles', (self and Dyer), and besides, Capt. Hooper and Mr. Morison[83] of Milton, who is on a plantation near Land's End.

The dinner was very successful, and the party a very pleasant one. Capt. Hooper was the life of it, full of stories and talk. His position enables him to know more of what is going on than most people, and he is wide-wake to everything ludicrous, and earnest in all good works. He says it is very doubtful what will be done after this with the plantations. Gen, Saxton will probably give up the charge of them very soon. At the sale last spring, the tax-commissioners legally came into possession of those which were bid in, but as Gen. Saxton had already begun the year's work upon them, they agreed that he should continue as he had been with the government plantations, through the season. Now they demand them, the crop being gathered and the general will probably have to give them up. Consequently he has ordered all work to stop, as there is no authority to pay for labor after this. Meanwhile everything is in a muddle.

The work for the next crop ought to be going on, but nobody is interested to carry it on, because nobody knows whom it is to be for, or who is to pay for it. Nobody knows when the plantations will be sold, or whether they will be sold at all. It was for this reason that they wished to sell to the negroes, because they wanted to give them some certainty of their future. But the lands will not be surveyed for a year to come, and if the negroes settle upon their twenty-acre lots, as directed, there seems no guarantee that they will not be sold over their heads. For the price for the negroes is a dollar and a quarter an acre; but the lands will certainly bring much more than that at auction. If Gen. S. gives up the plantations, the whole system of superintendents etc. on government plantations will cease; precisely why, I don't understand. I suppose the special appointments that have been made depend personally upon him. Where the pay comes from, I don't know—I suppose from the profits of the crop. But there are so many inefficient superintendents, and so many plantations where from special causes the crop is small, that the expenses of the concern are probably greater than the income. One of Mr. Morison's plantations reported one pound of cotton in October, and a pound and a half since. The great curse to the department is the hangers-on of Missionary Societies, who are sent down here because they are fit for nothing else. Capt. Hooper was very severe upon some of them, who are good for nothing, but who can't be got rid of. Some are worse. Clergymen have taken government stores, provided at a certain price to be sold to the negroes as a charity; sold them to them at a large advance, accounted to government for the cost price, and pocketed the balance. Of course such as these are expelled at once, but there are plenty of hypocrites and fools left, who seem in a fair way to be permanently saddled upon the department. As to the sales of land to the negroes, everything promises well. Upwards of $4000 have been paid in by them within eight days, as preemption money. Part of the land is sold by private sale, part by auction, and if they fail to secure the land at the auction, their money is in safe hands and will be refunded. Obviously the sooner the land is all in private hands, the better.

There wasn't much jollity, because everybody is in the midst of business, and couldn't keep it out of their heads; but I think all enjoyed themselves. I spoke the Dumb Orator,[84] Charley making the gestures. At about eleven we broke up Capt. Hooper, Ruggles, Dyer, Mr. Morison, Molly and Katy spent the night. Folsom and I rode along with Mr. Gannett and Miss Rice as far as our roads went together, and then pretty rapidly home—Nelly making very good time. It was a perfect moonlight night, and the Hamilton Fripp woods were very beautiful.

Yesterday and to-day I have had some of my scholars, and given out some books, which I got at Coffin's. We shall have a large class for afternoon, of those who work in the morning. The men are quite well advanced, and will be an interesting class. The women will come earlier, and have hardly learned more than their letters. In the morning I shall have the regular school for the younger scholars, probably in three classes.

Nov. 29, 8 p.m.

It poured all the night, and has rained almost all day, but has cleared up cold to-night with considerable wind. So we staid in the house all day until towards night. Mr. F. and I went to Mr. Harrison's (T.B. Fripp place), to witness a wedding. Mr. H. is an Episcopal minister, and our nearest neighbor. He is a pleasant, gentlemanly man, and his wife is quite agreeable I should think. It was four of my scholars that were married: Paris and Laura, Henry and Jane,—the beauty, who I thought was already married. There was nothing special in the ceremony. Mr. H. read the service; his wife and we sat in the room, and out on the piazza was quite a crowd from our plantation, the parents etc. of the brides and grooms. The men both stood erect and appeared very well. Laura looked interested and happy, Jane had a handkerchief up to her face all the time.

Dec. 1, 8 p.m.

Yesterday was a cold blustering day, but as there were several things we wished to buy, we decided to go to Mr. Hunn's for that purpose. Friend Hunn is a Philadelphia Quaker, who keeps a store on the Edgar Fripp place, in behalf of the Philadelphia Freedmen's Society.[85] He has been established here a long time, and keeps a larger assortment than Mr. Philbrick's stores, selling to all comers, while all of Mr. P's (except Ruggles since this last schooner) only sell to their own plantations. I had Nelly put in the sulky. I sat in a chair and Molly on a box, and off we started. The sulky was very comfortable, but the axle is weak and sags so that the wheels bend inward, and our appearance was somewhat as follows. Rear view. Consequently it was rather hard for my architectural steed, as Orpheus C. Kerr[86] would call her, from the gothic style of her build, to pull the go-cart though the sandy roads; and it was much as ever that we got her out of a walk. Add to this that the wheels hadn't probably been greased since last winter—when the sulky was last used—so that when we got to Edgar Fripp's I had them greased. It was a very lovely road, and if it had been warmer or our beast faster we should have enjoyed it very much; as it was, we were so long on the road that we were thoroughly chilled.

We went first towards Beaufort a few rods, then struck a cross-road to the left, which brought us into the Seaside road in the Mulberry Hill plantation. I don't know whether there are any mulberries on this place; I know there is no hill, only the house is in a spot which rises slightly above the surrounding plain. Here we turned short to the right, in a road all overgrown with grass and for some distance through beautiful woods. Mulberry Hill is under Mr. Folsom's charge. Next is the Hope Place, very low and wet; a wicked, unhealthy-looking spot, but wonderfully beautiful with tangled vines and hanging moss and thick undergrowth rising out of the standing water. Then Woodland, a small plantation, the road running through a fine, dry forest. From this forest we came into the open fields of Frogmoor, a very large plantation (more than a mile through) and then to Edgar Fripp's (Seaside Place) where the road comes very near the sea, crossing an arm of it. [See Port Royal Map and Key (No. 20).] The view along here of the sound, the marsh and the hunting islands, which line the coast, is very beautiful. We had rather more than half a mile here, before we reached the road leading up to the house.

Edgar Fripp's must have been one of the leading plantations, for it is a large one, and the house is the largest and finest we have seen—more stylish than Coffin's if not larger. Here we were shown into a pleasant room with a jolly oak fire on the hearth, where Mary sat talking with Mrs. Hunn[87] while I inquired for the various articles we wanted—none of which they had except a wood-saw that Mr. Folsom wanted. We couldn't stay long enough to get thoroughly warm, for I had an afternoon school, and we had ordered dinner at half past two, and it was now two, so off we set. On our way we met Mr. and Miss H.,[88] and exchanged a few words with them—a new white face on the island is instantly challenged—they seemed pleasant people.

We were glad enough to get into the shelter of the woods from the cold wind, and gladder still when we were fairly at home and before a warm fire. At Mr. Hunn's I saw ice standing. After we came home we had dinner and then school; then I went out and picked some roses and a beautiful white camellia japonica—which has just come in blossom. I gathered another to-day. Just as it became dark, Mr. Philbrick drove up and spent the night. Our guest-chamber wasn't furnished—except with the iron bedstead we had of Joseph[89] and a chair; and there was a great pile of apples in the corner. But luckily Taffy had been stripping shucks all day, and there were enough to fill a bed-tick. A wash-stand was moved in from Katy's room, the apples were picked up, and the room made presentable. We spent a very pleasant evening Mr. P. is an excellent talker—and this morning he went on to Ladies' Island.

To-day school, morning and afternoon (evening they call it). We have seventy now, including ten from the Hope Place, which does not properly belong in our district; but as long as we have room, we don't wish to turn any away, I have fifteen grown up men, mostly young, but among them Paris, the foreman at Mulberry Hill, a fine, intelligent-looking man, whom Mr. F. thinks the best man he has. Katy has a class of as many women, mostly less advanced. In my spare time to-day I have been putting up my curtain—fixtures, and one curtain as an experiment. It works very well, and now I have only to make three rods, and the tassels (bags of sand). A book-case is a great desideratum, for our books are piled all about the room. When that is up, and our curtains, we shall look quite civilized. Harriet came to dinner to-day, riding over alone, as is her wont. We have been hearing constant guns to-day in the direction of Charleston. Something doing.[90]

We are much perplexed how to arrange our after-noon classes, as the men and women have to come at the same time; but the men read quite well (Hillard's Third Reader), while the women are only beginning. They all seem very eager to learn, and the men are particularly anxious to learn to write. I think we shall have to have them come alternate days. In the morning school I have three classes, of about a dozen each. The first reads in Sargent's Second Reader, and I am teaching them Geography and Arithmetic. On the outline map of the United States, I have taught them N. and S. Carolina and Massachusetts; they are adding simple units. The second class is beginning Sargent's Primer; the third is just beginning to learn.

We are quite well served; better I think than most families. Dick is a very intelligent and trusty fellow, and I hope his care will renovate Nelly. He was one of Capt. John's house servants, and was carried off upon the main when the whites skedaddled, but afterwards ran away and joined his family, thinking if they were sold to Cuba (as he was told would be the case) he might as well go with them. He has faults. He will leave the door open and the wood-box empty. He forgets things he is told to do; disappears mysteriously to grind corn or bring potatoes; is slow and dilatory. He delights to wait on table in restaurant style with a towel hanging over his shoulder, striding round the table in heavy boots to hand us dishes we could reach ourselves, bringing us jelly to our potatoes and milk to our waffles; and evidently longs to carry round the white pitcher that has served as tea-pot to replenish our cups as he does our tumblers. We agreed upon 1½ as our dinner hour; and shortly after Dick asked Mary if she wanted dinner at 1½, "'coz, ma'am, I don't know what you likes, but we likes to be punctual."

To-day we sat down at quarter before three. Ann (Anacusa, is her full name, and her brother is Wakazeer) is his wife, and she does our washing and chamber work. She is as quiet and sober as Dick is merry. Her mother Phoebe is cook: a hideous old woman who cooked for the Fripps six years, having learned her trade in Charleston. When she has fairly got the hang of the new stove, I think she will give very good satisfaction, as she cooks already very well. It being all in the family, there is rather a disposition to give Dick the lion's share of work to do. For a while he washed the dishes, as the cooking was done at his house, and Phoebe didn't come here at all. But when we got the stove a-going, the dish-washing naturally reverted to Phoebe, who wasn't quite pleased at it. Mary overheard her the other day muttering to herself—"Dick's work for wash tumblers; cook wash plates but Dick wash tumblers." It being all in the family, it may safely be left to themselves to settle among themselves.

It is queer how the mail comes dripping in. Last week the Arago came in on Monday, and Wednesday Mr. Philbrick came along with a great pile of letters, but nothing for me. Two or three days afterwards Mr. Folsom went to Ruggles' and found a letter for Katy; yesterday he went to Beaufort and brought her home one; to-day Mr. Harrison brought a letter for Mary and my Commonwealth[91]—but still no letters for me. It is very strange.

Dec. 3, 1863

Now that we are settled and the school is fairly under weigh, there seems less to write. We are very busy in organizing the school: scholars drop in every day, and we have now nearly ninety. About twenty have come from the Hope Place, which is not one of our plantations; but they have no school there and I don't like to refuse them as long as we have room. I am in hopes to get the appointment for Katy, and then we shall join forces and try to make a first-rate school. At present they join our classes, and Katy and Mary both assist me. I have the two younger classes first; then, at eleven, the two older classes. In the afternoon I have my men, sixteen in number, who can read tolerably well, and are beginning to write. I am teaching them numeration now, and giving them simple numbers to add. Sixteen women come too, and Mary and Katy have divided them into two classes.

I have got my curtains up to-day, and they work very well, only the cotton is so crooked that they must be taken off again to be stretched. Last night I read one act of Philip van Artevelde[92] aloud. To-night Mr. Folsom is away, and while I am writing, Katy and Molly are reading German, and we can hear the sound of singing from the Praise House. We have just roasted and eaten some "grun-nuts" (peanuts), of which I bought a peck yesterday for 80 cents. I give on the other page a plan of our house, and will try to draw an elevation another time. You will notice that there is a roof over Mr. Folsom's room and over the kitchen, leaving only a small room for a guest-chamber. The furniture of our bed-room is an iron bedstead (a), two chairs, a bureau (b), a wash-stand (c), towel-stand and three trunks (d). The wash-stand we had from Pine Grove, in exchange for one of our small ones. The towel-stand I made myself, and it would be perfect except for an unfortunate habit it has of tumbling to pieces. The bureau is that old one from Northboro'. In the sitting room we have at present three tables and seven chairs—including Molly's sewing chair and Katy's barrel-chair, which is not yet finished, and so is far from ornamental, altho' very comfortable. The Sistine Madonna hangs opposite the fireplace; the Seggiola[93] and those two heads that used to be at Northboro', in the large space next the door the Immaculate Conception[94] in one corner, and Washington in another, a photograph of little Annie[95] between the windows, and over the mantel three small colored prints. We also have a few little pictures upstairs. Our andirons we use in the sitting-room, and find them better than the dogs.

Dec. 4, 1863, Friday, 8 P.M.

I am beginning to get my school organized. The greatest obstacle is that the scholars have no means of telling time, and it will be impossible to insure punctuality. My plan is to have the younger classes (in the primer) come early and be dismissed as soon as they are through, and then have the regular school for the first classes begin at eleven and end at half past one. It worked tolerably well to-day, but about half past ten, the great herd of older scholars from Hope Place and Mulberry Hill began to swarm upon the piazza, and flatten their already flat noses against the window panes. Now I am trying to teach them that looking in at the window is impolite, and to impress upon them that they must stay to the ground, and not come up the steps until I call them. So I went out and sent them off, and went on with my class. Pretty soon my attention was called to a loud chattering upon the piazza, and to the fact that in spite of my prohibition they were all there—black as night. Seeing Molly however in the midst of them, I was satisfied, and waited in patience until they gradually dropped off again, all but ragged James from the Hope Place, and sober John from Mulberry Hill, and two or three other fellows who staid hanging upon the stair-railing. It seems Molly saw that one of the girls looked as if she wanted to speak to her, so stepped out, and was instantly surrounded by them, with their "good mornin' ma'am," and then presently deluged with eggs. Fourteen she pocketed; and as they are now thirty to fifty cents a dozen, it was really no trifling gift from these poor people. Then she asked the name of one, and at once there was a chorus—"dis my egg ma'am—my name Hannah, ma'am;" "my name Queen, ma'am;" "my name Rinah, ma'am;" "my name Celia, ma'am"; and so on. Pretty soon I let them in; but as I have only benches enough for one class, I had to stand half of the scholars round the room to recite while the others were studying. I am in hopes to have more benches by Monday.

We had oysters for dinner, which Dick got in the creek,—yesterday we had a duck which he shot, and after dinner I walked into the garden and brought in a fine bunch of rose-buds. Found Mr. Philbrick in the house with our mail, which gladdened our hearts. By the time we had read our letters, it was time for the "evening" class; and while we were hard at work, a gentleman and lady drove in the yard in an open wagon. It was Mr. Thorpe the superintendent of the T.J. Fripp place—near St. Helena Village, across the creek [See Port Royal Map and Key (No. 7)]—and his niece, Miss Richardson, he seemed a very pleasant man, and made quite a little call.[96] It was now too late for our classes, so we dismissed them, and I told my class of men to come to-morrow—I shan't usually have school Saturday. Billy (Lucy's son) brought a basket with him which Mary had got him to weave out of grass—a very handsome strong one, which we shall certainly keep. It costs a dollar. Miss Rice now drove up in a gig, with Daniel behind, and made a short call—short, because it was already sunset.

Out of about 33 head of cattle on the place, one cow is milked, and affords us a quart to three pints of milk a day—when we get it. Sunday it was too rainy to milk. To-day Lucy came up (her husband, Jimmy, is cattle driver) and said that as Jimmy was away yesterday the cattle were not driven, and we should have no milk to-day; so she came to tell us, "that we might not be disappointed." Lucy evidently is of the aristocracy of the plantation, and yesterday brought the milk in a large pariah pitcher, really quite a handsome one, which she probably cribbed in Beaufort. She has a rocking chair, which she bought there.

In this cold weather we have found it hard to keep up the fire, as we have nothing but green pine to burn, and all the wood has been chopped. But I got a wood-saw at Mr. Hunn's the other day, and William the carpenter has made a saw-horse, after the model of one which he saw in Charleston once. Then some oak has been ordered, and by another week we shall be ready for any weather. I finished my curtains to-day, and yesterday mended a broken pane in this room by puttying on a triangular piece of glass.

Dec. 6, 8 P.M.

When I came down stairs yesterday morning, I heard wheels drive up, and going to the door found two men with a mule-cart well stocked with fine fresh fish. They were Limus' men. Limus is quite a character here—a Yankee among the negroes. He lives at Pine Grove and has boats with which he carries on a brisk trade at Hilton Head in fish, eggs, fowl, potatoes etc. He has a seine for which he gave a hundred dollars, and lets it out to other men. He is a great hand at shooting deer on Hunting Island, and has a contract for supplying Gen. Gillmore at Morris Island with venison, fish, eggs etc. He has horses and carts (I believe only one however) at Hilton Head which he lets out, and in fact is making money hand over hand. We were very glad to see the fish, as we have so little fresh food, and speedily purchased a large drum fish for .75 and two small bass for .25. Soon after somebody came to ask Phoebe if she would have any fish, and she answered that if he had so-and-so she would take it, but "she didn't want any of their mean little twenty-five cent fish."

By the way, all our servants "eat and sleep themselves." Phoebe is not at all disposed to have anything second-rate, and packed off the sweet potatoes that were brought her one day—better than what we have been eating—"she warn't goin' to have none of those mean leavin's." It was a question whether to have the big fish yesterday or to-day, but Mary decided to leave it till to-day, and cooked the bass yesterday. It isn't a first-rate fish; the drum is much better. Just as we were nearly through, Dick announced Mr. Philbrick, and pretty soon in came Mr. P. and Charley, hungry as a ten miles row from Coffin's Point could make them. We were sorry we hadn't the big fish, but eked it out with cracker and cheese and some ration bread which Mr. P. brought from Beaufort the day before, and four loaves of which he kindly brought us. They didn't stay long, but hastened to make the most of the tide.

William Hall called in the morning on his way to Beaufort with letters for the mail, and early in the evening appeared again and spent the night. We find it impossible, from our deficient transportation, to get to Coffin's on Sunday for the services, so we staid at home all day reading quietly, and after dinner Molly and Katy took a walk in the woods, while I rode some distance on the Beaufort road on Lucy, Mr. Folsom's horse. Coming back, I fell in with Mr. Alden,[97] superintendent of Frogmoor, Woodlands and Hope Place, riding in an unpainted sulky drawn by a mule. I hadn't met him before, but soon scraped acquaintance, and rode by his side until our roads separated.

Capt. John Fripp, as I have said before, was a kind master, and the people all speak well of him. Still the whipping-post stands within twenty feet of the school-room window (which used to be the drawing-room)—a sprawling Asia-berry tree, leafless now and completely covered with long gray moss. It looks weird enough. Mrs. F. used to stand at the window to see the flogging. Dick brought us in some daguerreotypes the other day of Mrs. F. and her three daughters. He seemed to like them all very well, except that you "had to stan' out de way when missus come in de house," and one of the daughters was "corner-boned and spiteful at times." He has been telling us of Edgar Fripp to-night, who was probably the richest man on the island next to Coffin. He lived where Mr. Hunn does. He was a very proud and cruel man, and used to make the negroes work all night in full moon at cotton picking time. Any negro would go a good way round to avoid meeting him, for if he didn't take off his hat quick enough and bow low enough, he would lay his horse-whip upon them well. Dick says he changed with the moon: "when moon full, him grow bad, when moon grow less, him good." We were speaking to-day of a Mrs. Fripp that used to live at Mulberry Hill, and asked Dick what relation she was to Capt. John, and he answered "he call him aunt." This the way they state such relationships. As to the grammar, Dick has attained some faint notion of case, but no gender yet. He calls his wife "he" instead of "him."

It is a curiously mixed-up way we have of speaking of the various plantations; sometimes by the name of the former owner, sometimes by that of the present superintendent, sometimes by the fancy name. It is always "The Oaks," "Cherry Hill," "Frogmoor"; always "Ruggles'," always "Coffin's." We speak indifferently of Gannett's and Pine Grove never of William Fripp's; altho' when I asked a little girl from Cherry Hill the other day where she had been to school, she said "Mas' William Big Place" (Wm. Fripp also owned Fripp Pt.) [See Port Royal Map and Key (No. 11).]. It is almost always Edgar Fripp and T.B. Fripp, and I rather think our place is generally known as Capt. John's.

Mary and Katy started a Sunday-school to-day, and after they were through undertook to teach them to sing. They take to singing very readily—so readily that there is a constant tendency to make up as they go along. They are musical by nature, and a tune is soon very much transformed by them. Robert, (Lucy's son) Flora, and Henry (Jane's husband) were the best. There are two younger children, about 12, Ishmael and Ellen, Robin's children that have pleased me very much from the first, and are also good singers. They always come up with such smiling eager faces, that they quite won my sympathies, and it really went to my heart last week not to be able to let Ishmael take a book home which he was very desirous of doing. Since then I have got one for him, but I always feel as if I ought to do more for him than I do. Then there is Thomas, of the same set, a real little gentleman, neatly dressed for these regions, bright, respectful, and very well-mannered. I have a peculiar feeling in communicating with them,—as if they were something between foreigners and dumb animals.

Their vocabulary is so small and their ideas so little developed, that it is hard to find terms which they have in common with us, and I feel as if in reading, it was mere empty, sounds I taught them. However, that is giving them a που στῶ,[98] and time must do the rest. Ishmael and Thomas are almost the only ones in the morning school whom I can speak to as to northern children, but the young men in the afternoon are really very intelligent, and understand very well. Still there are only two or three of these that can add units (abstractly), and I am not sure that anyone but Mulberry Hill Paris understands what he reads enough to give proper inflections. He is foreman of this plantation, and a very superior man. Then there is Henry, a mulatto, from Cherry Hill, who cooked Harriet's Thanksgiving dinner; a very intelligent and thriving man. Next these, Paris and Dennis from this plantation, both young men, are the best I have. Then there are three boys in the afternoon; Robert, Tony, and Taffy who have very good understanding, and are young enough to have a right to expect a tolerable education.

Dec. 8, 8 P.M.

I have been to Beaufort to-day, to draw our rations, Molly and Katy were busy yesterday making bags to get them in; Mr. Folsom lent me Lucy, as Nelly's back is not yet healed; and Dick was to go in a mule-cart to fetch the articles and learn the process, so that he can do it alone another time. We are eight miles from the ferry, and the first boat goes at 9½, so that I had to get off at 8 to be sure of catching it. I might have taken more time, but wanted to make sure, so hurried off with only half a breakfast, and left the bags on the table. The morning was cold and threatening, and I was glad to wear gloves; but riding soon warms one, and I had an enjoyable ride, except for anxiety that I might be late, and vexation at having left the bags behind.

About a mile from here is a tall tower (skeleton), built by the side of the road as a signal station, between Hilton Head and Morris Island. It is in Dr. Pope's plantation, where Mr. Barnard[99] and Mr. Phillips[100] both died, where Mr. Phillips (the Baptist minister) has been superintendent; but he has just been removed, and Mr. Alden[101] appointed in his stead. There is nothing of interest in this plantation, nor in the next, Indian Hill, except a magnificent oak by the side of the road, and an Indian mound behind the house.[102] The narrow field of the "Corner," one of Capt. John's four plantations, is very pretty indeed, surrounded by fine trees, and then we come to several meadows and creeks that diversify the road. Crossing the bridge to Ladies' Island, I was overtaken by Mr. Chas. Williams in a two-horse buggy, and soon after by Mr. Nichols, superintendent of Mr. Eustis' plantation.[103] He is a very sociable man, from Kingston, and rode along with me the rest of the way, I found I was early at the ferry, and we were soon joined by Mr. Tomlinson,[104] general superintendent of St. Helena and Ladies' Islands, and by an officer whom Dick picked up, and whom I at once suspected, from his shoulder-straps and resemblance, to be Lieut. Stone of the 1st S.C. [then the 33rd USCT (United States Colored Troops) Regiment]; from Newburyport, and a brother of Mrs. Hopkins of New Bedford.[105] He has been in command of the party building the signal station, and is expecting a lady by the next steamer to be married to. She will live at Mr. Thorpe's, near us.

I learned yesterday that I ought to have a descriptive pass, so that I might be in no danger of being arrested as a rebel or a deserter—the conscripts from the 55th Pa. have been deserting in great numbers. So I walked up with Lt. Stone to the Provost Marshal's office and got my pass. I had directed Dick to borrow some bags if he could, and meet me at the Commissary's to get my rations. I told them to deliver them to Dick, and then went to the Quartermaster's to get a cart for them. There is nothing here to be paid for, scarcely. Everything is government, and you either get it for nothing, or not at all. I found a notice on the Quartermaster's door that no transportation could be given except on an order from Gen. Saxton; so off I went to Gen. S's headquarters. It was Capt. Hooper's business, but he was sick a'bed, so Capt. Saxton gave me the order (and also some books for one of my classes), and the Quartermaster endorsed on it that I was to have a cart, and told me to hand it to the wagon-master; which I did, and he said I should have a cart as soon as there was one at leisure.

Back to the Commissary's, Dick hadn't appeared, and they were soon about to close for dinner—open again at two. It was now half past eleven, and there was little chance of hitting the 12 o'clock boat; still there was a chance, and I went along the whole length of the street to the Ferry, and lighted upon Dick at last, who had been patiently sitting upon his box at the Post Commissary's, while my rations were at Thorndyke's Commissary. He had got no bags; however, he shouldered his box and trudged back to the Commissary with me, and found it closed. No help but to wait for the 3½ boat. So I left Dick to meet me at two, and started off to kill time. First back to the ferry, to ascertain certainly about the boat; and while talking with Lt. Stone and munching a hard cracker, something went, and I found an old shell of a tooth had cracked. So now for a dentist. Mr. Tomlinson said he believed there was one, but nobody knew where to find him. Any physician would do for my case, and after inquiring at several places I was told of a Dr. Hayden,[106] near Gen. Saxton's, and after trying half a dozen houses, I found the right one, and a dentist too, who soon rid me of the broken bit for .25. Then I had my hair cut and got some dinner, and made some purchases; among other things some bags for my rations. And now "the water began to quench the fire, the fire began to burn the axe etc."[107]

My wagon-master put me on board a big team drawn by two handsome horses, which soon had me at Thorndyke's. Presently Thorndyke[108] opened and furnished me with a barrel containing 120 lbs, of flour (⅔ full); also 40 lbs. pork and 35 lbs. beef, 13½ lbs sugar, as many of beans, 9 lbs rice, 1½ lb salt; 1½ qt. molasses, 4 lbs coffee and 7 oz. tea, 6 candles, a bar and a half of soap—enough to last us thro' the winter. (Three rations). Then my driver drove me to the bakery, where I delivered my flour and took a receipt. As Dick's team was a small one, I thought I would not carry home any flour—we can have it from the shop this month. Then at the Post Treasurers they took my receipt and gave me an order for 88 loaves of bread. I took eight on the spot, and shall send for the others when there is opportunity. So the rations were drawn. At 3½ I returned in the ferry, and rode along as far as this island in company with Sergeant Ide from Saratoga Co. N.Y., a very pleasant fellow, who is in charge of the island jail, on the "Oaks" plantation.

Friday, Dec. 11, 9 P.M.

Another week's work is finished very satisfactorily. I have my benches at last, and I suppose about all the scholars who will come from these four plantations. I think the average in the morning is a little under 60. Katy has had the Hope Place regularly assigned to her, and we combined forces. They are very much afraid of the rain however, and to-day, when there was a light drizzle, none came from either Mulberry or Cherry Hill. This afternoon it rained hard, and nobody came at all, altho' the quarters are not a third of a mile off. Until the benches were made, I had rather a hard time this week, for these 60 scholars had only two benches, and it was impossible with no regular seat, and half standing, to keep any sort of order. They do not understand how to study to themselves, and the buzzing is tremendous when they are all studying hard,—as they do study. If I can once teach them to study in a loud whisper, I shall think my school is a quiet one. Their attention cannot be kept long, and they are soon tired. They will study for a while very hard and noisily, and then all be restless and play-ful. I find that a song, when they are so, is a recreation to them, and lets off the superfluous steam. As I do not know their songs yet, I let either Flora or Ellen or Patty from Hope Place start it up, and the others join in, singing with great spirit, very loud, and in perfect tune. Everyone sings, and I do not know that I have noticed a discord. It is very odd to see them sing, swaying backward and forward in their seats to mark the time, and sometimes striking one hand into the other, or the foot upon the ground. I have begun to teach them "the Poor Wayfaring Man of Grief,"[109] playing the tune on my flute, and deaconing out the words. They were hugely pleased with the flute, and when I asked what it was, only one ventured to suggest that it was an organ. I only know the first and last verses, and wish someone would send me two or three of the others. I showed them my compass the other day, which tickled them much. In the les-sons I think they are doing very well.

I find more variety and more beauty in the features than at first. I have spoken of Jane as being very pretty, and she has very bright and coquettish ways, which must make her quite a belle. Patty, of Hope Place, is really handsome. If you look at her profile, you see that her nose is somewhat flat; but the outline of her face is very regular, her eyes are handsome, and her complexion a very clear rich black. I was quite interested to see that the African type was capable of real beauty, for I had never understood how Story's Cleopatra[110] could be a success. Still, very few are attractive, either in features or complexion.

My work this week has been a book-case, which was hung this afternoon amid the plaudits of the assembled household. It is my greatest achievement. Katy's room was disfigured by three large rounded boards over the windows, which had served as curtain-fixtures. These I knocked down, and after brushing off the dust and cobwebs and wasp's nests, discovered that they were very handsome pieces of southern pine, and so reserved them for some use. At last it occurred to me that they were just the thing for a book-case. They were so heavy, that I sawed one of them into two—a very tiresome job, in this hard wood,—and then planed the new surfaces as smooth as I could, designing these new thin pieces for the two upper shelves. I rigged it then with a rope, and it was done. You can't think what a civilized air it gives the room, now it is hung and filled with books. I have also undertaken to weed and thin out a strawberry bed in the garden, so that we may have that fruit in the Spring.

We had an odd fright the other night. Mary and I were waked at about five by what seemed a violent shaking of our window-shutter. One of our windows looks upon a roof over Mr. Folsom's room, and this was open, and one shutter (or rather, solid blind) closed. I was completely puzzled by the noise. I felt sure it was a shutter, for I didn't think the lightning-rod could make such a noise. But why any sane person should do such a thing was more than I could divine. It was just such an incident as would be seized upon by a spiritualist. I struck a light, but could find no sign of any visitor; looked out of the window, but could hear nothing but a pig grunting below. Clearly, it was either spirits, or a crazy person, or the lightning rod; and on trying the experiment, we found that the latter would make precisely the noise we heard, if rubbed against by a pig; and as numerous pigs sleep under the house, we decided that this was it. Both nights since, we have heard the same noise.

To-night Mr. Folsom is away, he went last night to Mr. Gannett's, and I suppose has been kept by the rain. I have finished the first part of Philip van Artevelde aloud, while Mary has made a cushion for the barrel-chair—which has remained unfinished during the more pressing work of this fortnight. To-morrow I am to tinker up the fender and tea-pot, mend my towel-stands, and make eight buttons for the window-blinds.

Sunday, Dec. 13, 1863, 6½ P.M.

It rained torrents yesterday, and as our roof leaks badly, we caught quite a tub-full of water between the fire-place and our bed. Quintus came on horse-back from Coffin's, and carried our letters on to Ruggles', and coming back at about 4 brought our mail a good full one, for which thanks; letters from father and Prentiss,[111] and papers from Lucy.[112] Quintus was completely drenched, and the mail was pretty wet, altho' carried under a rubber coat. Mr. Folsom came back from Pine Grove yesterday, where he had spent two nights. He got wet, took cold, and is quite miserably to-day, altho' better to-night. Yesterday we disposed of our superfluous ration meat. I took two rations of pork and one of beef—

seven pieces of the former, and three large ones of the latter. Mary immediately cooked a piece of each—the pork we have already eaten, and it was very good, the beef we are to have. Then we reserved another piece of each, and undertook to exchange the rest with the negroes for their commodities. The piece of beef we gave to old Isaac, the only negro on the place who cannot support himself. Phoebe gave us 14 eggs for one piece of pork, Robin and Wakazeer each half a bushel of sweet potatoes, and the two other pieces I sold for a dollar. I bought a couple of marsh-hens which Wakazeer shot, for twenty cents—rather more than they are worth. All day yesterday I was tinkering over various small jobs, some of which I accomplished satisfactorily, others not.

To-day it rained just as we were about to start for church, so we staid at home, and had Sunday-school in the morning instead of afternoon. It cleared up afterwards beautifully, but continues oppressively warm. Before breakfast I hunted birds with an opera glass, but couldn't succeed in making any out. I have heard no mocking-birds here, altho' we had heard them constantly at Coffin's Point; but have distinguished four singers—one of them very sweet, a bird about the size of our linnet, as nearly as I can make out. Another is the fife-bird so common in the White Mts. There are a great many cardinal grosbeaks, but I haven't heard them sing yet. I read awhile in Levana[113] to Mary before dinner.

After dinner, which consisted of oysters which Molsy brought us, ration rice, both kinds of potatoes and oranges—we strolled down the avenue to the road. Then I went to the garden and brought away a couple of camellias, and Katy and I went to the Praise Meeting at Peg's house,—they have no Praise House here. First they had a sort of minor hymn of their own. Then Robin (Ishmael's father) deaconed out "There is a fountain filled with blood," which they sang to St. Martin's—just as I described Old Hundred before.[114] Robin then made a prayer, a very simple one, with a good deal of repetition in it; Dick deaconed out another hymn, Toby spoke a benediction, and we went away. Such meetings no doubt do good—the social and devotional effects must be salutary; whether their lives are manifestly improved I don't know, but it is at any rate one of the social agencies working towards civilization.

Peg lent me a daguerreotype of Capt. John Fripp, and we were quite disappointed to find that the old patriarch in whom we had become much interested, and whom we imagined a gray-headed serene old man, was a very ordinary looking person, with rather sharp and restless features. He looks as tho' there might be vinegar in him; but all the people unite in praising his kindness. Dick says he "nebber let anybody but massa whip him—jes like young chile whipping Massa use count one, two, tree, but missus whip till got tired." Mr. William Fripp (Pine Grove) he says used to carry a bible out to the field (he was a leading Baptist), show them Moses' law, and then flog them "accordin'."

When we came back to the house, we found Mr. Gannett and Miss Rice, who had driven up to make a call. We had at tea some preserve which Mary and Katy made with infinite pains out of some bitter oranges which Miss Rice gave her; it is very nice, and with sour cream delicious.

I was at first much troubled by my having here so large a class of able-bodied young men, who ought to be in the army. And Mr. Folsom tells many stories of the ingenuity with which they eluded the draft.[115] But on hearing how the whole thing was managed, one's wonder vanishes. For instance, last year, under Gen. Hunter's first draft, Robin was taken about planting time, kept all thro' the summer and until after harvest, and then dismissed without a penny of pay. The whole affair was unauthorized by government, and of course no provision was made for pay. This is only one instance. No wonder when the draft was renewed this spring they were beside themselves with apprehension. If the proper means of persuasion had been used, no doubt a large proportion of these young men would have volunteered in time; but the first thing done was to throw them into antagonism, and they took at once to the woods, where they could not be caught.

Their treatment as laborers has not been much better. It is rather trying to the people on the government plantations to have to wait three or even five months for the paymaster to come round, while on the private plantations adjoining the pay is prompt every month, To be sure they are always paid at last; but in the beginning of our occupation there were many cases in which they were never paid at all—careless or dishonest officials, who were here only for a short time to collect cotton, and then went off without concerning themselves about the pay of the laborers. When government was dilatory, Mr. Philbrick used to advance the pay out of his own pocket, but not many superintendents could afford to do that. So the wonder is rather that the negroes have done as well as they have, than that they have proved (as many of them have) idle, shiftless, vagabondish. They would rather earn a good living by hanging round camps and doing odd jobs at Beaufort and Hilton Head, than work soberly and steadily for small and irregular wages. Still, in spite of all these drawbacks, the industrial experiment is a success on the whole; in Mr. Philbrick's plantation it is a great success.

Dec. 15, 7 P.M.

A looking-glass and a rocking-chair, which came down in the schooner were added to our establishment yesterday—most unexpectedly to us, We hung the former, which is a good large one, 2½ feet long, opposite the fire-place in the sitting-room; we only need our sofa now, to have the room look completely civilized. Molly has nearly covered the barrel-chair. It looks tolerably well, and is very comfortable. Billy brought a curlew yesterday, which we bought for a dime, and to-day Dennis sent us a fat wild duck as a present. They made us a nice dinner to-day, but in the midst of all this game, in this warm weather, our piece of boiled beef spoiled.

Yesterday I had no fire at all in the school-room. Miss Richardson rode round on horseback yesterday, and made quite a call; then Mary and Katy drove part way home with her in the sulky. Rest and care have improved Nelly, and she went very well. Her back is still sore, and Lucy's back is in the same condition, as bad luck would have it; so to-day Mary took her in the sulky and drove to Coffin's Point, where she will spend the night. Tom (Dick's boy) went as "tiger," to open gates etc.[116]

Scholars continue to drop in, and I have now 101 names—several of these however, will probably never come again. The regular morning number is about sixty. We begin at 9½,—the earliest I can be certain of being ready—notice being given by a flag from my window. I read a short passage from the Bible, and then give them their books. Only the first class take books home, and as they hardly know how to find their places, this occupies some time. Then we hear the abcdarians, and let them go. Some little imps have appeared sometimes, who could hardly toddle alone. Sometimes I have kept them until they begin to holler, and sometimes packed them off incontinent under the convoy of the nearest relation. There is one pretty little thing, Sue, sister of Ishmael and Ellen, as full of mischief as she can be. I let her sit with Ellen the other day, and she behaved wondrously well; but at last it was too much for her—the whole experience was too awful, and she burst into a perfect tornado of screams, and had to be hurried off in disgrace. She hasn't appeared since.

Then I hear the third class read one by one, and let them go as fast as they read—ducking a curtsey or scraping the foot as they pass out of the door. Then the other classes, and singing interspersed. I give them a short recess as a rest. I have two classes in Arithmetic; the first is Ishmael, Ellen, Flora, Thomas, Robert, and two or three others. These can add units pretty well. The second class isn't up to anything harder than "five and two." About as many—and for the most part the same ones—know nine states with their capitals, and a few rivers and other towns. The others I think I shall have to make into a second class. The states—in the order learned—are South Carolina, Massachusetts, North Carolina, Georgia, Tennessee, Virginia, New York, Pennsylvania and Ohio. The best reader, and oldest scholar I suppose, is Robert, Lucy's son—a very nice boy indeed. In the afternoon my young men hold on very well, but the women are very irregular. Seventeen men came to-day, and usually as many. Bristol is a very entertaining fellow, with a good deal of dry fun. He considers himself very backward and stupid. "I look at un, an' try for larn, but can't come for unerstan'."

And when some bigger word than usual stands in his way, he shakes his head—
"can't fetch dat word, sar." This is a common expression, and it is queer enough
to hear Hacless (Hercules) a handsome young fellow from Mulberry Hill, spell
in a loud whisper "s-o: s-o: s-o:" then aloud, "can't fetch dat word, sar, nohow." I
am trying to teach them to read figures, and most of them get along very well.
I also teach them upon the map when I have time, and shall let that bring me
to a little more intimate knowledge of their ways of thinking. I haven't talked
much with them yet, however,—it is so hard to understand what they say, that
I don't try anything more than passing conversation as yet.

Dec. 19, 8½ P.M.

Until to-day it has been very warm and wet this week, and when Paris (Mulberry Hill) brought us half a hog Wednesday night, which we had bespoken, we
were very much afraid it would spoil before we could dispose of it. However, we
managed to get two roasts and sent another to Pine Grove. The scraps we had
for breakfast, the trotters [feet] for dinner to-day, Molly is jubilant over a big
pot of lard, Mr. Folsom has both quarters and one or two other pieces in pickle,
and a bag of sausage meat (guiltless of sage) attests Phoebe's powers. Phoebe is
invaluable at any such emergency; she knows just what to do with everything,
altho' she despised the scraps and was mistrustful of a Yorkshire pudding which
Molly put under the roasting pork. Its success raised her very much in Phoebe's
esteem. Quash from Mulberry Hill (father of a host of our prettiest children—
his wife, Rosina, is Lucy's sister) sent us a duck the other day, much to Phoebe's
disgust—"what for he no pick um?" she exclaimed. I have set out three little
strawberry beds this week, and have done one or two other small jobs.

The school has been satisfactory, and is now getting quite regular and
orderly. But it is very hard for them, to learn school ways, and especially to get
into the way of referring all matters to me. If I tell a boy to do a thing, all his
neighbors want to add their words of command and instruction. And if one is
encroached upon by another, he does not wait for the, slow process of the law,
but takes his redress into his own hands. Ishmael, yesterday, in taking his place
in the class, trod on the bare toes of Wyna, a pretty little girl from Hope Place.
I don't suppose he knew his feet were anywhere near hers, and in fact they were
not—but the extreme end of his boot is so far from his foot that he has very
little control over it. "You boy," cried Wyna fiercely "you mash my foot," and
proceeded to fisticuffs. However, they give me very little trouble now, and I
seldom have to speak except about their studying aloud.

Yesterday, in the evening class, I read to them Gen. Saxton's circular inviting the freedmen to a New Year's celebration at Camp Shaw, near Beaufort.
There were about twenty present, and altho' there was very little said, I think

they looked very much pleased. I have been asking them this week where they learned to read. Two (Dick and Paris Gregley (Mulberry Hill)) picked it up from their old master's children, who would tell them a letter at a time. Paris says he bought a book in Beaufort, and that several of the people could read hymns, which they knew almost by heart. Dick says his master took two or three books away from Ann. London learned from old Tim, a negro who kept a school here this summer. Henry learned from the "bukra [white] ladies at church," Miss Towne[117] and Miss Murray. Ned never was taught, but picked up his letters here and there, and now can read easy sentences—Williams First Reader. He used to belong to Mr. Eddings[118] and afterwards Dr. White, at Woodlands—both very "tight," as they call a hard master.

They used to give them a peck of corn a week, and 8 yards of cloth twice a year. Perhaps twice a year a little meat. They also had one "task" (about 1/4 acre) of land apiece to cultivate extra corn, and Dr. White used to give them molasses sometimes. One day was given them in the spring to prepare this extra land—all the rest of the work they had to do when they could. I asked if they used to whip them. "Talk o' lick um, sar? yes, sar, nebber did noffin but lick um, sar." When did they whip you, when you didn't work? "When we work hard, lick um all same, sar," and Jeffrey, standing by, added "take off shirt and lick um naked." Of Mr. Alvira Fripp (Hope Place) Patty says that "him was bad too much." These masters were among the worst. Mr. Coffin, Capt. John, and Mr. William Fripp are all well spoken of by their slaves. I was talking with Isaac to-day, an old broken-down man who does not do any work, but is supported by his nephews—Robin and Moses. He evidently regrets the old times, when he was maintained comfortably by his kind master, and "nebber use to hab to buy backer [tobacco]." But his brother, old Moses, who was also too weakly to work in "secesh time," does a good steady share of work now. I told once before of Limus (not Pine Grove Limus) who had been laid aside from "cutting marsh" for a dozen years, but this year earned $25 at it. And May, at Cherry Hill, I fancy would tell a very different story from Uncle Isaac. He belonged to a "cracker," or mean white, on one of the Hunting Islands and was so abused that he is a mere wreck of a man. When the "gun fire at Bay Point"—the great era with this people,—it was really a deliverance for him. But poor broken-down old creature that he is both he and his wife—they cultivated three acres of cotton this year, and tolerably well.

Molly and Katy went to Pine Grove to-day to spend the day, and I walked with Mr. Folsom over to Cherry Hill, through some fallow cotton fields and fine woods. Cherry Hill is rather a forlorn place, with only eight negro houses (no white men's house) and a few out-houses, standing in the bare open field. Only the marshes and creek are in full view, and you get a fine sea-breeze.

Mr. Philbrick is talking of building a house here for us to live in next summer, as being a more healthy place than this. If he does, however, I wish he would put it on Mulberry Hill instead, for that is a very pleasant place, directly on the creek, and with pleasant trees and the drive-way lined with a beautiful hedge of casina and other shrubs. Then there are nicer people at Mulberry Hill—Quash and Paris especially. We came round that way home. The ground rises slightly at each, altho' on Sudbury Meadows they wouldn't be recognized as hills. Mulberry Hill takes its name from a huge mulberry tree in the field near the sea-side road. They were ginning in each, and Mr. Folsom weighed the cleaned cotton, which was then piled in a huge snowy mass ready to be packed. I witnessed quite a scene at Cherry Hill. A young scape-grace named Jimmy came up to Mr. F. and complained that he had taken away his gin. He had neglected his work, and Mr. F. had given his gin to another man, but told him he should have it again when Morris had finished his cotton, and he would let him have it a certain number of days; then if his cotton wasn't finished, he would send it to the steam gin at the Big Place. This is the rule: They are paid by the pound for ginning, and the work must be done speedily so that the cotton can be got to market. But Jim fumed and sputtered, evidently in a tremendous passion, and his grandmother, old Deborah,—a good old soul, who devotes herself to the ungrateful scamp—stood by trying to calm him. "Peace, peace, patience," she said in a very sweet and gentle voice, "peace make half the road to heaven, and patience open the gate wide." The whole scene—he furiously brandishing a ramrod and vociferating his complaints, and she making gestures of entreaty and soothing was very dramatic and touching.

We went from Cherry Hill to Mulberry Hill by way of the marsh and creek, saw lots of curlew—Mr. F. had his gun—but failed to get within shot. The Fulton isn't in yet, and no knowing when this letter will go.

Sunday, Dec. 20, 7 P.M.

Mr. Delacroix, superintendent of Dr. Lawrence's plantation near Land's End, called to-day and staid to dinner.[119] He is going north in the Fulton, which he told us arrived yesterday. His wife is from Newburyport, and Mary and Katy used to know him. Dr. Lawrence and wife (daughter of Mr. Train of Framingham) have just come to spend the winter on their plantation.[120]

Today has been cold and clear.

Dec. 24, 1863, Thursday, 7½ P.M.

We are well through our preparations for the Christmas tree to-morrow, which have occupied us the last two or three days. Tuesday evening as I came in birdless and squirrelless from a stroll with Mr. F.'s fowling piece. I found two boxes just arrived in incredibly good time from Boston,—one for Mr. F., the other for us. Ours contained, with lots of jelly, preserves, sardines, olives etc., a Christmas pudding, and a small box of toys. Mr. F.'s was almost wholly made up of toys and candy. Katy had a large bundle of little books and picture cards, and an endless amount of combs. We also had 3 dozen combs, which I bought in Northboro', and some beads and ribbon. So we were well stocked. While we were gloating over our treasures, in came Mr. Phillips, the Baptist minister, whom I had never seen before. He had appointed a meeting on this plantation, and, being a little early, came up to see us. I soon saw that he would like the school-room, so invited him—altho' he is a man whom nobody speaks well of. The room was pretty well filled, and Katy and I went in.

The sermon was thin, but after the services were over the people sang some of their peculiar hymns—"The Lonesome Valley"[121] which I used to sing from the Continental[122] last summer. Jimmy (Lucy's husband) led, singing or rather talking in hoarse voice "Say brudder Moses, you want to get religion?," and the rest joining "way down in de lonesome valley." But I was most pleased with one which Billy led—"Praise, true belieber, praise God—I praise my God until I die," and the chorus "O Jordan bank was a good ole bank, dere aint but one more ribber to cross—O Jordan fight was a good ole fight etc."[123]

When they were dismissed we went hard to work on our preparations, and didn't go to bed until 12½, nor last night until 11½. We have a book, a picture card, a candy bag and two toys for each one in the morning school (about 70), and bibles, testaments or hymn books for all of the evening school (also candy and picture cards). When all were labeled, we had so many left that I drove down to Pine Grove this morning to see whether Miss Rice would like any. Her box had come, but she hadn't many small toys, and was very glad of some of ours. I got back soon after 12, and went to work to erect the tree—a young magnolia which Mr. F. and I cut last night. It is now all hung, and looks very well.

We had a queer scene last night. Just after tea there was a tap at the door, and Flora appeared. She is one of my first class, not pretty and not remarkably bright (altho' the best there is in Arithmetic), but so pleasant and cheery that she is a favorite of us all. Taft, her father, followed, on business connected with going to Beaufort to-day; then Ishmael, Rinah of Hope Place (a Topsy sort of girl, good-natured and troublesome)[124] and Billy. I was just wondering how I should get hold of the young men's names to write in their Bibles, so I seized upon Billy and pumped him. Every person picks out his own name, without regard to his father's or brother's. Thus—Jimmy's name I don't know, but his three sons are Bristol Singleton, Billy Field and Robert Middleton. Billy's name used to be Bowman, but he has lately changed it to Field. Then Moses, the foreman, has Moses Burbian, Robin Rivers, London Simmons, Paris Simmons, Isaac Jenkins and Gabriel Wig. We had a good deal of laughing, and finally—Taft had gone—Dick took a riding-whip which was hanging up, and drove them all out. Just before tea to-night the door slowly opened, and there stood Taft, silent and erect with a large bag of bread on his head, some panes of glass in one hand, and one of those counting frames in the other, which he brought for me from Mr. Ruggles'. It was a very comical sight, but if we hadn't been used to it, this sable apparition might have been appalling.

Mr. Folsom has had a beeve [beef] killed for each plantation—two for this—and distributed among the people. Also a sheep for the white people—we have the only flock of sheep on the island I believe. Yesterday I noticed a flock of twenty or thirty large birds hovering over the yard, and asked Dick what they were, who said they were turkey buzzards, attracted by the smell of blood. I know the bird near to, and an ugly creature he is, but very useful as a scavenger.

None of my young men came to school yesterday except Paris from Mulberry Hill: the others were all out finding something to eat Xmas. I was quite amused with Butcher, foreman of Cherry Hill, the other day. Mr. Folsom was complaining that the men didn't gin well, and he said in an apologetic way that wouldn't do much till after Christmas—there being three good full working days, which he seemed to think so small an affair that they might as well wait and take a new start.

Dec. 25, Friday, 7½ P.M.

Well, our Christmas festivities are well over, and I think it will have a good effect on the children. We had a few more preparations to make this morning, but we expected the children very soon after breakfast. I suppose if it had been a bright pleasant day, they would have come early; but it was windy and raw, and we waited a long time for them. At last as we were up stairs, the Hope Place children came in sight round the circle in front of the house, heralded by pleasant singing, which we heard some time before we saw them. They waited in the yard, and gradually the children from this place clustered around them, and last of all the pretty Mulberry Hill children, and Paris their foreman on his bay horse. While they were waiting the young men amused themselves with Dick's saw-horse, by turns, and bungling work they made of it. We had full time, by the way, after the Hope Place procession arrived, to walk rapidly—Mr. F. and I—to the woods, hunt up some holly, and bring home a lot of berries to adorn the tree. Cherry Hill didn't appear at all.

At about 11½ we began, admitting a few grown up people first to see the tree, and then the scholars, who crowded round and gazed with great interest but not much demonstration at the novel sight. We had it in the day-time because we knew they wouldn't come in the evening, and as it was all the young ones from Hope Place staid away. We began with singing "Marching along"; then Mr. Folsom made them a very neat little address, and began to take down the presents, handing them to me. I read the names and handed them to Mary and Katy for distribution. I noted them down too, and found the whole number to be 485 besides a number of small candy figures, which Mr. F. tossed to the old people present. The children didn't take it as white children would. They were eager and interested, and crowded up about us, so that we had to keep telling them to stand back, but they were perfectly well behaved and generally very silent. They have the look and manner of having been always kept down, and don't understand things as northern children do. It was very pleasant to see how pleased they were when anything was handed to them, and at the same how puzzled they seemed to be often at it. Bristol was the only one who made any fun, and he is always full of it. I think Patty was the only one who was discontented with her presents, and she cried bitterly because she hadn't a necklace—she has already one handsomer than most that were on the tree.

When all the presents were distributed, they sang America, and then several of their own songs, then Billy came to Mary and asked if she wouldn't like to have a "shout:" so forthwith the tree was shoved into a corner and the floor cleared. This "shout" is a peculiar custom of these people, and is well described in that article in the Continental "Under the Palmetto."[125] Mr. Eustis told me to-day that so far as he knew (and he is a native of South Carolina) it is not only peculiar to these islands, but to some plantations. Perhaps it is of African origin, with Christianity engrafted upon it just as it was upon the ancient Roman ritual. At any rate, it arises from that same strange connection between dancing and religious worship which was so frequent among the ancients, and which we find in the dervishes, shakers etc. These people are very strict about dancing, but will keep up the shout all night. It has a religious significance, and apparently a very sincere one, but it is evidently their recreation—just as prayer meetings are the only recreation of some people in the north. They do not have shouts very often, and were very glad of the excuse to have one in a large open room.

We went to see their regular Christmas shout in Peg's house last night. They had a Praise meeting first, and were so late that we went back to the house, and when we went out again at 10¼ wandered around for some time in the bright moonlight for them to finish an endless St. Martin's. At last they cleared the room and began, and a strange sight it was. The room is no more than ten feet square, with a fire burning on the hearth,—on one side of the hearth sat old Moses the foreman smoking his pipe peacefully, on the other stood Peg and Sandy her husband. On one side of the room is a table, and in front of it stood young Paris (Simmons), Billy and Henry, who served as band. Billy sang or rather chanted, and the others "based" him as they say, while Jimmy, Lucy, Joan (Moses' wife, and a fine striking looking woman), Dick, Anacusa, and Molsy (daughter of Jimmy and Lucy, and a very nice intelligent woman), moved round the room in a circle in a sort of shuffle. This is the shout. Some moved the feet backward and forward alternately, but the best shouters—and Jimmy, I was told to-day, "is a great shouter,"—keep the feet on the floor and work themselves along over the floor by moving them right and left. It seemed tremendous work for them, but Jimmy remarked to me to-day of the young people shouting "dese yere people worry demselv—we nebber worry weselv,"—and I saw that the most skillful ones moved very easily and quietly.

The shouters seldom sing or make any noise except with their feet, but work their bodies more or less; while the singers clap their hands and stamp the right foot in time. Tony, Taffy and Ishmael sat or stood about and joined in the "base." When they had shouted in this way for several minutes, they stopped and walked slowly round while Billy sang a sort of recitative interlude; then, when he began a new tune, they started off again. And their shouting varied a little according to the tune. In some they kept along with scarcely any change, and in others they would half stop, with a jerk at every change in the tune, and shift the foot in advance from right to left or left to right. Presently Billy joined the shouters, and Henry led the singing. We staid about half an hour and then came home.

To-day I was very glad to see the shouting again, to understand it a little better and catch the words. First there was a circle of the young people,—Rinah, Patty, Robert, Ellen etc.: afterwards Jimmy, Molsy etc. had one. Church members are sometimes unwilling to shout with outsiders. The singers were the same as last night, and they entered into it with great zest. Billy's face was all aglow, and Robert's was perfectly drenched with perspiration. I caught some of the words, which are evidently original. "Jesus call and I must go—I cannot stay behin' my Lord,"[126] while the base sang "I must go." Another was "Pray a little longer, Jericho do worry me,"[127] while the base was "O Lord, yes my Lord." In singing this Billy sang very fast "Jericho, Jericho, Jericho etc," while the shouting was very rapid and excited. Another "Bell do ring,—wan' to go to meetin' bell do ring, wan' to go to shoutin',"[128]—base "bell do ring," and here he sang in the same way "heaven bell" so fast that it sounded like "humbell-a-humbell-a etc." These two were very fascinating. Another was mournful—"Jesus died—died on the cross,"[129] while the base was minor, "Jesus died," and the singer repeated "died, died, died etc." as he did "Jericho," only slowly and mournfully. Altogether it was one of the strangest and most interesting things I ever saw.

base
O Jericho do worry me.
O Lord, yea my lord, (*bis* [two times])[130]

When the shout was over they went off, all in good humor, and soon Mr. Gannett and Miss Rice drove up, whom we had invited to dinner. Shortly after, Mr. Eustis rode up on his way to Coffin's, and staid a few minutes. He is a native of South Carolina, but lives in Milton. When the estates were confiscated, he secured one on Ladies' Island, that belonged to his mother (I believe) and carries it on with Mr. Nichols for his superintendent. He is a very agreeable person, and asked about Joseph and Prentiss, whom he knows. Our dinner consisted of a roast shoulder of mutton (oysters first), and the plum pudding from home. We had a very nice time, and early in the evening our guests went.

Sunday, Dec. 27, '63

Mr. Folsom and I walked to-day to the church, about 3½ miles, and were rewarded by the mail, containing your letters of Dec. 14. It was pretty much the only thing that did reward us, for Mr. Phillips, the minister, is very little worth hearing. It is astonishing that the Baptists won't send here some man of the right stamp, who might do some good among these people. Mr. P. is very much disliked by them, and they accuse him of all sorts of things—defrauding them, bringing the soldiers upon them etc. Whether these accusations are true or not, it is certain that he has no influence upon them, and had much better be away. He has been removed from his office as superintendent of Dr. Pope's and Indian Hill plantations, and it was hoped that now he was got rid of. But he declares his intention of staying as a missionary. Capt. Hooper makes no bones of calling him dishonest, and I must say that when he sold me 11 bibles for 15 cents apiece, and 3 testaments for 11, protesting again and again that they were for gratuitous distribution and he only charged the freight,—I didn't more than half believe him. Then he calls a dolphin a bird (so I am credibly informed) and spoke in his sermon today of "lasciviciousness." When I went in—I lingered outside to read my letters—he was comparing something in the Holy Land to the cone of Vesuvius, and the most of his sermon was a description of Bethlehem.

After dinner, Molly and I went in the tumble-down to carry the mail to Pine Grove. We went with Lucy, and had Nelly tied behind, so that we might bring back the splendid vehicle that I described in my first letter as Mr. Gannett's. Mr. G. received a new buggy by the schooner, so the old one was turned over to us. It took some time to fit the horses to the concern, and then we started off, with the "wheelbarrow" as Mr. Folsom irreverently calls it, tied on behind. But in turning round the strings broke, and we left it at the corner of the road to send for to-morrow.

Yesterday there was an excursion to Hunting Island in two boats, from Coffin's Point and Pine Grove. We were to start very early, to catch the tide at about ten. But when we got up the sky was entirely clouded over, and it threatened a bad day. So we gave it up. But just when it was too late to start, the sun came out brightly. As it turned out, they waited for us until 12, and had a very successful trip—much to our chagrin. However, we made the best of it, by doing what we had intended for a good while—visiting our sea-side pupils. Katy and I went in the tumble-down, and Molly rode Lucy—the first trial of my side-saddle.

First we went to Hope Place. It was as beautiful and as unhealthy looking as when we passed thro' it before; but the "nigger-house" (as the quarters are always called) lies high on the bank of the creek. Lucretia, one of our largest scholars, a bright pleasant girl, full of fun, saw us coming, and greeted us very warmly. Two of our scholars, Lucy and Betty, are very sick, so Mary and Katy went in to see them, while I distributed the presents from the tree to those who didn't come the day before.

Then I drove along towards the house where Mr. Alvira Fripp used to live, but was soon stopped at a house, by seeing Queen and Benjy at the door. Their mother, Clarissa, seemed a very nice woman, and began by begging me to take care of Benjy, and assuring me that if he was late at school it was his own fault. She had begged Molly—who was riding ahead of me—to look after Queen, who is a tall, awkward, good-natured girl. Mr. Palmer,[131] her former teacher, had said that she "could read right smart but she was clackety, clackety, clackety." She amused Molly very much by her description of "Massa Warra (Alvira)." "Before he got religion he use to cuss and cuss and cuss; but when he joined the church, that perwented him you know, so he used to lick'em instead." Massa Warra's house is situated very pleasantly on the creek with a beautiful view of the islands—very much like the house at Mulberry Hill. It is now occupied by a negro family. Clarissa brought us a dish of ground-nuts which I poured into the box in which I had brought the presents, and before we had got thro' the village (we had to drive back the entire length of the quarters) we had as many as half a dozen dishes poured into the box.

They told us we could easily go across to Mulberry Hill, and a dozen children undertook to guide us, the girls clustering round Mary, the boys round us. A merry set they were, running and leaping and tumbling in the mud, and they led us by a cart path thro' the fields and round by the beach, and finally where Will, who met us with an axe, had to cut a path for us thro' the bushes.

However, we got thro', and the Mulberry Hill people welcomed us as warmly as the Hope Place. It is a much smaller plantation, and two or three families pretty much exhaust the list. Rosina and Lucretia, sisters of our Lucy, are married to Quash Fortune and Paul Scott. Then there is Maria, mother of our Dick, and her children Will and Tamar. Rosina is a fine looking woman, and it was with a good deal of pride that she singled out a couple from a throng of children, and pointed to the rest—"all dese yere mine." A very pretty set they are. Polly is a beauty—very much like Sarah Bassett,[132] only taller—and is married to Will. We can't decide which is prettiest, she, or Patty (Hope Place) or Jane. Then there are Betsy, Lucy, Minna, Elisabeth, Lucretia and Flora—Elisabeth and Lucretia very pretty children indeed. Lucretia Scott has a smaller family, but a very nice one. My handsome pupil Hacless, Ned's wife Bella, and little Paul. The people here brought us eggs mostly.

We drove along from Rosina's door to Paris Gregley's, who had been waiting to receive us. Paris is a man of an unusual degree of character, not particularly enterprising, but firm, cautious and persevering. He is my constant scholar, and last Wednesday he succeeded with my help in adding together on the black-board two numbers of two figures each, where there was no carrying. Isn't that a comment on the divine institution—a man over fifty, who would be an intelligent man anywhere. He is very polite and courtly in his manners, and introduced us to his wife with considerable ceremony. Having no eggs, he brought us a large dish of ground-nuts.

We had had enough of cross-cuts, and went round by the road to Cherry Hill, with very pleasant recollections of Mulberry Hill. We only have four scholars at Cherry Hill, but they are very nice ones. Gilead is a very comical little fellow, who wears an enormous glazed cap with the glazing all gone. He lives with his uncle Henry—a mulatto who is very intelligent and enterprising, and has much the nicest negro house I have seen. His wife Mary is as white as half the people in the north, and nobody would suspect her of black blood. She claims that she was born free, but was cheated out of her freedom; and used to tell her master Mr. Coffin (who owned Cherry Hill) that she wouldn't work— she was as white as he, and had as much right to be free. This had soured her, and she has an ungracious, disappointed air about her, altho' Mr. Folsom says that she is much more cheerful since sunny little Gilead came to live there. Gilead had been in our sitting-room two or three times, and had always been very such taken with our feminine match-box, Mrs. Harris (which sister Mary[133] gave me). So we put on the tree for him one of those little porcelain babies, and it was pleasant to see his eyes shine when he received it. Several other women came in to see us at Henry's house, and brought us eggs and ground-nuts, and then we went along to see old Mary and Deborah, of whom I wrote in my last letter.

Deborah has great-grand-children living, but she cultivated this year three acres of cotton (a full man's task in old times; only one other person at Mr. Folsom's places cultivated as much) besides three of corn and one of potato; and did probably half the work on her worthless grandson's land. She thanked the Lord fervently for living to see this day, and insisted on giving us a dish of ground-nuts. We reached home with nearly half a bushel of ground-nuts, and 14 eggs. Quash had come over while we were away, and brought two ducks, and in the evening Margaret (Dennis' wife) sent us half a bushel of sweet potatoes.

The school has been rather unsatisfactory this week, by reason of irregularity of attendance. I have spoken to a good many of the parents, and hope it will be remedied. At any rate, I shall make some regulations to prevent it, and if necessary shall have the doors closed at a particular hour, and none allowed to come after that. My evening school didn't amount to much this last week, either, and I am afraid it will be still more broken up this week, for the soldiers have taken to hunting deserters again, and our young men are all in a panic and sleeping in the woods. There are only two or three deserters among them, (one of these is Bristol), and it is promised that none other shall be touched. Still the soldiers are not very nice in their discriminations, and carried off some from Coffin's and Pine Grove last night who were not deserters.
Monday eve.

(These have all been returned to-day.) It is a shame to turn our army into a press-gang without the pretense of any lawful draft—only a military order—and upon these simple and ignorant people. Mr. Philbrick has gone to Beaufort tonight to see Gen. Saxton—I suppose about this, and I hope it will have some effect. I wish sincerely that something would turn up to make these men more willing to fight for their freedom—they have got it altogether too easily. But forcing them into the ranks at the point of the bayonet is only driving them away. Aleck and William (the carpenter) have been sick this week with small pox; but it is of a very mild character, and Aleck is already out. Little Sue was burnt pretty badly the other day by her clothes catching fire, but luckily it was soon put out, and she is getting along very well.

Praise, (true belieber), praise God.[134]
 (brudder Moses) Praise, true belieber, praise God
 (Aunt Phoebe) Praise God before I die.// An' reach d' heaben my home.
 1) Jordan (bank) was a good ole (bank) sight 4 To help me bear
                     the cross
 (fight) 2 / I haint but one more ribber to cross
 3 I want some   cross.
  I want some valiant soldier   4 / To help me bear the

Jan. 1, 1864, Friday, 8 P.M.[135]

A happy new year to all, and a merry Christmas I hope it has been. This has been a quiet week, and I have had very little to write about. Dick went to Beaufort Tuesday, and carried our letters. He went to sell his pig, and was up all the night before, to slaughter it. The same day Harriet and Miss Rice came to dinner, and the next day Molly and Katy went to Coffin's in our new two-horse buggy. They didn't start until after Katy's classes were all heard, and intended to be back in time for the afternoon class. However, they were longer than they expected, but fortunately not many of their scholars came, and those I heard. They came at last with a cargo of castor oil, Perry Davis' painkiller,[136] rock candy and writing books. Yesterday it rained, and we had a very small school. Our Christmas festivity and our visit to the Sea-side plantations have given quite a start to the numbers—four little girls and four grown women from Hope Place, and a very pretty little boy, John, from Mulberry Hill—Rosina's boy, and brother of a host of pretty sisters. He has an uncommonly delicate and refined look—chubby and boyish too—and is only about knee-high to a grasshopper.

I find that there is a great deal of irregularity by reason of the scholars having work to do. Morning has always been the time for work, and it is hard to induce them to believe that there is as much time after twelve as before. When the spring work fairly begins, in two or three weeks, it will be still worse, so I am devising some plan for having my principal school in the afternoon, as Miss Rice and Mr. Hall do. The difficulty in my case is that I have such a number of grown persons, who must come towards night, and that it would be hard for the seaside young children to come alone in the morning,—as in that case I must have the primary school then. But I must do something.

My young men are getting along very well with writing, and I have just got writing books for them. In ciphering (some of them) can do a sum in simple addition, and are beginning to have a glimmering notion of carrying. With my class in Geography I have begun now the states in order—having taught them a few of the principal ones, and the general divisions of the country. I have put them into a Spelling Book—"Spelling and Thinking combined"—in which they do fairly. They are improving in capacity to sit quietly and study.

To-day was appointed for a celebration at Beaufort of the anniversary of the proclamation of freedom.[137] The celebration was to consist of a procession from Beaufort, to Camp Shaw, presentation of swords to Gen. Saxton and Col. Higginson, etc. Boats started early in the morning from Land's End and St. Helena Village, and at Mr. Philbrick's request the boat from the village was requested to stop at Fripp Point, which would be much nearer for the Coffin's Point and Pine Grove people and also for us, altho' not much. We should have done as well to go by land to the ferry, but we thought the sail round the islands would be a pleasant one, and our 3 families agreed to meet at Fripp Point.

Yesterday was rainy and uncomfortably warm, so that we only kept alive an apology for a fire, and all the night there were heavy showers at intervals with some thunder and lightning. The boat was to leave the village at 7, so we had to get up at an unearthly hour, and as both Dick and Phoebe were going, we had to depend upon our own resources for breakfast. Phoebe made up a quantity of "doughnushes," as she called them, yesterday, and Molly and Katy got the pails ready with our provender last night. At 4½ this morning Katy came and called us, but it was still very cloudy with considerable wind. However, I felt confident that it would be a bright day, and with many protests we crawled out of bed. Dick wasn't up, so I had to rouse him, and he got the carriage ready for us. Mr. Folsom insisted on walking, while we took both horses in the buggy. It was now bright moonlight, with considerable wind, but a warm balmy air and when we set out Mary half protested against my taking on overcoat. However, I never go where I am to sit, without extra clothes, so took my light overcoat and shawl, and half by accident a pair of gloves.

It was past six when we started, but there was a cross-road thru the woods in the Hamilton Fripp plantation, although we were not sure that it was practicable. We were drawing near the place where it turned off, and debating whether to risk it, when we looked behind, and there was Phoebe in a little go-cart, with a boy named Sammy (one of Ishmael's mates) driving her; and on foot, Billy and Taffy. Billy, being appealed to, thought the road feasible, so we let Phoebe go ahead, and, turned into the pasture. Presently we came to a strip of woods, and lo! Mr. Gannett had put up a beauteous new fence, tall and shapely, between his land (Fripp Point) and Hamilton Fripp. However, we were driving slowly, and by the time we were up there, Billy had the fence half demolished, leaving it for Sammy to put up again on his return. On we pushed, over the bumps, thru a narrow strip of woods, over some heaps of rails, and in a few rods were in the regular Fripp Point road, having saved at least a mile, and there was Mr. Gannett's buggy ahead of us. Now we felt safe, and drove more slowly, and soon were at Fripp Point "nigger house," which lies directly on the creek, and across the meadows we could see the white houses of the village among the pine trees and the steamboat lying at the wharf. The wind meantime had risen and grown colder, and we stood there for some time talking to Mr. Gannet and Miss Rice, and wondering whether we should see them from Coffin's.

It was twenty minutes past 7 when we arrived, and in about half an hour we could see the boat leave her wharf and move along the crooked creek. Just then, as we looked along the road, there dashed in the Coffin party—an open buggy drawn by two mules at full speed, with Harriet and Rose (her black girl) on the seat, and Winsor perched on the place where the dasher would have been, his hair blowing in the wind—William Hall in a sulky,—and Demas running after them with Winsor's cap, which had blown off, all shouting at the top of their lungs—"Has the boat gone?" "Have you all started etc?" They hastily disposed of the horses and mules, and awaited with us the coming of the steamboat. The "Mary Benton" meanwhile found it no easy work to reach us.[138] It was low tide, the channel was narrow and crooked, and the wind was so high as to prevent her from minding her helm, so at last in rounding a point she had to let her stern swing round and back down to the bluff where we were standing. Then at last, at nine o-clock, we got on board, and found several of our Hope Place scholars (Patty, Lucretia, Rinah, etc.) and Mr. and Mrs. Harrison, Mr. John Alden (superintendent of Dr. Pope's etc.) and others. Then followed a succession of futile efforts to turn the boat round—for there were bars and shoals ahead, and they wanted to go bow foremost. And at last Harriet and her party, tired of waiting left the boat, and determined to try to reach the ferry with their beasts.

Then it was 10½, and we began to discuss our own future. It seemed impossible, even if we got off, to reach Beaufort before 3, when the whole affair would be over; it was very cold and windy,—we should be seasick and chilled,—and the prospect was that we should not get back until late at night if then. The gangway had been put down while the boat was lying still, and a hasty council decided that we would avail ourselves of it. So down we went, and Molly, Katy, Mr. Gannett and I were safely on land when the gangway was taken up, leaving Mr. Folsom and Miss Rice on board. Now these two were perhaps as indifferent about going as any, and it was rather a comical predicament that they should be carried off to Beaufort and we left behind. Mr. Folsom's face expressed infinite disgust. However, the steamboat wasn't off yet, by a good deal, and Limus, seeing the crisis of affairs rushed for a "dugout" or canoe, paddled deftly to the boat side, seized Miss Rice, and, had her back to the shore in a twinkling; then back, and Mr. F. and two women came back, standing like the masts of a ship. The whole scene was very amusing, and not least so was Dick perched on the hurricane deck, with Phoebe's shawl on—she had possessed herself of his coat—his merry face a broad grin all the while. Our horses had been taken up to Pine Grove, so there was nothing for it but to walk up there. We stayed there to dinner, and had a cold drive back about sunset, thankful enough to have escaped from the Mary Benton. I pitied the poor negroes however, cowering on the boat in every corner, thinly dressed, and spending the day in this forlorn manner rather than in a gay festival;[139] and I was very sorry for Phoebe, for she was anticipating a great deal in seeing her son Waberlee [Waverly] who is in the 2d. S.C., which regiment was expected from Morris Island for this occasion. This evening we have had a roaring fire: the wind is howling outside: Molly and I have been writing, while Katy and Mr. F. dozed in their respective chimney corners.

Monday, Jan. 4, 8 P.M.

We had a good right to be cold, for this was called the hardest snap for years—at any rate, all agree that there was nothing like it last winter. In Beaufort ice was measured 1½ inch thick. We had our own work to do Saturday morning; I cut wood, and Molly and Katy cooked breakfast. After breakfast I read aloud the Tale of Two Cities[140] and we spent the forenoon very comfortably in that way. About one, Dick came in with a grin on his face, and gave us an account of his adventures. They got off soon after we left, and reached Beaufort at about three, after all the ceremonies of the day were over. Thro' the exertions of Mr. Harrison and Mr. Tomlinson, (General Superintendent for this island) rations were got for the people, and they slept on board the boat. Two children were frozen to death, and poor Phoebe, after all she went thro', failed to see her son after all. The boat came back the next morning, and altho' it was so cold the sun warmed them a little, and they had a merry passage back, singing and "shouting." I should like to have been among them. Harriet and Winsor came in to dinner, and she had been hardly more successful. They reached the ferry in good time, but no arrangements had been made for crossing. A steamboat was to have run across and back all day, but by some blunder in the order it only made one trip. So after sitting some time by a fire which they kindled in the woods, they went back to the "Oaks" and spent the night.

Yesterday it was cloudy and a good deal milder, and Mr. Folsom and I went in the buggy to Pine Grove and Coffin's Point—the first time I have been there since Thanksgiving. Dinner was late—five o-clock—and then we sang awhile, and reached home soon after eight.

To-day has been cloudy with a little occasional rain, and the school has been small and not very satisfactory. The afternoon however was very good. I have got writing books for them lately, and have got them along so that most of them can write down numbers of four places, and add or subtract them. I am now teaching them the mysteries of carrying. The irregularity of the scholars has troubled me very much these last two weeks, so to-day I made a rule that whoever came late should not be allowed to come in, and also I put the time of opening half an hour later. Then before school I went over to the Cotton House to speak to the fathers of the children about their work—they have been kept a good deal to "rake trash," that is dead pine leaves etc. for manure. All assured me that the children could rake as well out of school hours, so I hope to have the evil obviated. I found people hard at work; ginning, moting[141] and packing cotton. I described once before how they pick the cotton into great sheets, which are carried to the cotton house and weighed, and then put in heaps, each person having his own heap—a very obvious proof who has done most work. These heaps, by the way, are of families, not individuals. Next the cotton is sorted. The women take, each her own cotton, out upon a sort of shed, called the arbor, where they pick out the yellow cotton, and dry the whole in the sun. The yellow cotton is ginned and packed by itself. The ginning is done only by the strong men here, altho' at Coffin's the women gin, and Cherry Hill the other day I found Linda, one of our scholars about 15 years old, hard at work. I was surprised to see how simple an operation ginning is. The gin consists of two rollers turning upon each other in different directions, worked by a treadle. As they turn, they catch the fibre of the cotton, which is drawn thro' leaving the seeds behind. The seeds are about as large as small beans, and form about three quarters of the weight. Upland cotton is ginned by the saw-gin, which does a great deal more work than these, but injures the staple of this cotton.

Each man has his own gin, and besides that there is a steam gin here which is expected to be got into operation to-morrow, and which will gin whatever cotton is left by the men—a very wholesome admonition to them to work well. The engine was almost ruined by an officer from Beaufort who carried it off to work in a ferry boat, and it has been a long job to put it in order. It has been repaired by a very intelligent refugee from Edisto, named Nero. Altho' ginning is so easy that I ginned a little cotton myself the first time I tried it, it must be very tiresome, and there is considerable skill in feeding well. After the cotton is ginned it is moted, that is, the motes and specks are picked out by the women. Sorting and moting are paid a cent a pound each, picking 2½ cents (stone cotton) ginning two cents. Then it is piled in a great snowy heap, and packed, carefully picked over again by a woman, who hands it to the packer. When I went in the Cotton House this morning it was a very busy scene,—the gins rattling away in one room, and another filled with women sitting and standing at their work of moting, while in a third there lay three huge bales, marked 350 and 356 pounds. I went into a higher room, and there was Robin's round, handsome, bearded face rising out of a hole in the floor, while Peg was supplying him with cotton. The bag was hung down from this hole, and he got into it, and with his feet and a sort of huge pestle packed it down so tight and close that the packed bag feels as hard as wood to the hand.

It is curious how little grammar these people have. I don't see that they use a single inflection, altho' of course I may have overlooked them in the difficulty of understanding. They say "Sandy House," "Robin wife" etc. They use the past tense for the verb, as "loss" for "lose," in a good many cases, and express the past tense by the use of "done" or "been." Moses (Young) told me this morning of his daughter Hetty—"I been kep' him home two day." "Stand" they use very much as the Italians do. Flora (whose father Taft, occupied part of this house before we came) came prowling up stairs one day "for see how de house stan'."; Robin told Mr. Folsom his back "stan' like white man" (that is, was free from scars). And Katy on the boat the other day found it necessary to put up her hair in the presence of a lot of girls, who overcome with wonder and aided her with their advice; and when it was finished assured her that "him stan' splendid now, ma'am." So too, when Katy asked one of the scholars if her seat was not uncomfortable, she answered "stan bery well, ma'am."

Tue. Jan. 5, 9 P.M.

Two dull days. A very poor school yesterday, very good one to-day, and both days very full in the afternoon. I put my new rule in operation this morning. All the scholars came in good time except three, whom I sent away. I think the effect will be good. I gave the scholars a "general lesson" to-day about paper, and they seemed quite interested. I dismissed most of them early, as it began to rain; and to those that stayed I showed my microscope, which pleased them very much. They looked at a needle and their own hands thro' it. Katy has an enormous quantity of little combs, which were given her to distribute, so to-day she has been giving the scholars one apiece. I told her she had provided them with a uniform, for their first act was to stick them into their heads over one ear, which gives them a very comical look—boys as well as girls.

In the midst of school this morning Quintus appeared from Coffin's for our mail, which he was to carry to Coffin's. I had no notion it would be sent today, and had not my letters ready; I didn't want to leave school, so just put two sheets that were finished into an envelope, and sent them off, leaving a sentence incomplete. When my afternoon school was just finished, he appeared again with our mail from the Fulton—father's Christmas letter, and newspapers etc. from Lizzie[142] and Ned.[143] Thanks.

Mr. Philbrick—an always welcome guest—spent last night with us, and left to-night for Beaufort. (By the way, we are not at Coffin's Point, as somebody directed, which is five miles distant. No address but Beaufort S.C. is necessary, altho' you can put on "St. Helena" if you like.) Did I ever mention that we have arranged with Mr. Tomlinson, general superintendent of St. Helena and Ladies' Islands, that Katy is to have Hope Place as her special charge? She came down hoping to have a school of her own, but not certain. I am employed only for Mr. Philbrick's three plantations,—Capt. John Fripp "Big Place," Mulberry and Cherry Hill. So it is very opportune that this large neighboring plantation was unprovided with instruction, and that the children came to us of their own accord. One of Dennis' hogs strayed across the creek at low tide on Sunday, and was shot and carried off by somebody. He has lost two or three hogs before, but still the people can't be persuaded to keep their hogs shut up. At any rate, they make better pork when they "run."

The bashfulness of these children is something marvelous. It is almost impossible to induce one look you in the face, or to speak audibly. They have learned to speak up in their classes tolerably well, but if there is a door or a tree or a child to slink behind, they will do their talking from it; and if there is no such refuge at hand, it is hard if they can't get their face into their hands, or an end of a shawl into the mouth. To-day I called to Hannah to ask her how she enjoyed the trip on Friday. She hung her head. Then I tried Queen, who immediately got behind Hannah. Chloe next, who made for Queen's shelter. Each murmured some undistinguishable words, but to this hour I don't know whether they had a good time or not.

Sunday, Jan. 10, 7 p.m.

Thursday and Friday were dreary cold days, with rain. Very few scholars came, and they sat up round the fire. I had hardly any regular exercises, but taught them Portuguese Hymn,[144] showed them my microscope etc. It was very comical to see them look at their hands thro' the microscope, and laugh and exclaim.

In the midst of the rain on Thursday, Mr. Philbrick drove up, on his way from Beaufort with part of the mail—Ruggles got part on Tuesday, and there is still more to come, newspapers, which Mr. P. left by mistake at B'ft. My Examiner[145] and a letter from Lucy were received. Saturday, Moses the foreman brought an extra mail from Ruggles', which must have come by an extra steamer, with my letter of Dec. 30 from Lizzie, Joseph and mother[146]—very welcome letters. Two or three have asked whether I like to receive papers. Of course it is very pleasant to, as we have no dailies. Mr. Folsom receives the Advertiser,[147] I the Commonwealth, and Katy the Congregationalist.[148] At Coffin's they have the Evening Post[149] and Army and Navy Journal;[150] so that I can see these when I go there. They have Littell[151] and we the Atlantic[152] (a Christmas present from Mary's aunt), so we shall exchange these, and I think I shall arrange to have their Army Journal also. Mr. Folsom receives the Independent[153] now and then, and I have the Anti-Slavery Standard,[154] and William Hall receives a bundle of Inquirers,[155] from which I take toll as it passes. So we are pretty well off for Weeklies, but I want also a regular news weekly of my own, to keep on file—the Commonwealth is no newspaper.

Mr. Stetson, brother of Mr. Stetson of New Bedford, spent Friday night here. He is a superintendent on the north end of Ladies' Island,[156] but from his own account among a rather shabby set of people. He is genial fellow, and we enjoyed his visit—spending the evening in playing Five-Handed-Euchre. Yesterday it was too cold to set window glasses as I intended, so I painted some blackboards and did some other small jobs. Mr. Philbrick and Winsor drove here in the morning, but didn't stay to dinner.

Friday morning after school we drove to call on the Harrisons (T.B. Fripp), Mr. H. was away, but Mrs. H. and her sister[157] were at home. From her account Mr. T.B. Fripp was a very good sort of a man, and was well liked by his people. He has been killed in battle. The government superintendents are expecting to receive their dismissal every day—those on Port Royal Island have already been ordered to settle their accounts. This means that Gen. Saxton gives up the management of the plantations to the Tax Commissioners (Brisbane, Smith and Worden [Wording]).[158] They intend to get all the plantations out of the hands of government very soon. Certain ones, as Hamilton Fripp, Hope Place and Woodlands, are to be sold outright by private sale to the people in lots of ten or twenty acres, at $1.25 an acre. Others, as T.B. Fripp, T.J. Fripp, McTureous, and Frogmoor, are to be sold in the same way, with the reservations of 160 acres for a school farm. A few, as Dr. Pope and Edgar Fripp, are to be sold at auction in lots of 320 acres or less. So the occupation of the superintendents is gone, and Gen. Saxton will have nothing to do except as military governor. The General Superintendents, however, are kept—Mr. Judd[159] for Port Royal Id., Mr. Tomlinson for St. Helena and Ladies',—as their position is too important to be vacated.

There is quite a row in the church here. Mr. Phillips is one of the hungry missionaries whom Capt. Hooper is so bitter against. He was sent down here as a missionary by some society, and like enough receives a salary from them. At any rate he had a salary from government as superintendent until this last month, besides house-rent, rations etc. Still, last Sunday he demanded half a dollar from every church member for the half-year ending Jan. 1—rather steep, as there are some thousand members, and this would make a salary of a thousand dollars besides his pay—and what he makes in distributing bibles gratis. I wanted to get some to give to the scholars on the Xmas tree, and he told me he had some, put in his hands for gratuitous distribution, only he would charge me just what they cost his in freight. So I took eleven miserable bibles at 15 cts., and 3 good large testaments (with psalms) at 10 cts.—in all $1.95. Well, this new demand has stirred up the people who didn't like him over and above before, and they had a meeting today to decide about dismissing him. I don't think any decision was come to, but Moses said it was proved at the meeting that he "cusses." Another missionary of like kidney on Port Royal Id. Mr. Root,[160] whom Mr. Stetson says he has convicted of lying and stealing, has been packed summarily out of the department. A similar character is Mr. French[161] at Beaufort, the man who got possession of the New Bedford contributions and never accounted for them. He seems to be Capt. Hooper's "pet aversion," and I rather think, from all I can hear, he deserves the distinction. His wife has written a history of the Port Royal mission[162]—one of the most ridiculous books I ever looked into. Why won't the Baptists send some of their good men here—not scoundrels who come only to speculate for themselves and their sect?

I like to make you acquainted with these people who are about us, and in whom we are interested, but I don't speak usually except of those who are interesting in themselves. Three or four families pretty much exhaust the people even on a plantation so large as this. Moses the foreman, an old shrewd looking man, working hard and thrifty. His wife Joan is a fine looking, stately woman, and a woman of a good deal of character. Young Moses and Robin are his sons, as well as several others—Robin, father of Ishmael and Ellen, is I suppose the best man on the place; and his wife, Rinah (daughter of Joan by a former husband) seems to me a very nice woman. The children of Moses and of Joan count up to a great many. Then there are Sandy and Peg. Sandy is a trusty carpenter, but not very skillful; Peg is Joan's sister, but evidently less of a woman. Also her large family seems inferior to Joan's. Jane, however, who is very handsome and bright, is her granddaughter. The third family is Jimmy the cattle-driver, and Lucy his wife. Jimmy is a "real black nigger," and so is his son Robert—Bristol and Billy less so. These three are among the most interesting young men, and his daughter Molsy, married to young Moses, is much the most satisfactory scholar among the women. William the carpenter is brother to Jimmy; intelligent, but "crooked." His wife Dido is one of the finest looking women on the place. John the mulatto is brother in law of Lucy; his son Thomas is one of my best scholars. These three families pretty much exhaust the plantation, for Taft (Flora's father) is brother of Joan and Peg; but there are two large families of children,—Frank and Limus. Frank is a nice man, but his children are all dull and ugly—very light. Limus' wife Clara is Dick's sister, and his children are generally very nice. The two boys, however, Adam and Abraham, are perfect scarecrows—their rags hardly hold together, and are really not decent. Mary spoke to Clara about it the other day, and they have looked better since. Limus and Taft lived in this house before us, and Limus now lives very near, so that his children are in the yard a good deal. Margaret is a nice pretty girl; Adam is tall and stupid; Abraham is a bright-faced little fellow, a crony of Dick's son Tom. The other largest family is that of young Moses, who has a perfect host, mostly nice children—particularly Judy (whose hair stands up like slovenly Peter's) and Mylie, a very pretty little girl, very black and with beautiful soft black eyes. My three largest boys are Tony (son of Moses), Taffy (son of Peg) and Robert.

Monday, Jan. 11, 8 P.M.

We had a pretty good school to-day, but turned away several scholars for being too late. I think they will be more careful to-morrow. Mr. Soule came here this morning for a few minutes, and at about twelve Mr. Philbrick rode into the yard with Mr. Waters (the one whom I met in coming over from Beaufort); Mr. Waters is superintendent with Mr. Morison at the T.B. Chaplin place, near Land's End.[163] He is from Salem, of the class of '63. After school was dismissed I walked up and down in the yard with him for some time, and had a very pleasant talk with him. He and Morison have five plantations, but only two of them have any people on them, as a large part of Land's End is occupied by camps. One of their plantations returned 1½ lb. of cotton for October. He has had the charge of Parris Island for a month, during Mr. Hammond's absence, and says that neither there nor at Land's End do the negroes take much interest in buying land, while on Port Royal Island they are very enthusiastic about it. He says that he understands that Mr. Fairfield[164] (superintendent at the Oaks) has leased the school-farm, either at the Oliver Fripp place where he lives, or at Frogmoor.

Mr. Arthur Sumner[165] is quite a character here, but I have seen him only once. He is a friend of Mr. Potter's[166] of New Bedford, a Bridgewater graduate, and has lived in Cambridge of late years. He came down here among the first, and has been at the Oliver Fripp place ever since (on the west side of the island, rather beyond Edgar Fripp's). He lately found some letters to and from Mrs. Wallace (whose plantation is near Oliver Fripp's), relative to a slave whom her nephew and Edgar Fripp had killed for some trivial offence. Another nephew in Washington wrote very indignantly about it, saying that a man who would abuse these poor creatures who had no protection from the law didn't deserve to be called a man. He urged his aunt to leave this region and go to live with him in a better state of society. She answered that she should be glad to, but couldn't very well disconnect her various ties here. All the letters are in a sad tone and evince great dissatisfaction with the state of things. They were written in 1860, and the nephew writes that it wasn't the Abolitionists but the Charleston newspapers that are making trouble. One is astonished at the evidences of a moderate feeling here, among many of the leading men. Capt. John Fripp, Mr. Coffin and Clarence Fripp (son of "Good William") are represented as Union men by the negroes; and Mr. Waters said that besides Mrs. Wallace there were Lawrence Fripp and Ben Chaplin at that end of the island, who had to be forced away by their friends when our troops took the island.

Mr. Philbrick and Mr. Waters staid to dinner, and just as we were through Charley Ware drove up, on his way to Ruggles'. So he ate some dinner and staid till half past five. He is going to Beaufort to-morrow and will fetch our mail and draw our rations. We had a pretty good afternoon school. I have divided my class of men, as Katy had very little to do, and I too much. She is to have the less advanced ones,—Dick, Bristol, Gabriel, Wake, Isaac, Toby, Henry, and bye and bye Ned, who is getting along very fast; I keep the two Parises, London,

Dennis and Billy, together with Robert, Tony and Taffy who frequently come in the afternoon. This will give me more time for the blackboard and map lessons.

Mr. Folsom has told us of some of the barbarous stories he used to hear on Port Royal Island, where he used to be superintendent. One woman was buried up to the neck in the earth—a few days after she had a dead child born. A man, for not saluting his master respectfully enough, was ridden down and over, and left in the road until night, when a cart was sent and brought him in, more dead than alive. Another man helped his wife finish her task besides doing his own. He was ordered to flog her but refused, and his master gave him 500 lashes with his own hand. He was before one of the strongest slaves on the plantation, but is now completely broken down. This was Mr. Smith, one of the kind masters whom Southside Adams[167] visited, and whom he takes, I believe, for one of his models. *Per contra*, Mr. F. visited Barnwell Island, where Mr. Trescott[168] had a plantation, which Mr. Russell[169] describes. He asked whether they had a good master, and was answered "Can't you tell by look on de nigger?" Everything was very neat and well-arranged; the negro houses well built, comfortable and well kept.

The subjoined work of art will give something of an idea of how our house looks. It is not quite high enough in proportion, and you can't see how shabby the paint is. I am represented going in at the front door, and Mr. Folsom up the back steps. Tom Dick's son is in the foreground. I would have delineated more living characters if I had thought of it sooner, however, I think I can put Mary on the upper piazza, Katy at her window, and Phoebe under the house. I forgot to put the pile of wood under the school-room window. A. Dining room. B. Our bed-room. C. School-room. D. Katy's room. E. Kitchen.

Tuesday, Jan. 12, 1864

It has been a dull day, and to-night it rains. Charley went to Beaufort to-day and drew six rations; for us, Miss Rice, Harriet and William Hall. We sent Moses to the ferry for them, but by some forgetfulness the barrel of flour was left at the landing, where it is now probably either stolen or soaked with rain. Charley brought the mail, welcome letters from Mary and Ned, and papers from Keene and Lansingburg [Lansingburgh, N.Y.]; and he and Mr. Philbrick are spending the night here.

Jan. 14, Thursday, 8 p.m.

We were quite shocked this morning at the news of the death of Lucretia from Hope Place, one of our largest and pleasantest scholars. She was particularly bright and cheery, and seemed overcome with delight at seeing us when we made our jaunt over there. She took cold on New Years, on that ill-fated excursion; but was at school since, and must have grown worse very suddenly. I suppose it must have been congestion of the lungs—they say she never could speak after she became sick. The funeral was this afternoon, and I was inclined to go; but both Mary and I had colds, and I didn't like to be out so late.

We took a drive after dinner as far as the Signal Station—a lovely afternoon, the first really pleasant day this year. Charley staid here all day yesterday, and went off this morning. Yesterday was a warm rain, and I set one or two window panes in the school-room. Tony went in the "tumble-down" to Coffin's to get their letters, which then Mr. Folsom carried in a heavy rain to Ruggles', getting back at about 8½. To-day Mr. Gannett and Miss Rice called before dinner, but had dined themselves.

Mr. Charles Williams is the only government superintendent retained on this island, to act as justice of the peace etc. I am afraid the school farms do not promise a very successful experiment. Mr. Fairfield has leased the Oaks and McTureous, and is trying to get others. He is, I believe, a well-meaning man, but not a skilful superintendent; Quash at Mulberry Hill calls him a man with a "ractified" mind (ractified meaning "knocked to pieces"). When it was first proposed to sell twenty-acre lots to the negroes, Mr. Fairfield (who used to be superintendent of Mulberry Hill etc.) sent for Paris and tried to persuade him to buy at the Oaks, but Paris told Mr. Folsom he had seen something of Mr. Fairfield's pie, and didn't want to have his finger in it again. Certainly I should doubt Mr. Fairfield's ability to carry on so many farms so far from each other. Mr. Sumner too is trying to get one, but says distinctly that he wants nothing but the school—he doesn't want to be at any trouble or expense about the land; if the negroes want to cultivate it he shall let them. I don't think this is right— the industrial experiment is quite as important as the educational.

Ned asks several questions about my position, which I will try to answer. I am hired by Mr. Philbrick, but have by necessity an appointment as teacher by the Educational Commission, which entitles me to rations. Mary and Katy have similar appointments, and draw rations. Mary has no salary, and Katy has none from Mr. P., but hopes to have one from the Commission as teacher of Hope Place. All things which are supplied by the plantation,—use of house, horses, fuel, milk etc., as well as a certain amount of furniture are without expense. Servants and food we have to pay for, but as I haven't yet settled the December accounts with Mr. Folsom, I am unable to say how much they will come to.

The superintendent has the entire control of all out-door matters. He has a foreman on each plantation—old [Elder] Moses here, Paris at Mulberry Hill, Butcher at Cherry Hill. He gives the people work to do, according to their desires—each person takes as many acres of cotton as he thinks he can do. He has a right to dismiss people from the plantation, unless they own their houses as they do at the McTureous place. But this right he only exercises (so far) indirectly; Charley tells one family with whom he was dissatisfied that he shall give them no land this year, and I suppose they will naturally migrate. The land that they take they work as well as they please. The superintendent can take away land if it is neglected, but this is seldom done. Each time they hoe and haul the crop they receive so much, and the more thoroughly it is worked the larger the yield. So they are paid two-fold for every hoeing—for the work itself, and for the amount they pick. The pay for tilling the crop is very inadequate; but it is made up by a very high price for picking (2½ cts. a pound). The yield of course varies very much. Tony (Cherry Hill) got over 500 lbs. to the acre (stone cotton); others get under 250. Amaritta at Coffin's Point, with an old husband and four children cultivated 14 acres, and got over 400 lbs. to the acre. She is a remarkable woman. Of course the hours of work depend upon the inclination of the people. They like to do their work as much before noon as possible, and this is the reason, so many children were kept out of school to "rake trash," which they might just as well do in the afternoon.

Mr. Folsom says the people are going to take so much land this year that the school will be very much affected. Quash is going to take 14 acres. I suppose in March I shall have to have my first class in the afternoon, as the children will all be at work in the morning. X [unspecified quantity] lbs. of cotton were brought here from Mr. Gannett's to be ginned in the steam gin; but as the young men were anxious to have work, he let them take it among them; and they had it all sorted to-day and divided among 14 of them, ready to gin. Out of school hours, I am able to observe the work of the plantation as much as I please; and I think I understand it tolerably well so far. The work for the new crop has begun already. Isaac, Ned and Jimmy are busily carting away the "marsh" and laying it in the furrows where the new rows of cotton are to be. This marsh grass was cut last September, and stacked up along the creek to dry and rot. It contains saline matter, and so makes a capital manure for this crop, which requires salt manures. It has been an unsightly and noisome object, hiding the view of the creek from the house, and now that it is removed, the creek looks very pleasantly at high tide, with a row of fine oaks along the bank, with moss hanging almost so as to dip in the water. At high water it looks like a lake; at low water it is nearly dry.

Mr. Philbrick was telling us the other day about his early experiences here. Soon after the occupation of the islands, one Col. Reynolds[170] of R.I. was sent down here (thro' Gov. Sprague's[171] influence) to collect the cotton. It was all done at the expense of the government, who furnished him a steamboat etc., and he received a salvage of five per cent, on a crop that was worth a million dollars. These cotton agents had possession of everything here, long enough to spoil the chances of the new crop; and they laid their hands on anything they pleased—pianos, furniture etc., and carried it North. They were very insulting and annoying to the superintendents, calling them "d— abolitionists" etc., and one of them knocked Mr. E.L. Pierce down. It was not until Gen. Stevens[172] came to command the post of Beaufort that the superintendents were well treated. Gen. S. had the reputation of being a pro-slavery man, but Mr. P. says the worst thing he ever did was to collect the corn etc. from the fields and give the people rations, saying that they ought to have more variety of food—bacon, molasses etc.,—the effect of which was to render them dependent. Dick used to be Gen. Steven's servant once, and bears testimony to his profanity, "should tink he been school for larn for cuss."

We have great fun watching Dick's children and others playing in the yard. Tom and Abraham generally have a "chile for mine" (child to mind), which they cart round in various postures. Then Archy, Tom's brother, is a sturdy roguish little fellow of about 4; and Seline [Selina?], his sister, about two, a pretty little thing. Tom and Abraham are perfect quicksilver, running round with the baby hanging over their shoulder, then setting him down in the shape of a right-triangle, turning somersets, and playing all manner of antics. Abraham's baby tumbled down in the dirt when it had been left in this way—"Dat de way you mine dat chile" shouted Tony, as Abraham ran up and began to comfort it. Presently the child was in the same position again, with Abraham jumping over it. Of course he knocked it down, and was covered with mortification. A little after, Archy, jumping on a spring board, tumbled off, and governed by a vague notion that somebody knocked him off, rushed madly round in pursuit of both the others. Then they seized him in their arms, carried him in triumph to an empty cart and dumped him in; by the time he had clambered out his wrath had evaporated. In two minutes more the three children were "shouting" in a row, a vociferous tune. As I was standing looking on, a little two-year-old-er named Isaac, walked gravely up to me, looking in my face and holding out an unbent hand for me to shake. I think I have never seen Tom or Abraham out of temper. The children in the yard are constantly singing. Margaret (Abraham's sister, about 12) comes to the well, draws her pail of water, puts it on her head and walks off, singing "shall I die"[173] (mi mi re; mi mi do); and then Tom and Abraham follow, galloping along on bamboo horses, and shouting "my body rock' long feber,"[174] while Archy trots at a distance behind.

Sunday, Jan. 17, 8 p.m.

William Hall remarks that Coffin's Point has had its head-quarters at Capt. John's this week, and Katy says that everybody has been where they didn't belong all the week. It is understood here that every house is a hotel, and if you don't provide liberally for chance guests—the worse for them. Friday morning was lovely, and Katy started off for Coffin's about the middle of the morning, I hearing her classes. She was to bring Harriet back with her to spend the night. Tom couldn't very well be spared to ride behind (to open gates etc.), and Abraham had no jacket; so, queer enough, Adam went, even more ragged than Abraham. Just as we were thro' dinner Harriet drove up in a Concord wagon drawn by a mule. She had been to Frogmoor and came across here from Mulberry Hill, so that of course she missed Katy. Just then it began to rain, so Harriet hurried off, met Katy and carried her home with her, leaving Adam to drive our carriage home. Just before Mr. Gannett came in, drank tea and carried Mr. Folsom off with him to spend the night—Miss Rice was alone and half sick. As it turned out, Charley and Winsor both went and spent the night there with the same laudable purpose of keeping Miss Rice company, supposing Mr. G. was away. So Molly and I were left alone.

The next morning (Saturday) it was bright and warm. We took a stroll along the creek, I repainted the blackboards and hung a conch-shell for a hanging pot, filled it with earth and sowed Maurandya seeds in it, then read aloud. Dinner punctually at 1½, and just as we were thro' Mr. Folsom and Charley drove in. As soon as we could, Molly and I went off in the buggy to Pine Grove, where we found a pile of slates, writing books, primary school charts etc. that did my heart good. We packed them in, and started off. Mr. G. and Miss Rice soon followed—they were to spend the night with us and go to church to-day, where it was rumored that Gen. Saxton would tell some good news. We spent the evening in playing Euchre, and this morning started for church at about 11—Charley and Mr. F. on foot. We took Abraham for tiger,—he has a new jacket and looks quite respectable. He wore no cap however, nor shoes, and his shiny, curly head thrust up thro' the top of the buggy (which was turned back) looked very comically, Sandy (young Moses' son, about 14) fell in with us soon, and ran the whole way behind, holding on to the carriage.

There was a perfect throng of people, dressed in very gay colors, and many of them very tastefully. As we drove up to the church the scene was very pretty. The church is just beyond an open meadow and a creek, and is surrounded by noble oaks hanging full of moss. The rumor that the governor was to be there had drawn together an immense number, and the road was full, horses and carriages were tied to the trees all about, carriages and queer old carts were driving up, and just as we came in there cantered up a large party of ladies and gentlemen from the opposite direction. A new mail was in—an extra one—nothing for us however, but papers; two from father and the Examiner. Services had already begun, and when we went in, Mr. French was reading and expounding a psalm. Then he said that he had just come from Washington, and had brought with him a paper which would be good news to all the people. It was an order from the President, which he read, relative to the sale of lands, providing that with the exception of the school and other reservations, all the plantations should be sold by private sale in lots of twenty acres, at 1¼ dollars an acre, to any resident—white or black. This simplifies very much the former arrangements, and is so much better. It still seems to me that, on this island at least, that had better have waited another year; but with that exception, it seems admirable.—

There has been a chronic quarrel in the board of Tax-Commissioners, between Dr. Brisbane and Judge Smith. The third member, Worden, is a man of straw, who had sided with Brisbane, and given him the majority. Brisbane is a South Carolinian, who emancipated his own slaves and carried them to Ohio. He is an earnest man, but is represented as being visionary and unpractical. Smith is that Wisconsin judge who declared the Fugitive Slave Law unconstitutional. When he is sober he is called clear-headed and judicious. Mr. Judd says if you catch him before ten, you will find him sober and clear; but then he doesn't get up till quarter of ten. The former plan I suppose was Brisbane's—the adoption of the new one is considered a victory of Smith. At any rate, Lincoln's order was, as might be expected, clear, concise, and judicious. We then had several speeches. Gen. Saxton spoke in a homely, satisfactory manner—rather common-place. Mr. Lynch[175] the colored preacher at the village spoke very well, as he always does to his people; but he delights too much in words. Maj. So-and-so made a regular spread-eagle [pretentious, boastful, exaggerated] speech (Mr. Folsom suggests spread-goose)—but it had one merit, brevity. After church I heard him talking to some people in a very common-sense way and giving them good advice—it is very funny that people will make speeches instead of talking. In this respect Mr. Tomlinson's remarks were a model,—brief, pertinent, and with no oratory. Mr. Hunn made a short speech too, but didn't say anything in particular.

Then Judge Smith ascended the pulpit, and, looking around at the audience, asked why—why—when hearts were bursting with joy, heads were bent, and tongues silent, and manly faces bathed in tears. As everybody was looking straight at him, and nobody was shedding any tears except himself (he occasionally wiped his eyes with a dirty pocket-handkerchief), there didn't seem to be any occasion to answer the question, so nobody did. He then relieved himself of a very large mouthful of tobacco, wiped the tears from his eyes, and went on to show that there were two kinds of joy, and this was t'other kind. He might have alluded to the 9th Symphony, but he didn't. He told what pre-emption meant, however, that it was *prae* and *emptio,* and went on to say a good many good things and a good many less good, until he got thro' and the people sang "Jesus lib and reign foreber" to the tune of "John Brown"—other verses being

"Mr. Linkum call for freedom" and "Gen'ral Saby call for freedom"—I have never heard any black man except Billy and Limus (Pine Grove) call him Saxton.

Then Alec [Aleck] of Fripp Point, who Miss Rice says is the most conceited person she ever knew, got up to ask how it was with Mr. Philbrick's plantations—for that Mr. P. had promised to sell land to them at cost (which of course he never did), and the General answered that these regulations had nothing to do with them—he might buy his twenty or forty acres, and if Mr. P. chose to sell him more, all well and good. Then they sang "Jehovia hallelujah, de lord will perwide—de foxes hab holes and de birdies hab nests, but de son ob man hab nowhere to lay his weary head."[176] Then Col. Elwell[177] said that everybody was tired, and it was nearly night, etc. etc. etc., and went on to make a speech about half an hour long.

I didn't notice that he said anything, so I went out and walked about reading the inscriptions on the grave-stones,—Fripp, McTureous, Pope etc. When he finally finished, we found a lot of people to speak to; several women from Hopes, Paris, Ned and Hacless, all well-dressed and looking not exactly like slaves. Flora and Ellen ran on behind us on our way home, with hideous little old-fashioned open-work bonnets on their heads—Flora bought hers at Beaufort, she said, for ten cents. Ishmael, too and Sandy. The road was perfectly thronged, and one man cantered by us with a striped afghan (Mary said it was) with a tufty sort of trimming, reaching from his shoulders to the horse's back. Droll enough. Harriet and Mr. Winsor in their carriage drawn by two mules, brought Katy and Mr. Folsom, Charley rode a horse which Demas had brought up for him. Mr. Gannett and Miss Rice drove up in their buggy, and Mr. Ruggles and Mr. Eustis rode along on horse-back, so that our yard was quite lively for a time. But no one would stay to dinner.

Tuesday, Jan. 19, 9 P.M.

Yesterday was a heavy rain and we had a very small school. To-day, cold and blustering, but pleasant. I find these two days that the slates have worked very well. It has been the great problem so far how to keep them out of mischief when they were not reciting, for nearly all the instruction must be oral, and with so large a school there must be a good deal of time when they have to be left to themselves. They certainly behave as well as could be expected. Now I shall let them use the slates as soon as they have learned their lessons, but not let them take them if they are troublesome. I took two or three away to-day. I have used some story books that Miss Rice let me have, in the same way; but they can't understand story books written for Northern children, and it is a great question with me what sort of reading they ought to have when they have any. By the Geography lessons and General lessons, I hope to get ideas into their heads by degrees. I have told them how paper is made, and slates are quarried, and to-day told them about the Pilgrim Fathers. A little book on Drawing that Ned sent me I made use of the day after I received it. The first class in Arithmetic is learning the multiplication table of threes. With the men, who will have but little schooling, I went directly in Written Arithmetic, which they will need to use. They are still laboring over Carrying—I don't know what they will do when it comes to borrowing. The women are very irregular, and the men not so regular as I wish. The two Parises, Ned, Hacless, Dick and Gabriel are pretty constant—the others are absent half the time.

I have had several talks with the men about the sale of land, which puzzles them very much. Two with Robin, and with Jimmy, Billy, and both Parises. All are "confused or worried" about it, and think it is rather hard that they don't have the same chance to buy land on their own plantation that others do. I told Robin he could stake out a lot on Dr. Pope's or Hope Place, and he said the people would knock him with a pole. Mr. French on Sunday urged the people to be considerate—not to wear horns and have sharp elbows; and Robin to-day said that he found "dis one hab horns and dat one hab sharp elbows"—he added "dey ought not send we for stake out land." And this is the great absurdity— setting three or four thousand ignorant people at a day's notice to staking out claims. Quash to-day staked out his 20 acres on Hope Place, to the immense disgust of the inhabitants; and then asked Mr. Folsom to look at it. Mr. F found he had really about 50 acres. Mr. F. also staked out lots for old Paris, Ned and John. They won't leave their present places, but want to secure land while there is a chance. He said that the people were quarreling furiously about their claims, and almost coming to blows.

I had a long talk to-night with young Paris and Billy, and I think they understood it better and felt better contented. Billy had a vague notion that the land ought to belong to the people, who had worked so many years for nothing, and I answered that the President thought of that, and the land was put at this very low price. I contrasted this with the way farmers have to buy land at the North, and showed them that they were as well off as anybody, except that they live a little farther from the land that was for sale. They were amazed when I told them of land being a thousand dollars an acre where I lived. Jimmy has staked out a lot on the Pope Place, and had the shrewdness to include a cattle-pen full of manure. Gabriel says he is going to take twenty acres in the creek, and charge for the right to fish. I had quite a talk with Robin about old times. He said Capt. John didn't give him his rights, but he was the best man on the island—from Coffin's Point to Land's End. Whoever came to him, white or colored, whether he knew them or not, he gave them what they wanted. The people never had to buy tobacco, nor "kettle for cook, net for fish, razor for shave they beard, lock for house"—everything he gave them. Robin was one of the crew that rowed the family to the main when they ran away. Massa say he wasn't going; [but he would] "stay so (putting his hands down by his side) and let Yankee do what dey please," but he was very old,—the oldest man on the island,—and his children over-persuaded him. However, he said he should be back soon.

Mrs. Fripp wanted to keep the men on the main[land], but "Massa say, no, let dem go back home,"—and told them to take good care of themselves and not do any more work. He said he never heard Capt. John talk about the Yankees, but some say he told them the Yankees would carry them off the Cuba. A very universal story. Phoebe, who gave Mary a long account of the affair, said they told them the Yankees would take the children and "knock out deir brainses against de treeses." Phoebe said "many tear for ole Massa, but nobody care for Missus." The kindness of Capt. John is, I suppose, one cause of the supineness of the people on this plantation. They hardly know what slavery is, and are not really so very much better off (physically) than they used to be. Robin, however, could see the difference between earning wages and getting liberal presents by asking for them.

Wednesday, Jan. 20, 8 P.M.

A pleasant day and good school. Mr. Folsom went to Beaufort to-day, and brought back our mail (letter from Joseph), and likewise a cat from Ruggles'. We hope she will prove an agreeable addition to the family. I have just subscribed for the Weekly Tribune.[178]

Sunday, Jan. 24, 1964, 8 P.M.

One might almost think these few days past that Spring was fairly upon us, and that we had dodged Winter. Ever since New Year's we have heard the frogs, and this last week the blue-birds have been about; but yesterday and to-day it has been uncomfortably warm—the thermometer to-day at 73 in the shade. Yesterday was an exciting day for us. The day before, Mr. Gannett, Mr. Folsom, Capt. John Scott[179] (a friend of Mr. G's) and Winsor, with some black men, went over to Hunting Island and camped out. Then yesterday morning they set out to find game, but very soon Mr. Folsom, by some accident, shot himself thro' the arm. He had a very heavy charge of duck-shot, and his arm being directly over the muzzle, the whole charge passed clean thro', some of the shot grazing his neck, ear and head. It was an exceedingly narrow escape, for a very slight inclination would have sent the whole charge into his head. He had to walk a mile and a half to the boat, which carried him at once to Pine Grove, where he now is. He lived there so long with Mr. Gannett and Miss Rice, that he feels much more at home there than here, and it is probably better for him to be there. Mr. Philbrick brought us the news. He came in while we were at dinner, having just seen Gabriel, Billy and Frank (who were on the excursion); and immediately afterwards Frank brought in a note from Mr. Gannett, asking me to send clothes etc.

We had Nelly put at once in the tumble-down, and Mary and I drove off to Pine Grove. We found Mr. F. sitting in the dining-room with his arm on a cushion and his head on one side. He couldn't lie down, and his arm pained him a great deal; but he was very cheerful and courageous. He asked me to send Moses to see him this morning, and Moses brought me back a note giving some directions about weighing and packing the cotton, which I am to see to. We had the buggy with both horses, and drove down about noon to see how he was. We met Dr. Hunting[180] on the way—he hadn't been able to get to him until this morning—who told us that the wound was a pretty severe one, but that no bone or artery was injured. Capt. Scott had gone to Beaufort to-day to get a regular surgeon, and Mr. Philbrick thinks Mr. F. had better go to a hospital in Beaufort. I am afraid he will have a hard time with his arm, as this climate is said to be a very bad one for healing wounds. He was asleep when we got there, so we only staid a little while. After dinner we took a very pleasant walk thro' the woods into the Cherry Hill plantation.

I was glad to see how much concerned the people here seemed about Mr. F. They are so undemonstrative that they often seem unfeeling; but they showed more this time that I ever saw them before. Moses was waiting when we came home last night, to learn how he was, and Taft came in this morning and said that "heap" of the people were going down to "shum" (see him). I have always maintained that this seeming heartlessness was really undemonstrativeness; but there is one very serious fault of character that I can't acquit them of. They seem to me, as a whole, very selfish and disobliging to each other. There are exceptions of course,—Abraham always helps Tom get in his wood, and Tom helps Abraham carry water; and last Sunday Jimmy and Lucy driving home from church overtook Butcher who is lame, when Jimmy got out and made Butcher get in. Still, it seems to me that there is very little consideration and helpfulness towards each other. Here is one point in which they are very different from the Irish. I suppose it is because they are rather an undeveloped than degenerate race, and that this is one of the vices of the savage state that they retain. As an instance; last Sunday Mr. French advised them to lend money to one another, to enable them to buy land; and at once there was a very general murmur of dissent—quite painful to hear. So I have observed at school that the children are not at all disposed to share their food with each other—even brothers and sisters.

I haven't heard much of the excitement about the land these two or three days. I only know that nearly all the men have been out prospecting in one quarter or another, but with very little success. I only know of three men from this place who succeeded in staking out lots—Frank, William and Jimmy—and every one of theirs had been pulled up by other parties. Everyone says he is "all confus' 'bout dis land"; and I don't at all wonder. Among other absurdities, all the lots must run North and South; twice as long that way as East and West. Now all the cleared land is in large square fields separated by belts of wood, and all lie square upon the roads; which none of them (on this island at least) run either North, South, East or West. So all the new division lines must run at sharp angles to the roads and belts of wood, and there will be all sorts of queer nooks and corners left. For instance, the McTureous school-farm (160 acres) can't be laid out in a solid lot, but has to consist of a series of parallelograms lapping over each other thus—[lattice-like hand sketch here]

Of course it was the intention to ignore all plantation lines and divide the island up *de novo* [from the beginning], just as France was into departments —and I suppose with the same political purpose. But they don't say this, and merely direct the people to stake out only these plantations; of course the people, to whom the plantation lines have a historical value, observe them religiously. So the result will be a queer patchwork of these oblique patches, little three-cornered lots, and every now and then a private plantation sold whole, carried on still by the old lines.

It seems to me that printed "nigger talk" is very incorrect, or else that it varies very much in different localities. I think I have never heard "am" used here in any way (certainly never incorrectly)—indeed, I am not sure that I ever heard a copula [linking verb] used at all. They omit words a great deal. Dick was telling us of a snake called coach-whip. "Say dey tie round you wid one leg and whip you wid todder." I am not sure whether I ever heard an article. Then they have some very curious combinations and corruptions of words—"shum" for "see them" or "see him"; "yedde" for "hear." They use the auxiliary "do" a good deal. The other day I gave Abby a new book, and the next day it was very much soiled, so I took it away and gave it to Adaline. Pretty soon after, I saw there was a row between them, and asked Adaline what was the matter—"Abby do cuss me, sar." They pronounce short a very broad (hât, mât, etc.). Abraham the other day knocked Nat on the head, and when I asked him what was the matter, he answered that Nat "did cuss" him. Inquiring what the "cussing" consisted in I learned that Nat called him "black slink"—a term of opprobrium whose meaning I am wholly ignorant of. V and W are constantly interchanged—"woices," "perwide," "pumpkin wine," "veeds," etc. And it seems impossible to keep them from it—you pronounce it right to them, and they still get it wrong. Occasionally I hear an h misplaced, but not often. Some can pronounce th very well, some not. By the way, this confusion of v and w explains the enigmatic name of our pretty Wyna from Hopes; evidently it is a corruption of Lavinia or Melvina, just as they always say Nelia for Cornelia, Becca for Rebecca etc. "Studdy" (steady) is a great word with these people. Ishmael and Abraham had a little row, and Ishmael excused himself by saying "Abraham studdy 'buse me." And young Paris said "You studdy teach me, I studdy larn."

Jan. 27, Wednesday 7½ P.M.

Mr. Folsom, we understand is considerably better to-day. Arrangements have been made to have him go to Mr. Eustis' on Ladies' Island, in order to have surgical aid at hand if there should be need. Mr. Philbrick and Winsor came here yesterday and saw to some of the affairs of the place, and went over to Cherry and Mulberry Hills. Winsor opened the shop in the afternoon, and staid to tea; Mr. P. went on to Ruggles' and is going to Hilton Head. Of course all important matters are suspended until Mr. F. is better, but Moses and I are able to attend to the regular routine of the plantation. I have weighed the peoples' cotton and seen to its packing (it is now nearly finished), and done a few other little jobs. Yesterday and to-day I got a bed ready in the garden, and this evening sowed some peas; to-morrow I hope to put in some white potatoes and turnips. Mr. P. is expecting a large lot of seeds by the Arago to-day. For nearly a week we have had weather like our warmest May days—thermometer at 72.

I have put on a thinner coat and worn my straw hat to-day. Fleas have re-appeared, which were dormant during the cold weather; also red ants, with which the house swarms. School was very pleasant all last week. Yesterday and to-day it has been more troublesome and I had to be pretty severe. Yesterday the trouble was with the Seaside children going home. The classes are dismissed as fast as I get thro' with them—the first staying nearly an hour after the second. So I have made a rule that the little children may stay around the school-house until the 2d class is dismissed, which contains scholars large enough to take care of them; and that then all must go home. And I have directed the Hopes children to go by the road and Mulberry Hill thro' the woods, because I found that they quarreled. They have several times troubled me by loitering, and yesterday I couldn't get them off; so I made them all come in and wait until after the 1st class were gone. But some of the 1st loitered, waiting for the others, so I called them in too; kept them all a sufficient time, and sent them off.

To-day I had no trouble on this score. There are only four scholars from Cherry Hill—Linda, in the first class, a nice looking girl—a genuine negress—the neatest and most tasteful in her dress of all the scholars. She is the one I found ginning one day. Her mother, Dinah, is a very nice woman, who came over here one day to "see the gals." Menia is a nice little girl, 2d class. Gilead is a great favorite of ours, a bright, sturdy, comical little fellow. Reddington is less pleasant. He and Gilead were late today, and I wouldn't let them in. I afterwards saw Tony (R's grandfather) in the yard, and he said he would lick him for being late. I told him that being shut out of school was punishment enough for one day, and we had better try them again. My Geography class is getting along very well, altho' I don't hurry them.

Once in a while instead of giving them a lesson, I tell them about William Penn, King Philip etc., or draw a map of the plantation or island. They now know all the states as far as Georgia, their principal productions etc. The first class in Arithmetic is learning the table of 3's and can write the numbers up to 20. I have been giving some general lessons on lines and angles, and practicing the 2d class in drawing. My 3d class Mary hears read—Tom, Abraham, Gilead, Margaret, Rose etc (Rose is a very pretty girl from Hope Place). The 4th have sentences on the board. To-day I wrote "Nat has a big cap"; and it was very comical to see Nat (a nice boy from Hopes) open his eyes and look round with a puzzled and astonished look. They are beginning to have words of four letters. The afternoon school has been very satisfactory lately. They are still stuck in Addition and Subtraction. They carry pretty well in Addition; but I shan't dare to introduce borrowing for some time yet. They are getting on very well in writing.

Did I say that I had divided the men into two classes? I keep the two Parises, Billy, Dennis, London and Robert, Tony and Taffy who often come in the afternoon; while Katy had Dick, Wake, Gabriel, Isaac, Bristol, Toby, Henry and Ned, with Molsy. Molsy is a very nice woman, daughter of Jimmy, wife of young Moses, and mother of Judy, who is a real beauty when her hair is covered, and very bright. Judy's father was sold to New Orleans, so Molsy has consoled herself with another husband. Moses' former wife, who is dead, was mother of our little beauty Mylie.

Mary's afternoon class consists of a number who are mostly women and beginners. The most advanced are Hacless and Jane—both very handsome. Mary says that Hacless has the most beautiful face she has seen here, and he is certainly very ingenuous and amiable in his looks. His mother is Lucretia [Scott], (Mulberry Hill) sister of Lucy and Rosina, and Mr. F. says one of the best women he knows. Her husband has deserted her, and lives on Ladies' Island with another wife. Dick entertained us last night with an account of the superstitions of the people. He is a firm believer in Friday's being unlucky—how much he believes in these other things we couldn't make out. They say it is "The Evil" that leads them astray in the night, and pitches them into ditches. Tony, he says, was born with a caul, and is constantly running foul of "the Evil," so that none of the boys will go with him in the night, he is such an uncomfortable companion. One night he woke up and told his father there was a big man standing in the doorway. But the doors were all locked, so his father (Moses) wanted to "knock" him for his false alarm. He will mutter and talk to himself when he is alone—"Get out my way—move—let me pass" etc.

We were rejoiced yesterday to receive a sofa from Coffin's, which Harriet had made from some pieces she found there, and covered. Mary and Katy made a seat for it when we were there, and stuffed it with moss. It hasn't been brought before, because it is one of the articles which will be sold by Mr. Browne.[181] But it seemed not worthwhile to wait any longer so it was sent along. I forgot to say that Mr. Folsom found that one shot entered the skin directly over his heart—he pulled it out yesterday. William the Carpenter, said that all the people "sent huddy" (how do) to Mr. Folsom.

Thursday, Jan. 28, 7½ P.M.

Flora and Hetty are sitting on the other side of the table taking a lesson in sewing. Hetty is a nice girl, Judy's elder sister, not so bright nor so pretty as Judy, neither does her hair stand up so erect. She is very bashful, and whenever she is spoken to tries to hide her head behind her shoulders, and failing in that, runs her tongue out of her mouth and rolls her eyes in a manner fearful to behold. Judy, Mylie, Minnie and Venus came up as spectators, and ranged themselves in a row near the door, but Molly ruthlessly sent them home, and Phoebe who is a sort of gorgon followed them with the spurs of her speech. Altho' Dick said "Dey frighten in dark," I suspect Phoebe was a greater terror to them than even the "Evil." This of Dick's is by the way a specimen of one of their curious usages of speech—the omission of "be," either as copula or auxiliary. They seem never to use a passive. Paris to-day said to me "I can't certain, sir." Such expressions as "the door didn't fasten," "the bag won't full," are very common.

Mr. Folsom went to Mr. Eustis' to-day. He passed the head of the avenue with Mr. Gannett, and sent up to the school for Thomas (son of mulatto John) to go with him to wait upon him. Thomas is, I think, the most trusty and steady boy in school, and will do very well for him. I went down to the road and spoke with Mr. F. and G. Mr. F. looks much better, and is doing as well as possible. Mr. G. will stay with him until Saturday, when Charley will go. Perhaps next week I shall take my turn, altho' I believe he expects to be out of danger by that time.

Dick went to Beaufort the other day and came back with a cock and bull story of a new draft which would take not only the able-bodied but all who could work on entrenchments etc. The next morning I was in the garden and all of a sudden a dozen men ran by, dashing thro' the bamboos and plunged into a bit of woodland by the creek. I found soon that two soldiers had been seen passing, and they thought they were after them sure. It turned out they were on their way to McTureous after a white man named Smallwood[182] who is working for Limus, and whom nobody seems to know anything about. Here everybody must account for himself. I wish you could have some of the pink and white camellias that I bring in every day—three beautiful ones to-day, and more in promise to-morrow. The cold weather destroyed the buds as fast as they matured, but these June days bring them on finely. Daffies and jonquils in full bloom.

Jehovia, hallelujah, de lord is perwide (*bis*)[183]
(or iah)
De foxes hab holes an' de birdies hab nests, but de son ob man he hab
nowhere to lay his
weary head

Friday, 4 P.M.

Mail just came—father's letter of the 22d. On looking over this letter, I think I have written too many details. I will try to avoid this fault.

St. Helena, Jan. 30, 1864, 7½ P.M.

It was warm, but cloudy when I came down stairs this morning, and I was immediately hailed by Robin, who wanted me to go and weigh cotton for him to pack. They bring the cotton in large sheets tied at the four corners, and two pounds are deducted from the gross weight, for the sheet. I weighed three sheets for Aleck, weighing 48¼, 31¾, 34½ lbs respectively, then came into breakfast. Just then Robert came with the pail of milk on his head, and I got him and Taffy to go up to Mr. Harrison's to see if we could have his boat, as we wished to go to call on Mr. Thorpe. Also I sent Ned, who is carting marsh, over to Mulberry Hill to get some cotton that was to be packed with this.

After breakfast I prepared some earth for Mary's new hanging pot, but was interrupted by Robin calling me to weigh the Mulberry Hill cotton. From the Cotton House, I went to the garden, fastened on a rope to keep the gate shut, picked a handful of camellias and carried them into the house. Soon William Hall appeared on horseback, took our mail and carried it on. We would have sent the flowers to Mr. Folsom, but William couldn't carry them. He is going to stay with Mr. F. overnight, and Charley is going there to-morrow. By this time Aleck had another sheet ready to weigh. Frank and Clara were working on some yellow cotton, for which they declared they ought to get higher pay, it was so dirty.

When I was half way to the house, I was called back—Aleck had found another pile; and this made the last white cotton on the place. It was now clear and very hot, and tide was high, still the boat hadn't appeared. I read awhile to Mary, and at last, when we had fairly given it up, the boat appeared. They had had to go across the creek to Mr. Thorpe's to get it, and now there were no oars and no rudder, only two rude paddles. However, an oar was found at Robin's house, and off we started—the tide was already ebbing, and both our house and Mr. Thorpe's are inaccessible at low water. Taffy took the oar, Robert one paddle and I the other, with which I did my best to counter-act Taffy's strong pulling. But my stick was about as limber as a lath, and every two minutes I had to shout "Hold up, Taffy," as he nearly drove us into the bank. The creek is a very pleasant one, and having the tide with us we were soon at Mr. Harrison's, opposite to which a narrow channel runs up to Mr. Thorpe's.

We thought we would stop at Mr. H's, as the boys said they had carried a lady across there from Mr. T's. We found it was Mrs. Lieut. Stone,[184] and that Miss Richardson would probably ride round there, so that we shouldn't find her at home, while Mr. T. was certainly in Beaufort. So we made our call at T.B. Fripp's instead of T.J. Miss R. however didn't appear while we were there. Mr. Harrison furnished us with oars, so we came home in very good style. Dick was waiting on the bank with his white apron on and a broad grin on his face. "You seen Miss Torpe, ma'am? I seen him. I tole him you gone wid intention call on he, but de boat didn't ready in time. He catch you at Mr. Harrison, ony de horse bodder him." (They always call Miss Richardson "Miss Torp.") (I noticed particularly that Dick used the article.) We were now ready for dinner, but Phoebe had gone off to the "nigger house," and we had to wait some time for her. After dinner I finished the hanging pot. It is made of the end of a calabash, shaped so [hanging pot sketch here] and at the bottom I glued a curious sort of burr that we found in the woods. Then the whole is covered with lichens and hanging moss ad suspended from a tick fastened to the top of the window. It looks very pretty.

Mary sowed some lobelia seeds—the maurandia in the shell is already up. Then I sat down and read the papers—bought some eggs of Gabriel, and when the sun set we strolled down the avenue. Coming back, went to the garden and picked some more camellias, then to Robin's putting up a fence to enclose a garden plot, and talked with him a while, then met William and talked with him. Found a fire in the sitting-room, and presently tea. Just as we were thro', the door opened and Mr. Gannett walked in with four loaves of bread in his hands, which he had bro't from Beaufort, with a letter for Mary. Mary read her letter aloud to us. Mr. Gannett wouldn't stay—and then we sat down to write. Mr. G. says that Mr. Folsom is doing very well, there is no marked change, and that he will probably come back in a few days.

Now let me describe our room. We are sitting at our dining table, with a checked cloth on it by the light of a kerosene lamp. Mary is writing on the side next to the fire, Katy reading at her right hand, I opposite Katy. On a plate on the table are four huge loaves of bread. There is a very small fire, and in front of it a very dilapidated fender—in front of which is spread a piece of blue bocking.[185] A large wooden mantelpiece painted black—Mr. Folsom didn't have enough linseed oil, so used castor oil, and the paint is sticky to this day. On the mantelpiece a pretty little clock, two small kerosene lamps, three candlesticks, match safe etc., and a little vase I rigged out of bamboo to hold one camellia. The vase is ugly, but the flower shows well. Over the mantelpiece three little oil-color prints, and a large twig of casina,—the berries pretty much faded. Opposite the mantelpiece, the looking-glass, and a branch of cypress over it; under it the yellow table from Northboro', covered with a blue and white cloth of Mr. Folsom's. The black table is behind me—each has books on it and a tumbler filled with camellias. Under the black table is the basket Billy made, which we use to hold newspapers. Over it, the Sistine Madonna, the St. John, and the two saints that used to hang in the parlor; each with a sprig of cypress over it. Behind Katy, between the windows, our new sofa, covered with a dark reddish calico, and over it the photograph of Annie Lambert—under it a bunch of pressed flowers, and at each side some autumn leaves pasted on sheets of paper. On the same side of the room, towards Mr. Folsom's room, is the great map of the Southern States—towards the front of the house the bookshelves. Under the bookshelves the barrel-chair, in the corner by the door the rocking-chair, and Mary's sewing chair near Mr. Folsom's door. Other chairs and a few little pictures. The shell hanging at the window between the sofa and bookcase; the new pot at the one between the bookcase and looking-glass.

Sunday, Jan. 31, 7½ P.M.

A very hot day, but with a delightful breeze in the afternoon. We should have gone to church today, as it was the quarterly meeting and several were to be baptized; but we have no horses. Charley's Rob Roy got hurt the other day in the head and being neglected the hurt got pretty bad, so he was brought for Dick to take care of, and Lucy carried off in his place. Of course we can't go in the buggy with only one horse. Mr. Philbrick came along this morning on his way to Coffin's, and brought a detachment of our mail, and towards night Charley called, on his way to Mr. Eustis' to relieve Wm. Hall. Mr. P's account of Mr. Folsom is not very encouraging—he is no worse, but no better, and very blue. This morning there was quite a panic among the people from a story that the soldiers were after them—that "in Beefut yes'day dey took eberyting under fifty year old," and some even had a story round that they were to be carried to Cuba, as their masters had told them the Yankees would do. I had quite a talk with Robin, Toby, Billy and Dick, and told them about the draft in the North;

about the millions of troops we had raised, less than 100,000 of them black; how I was drafted myself; that this was a great war and everybody must suffer from it—they didn't suffer anything compared with those who were still in slavery or with people elsewhere; that the government had a right to call upon every man if it was done in a lawful way; but that I didn't think Gen. Gillmore had a right to seize them in this way, and I didn't believe he had given the order—they would find that the stories were exaggerated.

Robin was quite wrought up, for his former experience was rather a hard one. "Look here sir, I poor man, wid large famerly—my wife Rinah she can't work (Robin sometimes says "she")—she sickly woman can't work wid de hoe for more'n twenty year.—Dey took me an' kep me tree mont' an' nebber pay me, not one cent. My wife hab notting to eat—mus' starve." I think he felt considerably reassured after my speech, altho' I must confess that the stories were so positive that I felt half guilty all the time, as if I were deceiving them. However, Mr. Philbrick told me he had seen Gen. Saxton, who told him that the orders were only to enlist all that they could. But isn't it too bad to stir them up in this way every few days?

Thursday, Feb. 4, 9 P.M.

Our pleasant weather continues, but colder; yesterday quite blustering. In spite of the raw wind, Mr. Folsom came back yesterday. There was no object in his staying any longer at Mr. Eustis', and he would be much more comfortable at home and with women round. He was quite tired last night, and I got up seven times to attend to him—changing his position etc. (I slept on the sofa in the dining room). But to-day he has seemed very bright and like himself. I think the wound is doing as well as possible. It seems too hard that he has been suffering all this time from an ulcerated tooth; but he thinks it broke last night, and at any rate it has been easier. Fearing that the noise might annoy him. I gave notice yesterday that the school would be suspended; but he insists upon it that it won't trouble him, so to-day I sent word to the adults to come. We shan't have the children until Monday, and then must reorganize the school. The spring work has been taking off one after another of the first class, and when we commence again we must have the first class and one at least of the second in the afternoon. That is, we must have our principal school in the afternoon, and only the youngest scholars in the morning.

I wish very much that some of us understood medicine a little. The people come to us for their trifling ails, for which Mary gives alternately castor oil, Perry Davis Pain Killer, and Jamaica Ginger. But anything serious is another matter. I think Ishmael is really quite sick—it appears to be of the nature of pleurisy—and Dick went to bed this afternoon quite miserably. I told him to go to bed and I would cut his wood, which I did with great satisfaction, except that these live-oak knots are the toughest I ever tried to split.

There has been coming and going this week as usual. Rufus Winsor has come to stay and be Mr. Folsom's mouth-piece, so that the people may not worry him. Monday he and Mr. Philbrick and Wm. Hall met here; the latter was on his way from Mr. Eustis' to Coffin's, and carried off Molly with him. He brought her back the next day, and went on himself to take care of Mr. F. another day, while Charley went to Beaufort. He brought Mr. F. back yesterday and went home himself. To-day Charley stopped here on his; way back from Beaufort, and at the same time Miss Rice called. Mr. Philbrick went from here Monday to find a schooner to send his cotton North. He secured one, and will pack it off as soon as possible. Mr. Harrison too made a call on Monday, waiting for Mr. Philbrick. He says that the truth about the draft is that Gen. Gillmore has ordered an enrollment of all the militia, white and black, who are liable to military duty. So I tell the people boldly now that if there is a draft, there will be no grounds of complaint—it will be made fairly and legally, and everybody must do his duty.

I have just finished Mrs. Kemble's book,[186] and remarked to Mr. Harrison that so far as I could judge the slaves were much better off on these islands than in Georgia—one reason is no doubt that the plantations here are much smaller, and so were more immediately under their owner's eyes. Capt. John, for instance, altho' he owned four plantations, never had an overseer. I never have seen any cabins so wretched as Mrs. K. describes. Mr. H. answered that they were quite as bad on the McTureous place, but that the people had built themselves better ones since their masters had run away. As to cruelty, Mrs. Kemble tells nothing to compare with the stories we hear of Eddings, Smith, Pritchard, or even T.J. Fripp. Pritchard was the owner of old May, of whom I wrote; he still lives on Pritchard's Island, altho' his slaves have all left him. He is wretchedly poor, and comes begging to them. The stories of Mr. P.'s barbarity are too shocking almost for belief—putting a hot poker in a girl's mouth, and sprinkling red pepper in her eyes. Mr. Harrison says this is told him by a perfectly trustworthy woman who saw it done. Also of T.J. Fripp (where Mr. Thorpe lives) that he beat a slave in the hall with the tongs until she stood in a pool of blood. A man from the main[land] has been at work here to-day, whom you would never suspect of having any negro blood in him. He told me he was born free and had been sold into slavery by fraud, and that he had often been beaten with a saw. It is refreshing to turn to our good old Capt. John, who once asked Phoebe if she would like to have him buy a son of hers who belonged to another man. She answered "Just as you please, massa," knowing very well, as she told Mary, that she didn't need to say anything more. It is quite a striking fact that the people here are almost the only ones on the island who didn't plunder their master's house, and I think it must have been in part from their affection for him.

Friday, 8 P.M.

Mr. Winsor went to Beaufort to-day and brought back an installment of our mail—papers for me from Prentiss, and the two volumes of Merivale,[187] which I am very glad to have, altho' I only expected the first. He also brought some seeds which I have been peddling out to the people since. I find my peas and turnips are up, and I have also made the valuable discovery of celery and parsley in the garden. The strawberries are in blossom too, and some other very pretty flowers in front of the house. Mr. Folsom seems quite nicely to-day.

St. Helena, Tuesday, Feb. 9, 1864, 7½ P.M.

I hardly know when I wrote last for I have been busy about other matters for two or three days. Mr. Folsom has been growing better very fast, and to-day rode on horse-back for several hours about the fields. He requires a good deal of care, however, his poultices have to be changed three times a day, and Mr. Winsor sleeps in the room with him every night—I slept there two nights. Saturday morning Molly wanted some oysters got for him, so I went out into the field to find some boys to send. I found the people at work mending the fence between this plantation and Cherry Hill under Moses' supervision. Robert and Taffy were armed with axes—"look yere Mr. William" said Robert as he aimed a blow at the root of a small tree "dis de way de lumbermen cut down tree." (Robert is one of the scholars who has made out to remember that the lumber business is the principal one in Maine.) The way of cutting trees here generally is to hack them off about three feet from the ground. Ellen, Hetty, Sammy, Adam, Margaret and other children of that age were bringing the rails one at a time on their heads—Ellen had fashioned a cushion of hanging moss for the rail to rest on—while the women were laying the rails zig-zag fashion. Taft and Limus were staking out the field into tasks of about a quarter of an acre each. I engaged Adam and Sammy to get oysters. For the best ones they had to paddle in a little canoe or dug-out below Mr. Harrison's, and they brought a quantity which we emptied into the water behind the house, where they will keep and can be used as we want them. I then sowed peas, cabbage, lettuce, radishes and beets, and wrote a while.[188]

Sunday was rather a confused day. Only a few scholars came to Sunday-school, and at about 12 Mr. Eustis came in to see how Mr. Folsom did. We had a very pleasant call from him, but he wouldn't stay to dinner. He gave us an interesting account of the trouble he had in securing his plantation. It was absolutely impossible for him to find out whether the plantations were to be sold or not. The sale was advertised only in the Beaufort paper—as good as no advertisement at all—and it had been ordered and forbidden and put off so many times that nobody in the North knew anything about it. At last he determined to come down himself and find out—started at a day's notice, and on stepping on the wharf at Beaufort was informed that the lands were all sold. Luckily he had deposited his money beforehand with Dr. Brisbane, one of the commissioners, (the sale was for the taxes), and so his plantation was saved. He says that the hostility between the commissioners—especially Judge Smith and Dr. Brisbane—has reached such a pass, that if you know the opinion of one, you can be pretty certain that the other's will be directly opposite. Dr. B. insists that the sale of the land shall come off on the 18th Feb., as advertised, in spite of the President's order, and the advertisement is still kept up in the Free South. I rather think there's fun afoot. I asked Mr. E. what had ever become of the cotton found here when the islands were taken. He says that both the Secretary of War and of the Treasury were afraid to touch it, so it was given over to Mr. Barney, Collector of New York,[189] who acknowledges the receipt of some $650,000 from its sale. Since then it has been drawn upon by Gen. Saxton to meet the expenses of the industrial enterprise, but what has become of the balance, nobody knows. As there is no legal receipt for it, it may have melted away as so many such things have done. Mr. Eustis thinks there are some $13,000 of it from the cotton on his plantation—it was a very large crop—but he can't succeed in getting hold of any evidence. Two or three of the people here have intimated that as they raised the cotton, and "massa" ran away, the cotton "belong to we." There is considerable justice in this view of it, but it would certainly be the best disposition of it to have it left as a fund for the benefit of the freedmen.

Just as we were sitting down to dinner Mr. Gannett and Miss Rice came in. Their buggy had broken down, and was a melancholy wreck. As Mr. G. refused to accept the loan of ours, they both walked home. Harriet and Mr. Soule made us a short call in the afternoon; H. will probably go home with Mr. Philbrick next week. Yesterday we sent Dick to Beaufort to draw our rations, and their weight broke the back of our poor old tumble-down, which had just been mended in the most splendid manner. Two vehicles ruined in two days. Today, just as we were thro' breakfast, Quintus rode up from Coffin's with a note saying that the schooner, which Mr. P. has engaged to take his cotton North, was just coming in and that our cotton must be carried down at once. So it was loading in the flat, and Mr. Winsor, Robin, Frank and Bristol went off with it. Mr. W. being away, I took his horse as soon as school was over, and rode to Mr. Hunn's to get some garden seed for the people. We got some last week in Beaufort for ten cents a paper, and few seeds and paper, but at Mr. Hunn's I found them for five cents, and nice full papers. Several kinds which the people most desire, however, I couldn't get. It was a perfect day for riding. I had heard that a bridge on the Seaside Road was repairing, so I went round by the Signal Station, the road leading thro' monotonous pine barrens, past the little white Episcopal church, and then by a crooked wood-path, bringing me out in front of the Edgar Fripp house. I found the bridge was in order, so went back by the Seaside Road,—through the open Frogmoor fields, the beautiful woods of Woodlands, and the low, wet Hope Plantation. As I was passing thro' Mulberry Hill, I heard a shouting, and Ned came running after me, from mending a fence; and soon there followed him John, a fine looking middle-age refugee from the main, who went thro' a great deal to get his freedom, Quash, Rosina, London and Will—all eager for turnip seed. I had got just enough to go round, and as the people at the Big Place were already pretty well provided, I let them have them all.

Our school is in rather an unsatisfactory condition. The children of the first and second classes have to work in the field in the morning so our morning school is a very small affair now, and for the afternoon we have too many scholars in too short a time. I think it will be more satisfactory when we get fairly under weigh in the new arrangement, but at present we are rather mixed up.

Friday, Feb. 12, 7½ P.M.

The weather has been rather unsettled these days—a storm brewing I think. They have passed rather monotonously, with small and irregular morning school, and very busy afternoons. It would be very satisfactory if we had more time, as I think we shall before long. My first class in Arithmetic—Ishmael, Sammy, Ellen, Flora, Robert, Taffy, Thomas, Celia etc.—are learning the table of fours, knowing the others pretty well. The second class, which Katy hears, is learning the threes. My class can make the figures, and will begin to cipher as soon as we get time. I am giving them writing lessons now on their slates. I haven't been able quite to make out how much the scholars understand of what they read. If they get mechanically correct I am satisfied, but they sometimes make emendations which seem as if they understood. One scholar read for "tired," weary,—a word they use a good deal more. Hacless read to-day "too old for play with dolls," for "to." They never sound the s in plurals, which it seems to me they would if their reading was merely mechanical. The other day there was a picture of a boy with a parrot, which the piece was about. I asked Tony and Taffy if they knew what a parrot was, "Oh yes, sir" said both, "I shum." Whether it was a real parrot or a picture that they "shum" I don't know. Katy hears the first class read—a quite large one. I have the second, which is a very nice little class, and nice readers. Minna, Quash's daughter from Mulberry Hill, is a rather large, pretty girl, who parts her hair. Her sister Elisabeth is small and very pretty, with a round chubby face and handsome eyes. Her elder sister, Polly, is one of our three beauties. She is married to Will, Dick's brother. This morning Mylie came into school with a pickaninny on her back nearly as big as herself. Presently I called her up to read, and she lugged the "chile" along with her, and stood it up by her side, where it clung for dear life to her gown and gazed up with awe in its face until Mylie was through.

Yesterday after school we (M., K., and I) drove down to Mr. Harrison's to attend the wedding of Frank with one of Mr. H's women. Frank is quite an old man, father of Laura, who was married to young Paris soon after we came. He is a tall, awkward man, quite light, with a hare lip—very good, and very homely. Hannah has had 15 children, of whom six are living. As we were just driving out of the yard, Frank came shambling along with an axe over his shoulder, in his working dress—quite to our consternation, for we had rather hurried, as it was already five. "Aren't you going to Mr. Harrison's, Frank?" I called out, "Oh yes, sir, d'rectly," said he. Just then Robin and others came along, and began to chaff him, advising him to jump up behind the buggy to open the gates for us. Off we drove, but Dick had harnessed so carelessly that whenever the horses trotted, the pole would wag up and down, and bump Nelly on her nose. So we had to let them walk most of the time, and they rewarded us for our consideration by spending all their strength in trying to push each other out of the middle of the road. I am sorry to say that Nelly hardly held her own in this contest.

We had to wait nearly an hour for the bridal procession, which we passed very pleasantly in conversation. Mr. H. entertained us with an account of the squabbles of the tax-commissioners. Dr. Brisbane, the chairman, refuses to carry out the new instructions, which he considers invalid. The sale of land, according to the old order, is advertised for Feb. 18, and he says it will come off. So he gives the superintendents instructions totally at variance with the President's orders—rather embarrassing for the poor superintendents. Then Dr. B. lays down some quite arbitrary rules. There are a great many St. Simon's people on the Hamilton Fripp place, who have preempted there. But Dr. B. tells Mr. H. that the St. Simon's people are not to be allowed to preempt until all who belong on the island have had their pick. Also, he has made a rule that the people who live on a plantation are to have an opportunity before any others—a rule which I suppose will shut out Paris, Quash, John and others. The rule that heads of families are to receive preference works queerly in some cases. Charley Ware has staked out a claim on the McTureous; but one of the negroes wants the same, and being a married man will get it. Mr. Alden, superintendent of the Dr. Pope place, (who superseded Mr. Phillips) put in a claim for twenty acres on that plantation including the house; he got the start of Mr. P., but the latter, being a married man, had precedence. We hear, by the way, that Mr. Phillips died to-day. The vote to dismiss him was not passed, I believe.

After we had waited nearly an hour, the happy couple came in, and the ceremony began. Mr. Harrison used the Episcopal form, and read it very well. The bride had her face covered all the time with her handkerchief. Both wore white gloves,—indeed the wedding had been deferred several days that Frank might procure a pair. When they were told to take hold of hands, they shook hands quite vehemently, and then let go, so that the minister had much ado to get them together again. We didn't kiss the bride, but shook hands and wished them joy. Aunt Jenny, an old woman, very straight and active in her motions, was just going out when Mr. H. told her to wish them joy. So she turned and said "Wish you joy, a girl and a boy," curtsied, and was just starting again, when Mr. H. asked her to tell us her title. She hesitated a moment, and then said with quite an air "Sarah McKee, the belle of Beaufort, the gold-wearer." She says that at balls she never used to dance with any but white people, and I can very well believe that she was handsome and graceful. She wore a stunning turban, gathered into a sort of mitre above her head.

I have been busy this week in selling the seeds that I got at Mr. Hunn's and our ration meat. The latter we prefer to exchange for eggs etc. There is a great demand for the pork, but the beef they don't care for. Eggs have been as high as 50 cts. a dozen, but we are giving now 35; and for the meat we ask 10 cts. a pound. To-morrow I am going to sell them the last ration flour. It was poor to begin with, and as it was left out doors over night in a pouring rain, it isn't such as we like to use; and now we have a fresh barrel—if we can ever get it from the ferry—so we will get the old one out of our way. We had a nice row after morning school in Charley Ware's boat which is here for a day or two. If I had known how we were to be situated, I would have brought down a row-boat.

Saturday, Feb. 13, 9 P.M.

Another pleasant day. A delightful row on the creek; trimming trees and grape-vines, and a little writing. Mr. Philbrick called after dinner on his way to Coffin's, and astonished us by saying that he is going North in the Atlantic, Tuesday. He has his cotton all packed in two schooners, and is off. We shall miss him very much. He says that Mr. Chase[190] has sent a new order down here about the lands—that Mr. French grossly misrepresented the state of things to him, and that the old order is to hold good. Isn't it odd? (Rev. Mr. French—Mendax[191] they call him.) So now the sale will come off next Thursday.

I wonder where all the children learned the alphabet. They all seem to know it straight along, and can spell small words even when they do not know the letters by sight. Archy, now, doesn't know a single letter, and yet he will shout out "m-a-n, man" with the best of them; and they also have a great fancy for spelling words in the yard at the top of their voices. As they all know the letters more or less, it is hard to try any experiment of teaching reading according to any plan, for they will constantly upset you by displaying some item of knowledge that they oughtn't to know for a week or two yet, by your system. But I really think that the names of the letters help them, and that they will determine the work sooner if they say the letters first. "M-a-n" doesn't sound like "man," but it brings in all the consonant elements, and is a sort of rude guide, and at any rate a pretty effectual one. The chief trouble is with the vowels, and I think the books are at fault in mixing as they do from the very first the long and short vowels. I find my children learn words of three letters quite as easily as two, if only I keep the vowel sounds consistent.

When I carried Mr. Harrison's boat back the other day, Paris, Tony and Taffy went with me, and I got them to sing some of their boat-songs. It didn't amount to very much, because, as Paris said, "dem boy" couldn't row and sing too well; still they gave me two or three simple ones. "Oh Michael row the boat ashore, Hallelujah, Hallelujah." "My name, my name in de book ob life, Hallelujah etc."[192] Paris sang the words and they the chorus. He said the boat songs were sometimes the same as the shouting songs, and sometimes only used for rowing. One that they sang I recognized as having heard at the shout, with the chorus "Archangel open the door,"[193] Do, do, mi, re, do, re—do, do, do, do, si, si." I have only heard good boat-singing once—in crossing the ferry to Beaufort. That crew sings finely. I haven't heard a single piece of music here that was not religious, except the children singing "O come, come, away" which I suppose they learned at church. Flora says they have songs that are not hymns, instancing "Grandmother in the graveyard"[194]—a very jolly carol I suppose. Phoebe divides all their music into "spirituals" and "running spirituals," that is, shouting tunes. This is one of the prettiest of their hymns, that we have heard.

(better with crotchets [quarter notes] for quavers [eighth notes])

> Travel on, O weary soul,—An' I yedde from heaven to day (*bis*)[195]
> O my sin is forgiven an' my soul sat free,—an' I yedde—etc. (*bis*)
> O a baby born in Bethlehem etc. (*bis*)

> Boat Song

> Michael row the boat ashore, Hallelujah (*bis*)
> Jordan bank de bank I stan'; Hallelujah (*bis*)

Sunday, 1 P.M.

A warm hazy day. Mr. Folsom is gone to Pine Grove to spend the day. We had a small Sunday school to-day, and a good deal of it singing. They know now Portuguese Hymn (three verses) and one or two of Coronation, Poor Wayfaring Man, and Rest for the Weary.

Evening

Dick and Phoebe went to church to-day to Mr. Phillip's funeral. Mr. French spoke to the people telling them to hold on to their 20 acre lots, and he was sure it would be all right. I think the people must be in a delectable state of mystification by this time. Hyacinths, crocus and snowdrops in the garden.

St. Helena, Thursday, Feb. 18, 1864, 8½ P.M.

We have been having cold, blustering weather this week, and this evening it has squeezed out a little snow, for the first time this winter. Robin and Bristol took Charley's row about down to Coffin's Point early Tuesday morning to leave it there and bring the flat round by Station Creek to Mulberry Hill. Yesterday afternoon, when school was nearly through, Bristol came in and handed me a package. He looked hearty and jolly as ever, but when Toby asked him if he hadn't had a pretty hard time, he said he never had such a hard time "since your name was Toby." It seems they set out from Coffin's at about ten o-clock Tuesday morning, but when they got into Station Creek the wind was so hard against them that after working in vain all day they had to put in to Harbor Island, where the waves landed them high on shore. They spent the night there, not having had a morsel to eat since they started from home, and I suppose not since the day before, for the negroes never eat in the morning. Then yesterday they had to wait for the tide, and at last they managed to get to "Massa Williams's," that is Pine Grove. Robin said if he had been smaller he should have cried, his hands pained him so with the cold.

As soon as I got a chance I opened the package, which was that from Northboro' which Mrs. Lambert[196] had put into Harriet Ware's box. Many thanks for its contents. The napkin rings have gone into use already, and the book from mother we shall read very soon. The account of the battle of Gettysburg I read last night. Mr. Gannett spent last night here, on his way to the land-sales in Beaufort; and at about 11, Mr. Stetson appeared on his way from Land's End. We had to put two of them into Mr. Folsom's bed, while Mr. F. himself slept on a sofa, as he prefers. Winsor went with Mr. Gannett to-day, and they give an amazing account of the sales. Dr. Brisbane and Judge Smith kept contradicting each other, and the audience asked all sorts of questions, which each would answer differently. Our mail was brought Saturday and Monday, but no letters for either Mary or me. I had a lot of papers from Prentiss, Ned, and Lucy, and "Pet Marjorie"[197] from Lizzie, and I haven't got thro' the pile yet.

Our school has been ridiculously small last week and this—the morning school a mere farce. The children who should come in the morning many of them have to "mine chile," and those who could come don't like to come alone. The other day those from this plantation,—Venus, Mylie, Minna, Emma, Charlotte etc.,—all turned up with the children in their arms, and there were so few in all that I let them come in. They behaved very well indeed, except that one little one toddled in hanging on to a hand of each Emma and Charlotte, and as these two sit on opposite sides of the room and neither would give up her half of the child, there was a catastrophe threatened and a scream realized.

The afternoon school has been exceedingly pleasant except for the interruption of the weather, and the short time. It is much more agreeable to have the older classes without the swarm of little ones. They learn more in an hour and a half now than they used to learn in three hours. My arithmetic class is doing famously—learning the table of fives, and practicing all the four rules in simple mental operations. I have them take places, and when any one goes up it throws the class into convulsions of laughter. Sammy is the best—a bright but saucy boy, Toby's son. Flora, Taffy, Ishmael and Ellen are about as good. I like Ellen very much—she has a very sweet, refined expression, and is a good scholar and more even-tempered than Ishmael, who is often turbulent and sulky. However, for all Ellen's gentleness, I found Thomas the other day in a sort of row with her, Flora and Hetty. He had a long switch and was laying round him, and justified himself by detailing their assaults on him—"Dat one (Flora) fling brick at me and fling stick at me and fling tin kettle at me. An' dat one (Hetty) fling oster-shell at me. An' dat one (Ellen) do wuss of all—she kick me," and he showed a bruise on his ankle. For the matter of that, there is very little "Kiss for a Blow"[198] among them, and the girls will hold their own against the boys any time. There are some very interesting scholars from Hope Place, and Rinah is perhaps most so. She is a slovenly, harum-scarum girl, always in trouble. In school she is all the time talking or studying aloud, or out of order in some way, and out of school she is a sort of leader and champion of Hopes against the Capt. John scholars—sputtering away at Sammy or Ishmael in an incomprehensible jargon with a very peculiar drawling cadence. She and Queen are the most troublesome girls in school, but both we like very much. Dolly is a sister of Rinah, a pretty, demure little thing, altho' she is in the first class. She is very intrepid in Arithmetic, answering every question promptly in a soft bashful voice, but hardly ever right. Yesterday by chance she answered 15 right, and got up near the head of the class; and was so emboldened by it that she answered every question after that, 15. This cold weather the children come to school in all sorts of costumes. Dolly wears a round soldier's cape; Rinah a rough sort of pea-jacket which gives her a very brigandish air; Abby, a white cape with a fringe all round it; Harry a pocket-handkerchief tied over his head; Benjy a pair of stockings and no shoes; etc. Patty, Linda and Hannah are almost always neatly and tastefully dressed. James, from Hope Place, is a perfect curiosity of tatters. Not so bad as Adam was, for Adam's clothes were 60 percent holes. James' are decent, the 60 percent of holes being patched and darned with every imaginable color and pattern. He is a queer, absent-minded boy,—stands with his feet very far apart, gazing round the room sitting in all parts of the room except in his own seat, losing his place in the book, and forgetting the question before he can think of the answer. But he is quite bright, and a pleasant, well-behaved boy.

I am afraid this cold weather will kill my lettuce, radishes and cabbage, which are already up. It has put an estoppels on our having camellias.

Sunday, Feb. 21, 8 P.M.

Mary and Katy went to church to-day, and I walked to meet them past the creek. They hoped to get the mail, but the steamer isn't in yet, or wasn't last night. We are quite disappointed, for neither Mary nor I have had any letters for two weeks. Mr. Stetson spent last night here, and he and Mr. Folsom rode to-day to Coffin's. Mr. F. has got along famously, and last night slept without anyone to take care of him. Thomas comes every morning and night to do his little jobs. Thomas is a very handy, bright boy, more like a white boy than any I have seen here. His father, John, is almost white, and is a very good carpenter, an intelligent man. Sober and steady as Thomas is, he is great at carrying on with the boys—standing on his head and tumbling the others round. The other day we tossed a copper each to him, Tom, Abraham, Archy and Peter. Thomas, by his quickness of eye and hand, secured the first one, and then stood guard to see that the others got one apiece—making a great show of scrambling for it himself.

Charley spent Friday night here, on his way from Beaufort where he had been attending the sale. There wasn't so much of a row the second day as the first,[199] still Smith and Brisbane stood guard, each contradicting the other to the best of his powers. When the bidders asked about the preemption, Dr. Brisbane told them that they needn't concern themselves at all on that score; to which Judge Smith added that there wasn't the slightest doubt that the preemption titles would hold perfectly good. For all this, the lands went enormously high. The Seaside Place (Edgar Fripp) sold for $7300—280 acres, with an excellent house. (Mr. Philbrick gave about a dollar an acre for his plantation, the houses being thrown in). I suppose that if the plantation is carried on skillfully, the purchasers can get a fair profit from it; but it isn't safe enough for absentee proprietors. There is a poor set of men on the place, and chagrined as they no doubt are at being deceived as to the preemptions, it is not at all likely that they will work very well—if at all—for the purchasers. As a specimen of the absurd way in which they have gone to work to cut up these islands, this lot of land,—the Edgar Fripp, containing the house—is described as Section 5, Town 2 South, Range 1 East. The first day of the sale a speech was made by a colored soldier named Prince Rivers,[200] and it was said to be a very sensible speech—justly indignant at the whiffling course that has been pursued about the islands. Dick says this Prince Rivers used to be President of a Mutual Aid Society[201] the colored people had—slaves and all. Each person deposited some money with him every week, and when anyone was sick his wife was aided from this fund—the money to be refunded when he became well.

By the way, we have come across a fact which shows Capt. John to have been mortal. Amaritta, the very best woman at Coffin's Point, met him one day in front of the place, and called to him for some reason "Take care of your dog, Capt. John"—not putting on "Sir" or Massa." Justly incensed at the insult, Capt. John made at her. She ran, but as he was on horseback, he soon caught her, tied her to a tree and gave her a deserved castigation with his own hands. Capt. John's liberality to his people spoiled them in one way—they were so petted, so encouraged to ask for everything, that it crushed all manliness. There is very little spirit on the plantation, no patriotism, and a great deal of begging. They are generally a tractable, pleasant set, but less manly than at Coffin's, Gannett's places, Cherry Hill or Mulberry Hill. This proves what we have always said, that the demoralizing effects of slavery are inherent, and that where it is mildest it makes men most unmanly.[202]

Katy and I were talking the other day about our change of feeling about slavery. I had never laid much stress upon its cruelty, that being a thing of which I could know nothing certainly; whereas the degradation of the system was manifest. But here I find the people so much less degraded that I expected, and the barbarities so much greater than I supposed, that I have been led to place more stress upon them than I ever did before. As a specimen of the indifference of these people, I have had so little time for the afternoon school that last Wednesday I asked the men to come in the evening for an extra lesson. Not one came. It was very cold, which I suppose was their excuse, so I shall try again. Our most constant adult scholars are from Mulberry Hill—Paris, Ned, Hercules,

Dolly, Betsy, Chloe, Lucy and Bella. Only Paris and Dick here are as regular as Paris Gregley. It is a real pleasure to have dealings with him. Mr. Folsom says he is a born gentleman. He comes in with such a modest, manly, respectful air, so grateful for the smallest crumbs of knowledge, that it seems a sin to teach him so little as I do. Paris Simmons, on the other hand, repels one by his air of conceit and a disposition to find fault if he doesn't get on so fast as he thinks he ought. Still he is very bright, and when I talk with him in private I like him better than in the class. Almost all the young men here have something of this self-sufficient way—particularly Bristol, Gabriel and London. Billy, on the other hand is very modest and pleasant, and so are Dennis, Ned and Hercules.

My radishes were not hurt by the frost, but all the narcissus and jonquils are cut down.

Tuesday, Feb. 23, 1864, 7½ P.M.

Yesterday and to-day have been lovely days. Harriet and Miss Rice, each in a gig, drove up yesterday before dinner, and Harriet spent the night, returning this morning with Mr. Soule, who came to bring along his letters. Mr. Winsor took them to Beaufort, and brought news back of the repulse of our troops in Florida.[203] This morning, after a tolerably good school, Molly, Katy and I walked to the "Hill," to see the people at work. The "Hill" is a slight elevation, very sandy, the large field directly at the end of our avenue (or rather of its continuation) thro' which the path to Cherry Hill leads. We shouldn't even call it a knoll. This is the best cotton land on the plantation, and each person has some tasks here and some in another field, while the low land around is given out for corn and potatoes. They have taken cotton land at about the rate of two acres (eight tasks or 2½ to a full hand). Robin, I think, has the largest proportion 4½ acres, as Rinah cannot work in the field, and he has only Ishmael and Ellen to help him. Then they are allowed 1½ acres to a full hand for corn etc.

On our way we met Justina (Phoebe's daughter and Billy's wife) with a basket on her head and a hoe over her shoulder, "too weary for turn out for get wood." In the field, the first tasks we came to were Frank's, and he was listing away, while Mary (his daughter) was spreading "marsh" for manure. The marsh grass, which Isaac, Ned, Jimmy and Paris have been busy carting these few weeks, is distributed in heaps thro' the field, and children take it and lay it in the "alleys" as the hollow between the beds is called. Then the "lister," with a huge, clumsy, long handled hoe draws the earth over from the bed, so as to cover the manure—going the length of the row and returning on the other side, so as to cover it in the two hoeings. We then turned to the left, where Joan and Tony were listing corn-land, using cotton seed for manure. Mr. Folsom gave out the seed to them last week. Molly and Katy then went back to the shade to wait for me, while I went on some little distance to where Taft and Flora were at work—Flora with her gown tucked up about her waist—while Tyra (Taft's wife), too infirm to work, sat by a little smouldering fire, to get water or cook food for them. Taft is an elderly man, whom Mr. Folsom considers the most faithful man on the place. Pretty soon Dido came up, William's wife, a splendid figure of a woman, and sat down on the ground by Tyra. I began to ask what was their work in old times, a task and a half to list, which they could easily finish by noon. And then they went on to expatiate on "massa's" kindness—if it rained, or was wet or cold, he would send them indoors, and when a task and five beds in the heavy land was too much, he would take off the five beds. I asked them whether they worked more now than then, and Taft said he had already finished a day's work on the old system, while Dido said that she had done a task and a half, and might have finished the second task if she had kept at it. I thought from the warmth of their encomiums that it might be they regretted the old times, but I soon saw it was no such thing. Taft said the money was for himself now and "I work as long as I kin." They evidently appreciate independence thoroughly.

I forget what led Dido to speak of her old mistress, but when she did, it was fine to see her wrath and vehemence. She turned up her sleeve and showed me the scars on her arm and said her back was covered with them, and it was so with every house-servant (this was probably an exaggeration)—and that she was thankful when she was sent to work in the field, where she was under massa, and away from missus. Once, she said, missus had her clothes stripped off her back, and had her tied to the tree in front of the house—her arms put round the tree and her wrists tied together—and flogged till she was covered with blood. Then she went behind the garden and cried, and when massa came home from Bee'fut he found her there, and "went in de house an' tole missus not lick de nigger so." I asked her who did the flogging, and with what, and she said "Driver Mosey" with a raw cow-hide—not a square cow-hide, but plaited together. She seemed to despise Mrs. Fripp (who was an Irish school-mistress) as much as she hated her; that she didn't bring "not one nigger" to massa—and at every wrathful torrent of words from Dido, Tyra would feebly mutter a confirming echo. She accused Mrs. Fripp of having sat by when Capt. John was very sick and was making his will, and contriving that every strong healthy slave should be given to her, and the old and feeble to "Miss Marta an' Miss Car'lina," the daughters of a former wife. Whenever Capt. John flogged, he would never strike the same place twice; and he never licked Dick hard but once, and that was when he watered the garden with salt water—it was easier I suppose to dip from the creek than to draw from the well.

9 P.M.

We have just had an amusing episode. We lost our cat the day after she came—
and with all our searching we found her not. But just often enough to revive the
dying embers of hope, there has appeared a vision of a cat, either vocal or visible,
which we thought might be ours. So we have never given her up, and when the
mice gnaw my seed-peas or drink up the water that the sugar-bowl stands in so
that red ants get into the sugar, or make holes in the table-cloths and napkins,
our hearts yearn for pussy, and we almost believe she is coming back. Well, to-
night we heard steps on the piazza, and then a tap at the door, and Flora and
Mary came in for some medicine. Just as they came in, we heard a cat outside,
and I looking out, I spied her cautiously creeping toward the door. By skilful
maneuvering we got her into the house, shut the door on her, and lit a candle
to see whether it was our lost yellow outside. "Did you see the cat, Flora?" "No
massa, but I yedde him holla." We "yedde him holla" very decidedly, for when
she found she was caged, she set up a tremendous caterwauling, and we soon
saw that she was none of ours. "Is she yours, Flora?" "No ma'am, no own." So
endeth the episode of the cat.—This use of "own" is the only way of expressing
the possessive—"my own," "Tony own, Mosey own." Mary says she never heard
"ma" used for "mother" before. They generally say "tiddy," which must be a corruption of sister. Dick's children call their mother "Tiddy Ann"; Phoebe (their
grandmother), "ma," and their little sister Selina [Seline?], "mudder." For father,
they say "pa" and "pap."

Wednesday, Feb. 24, 9 P.M.

I have succeeded in having a sort of Lyceum to-night, or as I called it "map
lesson." Only Paris, Demus and Bristol came of the young men, but a good
many scholars of the first class,—Robert, Tony, Taffy, Ishmael, Hetty, and even
Tom and Abraham, who sat on a low bench with their backs to the map, and
probably didn't understand a word. The younger ones came first, and I had them
sing several of their pieces, some of which are very pretty. They sang two "shouting" tunes (running spirituals), one of which was I think the sweetest tune I
have heard—"I can't stay behind my lord, I can't stay behind, Room enough an'
heaven all roun', I can't stay behind."[204] Stoback means shouting backward, and
probably is a corruption of stand back. This is the other one.

I ax all de brudder roun',—brudder, why can't you pray for me (*bis*)[205]
I'm gwine to my heaben I'm gwine home—archangel open de door (*bis*)

I gave them to-night a little talk upon "what constitutes a state," telling them how the laws were made, and about the legislature. I illustrated by asking them what they would do if they sold a bushel of potatoes to a man and he wouldn't pay. "Sue him." Then if he not only wouldn't pay, but should knock them with a stick. "If he didn't kill me, I kill him," said Bristol, which wasn't precisely the lesson I intended to enforce.

I had a long talk this afternoon with Paris, Billy and Henry about the war, and told them very plainly that it was a shame to the plantation that there were no volunteers from it,—with so many able-bodied young men. They really talked very shamefully, and I very severely. Paris seemed to be a good deal impressed by what I said, and Billy, I thought, was rather ashamed of himself. He had said he would rather be a slave all his life than fight, and I told him he deserved to be. Finally, however, he said he would fight with a stick, but not with a gun.

I have a very nice little class in the morning school that I am teaching to read on the board, and this morning I wrote, "I can see the sky." Then I asked them if they ever saw the sky, and what color it was. Nobody could tell, so I had them all come to the window and look at the sky. Most of them stared straight at Jimmy, who was in the yard, and I half expected them to say "black." At last Abraham suggested "white"—"and red" he added. Just then Dick was passing the window, and I called out to him that none of these children could tell me the color of the sky. "Dey born so long time, an' not know dat,—ought to lick 'em" said Dick promptly. "Well Dick," said I, "here's a chance for you to lick Tom" who was appearing round a corner of the barn. "Tom, what's the color of the sky?" Tom stared at the sky, but said nothing. Dick grinned. "Tom, how sky stan'?" "Blue" shouted Tom.

Monday, Feb. 29, 10 P.M.

Our school has rather improved in numbers. Katy drove Lucy in a gig on Saturday to Hopes to see why the children didn't come more steadily, and found that there was a good deal of sickness, but that they would come when they got well. I intended to go too, and started on foot, thro' the fields, Molly accompanying me part way. When we reached the Cherry Hill woods, we found the fence on fire—the people have made a great many fires to clear their land of weeds and grass. Ruggles has lost about a mile and three quarters of fence, and all the fences about Frogmoor are gone. The fire looked too formidable for me to deal with alone, so Mary went back to tell the people, and I went on to Cherry Hill, where I told Butcher (the foreman) and then hastened back. By the time I had the fire checked at both ends, and was at work on a cross fence, Butcher and the rest,—women and all—appeared, and we soon had the fire stopped.

Thursday eve.

I was out in the same woods, with Mr. Folsom and most of the people from the place, and Friday eve. Mr. F. went out again.

Thursday Mr. Folsom and I went to Beaufort to attend the land sale, while Mary and Katy took care of the school. The fun was over, however, Judge Smith had retired in disgust, and the two other members of the board had it all their own way. The land brought enormous prices—too high for anything but the chance of there being a city sometime at Land's End. For anything else, I doubt whether the purchasers will make even a fair profit. Mr. Tomlinson crossed in the boat with us coming back, and when we landed he was surrounded by a crowd of women from a plantation near Land's End, complaining that their land—that they had preempted—had been sold away from them, and declaring that they wouldn't work for the purchaser. They said they would have given as much as anyone for it, but I suppose they didn't combine. The people of Wassa Island and of the Marion Chaplin place have clubbed together and bought their plantations or a part of them, and will carry them on in common for the present. Everybody in Beaufort was full of indignation at the Florida affair, which seems to have been miserably mismanaged. Gen. Seymour[206] is noted for his unjust treatment of the colored troops—he is a cousin of the two governors. He is however a fine disciplinarian and has done a great deal to weed out drunkenness from the army.

Yesterday Mary and I drove to Coffin's and staid to dinner. Coming back, Mr. Eustis rode by the side of the buggy, and we had a delightful talk with him. He says he is anxious to get his plantation into the hands of the negroes as soon as they are ready for it, so this year, as an experiment, he offered to let them have the use of it in lots of 10, 15 and 20 acres,—he to furnish teams etc., and extra labor, and pay them so much for every bale of cotton they would raise. Not one would take the responsibility—they would rather work for him for wages. He thinks these people must be civilized by colored people coming from the North—mechanics etc.—and he is going to try to get some down. He surprised me by saying that his people only worked for him last year an average of 25 days of 5 hours each. Mr. Soule told me to-day a remarkable fact. He has come across some old documents, showing that the average crop of ginned cotton on this island one year was 130 lb. to the acre, and that the hands took an average of over 3 acres. This last year Mr. Philbrick's plantations had about 75 lb. to the acre, the hands averaging about 2 acres. Mr. Soule brought us our mail to-day—letters from father, Joseph, Prentiss and Lucy, and for Molly from Mary and Eugenia[207]—thanks to all. Yesterday morning I began a sort of Bible class for the men—about ten came and they generally seemed to like it. I took the Beatitudes, which they said they never read before—they are mighty on John and Hebrews.

Tuesday eve.

Charley has just come in with more mail. The sales of furniture, cattle etc. is to begin tomorrow at the Oaks. They will get to us in the course of the week, and we hope to get some fun out of the affair, even if we lose Nelly and the tumble-down.

St. Helena, March 3, 1864, Thursday, 8 p.m.

Another cold snap—not so very cold—a prospect of frost to-night. Our peach trees have been in full blossom for a week, and look very handsome. The red camellias have gradually recovered from the last frost, and are in full bloom again; but the white ones haven't shown themselves since. The roadsides are white with the blossoms of the wild plum, and the beautiful wild jasmine, with its heliotrope fragrance, is just blooming—the side of the road beyond the avenue is lined with it. But the narcissus, jonquils, etc. were killed dead, and are now withered. I have peas, turnips, radishes, lettuce, cabbage, beets and spinach up, and have some sweet corn and tomatoes. I am surprised to see how slowly the trees come on however. I do not see that the buds are generally started more than they often are at the North at this season—they evidently have their fixed habits which they are not to be enticed out of by any warm days. There are fig and pomegranate trees near the house, which look as dead as ever; the orange trees are all shriveled up now, ready to put out their new leaves. Then there are three or four trees in the circle in front of the house which Dick says are olive trees—and they look like it—and I am curious to see whether they will flower. We have had quantities of blue-birds, but I think less now, and it has seemed very home-like to hear their pleasant twitter, but I have neither seen nor heard any robins or song sparrows. The mocking birds fill the air now with the most charming melody at all hours of the day—handsome, dapper little fellows they are too. Then there is the splendid cardinal grosbeak—redbirds they call them—brilliant scarlet with a kingly tuft on the head. Everybody declares that they don't sing, but I remember well that Audubon speaks of their note, and am probably the only person in the department who has noticed that they have three distinct notes; the most common a loud, very sweet whistle, "wheet," another a sort of rapid call, and a simple song, which I have only heard once, and which is not very striking.

School has been better this week—Hope Place has been quite regular, but Cherry and Mulberry Hills have hardly been at all. The Hope girls—Patty and

Rinah spokesmen—entered a complaint to-day against the Big House children "dey study 'buse an' cuss we." So I sent for Ishmael, Sammy, Tommy and Flora, and gave them a lecture. They declared that "dem gal" began it, and I think like enough—Rinah is not chary with her tongue. It seems they were not satisfied with the admonition I gave the Hopefuls a few days ago for shaking their fists at Ishmael across the school-room, and had taken justice into their own hands. They said that Hope was nine and they only six, and that Hope had come against them in extra force—"a gang of twenty head." Mulberry Hill doesn't agree with Hope Place any better—they say that there is a "bigger gang," which is very true—while the little children at Hopes excuse themselves from coming thro' Mulberry Hill on their way to school by their terror of Minna, the oldest of the Mulberry "gang"—"Minna lick we—we fight him an' den he lick we."

I believe I have lately spoken more of the faults than the virtues of these people. There is absolutely no profanity or drunkenness (perhaps there would be drunkenness if they could get liquor) among them. There is very strong family affection—Rinah cried bitterly the other day in school because I punished her sister Venus, and this affection is very marked between brothers and sisters. They are very polite and courteous—always bow and say "sir" and "maam" to each other. Paris came into the class late this afternoon, and Bristol was using his book. I asked him where his book was, but he made no direct answer until Bristol had got thro' and handed it to him. I have been quite struck with one usage which shows that their souls revolted against being classed like cattle. They are all of course called by their first name, and there is no title—no handle to it—but from an instinctive feeling of politeness the usage sprang up of calling everybody "Uncle," "Aunt," or "Cousin": and it is quite curious how "cousin" particularly has been clipped into a real title—"Co' Abraham" is Tom's constant way of addressing Abraham; "Co' Robin," "Co' Isaac," "Co' Venus," "Co' Margaret"—the o being sounded as slightly as possible.

Mr. Eustis has lately received a letter from his brother[208] in Natchez, from whom he has not heard for three years. He was a rich man, and an accomplished cavalry officer. He is now living on $16 a month, derived from the sale of butter. All their slaves have left them, and they pay $8 a month to their single servant. Tablecloths, napkins, everything, have been cut up into underclothes, and the children this winter have had nothing to wear but bed-ticking. And all the wealthy families in the neighborhood are reduced to the same straits.

Yesterday Mr. Folsom, Gannett, and Winsor rode up to the Oaks to attend to the sale of furniture, cattle, etc. But the sale was postponed on account of the commissioners not being able to find horses to get there. After school Katy mounted Nelly and Molly and I walked across to Cherry Hill. We found most of the people at work in the fields, and talked with them a while. Then Molly got on the horse and rode round by McTureous and Pine Grove, while

Katy and I walked back. Nelly's back seems quite well now, and Katy rode her to-day to the village. When I say there is no profanity among the people, I should mention a use of language precisely like one of the Germans—the habit of using expressions which we should call irreverent, but which are not so to them. Their favorite exclamations are "Jehovia," "Great King", "Jesus" etc. which church members use as much as anybody, but round anglo-saxon oaths you never hear.

Saturday, March 5, 9 P.M.

Yesterday forenoon William Hall rode up, and staid to dinner with the view of visiting our school. As we were at dinner—a full hour before school time— Hope Place marched up and camped under the window, whence presently preceded a sound of weeping and wailing. Thinking it my duty to look after my young hopefuls I went out and found Nat blubbering on the ground, and his sister Libby crying in sympathy. Benjy informed me that Nat "cuss Harry" and so Harry had chastised him gently; and Harry explained "Him cuss me 'git out'." Just the reverse of a northern school, these scholars never behave so well as when there is a visitor; and we haven't had so pleasant a school for a long time. The only drawback was that there were only two of my favorite second class. Just as school was nearly thro'—they were standing at the map and pointing out the states—when my attention was attracted by an elegant little dog running into the yard, the sure sign of a white man. Immediately there followed Messrs. Folsom, Winsor, Sumner, Harrison, Dr. Lawrence (of Boston, who owns the Dr. Jenkins place beyond Edgar Fripp's), the two agents of the Commissioner, Reed and Carter, and a certain speculator named Pickens.[209]

The sale was actually coming off. Mr. Sumner, spying out a class reciting, rushed in to hear it, and by the time we were dismissed all the household articles—sofa, fender, wash-stand, and big chair, were knocked off to Mr. Folsom, *nomine obstante. [nomine non obstante:* name not withstanding]. But Mr. Pickens was after mules and carts, and mules and carts Mr. Folsom must have himself. So Caesar went up to $195, and Tamar (worth about $70) to $190. An old mule, blind of both eyes, was knocked off to Phoebe for $10½. She was delighted at her bargain—"he carry me to church and back" said she triumphantly. When we drew near the stable, and a "grey mare" was mentioned, there were derisive remarks and laughter, on the strength of which Mr. F got Nelly for $15. But Lucy was run up above her value and he lost her. The tumble down Dick bought, and we the buggy. Mr. F. also bought all the sheep and meat cattle, and we shall probably have fresh meat after this. A small, mouse-colored mule, named Wind—old, but very swift, not good for working but for riding,—was not brought up till the sale was over. So he was put up this morning. Messrs.

Reed and Clark [Carter][210] spent the night here—and Mr. F. got him for $25. Lucy being gone, Wind must take her place in the buggy. So after dinner Molly, Katy and I set out to try the new team. Wind is very willing and gentle, but we soon found that when he trotted he nearly yanked Nelly off her legs. So after considerable experimenting we compromised by letting Nelly trot and Wind walk, by which we got along about as fast as we used with the old pair. We went towards Pine Grove as far as the Seaside Road, and then turned to the right and kept on thro' the McTureous place—which is quite beautiful, I think as pleasant a place as I have seen—to Cherry and Mulberry Hill, and then by the cross road home. Wind's back is sore now, but he will be a good riding-horse. I was going to say—when it is well.

Tu. Mar. 8, 8 P.M.

Mr. Gannett brought us a pile of newspapers Sunday evening—I had some Posts from Lucy and Election sermon from father—and to-day Wm. Hall brought some letters; only one for me, and that not from home. All the island is on fire to purchase horses. Mr. Gannett has just got a splendid iron grey from Morris Island,—the largest horse on the island, Mr. Soule says—and two or three others have been sent for. Charley Ware has bought a large horse from Limus, and Mr. Folsom has sent North for two horses. The negroes are crazy on the subject. Dennis bid today $162 for a tacky not so good as Lucy, Mr. F. says—and one man at Fripp Point gave $231 for a mule. Mr. Gannett's people bid against him, and bought several mules, cows and carts that he wanted—they are an independent and troublesome set. It is curious how variously the sales went—not agreeing with the doctrine that things will always fetch their value at an auction. Lucy brought $95 and Rob Roy $51. Mr. Ruggles gave $190 for a mule worth $70, and $40 for one worth $200. Mr. Folsom gave $24 for a pair of wheels (the rest of the cart belonged to him), and $20 for a first-rate cart, complete.

Yesterday, after morning school, as I was sowing some sweet corn, Mr. Ruggles, Nichols, Wells and a black man rode up on their way to the sale at the McTureous and Hope Places. So when I was thro' my work, I mounted Nelly and followed. I found them at McTureous, waiting for the auctioneers, and there we waited a full hour, having a very good time; Mr. Harrison, Thorpe and John Alden were there too.

Yesterday evening Quash came in, and I attacked him on the subject of his children being so irregular. He agreed that "eddication great ting in dese time," and promised to "lick em." "Dey so sloteful. When I make a resh at 'em, dey come studdy, and den I fall away an' dey stay home." Yesterday Hope Place was quite early, and as tide was dead low the whole gang were presently wading about after crabs, which they carry loose in their pockets, and are rather in the habit of taking out and playing with in school. The crabs are small as yet—soon we shall have large ones and shrimps—it is too late now for oysters, so these will be quite a resource. Potatoes too are nearly gone, of both kinds; chickens can't be had, and we must live on what we can get.

Wednesday, 2 P.M.

We were interrupted at dinner by a messenger that the steamer goes tomorrow, and our letters will be called for this afternoon. So we have to close in haste. I hope this is a sign that the steamers are to run once a week. I am going to Beaufort to-morrow with Mr. Folsom.

St. Helena, March 14, 1864, 8¼ P.M.

Our present weather is almost perfect. Glorious bright mornings, with the birds singing merrily; then warm forenoons, sometimes too warm; the afternoons always cool with a South or East wind; and the evenings cold enough to enjoy a live-oak fire. Mr. Harrison says that there is very rarely a day in the height of summer, when it is not comfortably cool in the shade after two o-clock; but the forenoons are fearful. Wednesday and Thursday nights there were heavy thunder-showers—Friday morning a tremendous rain. My peas, radishes etc. are getting on finely. The orange and oleander trees seem to be killed by the New Year's frost—I am much disappointed at losing the orange blossoms. The last week we have had a good deal of company and a good deal of going about. Mr. Folsom went to Beaufort on Thursday, and brought back with him Mr. Dennett,[211] a very agreeable person—very cultivated and well-read, and of a good deal of thought. Saturday, Molly and I took a drive to Mr. Ruggles to get some flour and pickles, and carry him a quarter of a sheep which Jimmy had just slaughtered—one quarter each went to Pine Grove and Coffin's Point. It was a very pleasant drive—Wind and Nelly went capitally together, the road was lined with blackberry and jasmine.

Yesterday morning, while we were at Sunday School, Charley Ware and a Dr. Westcott[212] (surgeon of the Kingfisher) drove up for a few minutes on their way to Mr. Well's. Soon after they were gone, in rode Mr. Gannett and Miss Rice,—and she on Feeble, he on his handsome iron-grey, Harry—on their way to church. Mary and Katy were just setting out in the buggy, and just as they were gone Mr. Gannett called out to me to ask me if I wouldn't like to take his horse and go. I was nothing loath, and saw that he evidently preferred to spend the morning with Folsom and Dennett, so in a jiffy we had changed places and

I was off on his colossus. I had a very nice ride,—met Messrs. Ruggles, Dyer, Wm. Alden, Wells and wife[213]—and then Mr. G. and Miss R. staid to dinner. Just after dinner Mr. Stetson rode up, and just before tea Mr. Tomlinson,—the former went off at about 8, the latter spent all night, and we had a very pleasant talk in the evening. I went to bed at about twelve, the others staid up till three. It was as pleasant a company as one often meets. Mr. Stetson is very lively and witty, Mr. Tomlinson a great talker and a good one. Tonight Miss Rice is staying here, Mr. Gannett being away. The Continental arrived the other day, and I was interested in looking at the music in "Under the Palmetto." I have heard all the pieces but one, and they are quite correct, except that he calls them all "shout tunes," while only one of them is, and that he gives only in part, and that differently from what I have heard. It is as follows

Hold your Light[214]
What make de Satan da follow me so—Satan hab nottin' 'tall for
   to do wid me—Hold your light.
Dear brudder
or Seeker turn back
true believer
dear brudder (*bis*) Hold your light on Canaan shore.

Wrestle Jacob[215]
Wrestle Jacob; Jacob, day is a-breakin'—Wrestle Jacob, Lord I would
   not let you go. I hold my
brudder (sister) wid a tremblin' han'. I would not let
you go (*bis*).
I fish all night an' I fish all day, I would not let you go.
I ketch no fish but I ketch some soul, I " " " "

There is considerable variety in singing these hymns, especially in the shout-tunes; so that I presume the copies in the Continental are as correct as mine.

Tuesday, March 15, 8½ P.M.

There is very little to write about now-a-days. All the excitement of the lands and the sales is over, altho' everybody is still talking about them. Mr. Gannett's people—a very unruly set—bid against him and bought some carts and animals which he wanted. Neither Charley's nor Folsom's did so. Gannett's people set out to keep the cotton seed, which they like to use to manure their corn. So this brought matters to a crisis. It is worth $2 a bushel, and of course belongs with the crop; after trying persuasion in vain, he got the promise of a guard of soldiers, which brought them round. The superintendents give out cotton seed to the people, but the principle needed to be tested. This preemption business has had a very unsettling influence upon the people, and Mr. French has a good deal to answer for, for meddling in the business. The people in many cases refuse to work for the new owners and talk so loud as to scare the poor fellows out of their wits.

Judge Smith has been removed from the board, or at least so it is stated in the papers, and altho' no official notice has been received, he refuses to sit any longer with the board, the effect of which is to put a stop to all proceeding until the new commissioner arrives. Brisbane's plan is the most judicious, and Smith behaves very factiously about the business; still some of Brisbane's performances are very queer. He lets Mr. Fairfield have five school-farms, most of them at two dollars an acre for the land cultivated, but for the Oaks he pays $500, which is however refunded if he keeps a school. Another gentleman has taken the school-farm at Cuthbert's Point, and has to pay $500, altho' the land is poor and there are no hands, and is not permitted to keep a school. Of course it is intended that these farms shall support schools eventually, but this year they are simply leased for money in most cases. The McTureous people asked Mr. Fairfield if he was going to give them a school, and he told them there were three within a mile, which was equivalent to saying that he would let Mr. Philbrick school them. The Frogmoor people declare up and down that they won't work for Mr. Fairfield or anyone belonging to him. So finally he has agreed to let Mr. Wm. Alden take the school off his hands—Mr. A. being, as I understand, to have all the profits. Alden is also going to keep a school at McTureous. The people at the Oaks also refuse to work for Mr. Fairfield, who seems likely to have a hard time of it. He has set out to have a Normal School at the Oaks, taking children in his family; and he actually got three, but I understand that they have all left. Mr. Fairfield has said a great deal against Mr. Philbrick's enterprise, as being a speculating affair; so that his getting five school-farms into his own hands is somewhat commented upon.

My school has been quite pleasant, altho' irregular, of late. The Geography class know all the states except California and Oregon, and the Arithmetic class are learning the table of sevens. Paul played truant the other day (Mulberry Hill), and when I told his brother Hacless, the latter advised me to "ketch him an' git him nasty lickin'." I had quite a row with Rinah to-day, who troubles me and Katy a good deal by not speaking loud enough to be heard. I kept her after school, and she put in an indignant defense—"I study talk hard but you no yedde me." "I hab too much work for do—I no come here only for larn."

Wednesday, March 16, 8 P.M.

Miss Rice staid all day yesterday, and till this morning. Wm. Hall dined with us, on his way to Mr. Sumner's to spend the night. Mr. Winsor also came to sell (as he does twice a week) and spent the night. At about half past nine Mr. Gannett came in from Hilton Head, with a pocket-full of letters and papers— two papers from Lizzie, Tribune Almanac and Examiner. Also my pantaloons, which were sent in a bundle to Mr. Severance.[216] He spent the night, and this morning Mr. F. and Winsor went to Beaufort and brought some more mail— no letters for me—and news that Gen. Gillmore is going to draft the negroes. It will be a regular, fair thing I suppose; still, I am sorry for it. The people here were sent into the woods last night at about midnight by a rumor of this sort, and I suppose now we shall be full of trouble. It has been a cold day, and Abraham was the only child who came to school this morning. This afternoon school was quite good. Both Katy and I are going to let our men read in the testament instead of Hillard's Third Reader—which is a most wretched affair. They like the change, and read better for it.

The following is one of the best shout tunes—very simple, but very jolly.

Pray all de Member[217]
O Lord   yes my Lord
1. Pray all de member—O Lord—Pray etc—Yes my Lord
2. Pray true believer. Pray a little longer.
3. Jericho do worry me. I bin to Jerusalem.
   Patrol around me. Tank God he no ketch me.
   I went to de meetin'. Met brudder Hacless.
   What d'ye tink he tell me? Tell me for to turn back.
   Jump along Jericho.

First, they sing to tune 1, then to 2, then to 3, the base coming in after every line.

Sunday, March 20, 1864, 7½ P.M.

It was lucky that Mr. Soule came for our letters on Thursday before they were fully ready, for they have a new arrangement, that the steamers are not to go every eight days as heretofore, but are to sail as soon as they are full, whether after a longer or a shorter time. So you must expect letters very irregularly now.

We had quite an excursion yesterday, which has been planned for some time, for our three families and the Oliver Fripp household, to spend a day at Hunting Island. The Oliver Fripp House is about six miles from here, beyond the Episcopal church,—not towards Land's End, but Parris Island. Mr. Sumner has been teaching there for two years, and I suppose has the best school on the island. Miss Kellogg[218] assists him, and Miss Forten[219] (a mulatto) lives with them, and has a school somewhere else. Mr. Chas. Williams was superintendent on the place, but it is now a school-farm, leased by Mr. Sumner; Mr. W. is however retained as a superintendent—a sort of assistant, I suppose to Mr. Tomlinson. It was cold thro' the week, and altho' Friday was rather milder, we still were afraid that it would be too cold and blustering for the expedition. However, we closed school early; Mary got into Mr. Gannett's sulky which he had sent, and Katy and I into the buggy with Nelly and Wind, to spend the night at Pine Grove so as to be ready for an early start.

I don't know whether I have ever described the manner of harnessing the beasts. The pole is fastened to the breastplate with ropes. Then we have two pairs of reins, but they are so short that when tied together they only make one pair long enough to reach. So one rein is fastened to the right side of Wind's mouth, and the other to the left of Nelly's, and their heads then joined with 2 straps. Each beast then goes along with mouth wide open, tugging at the other, and as soon as Nelly falls back a little or Wind turns his head out, the other is pulled towards the middle of the road. As Nelly always does hang back, Wind is as constantly pushing her to the left; so that in practice, in driving, I generally hold on to Wind's rein tight—sometimes with both hands— relaxing it when I want to steer to the left, and pulling with all my might to turn to the right. When we started this time, the two "Kettrypids"[220] set out in the two opposite directions—Thomas had forgotten to fasten their heads together, and each followed his rein. When we came back I found that the strap joining their heads together was at the left of the bit of each, which would have made a row if I hadn't discovered it in time. As the harness consists only of bridle and breastplate, and there are no D's for the rein to pass thro' the effect is of an extremely loose arrangement;—I really shouldn't like to drive skittish horses in this vehicle and harness.

Well, we had a pleasant drive and a pleasant evening. Mr. Williams spent the night with us at Pine Grove—somewhat deaf and rather taciturn, but quite agreeable. The next morning we started at about 9½, in Mr. Gannett's large boat rowed by six young men. A narrow winding creek brought us to Station Creek, the broad sound separating us from Hunting Island. Here we could see Otter Island, Egg Bank, the Kingfisher, and soon the little boat from Coffin's, which rapidly drew near—a smaller boat than ours, with a sail and four oarsmen. We made for the extreme northern end of Hunting Island, where are the ruins of a light-house, blown up by the rebels. The two boats landed at precisely the same moment, and the inmates of Coffin's,—Mr. Soule, Mr. Sumner, Winsor, Charley, Wm Hall, Harriet, Miss Kellogg and Miss Forten—immediately fraternized with ours—Mr. Gannett, Mr. Williams, Miss Rice, Katy, Mary and I.

Miss Kellogg, who had sprained her ankle, had brought a pair of crutches, but as she found she couldn't use them on the sand, she had to be carried across the island, partly in Rodwell's arms, partly sitting in a chair by four persons using her crutches to support the chair. It is only a few rods across thro' the woods, and we came to a beach—I think the best I ever was on, perfectly hard, smooth and white. It abounds in very pretty shells, of which we secured a good number, while Charley and Mr. Gannett came upon a more valuable prize,— some fifty crates of hay, which had been thrown from a schooner in distress. Mr. G. got six crates aboard his boat, and they are going with flats to-morrow to secure all they can. We had our dinner in the woods, and afterwards singing; then at about 4½ started for home. It was nearly high tide, and the boats lay so far from the shore that the men had to carry us out. Charley's boat soon outstripped ours, for it was light and the wind favorable. But we had wind and tide against us, and a heavy load, so we were not home until near seven. When we were across Station Creek, going up the narrow winding creek, it was exceedingly pleasant. The day had been a perfect one, warm and bright, and now altho' after sunset the air was balmy, there was a full moon and the men sang most of the way as they rowed. It was curious to see how their rowing flagged—for they were quite tired—the moment the singing stopped. It wasn't a very good set of singers, still I was very glad to hear them, for I have heard very little boat music. They sang "Michael row,"[221] "Hold your Light,"[222] and several others of which we were particularly struck by "de Grabeyard,"[223] "Ober yonder"[224] and "I want to go home."[225] The first of these is sung differently here—as I give it.

Graveyard you ought to know me—Graveyard etc. I know Graveyard—I ring
  de rosy lan' (Jerusalem?)
I hab a grandmother in de graveyard. (or dear sisters) Where d'you tink I fin'
  'em?—I fin' em in de boggy mire.

(When I asked Billy what he found he was completely posed.) We staid to dinner after we got to Pine Grove, and drove home by moonlight. This evening we drove down to a shout—they have one frequently, after praise. As we were going, Bristol overtook us, and we asked him if he was going to the shout. "No Ma'am, dey wouldn't let me in—I haint found dat ting yet (meaning religion). Haint been out on my knees in de swamp." These people have the custom when they are "on the anxious bench," of going "out in de wilderness" as they call it— wandering by night thro' the woods and swamps like the ancient Bacchantes.[226]

It must be this that the song above refers to; and they use the expression "fin' dat ting" for getting religion. They shouted to seven tunes—Heaven bell,[227] Archangel open de door,[228] I can't stay behin' my lord,[229] Jesus die,[230] Sinner turn,[231] My body rack wid feber,[232] and Jordan roll.[233] The Heaven bell is a pretty good type of these tunes. The introduction is sung, the shouters standing still or clapping their hands. Then begins the second part, the regular shout. I will try to send it some time. "Sinner turn" is very sweet—I hadn't heard it before this evening.

All in confusion again about the draft. The enrolling officers are coming soon to make their head-quarters at the "Corner," but nobody knows yet whether it is to be a sweeping draft, or not, or whether it is to be of both whites and blacks. In either case, as long as the draft has been suspended at the North, it seems to me that it is an outrage to put it into operation here. The two previous drafts with their incidents, and the way in which they have been deceived about the land here pretty much destroyed the confidence of people in government. I don't wonder they are not willing to fight out of patriotism, but I do think they show a pretty mean spirit in not being willing to fight for their freedom.

Monday, March 21, 9 P.M.

We were very lucky in having the only good day for more than a week for our excursion. Yesterday was dull, and to-day a cold rain-storm. Mr. Folsom went to Beaufort to-day on Wind, and came back on a fine prancing white horse, which has been neglected and abused, so that he is now in poor condition. He used to belong to the rebel Gen. Drayton. Mr. Gannett's horse belonged to Gen. Ames; Mr. Wells has a new horse which was Gen. Stevenson's;[234] and Charley has bought a grey horse of Limus. So gradually the various houses are getting supplied.

There has been a good deal of sickness in Dick's family, and to relieve Dick, we have had Thomas do his indoor work. We miss Dick's grin and chuckle, and his stories, but it is a very pleasant change to have a bright, light-stepping and quick-witted boy in place of a clumsy man. Ann (Dick's wife) has to give up the washing for the present, so last week Dido did it, and to-day I rode over to Cherry Hill to get Minda (wife of Tony, a very nice cook and washerwoman) to do our washing for the present. Nelly carried me very well. The jasmines are now in their perfection, and I gathered some pretty blossoms and leaves from trees, and rode a few rods out of my way for some violets that I saw when I went to McTureous a fortnight ago to-day. In the "Hill" field, I found Isaac and Paris ploughing with Caesar and Tamar. I described the listing before. This whole field is now listed, and the next process is to run a plough lengthwise between the new beds,—twice, so as to turn a furrow each way, the idea being to throw the earth of the old bed wholly upon the new beds. The next process is banking, of which I saw a small specimen at Cherry Hill. The earth thus loosened by the plough is hauled up upon the beds so as to make high, well rounded ridges alternating with quite deep furrows. Of course this process uses the same earth over again every time the land is planted. The plough only scratches the surface, and the subsoil is never touched—the old beds are simply divided and transferred to the old alleys to form new beds. It seems as if subsoil ploughing would certainly turn up something worth using. Still it is necessary to be careful in experimenting, and I suppose that these superintendents do wisely in simply following the old system for the present, meanwhile experimenting on a small scale—as Mr. F. is going to do at Cherry Hill.

Mr. Dennett told of somebody on Port Royal Id. who came down with fine subsoil ploughs and turned up a sort of red sand in which nothing whatever would grow, thus ruining his land for the present. I rode beyond the quarters, to see where the new house would probably be put; for Mr. Philbrick has decided to build one, and on the whole Cherry Hill is considered a better spot than Mulberry Hill. I got back at about 1½, just in time to escape a heavy rain, which made our school miserably small—we had in all fifteen scholars to-day. One day last week Abraham was the only scholar in the morning. We have had several new scholars lately,—one of them named Cuffee, the only person of that name I have ever met here. He is a nephew of Dido—his mother is dead, and he has come to live with his aunt.

Last night while we were writing, Adam came in to get a "pass for go Beefut." I asked him what he wanted to go for, and he said "I wan' to see how Beefut stan'—nebber shum since my name Adam." There are two words they use very oddly—meet and draw. The latter they use of anything they get, even of buying. Lucy has never been to school regularly, but we let her have a book, and she was quite grieved that she had nothing on the Christmas tree, seeing she "drawed a book." When Katy distributed of her combs to the scholars, they calling (sic) it drawing combs. And Joan expressed it as her opinion that the people ought not to choose their own surnames, but should draw them from Mr. Folsom. "Meet" is used in the sense of "find." Missing one of my school room chairs, which had strayed into the kitchen, I asked Phoebe always to bring them back when she took them. She felt quite aggrieved, "I meet 'em dar, an' he remain wid me. Miss Mary tuk 'em for strain jelly."

Mar. 23, Wednesday, 9 P.M.

A real equinoctial storm, cold and blustering. Only ten scholars showed their faces yesterday—three of them merely to get a copy in their writing books. I thought our change—having them read in the testament instead of that stupid Hillard's Third Reader—would have the effect of making the men more constant; but they are as irregular as ever.

To-day in my class only the two Parises, Robert and Taffy. Taffy, who is a real faithful good fellow, requested the chapter to be given over and over again until he could "ketch 'em"—"I wan' to ketch 'em very bad sir, very bad." To-day we had a new scholar—Gibb—a brother of Cuffee and Frank—a bright little fellow who came in with Abraham. I asked him whether he could read, which he answered promptly in the affirmative, so I tried him on Wilson's Primer, which has a lot of rather elegant pictures—boys on a rocking-horse with the text, "Is he on it?" etc. I gave it to him at this point, and he immediately started with the greatest energy—"h-o-r-s-e—horse. de boy is on top ob de horse"— adding some remark about a chair in the background. His eye then fell on an eagle at the bottom of the page, and he went on "De roben is big bird." The next picture that attracted his attention was a lion on the opposite page; so he began bravely "d-o-g—dog," but just at this moment a cut just above, representing two men and an ox, proved too strong for him, so he gave me the history of the man and cow, from which he immediately passed to the portrait of a youth with a soldier's cap on his head—arguing from the visible soldier's cap to an invisible sword. "Dis man hab sword—he tuck he sword an' cut he troat." At this I thought it best to examine his acquirements more closely, and found that he didn't know a single letter.

After school Katy and I took a ride—she on Nelly, I on Wind, who went very well with me. Charley and Harriet dropped in to tea and soon after they came, Mr. Folsom returned from Ruggles', bringing a chance mail—Lizzie's letter of the 8th for me. Thank her for the hymns, which are just what I wanted, and enough. Thanks also for the senna and recipe—I know it was mother's favorite medicine of old, and I hope these people will like it as well as castor oil which I think stands next to molasses in their affections. But you mustn't despise the Pain-Killer, which is said to be a very excellent remedy, consisting chiefly of turpentine and cayenne pepper.

My Geography class have learned all the states now, and I have been exercising them on general map questions. I try to vary and interest by alternation— sometimes I tell them stories of the early history, sometimes tell them about the occupations and productions of the various states. In writing I keep them for the most part on pot-hooks and trammels—writing on slates and without lines. They are getting to write them very well, and I encourage them by letting them form letters and words occasionally. This is the first class in school—the men use writing books, and some of them are writing quite respectably. They haven't made much progress lately in Arithmetic, but I drill them on what they have learned. None of the adults—unless perhaps Paris Simmons—will go beyond subtraction, I think. In the brief time that there has been for the afternoon school, (3 to 4½) we have neglected singing this past month; but now the days are so long that the men don't come until 5, and I mean to resume it. The morning school say "Busy Bee" very well, and will begin "Little Children" tomorrow.[235] I forgot to say that when Gibb appeared this morning, Abraham introduced him as "Cuffee brudder," but the little scamp insisted on it that he was Cuffee himself. Abraham didn't know his name, and I had to appeal to Thomas to learn what his name really was.

Friday eve., Mar. 25, 8 P.M.

Finding that I have time, space and matter, I will add another half sheet. Yesterday seemed dull and cold, but promised the end of the storm, and we had a pretty good school. The Hope scholars came early, and when I went out to give them "huddy," they surrounded me with protests against being obliged to leave our school for one upon their own place. It seems they think that Mr. Wm. Alden, who has Frogmoor, is going to start a school at Hopes—as he thought of doing until he spoke to me about it, when he gave it up. Patty and Rinah were spokesmen as usual, and I wish I could remember half they said—indeed I can no more understand Rinah that if she spoke Choctaw. They had a school once before, it seems, and were not satisfied—"he jump (omit school) two week at a time" said Patty—"he jump ebery day" said Rinah. "He no larn we anyting" said Patty. "True Paht" echoed Rinah. "We no wan' Mr. Alden for school we—we larn mo' yere dan we eber larn 'fore" said Patty. "We do Paht" echoed Rinah (rapid, without pause, and with increasing stress of voice) and then poured forth one of her voluble speeches of which I could hardly catch a word. The whole thing was very comical, but very gratifying—especially as there isn't a day passes but I have to scold Rinah for something. The other girls—awkward Queen, gentle Hannah (dull, but with a lovely face and disposition), bright little Dolly, pretty bashful Wyna, the sisters Lucy and Celia (homely but real good girls)—all stood round and ejaculated assent.

I got thro' my school early, leaving old Paris (who is always late) for Katy, and rode off on Wind to meet Molly who had gone to Ruggles' on Nelly to get the mail, by which I got no letters. To-day after morning school, in which Gibb distinguished himself by informing Katy of the names of all the boys, and giving various directions for the management of affairs, (yesterday as soon as he appeared he asked for "a book for larn me lesson, then for a slate, then for leave to go out," all in quick succession)—I rode Nelly down to Pine Grove to see if I could learn anything of the schooner. On the way I fell in with a man named Glasgow from St. Simons, who has preempted 40 acres on the Hamilton Fripp land (there is quite a colony of St. Simonians there). He said he used to live on the next plantation to Mr. Butler's, and that Mrs. B. was "a severe lady, he use to row himself. He was bery kind to de colored people." He would like to go back to St. Simons, where the land is much better than here. In the woods I heard a bird with precisely the note of one in the Pastoral Symphony[236]—"re-do, re-do, re-do."—We have been in quite a panic about the early starting of the schooner, for fear it might not bring the things we sent for. We hear now that she was delayed by a fortunate accident, and that everything is on board, but that there was so much that a second one started immediately. They are the Delia Kelly and Mill Creek—we begin to expect them now every day.

St. Helena, Mar. 27, 1864, Sunday, 7½ P.M.

Our letters were sent to Beaufort before we were up yesterday morning, and the steamer was to sail to-day. Yesterday was distinguished only by my transplanting beets and cabbages in the morning, and by a glorious ride in the afternoon on Mr. Folsom's horse. He is very much the best horse I was ever on—very swift, very easy, and perfectly gentle—as large as Mr. Gannett's. His only fault is that he has been ridden so hard that he wants to go on a run all the time, and he is a little hard-bitted. But he slackens his speed at a word, and Mr. Folsom will soon have him trained to be perfectly tractable. The native horses, "tackies" they are called,—Nelly, Rob Roy, Lucy, Feeble etc.—look ludicrously small by the side of these northern giants. To-day Katy and I went to church in the buggy, and found Miss Rice on a stupendous grey which Mr. Gannett has just bought—just a hair shorter and a shade lighter than his own Harry. Mr. Folsom is expecting another horse in the "Mill Creek," and two are coming down,—possibly three. I was rewarded for going to church by finding a letter from Prentiss. Not only northern horses but fresh meat is begging to abound—since the sale put the cattle into the hands of the superintendents. A fort-night ago Mr. Folsom killed a sheep, last week Charley killed a calf and sent us a quarter, and yesterday he brought us a leg of pork. This ought to be plenty now—Limus told me he should draw his seine to-morrow and would send us some—and we shall soon have crabs and shrimp; oysters it is too late for. My vegetable garden is flourishing, but the birds pull up the peas and corn, so that I hardly know what we can expect. Everybody is chuckling over the condign punishment of a man named McCrea[237] in Beaufort—one of the French set, Mr. Folsom says, one of the false missionaries. He is condemned to walk up and down the main street in Beaufort for seven days with a placard hung to his neck—"I sold whiskey to a private soldier"—then to pay a fine of $500 or be imprisoned at hard labor for six months, and finally to be sent out of the department.

My "Bible class" has been rather small for the last two or three weeks, but to-day they came in good numbers, and seemed quite interested. I am going thro' the Sermon on the Mount slowly, and it is entirely new to most of them. They can all read the first chapter of John and some of them Hebrews. My Wednesday evening class, I am sorry to say, has entirely fallen thro'.

Tuesday, March 29, 8 P.M.

Mr. Folsom went to Beaufort yesterday, and brought us back a box which has been more than a month on its way, containing a number of things which we were very glad for—among others a very pretty vase, so that now we shall not have to put our flowers in a tumbler. There was also a package of scarlet and white beans which I sent for to try the experiment of getting the people to plant. I think if they can get into the way of ornamenting the outsides of their houses, it will be quite a step. To-day I distributed a number of them round to the children, with directions how to plant them.

I have quite a number now who can add correctly, and two or three who can subtract. It is very funny the way they go to work, those who are only beginning. You set down a couple of rows of figures and tell them to add them up, and presently you find that they have copied them below—both rows. Isaac once added them up and set them down fairly (no carrying), and then improvised another row below—"I meet two row, and I set down two." Often instead of carrying they set down the number entire for each column, making a stupendous sum. My best scholar, Paris Simmons, has to be told distinctly at the start whether he is to borrow or carry. Taffy invariably makes his figures horizontally, as [figures "3" and "8" on their sides here]—indeed I have to work hard to keep them almost all from doing the same thing. If I would let them, all the scholars would hold their books even with the left shoulder at exact right angles with the usual way, so as to look at them side-wise. It is very comical.

We have quite a change in our house-hold. Dick has so much to do in the morning, what with the horses and all, that we have decided to let Thomas do his indoor work, which is a very pleasant arrangement. At the same time, as Phoebe is sick, we have Flora to help Mary about the house. Flora has always been a favorite with us, and Mary finds her very cheery, quick and bright in the kitchen. She and Thomas have high times together, and I think we shall have great fun out of them. Gibb continues as amusing as ever, and finds Abraham a congenial companion. Yesterday morning the first thing he did was to knock Reddington down for "cussing" him. I made him go and tell Reddington that he wouldn't do so again, but to-day after school he "knocked" Reddington, for which I must haul him over the coals. The next thing after his apology was to seize Lauretta and Charlotte and swing them round him, and then he and Abraham got up a "shout," which was as good as a play—Gibb leaning against a post singing, stamping and clapping his hands with all his might, while Abraham kicked up the dust—then they "shouted" together, back to back and round each other, ending in tumbling in a heap on the ground. As big-headed Edward (Robin's son) came up,—"Edward come base me" cried Gibb in the midst of his delirium.

We hear funny stories of the negroes bidding for horses etc. Quash wanted Mr. F. to buy a horse for him. He didn't want to give more that $56 "nohow," "but if dey strain you gib $57 or $55." At the auction at Coffin's Henry and Titus were bidding against each other for some article. Titus bid $6. "Well Titus," says Henry, "I won't strain you—8." "7" says Titus—"10" says Henry. "12" says Titus. "An' den Henry bid 14 an' tuk em for 15."—The people are now planting their potatoes; they would have planted them earlier if it hadn't been for the cold storm. We have had asparagus twice from Pine Grove—it has all run out here. Did I write that we are expecting a blacksmith by the schooner—a Mr. Hinckley from Cape Cod. He is to live here, as this is a very central position, and a blacksmith's shop here would have a good run of work. We are rather embarrassed, however, as to where to have him sleep, as we have only one spare chamber.

Friday, Apr. 1, 1 P.M.

Charley brought us our mail to-night—a letter from Ned, and papers from Prentiss, father, Lizzie, Lucy and some unknown person—14 in all. He told us that the Kingfisher was sunk—having run aground. The people had one of their periodic scares about the draft day before yesterday, and spent the night in the woods—even as old as Robin. Word was brought that the soldiers were at "Mr. Eusless" (Eustis), so yesterday Mr. Folsom went up here to find out what ground there was for it, and learned that no draft had been even ordered— merely an enrollment. Lt. Col. Strong of the 1st S.C. had been to Ruggles', and Ruggles and Mr. Tomlinson (who lives there now) had represented the state of things to him so strongly that he went back discouraged. Very likely he will state matters to his superiors, and have it given up.

Yesterday I brought in the first rose-bud, and to-day the first strawberry. It was laid carefully upon a plate, divided justly and devoured. It is surprising how much later we are than at Pine Grove. Our pomegranate trees are just putting out their red leaves,—as far advanced as theirs were at the time of our expedition to the Hunting Island a fortnight ago. The fig trees are also beginning to leaf out.

This is Mr. Folsom's favorite of the people's hymns.[238]

De talles' tree in Paradise   An' I hope dat trumpet blow me home
De Christian call de tree ob life   To de new Jerusalem
Blow your trumpet Gabriel, Blow your trumpet louder,
     An' I hope etc.

I have discovered a capital way to make the scholars look at me when they speak to me. They think a great deal of "manners," and being "perlite." Yesterday, for the first time in history, I prevailed upon Queen to face me. She and Patty were haranguing me with their backs turned towards me as usual. I told them that wasn't polite, and Patty immediately wheeled round. Queen couldn't bring herself to that, but when I went round in front of her she didn't turn round in the other direction.

St. Helena, Apr. 7, 1864, Thursday, 8 P.M.

We missed the mail last week, for the first time, I believe, since we have been here. We were informed on what was supposed to be good authority, that the steamer would sail Monday, so sent our letters Sunday; but after all, it sailed Sunday morning, so unless there is a chance steamer you will probably get that letter and my last on the same day. As we are all in the same box, I suppose you will guess the cause of the delay. Joseph will meet William Ware,[239] and father will meet Mr. Lambert[240] or Uncle Hall,[241] and by comparing notes will decide that there is no reason for uneasiness.

The long-looked for schooners have arrived. We had been tormenting ourselves with fears that they were lost, or at least would have thrown overboard a good part of their cargoes. Mr. Folsom professed himself willing to sell his "sorrel mare" cheap; The Cherry Hill house we thought would surely furnish timber for the mermaids; and our visions of rowing in the new boat and driving in the Concord wagon were growing very dim. We had even begun to reckon up the value of the paper collars, cider, hymn-books and dried apples, which we expected would prove a dead loss. But this morning a man came along from Ruggles' with the welcome news that the Mill Creek (which started three days later), was already there, and the Delia Kelly was at Hilton Head. And Mr. F., who made a trip to Ruggles' on Drayton, reported that the M.C. got aground and so was not yet quite at the dock, and that the D.K. was just coming in sight—a fearful storm, but the cargo all safe. The sorrel mare was badly bruised to be sure, and cannot be used for some time. The Mill Creek put into Newport [R.I.] during the great storm,[242] and so escaped the worst—it seems as if the Kelly must have suffered more. She is reported as having lost none of her cargo—which is very much the most valuable, valued at some $20,000. All our things are on board of her, and we are expecting to brew a delicious beverage of senna and dried apples steeped in salt water and cider.

Sunday, after my Bible Class (which I have early in the forenoon, so as to give time to go to church) I asked the men to sing, and they sang several of their best tunes. Billy wasn't there, so Henry (Jane's husband) took the lead. There were two that were new to us—"Happy Morning"[243] and "Gwine down Zion Hill."[244] Then a shouting tune, "Turn Sinner,"[245] very sweet and with a peculiarly dramatic effect.

Turn, sinner, turn to-day—(Base) turn, sinner, turn O Turn O sinner de worl's a gwine—Turn etc.
Wait not for tomorrow sun (*bis*). Tomorrow sun will sure to shine.
De sun may shine, but on your grave (second time with variation).
Hark, I hear dem sinner say—If you get to heaben I get dere too.
O sinner you make mistake.
(A cheerful dancing tune.)

We should have gone to Coffin's Sunday, but we heard that Harriet and Charley were away, so after dinner Molly and I drove to the village, taking Thomas as tiger. The road turns to the right a little this side of the signal station, and keeps through some fine pine woods for about two miles, when we emerged into a partially open country, and could see the creek at a few rods at our right, lined at intervals with houses of about the character of the one we live in. It was very odd to drive along a main street without a single house on it until we came to a few cabins recently put up for refugees. Here we turned in, and returned on the bank of the creek, where there was sometimes barely room for the carriage to pass. The bank here is a high sandy bluff (about ten feet high) and the planters had their summer residences here on account of the salubrity of the situation. Capt. John had one here as well as at Beaufort. At present these houses are occupied by Edisto refugees. Besides, Mr. Lynch the Methodist preacher at the village (a mulatto) and his sister,[246] Miss Howard[247] (she and Miss Lynch have schools at the village), and also Miss Towne and Miss Murray, the teachers of the school at the church, live here. We returned by a pretty road near the creek, passing directly opposite our house, and in full view.

Since then, there has been very little to interrupt the monotony of our life. Sandy has made a safe for Mary to keep her eatables in, and I spent two forenoons in tacking on the mosquito netting so as to allow ventilation, and putting on hinges and lock. Just as I got the lock finished, the key broke. The legs were set into empty tin fruit cans, which were then filled with water. This will probably keep out the red ants, but there are already indications that the mice have found their way into it. O for a cat! Other Spring-like vermin are beginning to make their appearance. Fleas abound, and sand-flies. We haven't heard of any rattle-snakes or moccasins yet, but the other day Dick killed a handsome red house-snake, a beast who destroys chickens and is fond of coming into the house to catch rats. It is refreshing to learn that some of our pests feed upon others.

For the rest, life is enlivened every day by about the same incidents. Jimmy driving into the yard in his cart with his handsome black oxen at a fast trot (they were the fleetest animals on the plantation till Mr. F. got his white horse), shouting "gee" and "haw" at the top of his voice and belaboring their ribs with his stick so that in some marvelous manner he always contrives to get where he wants to go. Young Paris cantering in from the field on Tamar, and invariably stopping at the window—"What's o-clock Sir?" "Little Isaac" (this distinguished from his uncle)—a tall, sober looking chap, with checked apron and exceeding short coat tails,—driving Caesar who generally manages to get away, and gallops across the field to a corner where Isaac pursuing him always secures him and brings him ignominiously back. Dick, discovering a dozen pigs in his corn-field, and bringing his gun from his house with a very grim face and peppering them with small shot—so that Dennis—whose own they generally are, and who lost some thirty dollars worth of swine last year by his negligence—may keep them up. Margaret and Abraham bringing water from the well, in which occupation they seem to spend their lives, almost always singing a snatch from some shouting tune—"O Lord, Shall I die,"[248] "My body rack long feber,"[249] "I can't stay behin' my Lord."[250] Tom, Archy and Abraham riding horse on bamboos at full speed round the house—the hollow ground echoing under them so loudly that I am often startled into looking out for a real troop of horsemen. Thomas, chaffing with Flora and Margaret; they call him "Buggy-top" in contemptuous allusion to a rubber cloak he wears in wet weather, and he retaliates by spilling Margaret's water and dropping candle-grease on Flora's newly cleaned stove. Store afternoons—Tuesday and Friday—there is always a noisy group collected, but as we are always in school at that time we lose most of the fun.

Neither is there much new to write about the school. Old Paris doesn't get anything now but his reading and writing. Being foreman at Mulberry Hill, he has care and extra work which keep him late. Young Paris is just learning to multiply. My first class in school are in the table of eights, altho' none of them are perfect beyond five. The Geography class have learned all the states, the countries of North America, the continents and oceans. I shan't have them learn any more at present, but drill them on what they know, and renew my general lessons, which have been suspended while we have had school in the afternoon. In writing too I feel pretty well satisfied. I think by summer they will make pot-hooks and trammels even and regular—a thing very few persons can do without lines—and I vary it by letting them learn a few easy letters.

Our larder is lean enough now—9 days, and the schooner has been eagerly looked for on that score. Flour and sugar we are out of—however we shall draw rations soon—and butter too. Meat we have been well provided with lately, and now we can get chickens, which has been impossible thro' the winter. Eggs are up to 50 cents a dozen again—we couldn't reconcile it with our conscience to buy them, but we exchange our ration meat for them. All thro' the winter we have had miserable sweet potatoes, but I bought a bushel of splendid ones the other day from Cherry Hill, and have more engaged. They only grow two kinds on this place—the "reds" and "common yams." The reds are white inside, and very insipid in taste. They only have the merit of being very early, but I don't know why it is that we have had a great many of them this winter. The common yams are good, but we have had them very small. These that I bought the other day are "yaller inside"—a handsome red outside,—I think the best quality that I have tasted. I have engaged some "yellow yams," but don't know their quality, except that they are considered good. The "Spanish" are long and slender, yellow outside and a sort of bluish white inside; a rather peculiar taste. The "Alabama" I don't know, but I believe it isn't very good. The "Georgia yam" is very large and of a deep yellow, very good, but rather coarse. Then there is the "Pumpkin yam," which is also said to be coarse, and which I have never seen; and perhaps other kinds. We had crabs for the first time to-day, some that Ishmael got us yesterday: they are very nice, but Flora opened them so as to leave the shell and the meat mixed together. Soon shrimps will abound, and prawns can be got at the "Corner"; also mullets are beginning to come up the creek.

Friday, 9 P.M.

It has been a dull day, with a small school. Most of my forenoon was spent in helping Dick catch Nelly and Wind, who had got away. First Dick had headed them off in the home field, and drove them into the yard, but as there was nobody to turn them into the stable yard gate, they slipped down past the corn house by the water fence along the bank of the creek. It was at this point that I came upon the stage, and walked up with Dick to the big bridge to drive them back. "Dat meer" he said, "wen he run 'way, nebber let nobody come nigh um," and as for Wind, we knew his fleetness. Dick assuring me that he could manage them here alone, I went back to the yard to stop up all cracks there disposing Tom and Archy at different points on the most approved principles of strategy. But the enemy slipped thro' Dick's hands by the branch creek at the "nigger house," and then there was nothing but to drive them round thro' the home field again. So I arranged my forces for the new emergency, and presently the enemy were cut in two,—Paris and I drove "ole Win'" in triumph into the yard, where Tom headed him off. Nelly however eluded all pursuit, and is at this moment, I suppose, enjoying the sweets of freedom. After what I have seen of her locomotive powers to-day, I am afraid I shall never spare the whip again out of a misplaced compassion.

Miss Rice was at dinner, and when we were nearly thro', we were startled by a handsome Concord wagon driving up with a white horse in the thills[251]—the first fruits of the schooner. Mr. Folsom had ridden to Ruggles' and brought the blacksmith, Mr. Hinckley,[252] back with him. He seems a very pleasant and intelligent man—a New England mechanic. He has a clock and thermometer up in his room already. The sorrel mare was tied behind the wagon, and a sorry figure she cut, with some awful bruises and gashes. She had not been put in the vessel properly. Both the schooners were at Newport during the great storm, and both had a very rough passage from there. Just as we finished tea, Mr. Gannett came in with Mr. Winsor's brother (Mr. Frank W.),[253] just from California. Two other persons have come—a Mrs. Walker[254] (colored) to help Harriet keep house, and Mr. Jackson[255] to assist Mr. Gannett. Mr. G. brought a mail—a letter from Lizzie and Joseph mailed Mar. 29.

St. Helena, Apr. 11, 1864, Monday, 9 P.M.

The day of the golden wedding[256] of which I was reminded by receiving the letter of Apr. 5, from Lizzie and Mary—by a chance mail. I wish very much that I could have been there. Saturday morning it rained heavily, and I staid at home; but after dinner Mr. Hinckley and I started in the buggy with Wind and Nelly for Ruggles'. Nelly seemed not to have got over her escapade of the day before, and set out to be obstinate—it seemed as wild an undertaking as for Florida to rebel—nevertheless, she managed to trouble us a good deal. When she backed, of course she pulled Wind's head to the right so Wind performed a circle about her, at one time actually carrying us out of the road into the pasture. At last we took a coil of rope which I happened to have, and rigged another pair of reins; Mr. H. drove Wind and I drove Nelly, and after a while we got on very well. I little thought it was the last time I should use "Ole' Wind"; Mr. R. had promised him to one of the negroes, as soon as his new horse should come.

The new horse has come, altho' unfit to use; and Wind has left us. As we approached Ruggles; the masts of the schooner looked quite maritime, and it was a busy scene at the wharf and the store,—several carts running, Mr. Soule, Dyer and Winsor superintending the unloading, and Mr. Ruggles stowing things away. We got Mr. Hinckley's trunk, and I managed to squeeze a pail-full of sugar out of Mr. Ruggles, in the midst of the hurry. Then I prowled round and picked up a half-barrel, a box and a bundle marked with my name, a box for Miss Rice, and bundles for Mr. Gannett and Mr. Folsom, and we managed to stow them all away, in somewhat the following style. Mr. H. is represented as driving, and I as licking Nelly, who still manages to keep behind Wind. The top of the buggy is turned back, and Miss Rice's box thus placed on top of Mr. Hinckley's trunk. We had a great time unpacking, and found lots of good things in the half-barrel (from West Newton). The box contained the cider, which is very nice. I at once opened a bottle and put in a lot of nails, for Molly's drinking.[257] The bundle contained the collars etc., which are very acceptable, as I am nearly out. By the time we had them unpacked, Taft, who had been up for a load of hay, brought in the bundle of hymn-books,—I think it a very good one, and I found in it almost everyone that the men asked for. Shortly after, seeing Taft drive by with Gibb in his cart, I stopped him. "Taft" said I, pointing to Gibb (Gibb is his nephew and lives with him). "That boy hasn't been to school for three days." Taft looked ruefully at him with the resigned air of a man who has drawn an elephant—"Dat boy" says he "dat boy de baddes' little debble eber I see." So he drove on lecturing Gibb on his naughtiness. I took our mail to Ruggles', and sent it along by Mr. John Alden, who said the steamer was to sail the next day: but we learned afterwards that it won't sail till tomorrow.

Yesterday Molly and I drove to Coffin's with Drayton in the Concord wagon—as perfect a team as one could wish. I read up all the Evening Posts and Army and Navy Journals I could find; and then we stopped at Pine Grove to dinner. Mrs. Walker, who used to live with the Wares, came down in the last steamer to relieve Harriet of some of her care. She used to be a slave in North Carolina, but I never should have suspected her of a drop of negro blood. Mr. Frank Winsor (Rufus' brother) also came down to stay there and get acquainted with the ways of the place. At Mr. Gannett's also they have a new-comer, a Mr. Jackson, who is to stay there and help about odds and ends. Mr. Gannett has Browning's new book, and while we were waiting for them to get back from church, I read the first act of Strafford,[258] which I think is splendid.

This morning, Mr. F. and Molly drove down to Coffin's, intending to return by Cherry Hill; so about the time I thought they would get there, I rode Nelly across to meet them. It was quite a gay party, as they came in sight—they were accompanied by Harriet on Rob Roy, Mr. Jackson on Harry (Mr. Gannett's iron-grey), and Mr. Gannett on Feeble (a sorrel tacky of his which Mr. Sumner named, but the name is a slander). We followed past the quarters down to a sort of peninsula, where the house is to be built, in order to decide upon the spot. The spot marked B has a lovely view in front and to the left, but none to speak of to the right. At A the view is fine in every direction, but not quite so fine in any as the left hand view at B. [See Port Royal Map and Key (No. 16). Allen's map of sites A and B is meaningless without knowledge of the terrain.] Mr.

F. and Molly drove round by Mulberry Hill, while Harriet and I rode across, and she staid to dinner. I then packed a half-barrel with winter clothes to send home by the schooner (to West Newton). I tried to get some ground nuts to send, but couldn't get any at so short notice.

I am afraid with our present family, we shan't do much reading aloud. We never have much [time]—what with company, letter-writing etc., we have only managed to read Philip van Artevelde, Tale of Two Cities and the Sanitary Commission,[259] all of which we have enjoyed very much. Two or three little things also, and we have begun Mill on Liberty.[260]

Friday, Apr. 15, 8¼ P.M.

We are having another cold storm, and to-day the school was very small. The Arago came in yesterday, and to-day we got a small mail. I suppose she came before her time in order to carry back troops, as we hear that all the white troops are to be sent North. The Fulton has been delayed for this reason, and hadn't sailed yesterday—Tuesday was her day—so I suppose our various letters will reach home very irregularly. Some Galignani's[261] from Prentiss came in the mail to-day. Wednesday we received our last package from the schooner—the box of dried apples and senna (all in good condition), and the box containing two barrels of currant wine from Nat. I am sorry to say that seven of the bottles of cider, in their haste to be drunk, opened themselves and discharged a part or the whole of their contents.

My garden is getting on well, and promises to furnish abundant provision for the birds and chickens. The peas have been in blossom for a week, and the potatoes are coming on finely. Most of the late peas and the corn were pulled up by the birds, still I think there are enough left to supply them well when they are fit to eat. The strawberries are coming on finely, but never one since the first has had a chance to ripen. I put up some contrivances the other day to scare the birds, and shortly after saw a mocking bird walking coolly round my scarecrow and examining the berries. The birds eat my lettuce leaves, and as fast as I sow more pick up the seeds. I had a fine little plantation of spinach which the hens have fairly torn up. However, I have already pulled four radishes, but nobody eats them. I get a handful of splendid roses now every morning.

Tuesday was a great day for the pigs. Dick shot one of Sandy's, and Sandy one of Clara's. We bought a leg of Sandy's hog to roast. Just as I finished school I looked out of the window and saw a rare procession appearing from behind Dick's house—Bristol, shouldering a large black pig; Billy and Taffy with another big one between them; Henry trundling one by his hind legs, like a wheelbarrow; and Cuffee hauling one behind him. As they passed the front of the house, the sweat pouring down their faces, all of which were stern and grim

Reuben (from T.B. Fripp) hauled in sight walking rapidly behind them—the whole procession then took up their position in front of the store, where Mr. Folsom was selling. It seems they were Reuben's swine, and had been uprooting Bristol's potato patch, whereupon Bristol had gone with *posse comitatus* and taken them into custody. The scene was a very comical one—Reuben standing in the middle, Bristol sitting on his hog (occasionally turning it over when it became uneasy), the others holding their pigs in various positions, and a gaping multitude around, one of which was I. After an earnest but not unfriendly discussion, Reuben agreed that if they would let his hogs go he would pay for all the potatoes required to replant Bristol's field. So the pigs were released and Reuben walked off well satisfied, and shouting back—that if it had been he, he would have shot every d—d hog.

The same day, I walked in the field to see the men planting cotton. (It is very late this year.) They make little holes about a foot apart with the hoe, in each of which they drop from a dozen to twenty seeds, which they cover with their feet. As they only leave two plants standing, this seems a great waste—the seed is worth $2 bushel—but it is impossible to persuade them to plant less. Speaking of this system, Gabriel said "I meet 'em so, and my fader (Moses) meet 'em so." Mr. Folsom gives them about 19 quarts to an acre.

We (i.e. Mary and Katy) have accomplished a great triumph this week in the shape of butter, which we had been without for some time. Molly professes herself desirous of turning dairy-maid. We bought to-day a huge drum-fish at the rate of about 9 cts. a pound. It is a very firm, meat-like flesh.

St. Helena, Apr. 17, 1864, Sunday, 9 P.M.

Mr. Winsor took our mail yesterday morning to Ruggles', but just missed the mail. So you will probably receive our letters very irregularly. I spent part of the day in arranging the Cotton House for our school. Our old school-room has always been cramped, and particularly inconvenient for two classes, and now we have put Mr. Hinckley's bed in it, and shall have school in the Cotton House. Then I read Vanity Fair[262] to Katy and Mary while they made bread and cake. Flora, who had promised to stay all the forenoon, had disappeared directly after breakfast. Tom reported her "gone in de creek for ketch creb, ma'am." But Flora herself said she had been to "see pa hen set." Then, Dick had left no wood and the fire in the stove (which Flora says "burns wood in secret") had gone out, so M. and K. spent all the morning in doing an hour's work. In the afternoon Mr. Folsom opened store (his regular days are Tuesday and Friday) to sell the schooner's goods, and there was a great trying on of waistcoats, and measuring of plaids, and carrying off flour and sugar in pails, aprons, head-kerchiefs, baskets or on boards,—dirt is not of the slightest importance. I mounted Nelly at about four and rode to Mr. Gannett's to get some seed peas. She never went so well with me, and I enjoyed the ride much. I found iris and honey-suckle in bloom by the road. Coming back I met Mr. Reed (the one who sold the horses etc.) at the gate, and he came and spent the night. In the evening Katy and I covered our new reading books, while Molly read Vanity Fair. We have a complete set of Wilson's Readers (the first four) for the school, but shall perhaps not use the highest.

This morning I gathered a handful of roses before breakfast. My Bible Class didn't make their appearance, so I spent the morning in reading. Mr. Hinckley and Katy went to church, and Mary and I were reading on the upper plaza, when Mr. Gannett and Miss Rice drove up in their new Concord wagon, and Mr. Jackson on horse-back; and soon after Mr. Frank Winsor. We had invited the first three to dine off roast pig—one which I have engaged of Clara—but this huge drum-fish must be eaten, so the pig was deferred. Dick was late in getting back from church, and I had to cut the steaks from the fish myself—it is as meaty as sword-fish—and to eke out the rather small quantity. Molly fried some delicious drum-fish roe which Miss Rice had sent. Mr. Reed, who had gone off in the morning, reappeared just in time for dinner, and our table was enlarged by placing the yellow and black ones alongside. After dinner I got another big handful of roses for Miss Rice, and when our guests were all gone stood talking awhile with Paris, Dennis, Bristol and others in front of the house. Then Charley and Harriet drove up on their Concord wagon, drawn by Rob Roy and Black Mink, and staid into evening, singing out of the books which Joseph sent, which contains excellent tunes. I picked a third handful of roses for her—some of them are very fine ones, and I shall try to bring home some slips.

The people are beginning to find out that we are likely to leave in the summer, and seem very sorry. Paris Gregley says he shall be quite "desicute," and Molsy told me that we must "studdy come back." ("studdy" here seems to mean "certainly"). The Hope girls are loud in their protestations—"What make you leff we, Mr. Ahllen?" says Rinah. "You nebber come for see we agin." I shall really be very sorry to leave these children, for I have become very much attached to them. These warm hearted girls from Hope Place are greater favorites as a whole, but there are particular ones, like Abraham and Judy, that we particularly like here, and for scholarship these are much ahead. My first Arithmetic is made up from this plantation, except one from Cherry Hill.

We had quite a breeze here a couple of weeks ago; it got about that we had been gossiping about the people, and they came up in great indignation,—Eliza, Dido, Laura, Clara and others,—to know who told us the stories. We convinced them that some of the matters were entirely trivial, others wholly made up, and others much exaggerated; and I told them that we had inquired about them from various persons,—Mr. Folsom, Dick and Phoebe—and that we had never asked nor been told anything but what was perfectly proper. We traced the origin of the stories to Phoebe, who spoke in her own house of her conversations with Mary and Katy; and then Billy, who married her daughter Justina, partly misunderstood and partly exaggerated them, and told the stories to "Co' Robin," not thinking they would go any farther. We were at first inclined to think that Phoebe shouldn't come back to the house; but we decided on the whole that what blame there was belonged chiefly to Billy; so Phoebe, who is now well, will come back in a day or two.

It is surprising how cold it continues—we had a fire nearly all day to-day. Harriet told us a fortnight ago that we should have hot weather enough within two weeks. Spring comes on much more slowly than at the North, and seems slower than it is. So large a proportion of the trees are pine and live-oak, that the delicate green of the new foliage is hardly noticed among the dark pines and dusty looking oaks. But the new leaves are not fully out yet. Locusts and Pride of Asia are in blossom. We hear that Capt. Hooper has gone home dangerously sick. He has had a congestive chill. He will probably be a greater loss to Port Royal than any other man.

Thursday, Apr. 21, 8 P.M.

Monday was a cold rain-storm, and we were disappointed in beginning school in the Cotton House. We did have the half-dozen morning scholars there, and with them appeared Rinah, Dolly and Chloe, who had spent the night here and were kept from going home by the storm. Then they came into the entry, with Flora, and sang two of their songs, which were new to us—"I'm hunting for a city"[263] and "Sister Dolly light de lamp and de lamp light de road."[264] Rinah and Chloe staid here all day, helping Flora, picking over split peas, and wading in the creek after crabs; and Mary bestowed the remains of the dinner upon them. Flora began to get some spoons, but "De fus ting God made fingers" (ng as in sing) said Rinah, and proceeded to help herself. She was very merry and comical all day, and advised us not to give a new book to Libby, who would tear it up, or put it in the fire—when Mr. Palmer gave her one she tore it right in two, saying she wouldn't keep a book for no nigger. It rained so hard that we had our half-dozen scholars in the kitchen. Having got new books for all the classes, we have put a large number of the first class into the second,—Flora, Linda, Hannah, Chloe, Wyna, Lucy and Libby and they seem to feel very badly about it. But really, none of these read better than my bright second class—Mary Ann, Minna, Judy, Sarah etc. The school has been a good deal larger, and I think it will be more regular and successful in the Cotton House.

The little altercations of these children—commencing generally, I blush to say, in school are very entertaining. I put Venus standing on a bench the other day, for whispering, and when I was ready told her to get down. She is a stubborn little piece (Rinah's sister), and wouldn't budge. So as I stepped toward her, to expedite her movements, Gibb, who never lets an occasion pass of airing his sentiments and commenting sotto voce on all incidents, remarked in a loud whisper "Co' Bena' [Venus] wan' Mr. Allen for tuk 'em down," at which Venus shot him a revengeful glance from her black eyes, and after school I found them at some go, and inquiring the row learned from Gibb that "dat same Bena' dar knock me," Venus' grievance being that Gibb "cuss me" in school. I might almost say that it was a family quarrel, for I found Rinah and Cuffee "cussing" each other in school to-day. It is pleasant to see how quickly they will take up the cause of a brother or sister. Sandy and Flora were squabbling today, and Flora's lips were out very far as she asked him "You tink you big enough for lick me?" It was with considerable trouble that I elicited from Flora that Sandy had threatened to knock "sister." "Sister" said I, for I can't always remember the relationships in a moment. "Talk Margaret, Sir." And then I found from Sandy that Margaret again had been abusing "sister"—that is Sarah.

I have been laying down some of the handsomest rose bushes here, to carry or send home. A mail came yesterday, father's letter about the Golden Wedding, and newspaper and also a note from a Mr. Graves [Greves][265] in Beaufort, who has a letter and package for me from the Doctor, asking how to deliver them. This morning Molly, Katy, Mr. Hinckley and I took a short row in Mr. Folsom's new boat, which came down in the schooner. Much to Mary's delight, Phoebe has come back, and lightened her work by a half. Flora is quick and good-humored, but careless and very un-neat. I think you will give me credit when I say that Paris Simmons, who could not write at all when I came, showed me the other day, written very neatly, "Paris Simmons wright a note to mister Allen and Miss Mary." Cuffee, who is a very bright, attractive fellow, but whose work makes him very irregular, has been here twelve times in five weeks, and I find knows nearly all his letters now, and I have exercised him constantly in forming small words. Paris did a sum in multiplication correctly to-day, having a multiplication table to refer to. He is the only scholar so far advanced as this.

St. Helena, Sunday, Apr. 24, 1864, 8 P.M.

I think we have really spring at last. After our cold rain of last Monday, it grew gradually warmer, and yesterday the milk soured for the first time, I believe, since January. This morning a copious warm rain, a good Bible Class, and after dinner a drive to Ruggles' with Mr. Hinckley, where we found no mail.

Bignonia[266] in blossoms by the road—Friday we had our first peas, from Cherry Hill.

Friday morning Rufus Winsor rode up to say that I was to have some callers, who had spent the night at Coffin's; and soon after a large wagon drawn by four grey horses drove up, and Mr. Graves, who brought me a letter from the Doctor and a package of delicious maple sugar, got out, accompanied by the new tax-commissioner (in Judge Smith's place) Judge Cooley,[267] and another gentleman.[268] We had a very pleasant call from them, and they came out to visit the morning school, which was under Katy's care. It happened to be pretty full, but Venus and Mylie were standing like statues on benches, and Gibb in front of the desk, as gentle discipline. It happened that the best class was reading,— Abraham, Edward and Lizzie,—and they were much pleased with the proficiency of the two first.

Mr. Tomlinson spent the night with us, being on his way round the plantations to witness the contracts for wages. There is a great excitement just now on this subject. The people have had it put into their heads that their wages are too small, and some meddlesome person put it into the head of the Fripp Point people—a very troublesome set,—to send a petition to Washington, to represent how they were oppressed. I arrived just as Judge Smith[269]—not the tax-commissioner, but a gentleman sent down here to investigate the land question on behalf of government—was about to start; and he was given a copy of the document with directions to look the matter up. So he spent Thursday night at Coffin's, and also Mr. Tomlinson, and it was this that brought Judge Cooley there, and they sifted the whole matter. The Fripp Point people came up there, and one John Major[270] was their spokesman, as he had been their leader. Judge Smith managed the whole business with great tact and sagacity, and finally told John Major that he thought him a troublesome, mischief-making fellow, and afterwards said that he had no doubt that Mr. Philbrick would sell land to all proper persons, but not to troublesome ones.[271]

From all I can learn I am inclined to think that their present wages are adequate. They sound small but the circumstances are not taken into account. For instance, a day's work is 45 cts., and this is what it amounts to. Isaac goes into the field in the morning and works on his own land until about half past eight, then comes to the stable, gets Caesar and brings him out to the watering trough. Caesar runs away, and Isaac after him—brings him back, harnesses him in the cart and goes to carting trash. At about twelve, back he comes, unharnesses, gives Caesar his dinner, and goes off to get his own. At about two he comes back and goes through the same process, works till five, and then comes in to school. The day's work, Mr. Soule says, averages 5½ hours. And all this time he worked with his coat on, and if it is cold, with an overcoat.

This is day-wages. When they are working at job-wages, it is entirely in their own hands. Perhaps at Coffin's Point, where the land is full of joint-grass (our witch-grass),[272] and in some places where the land is heavy, the wages ought to be somewhat higher; but here, a man can easily list three tasks in what would be at the North a working day, and for this he would get $1.20. Now when we consider that they get the rent of their houses for nothing, corn and potato land at the rate of an acre and a half to a full hand (paying a rent of about 1/15 of the corn they raise) the use of the plantation mules and teams to work their land; that they get their fuel out of the woods, pasture their own horses and mules on the plantation pasture, have no taxes, schooling free, are given half the milk of the plantation cows, and have a store on the place where goods are furnished at cost (their wants, too, being so much fewer than those of a northern laborer), I think there is no question that they are as well off pecuniarily as any laborers in the country. A dollar a day goes as far with them as two dollars with an Irishman in Massachusetts at the present time; and I have heard Mr. Philbrick say that as a matter of dollars and cents it would be better for him (to) bring down Irishmen from the North and pay them normal wages. But there is a set of meddling busy-bodies, some of them honest agrarians and sentimentalists, but some of them, I have no doubt, simply envious at Mr. Philbrick's success, who go round talking to his people and putting notions into their heads that they ought to have northern wages, and making them discontented. John Major told Judge Smith he thought he ought to get a dollar for listing a task which he confessed he could do in about three hours. It ought to be remembered too what a risk Mr. P. ran—and still runs—of loss. He has made a handsome profit, but he might have come out of it without a cent's profit, and I think everybody would have said a year ago that it was a very hazardous venture.

Another point of dispute is the land question, upon which I had a discussion with Mr. Tomlinson the other evening—or rather I got facts from him. There are about 80,000 acres within our lines. 13,000 were sold last year, 7000 are reserved for school-farms and 13,000 for military, naval etc. purposes. 20,000 are divided into small lots for the negroes, by private sale at $1.25 an acre, and the balance, 27,000, was to be sold by auction this winter (but only a part was sold). Of that sold by auction, negroes bought (this year and last) not far from 3,000. The school-farm reservations are of course intended entirely for their benefit, so that we have 30,000 acres already secured to the use of the freedmen. Perhaps it would have been better if there had been a larger proportion divided into small lots—I think it would have been—but I certainly agree with Mr. Philbrick that whatever they buy ought to be at the market price. When the Port Royal Islands come into the market, I hope the freedmen will combine—as they did at Warsaw Id., the Marion Chaplin plantation and the

Edgerly plantation—and buy some of the lots. But at any rate, we know that
Mr. Eustis means his plantation to belong to the negroes eventually, that Dr.
Brisbane bought one for that purpose, and that Mr. Philbrick has promised to
sell to them a part at least of his. So that it seems to me that it was a very injudicious thing for Gen. Saxton and Mr. French to interfere in the sales and cause
such confusion and misunderstanding as prevail now.

Well, Friday evening we all went down to the quarters with Mr. Tomlinson, the people were collected in front of Sandy's house, and Mr. T. read them
the list of prices which Mr. Philbrick engaged to pay, and asked whether they
agreed to them. Some evil spirit had got amongst them, and they didn't seem
to care for anything but to worry him—he says he hasn't had such a troublesome time at any plantation. Only two—Limus and Toby—said straight up and
down "Yes": all the others talked and beat the bush and said the same thing one
after another—Well, if I say I satisfy, I tell lie." "I don't ask you if you're satisfied,
I ask you whether you mean to work for these wages." "Well, I tink de wages
is too low, but I can' better myself, I done pit my crop in de groun' a'ready, an' I
can' help myself. You ought to come for we in Janiwary." "Well, do you mean
to work—Yes or No." "Well I can' better mysef, an' I will work dis year, kase I
done pit my seed in de groun' a'ready." "I put your name down then." "Yes, sir,
kase I can' better mysef, but I not sattify." Morris, Dennis, Billy and Paris were
particularly troublesome—the old men—Moses, William, Jimmy, John etc.,
were very much ashamed at the behavior of the young men. Robin's answer was
perhaps the best—if any answer needed be made at all, "Well, sir, I didn' sen for
you, an' you come. Ef you hedn' come, I should gone en work for Mr. Philbrick
same as I been begun, an' seein' you been come I shall do de same." Mr. Tomlinson came home thoroughly tired and disgusted—it was the fifth plantation
that day, I believe.

There was a comical affair the other day. Mary was sitting at the upper
window and heard the children talking at one of them—Emma—for finding
a spool of thread which she was going to keep instead of returning it to "Miss
Mary." Evidently they didn't know Mary was listening, for Tom came up to
ask me where Mary was. But when all their reproaches and threats not to play
with her were of no avail, Gibb, who was sitting on the saw-horse with his legs
crossed, threw his head back with a fragment of a cap cocked on one side, rolled
his eyes up, crossed his arms over his breast, and exclaimed "Oh Lord I'se so
sorry for Emma!" The other day I set him to pick all the F's out of some alphabet cards, and he kept finding E's instead. Finally, discouraged, he said "Dis yere
stan; sio a-r-um." The r is euphonic, the a, a contraction for as. A euphonic letter
is very often inserted. When I ask a child where her sister is, the answer often is
"He n-a-comin' sir." At first I thought the n was negative, but soon found that

the sentence was not a negative one, and I suppose then is simply euphonic. "Y" is used euphonically too: "Co' Rullus y 'own," said Gibb, when I asked him whom something belonged to.

Friday, Apr. 29, 8½ P.M.

Yesterday was a pretty hot day—as in our sitting room, with the sun shining on it and a nice breeze blowing in. At about four a violent gust came sweeping over the field, bringing a chilly sea atmosphere, and to-day it is raw and cold. We have had two or three nice rows in the new boat—Tuesday we rowed down and called on Mrs. Harrison. The school has been much fuller and more since we have been in the Cotton House and have had new books—also the work is less engrossing now. To-day, as I went to open the Cotton House, I heard some loud singing, and presently the Hope girls appeared coming up the avenue in full numbers singing very sweetly and clearly—as they didn't know they had listeners they threw their whole voices into it, and it was as good singing as I have heard here. "I can't stan de fire my Lord,"[273] and "I'm hunting for a city."[274]

I'm hunting for a city for to stay awhile (*bis*)   (Chorus) True believer has
    a home at last.
        Or—Go home Tiddy Ceely (or any other name) go tell my lord.
        (repeated three times).

In speaking of the wages, I forgot two points. Manure is given them—cotton seed for their corn, which is worth from $1½ to 2 a bushel, and of which Mr. Folsom has distributed not far from 500 bushels on this place; and when they plant their slip potatoes in July they will have all the cowpen manure which will have accumulated between now and then. But the chief point is that their current wages are understood to be rather low, the chief payment being made in the form of a premium for largeness of crop in the shape of a very high rate for picking—2½ cents a pound. A good picker in the height of the season can easily pick 80 pounds a day, which would make $2 a day. Mr. Folsom says that the previous labor on a crop will average about 14 days of about 3 or 4 hours for a good hand. They are paid (per task): listing, 40 cts.; banking, 20; planting, 10; thinning, 5; hoeing, 20; hauling, 20 the two latter operations being performed two or three times. Say twice, they get $1.25 a task = $4.60 an acre. Suppose they get 400 lbs. an acre, as any good hand ought to. There will be ten dollars, for perhaps 60 hours work. Their whole wages, about $15, will be for perhaps 120 hours work, about 12½ cents an hour. This very John Major, who has made such a row, has bought two horses, for $100 and 220. To be sure, he has been working at Hilton Head, where he made a good part of his money.

Sunday, May 1, 7½ P.M.

My May-basket consisted of a pan-ful of roses gathered, I believe, from 16 bushes; and I sent similar remembrances to Harriet and Miss Rice, by Messrs. Jackson and F. Winsor, who dined here. Mr. Folsom has been trying his new horse, Concord (whose hurts have healed marvelously fast), in the saddle and in harness, and the other day he put Drayton ahead of her, to try a tandem. She is young and very lively—a pure Morgan—and we all thought it was a great risk to try such a team with only one hand and a half. He went to Ruggles' and returned in triumph,—Concord was, I suppose, too much bothered by having a horse in front and a buggy behind, to undertake to cut up. Yesterday Molly and I were going out to take a row—Katy was at Miss Rice's,—when just as we were pushing off, Taffy came up saying that a gentleman and lady, unknown to him, had just driven up. We found it was Mr. Williams and Miss Forten, who made a short and very pleasant call, and then we had a nice row, Molly steering. Then I took Concord and rode to the Hamilton Fripp place and back. She is very easy, and altho' rather frisky, perfectly tractable. To-day after Sunday-school Molly and I had Concord in the new buggy and drove to church, accompanied by Mr. Folsom on Drayton, Mr. Hinckley on Nelly, and Mr. F. Winsor on Garibaldi (a handsome little grey which came down in the schooner). Mr. Harrison held services in the Episcopal church to-day, so we went there, and enjoyed it very well. We turned off at the Signal Station, and went a mile or two by a very pleasant, good road thro' the woods, to the point where the road struck the road from Land's End to Beaufort. It is a small white church, quite pretty and comfortable. In old times, none of the negroes were, I am told, allowed to attend here, except a few favorite house-servants, and there were to-day only half a dozen of them—for the matter of that, not many more whites; Gen. and Mrs. Saxton,[275] Dr. and Mrs. Lawrence, Dr. and Mrs. Hunting, Miss Wells, Mr. Dyer, Lt. Rhodes,[276] Katy and Mr. Jackson, and one or two others.

A good deal of rain these two or three days, heavy thundershowers etc. The following shout-tune has very odd words, and besides brings up comical reminiscences of Laura or Margaret coming to "draw" pain-killer for "pain in 'e head an' feber ma'am."[277]

Way my brudder, better true belieb,   Way my sister etc.,
    Better true be long time get ober crosses,
        An 'e get up to heabn at las'

O my body rock 'long feber, I wish I been to de Kingdom
(Base) O, wid a pain in 'e head To set long side o' my lord.
Or "my brudder," "my sister," "all de member" etc.

There ought by rights to be a sequel, to illustrate the invariable answer to the question "how does Jane etc. do?" "He feel a lee (little) better'n he been, ma'am."

St. Helena, May 9, 1864, Monday, 9 P.M.

We are in a dismal frame of mind enough with no mail for now near three weeks—my last letter (from father) came Apr. 20—with no news except some unfavorable items from North Carolina and a rumor from the rebel pickets that Grant is defeated. This may very likely be true, altho' the evidence is of very little weight. Mr. Folsom lived some months at Port Royal Ferry, where he talked with the rebel pickets every day, and he says their stories were notoriously false. I think if there had been a serious reverse we should have had more definite information from them. Still all this makes us rather gloomy, especially as it is announced that we are to have no more steamers for two months. Katy and Molly were for starting home at once in the Fulton, which is expected now every day; but I assured them that there must be plenty of means of communication by private enterprise with a place which is so important as this is now, and Mr. Folsom says he has understood that a private line is all ready to start operations, for weekly steamers to New York.

All last week was cool and pleasant, and I rowed every day, with some one. Twice I took out as many of the children as I could carry. We are all getting tolerably expert with the oars. Wednesday Molly went to Pine Grove, and Friday I drove up for her with Drayton. Saturday we at last got an opportunity to visit our parishioners at Hope Place, but we got off so late that it was hardly better than no visit at all. Molly and Katy drove Nelly in the Concord wagon, and I rode Concord, who went finely. I can't open gates with her yet, they frighten her. Yesterday was to be a great baptism, so we all hands went to see it. Molly and Katy drove Nelly, Mr. Hinckley rode Concord, and I rode him back—walking there. There was a great crowd of people—white and black—and Mary and Katy staid to church. They got rather more than they bargained for—a long sermon, a collection, two weddings and communion—so that they didn't reach home until 4, having left at about 9½. I rode back with Mr. Folsom, Rufus Winsor and a Mr. Warren[278] from Concord [Mass.] who was calling on Mr. F., and for the first time in my life I got thrown. It was a tremendously hot day, (94 on our piazza) and as we were coming through that dreary, sandy Indian

Hill field, I thought I would take off my coat. So I very carelessly laid down the reins, and when both arms were extended in the process of drawing them out of the sleeves, of course Concord was frightened and began to plunge and rear, and before I could get hold of the reins I was off. Finding my feet clear of the stirrups and myself uninjured, I hung on to the reins in hopes to hold her. But her feet were a good deal too lively round my head, so after being dragged about a rod and a half I let her go. Luckily she was easily caught, and I rode home pleasantly.

It was a very oppressive night, and the mosquitoes were very troublesome. We had a good big plate of strawberries yesterday—we have had a tolerably supply now for a couple of weeks—and to-day we had our first blackberries. Turnips we have had from the garden,—our plethora of roses is over, but we have as fine ones now as ever, and enough. The Pride of Asia trees—"Heth (Asia)-berry" the people call them—are in full blossom now; a pretty, delicate, lilac-colored cluster, with an ever-sweet odor. I confounded this with the locust when I wrote before that it was in bloom. To-day has been hot, altho' less so than yesterday, and I took a dip in the creek this morning. Mr. Hinckley is at work, with William, on the Cherry Hill house, which he has got almost ready to frame. He makes William stare at the style in which a Yankee mechanic can work—telling him too that he should be ashamed to work by the side of a real carpenter, being only a blacksmith. One day's work for William was putting in two horse-posts in front of the house, common trunks of trees rudely finished. John—the crack carpenter of the place (a mulatto, Thomas' father) has been a full week putting up a fence round the circle in front of the house— perhaps thirty posts, with two boards like this. [single-rail fence sketch here] Isaac and Morris, carting lumber from Ruggles' to Cherry Hill in two mule-carts, brought loads averaging 250 feet of boards: their idea being to trot their mules all the way, and get thro' the day's work as soon as possible. Two such trips were called a double day's work, for which they were paid double wages ($.90).

The wages question being settled, there is a great row about corn. Contrary to express orders, the people have planted corn in the cotton land, between the rows, and it is a problem how to deal with it. It being an old practice at Coffin's, where they have planted it too in moderate quantities, Charley has decided to let it remain. Only one man (Limus) has done it here, but several at Cherry Hill, and Mr. Folsom means to have it all up. But Mr. Gannett has had a great deal of trouble. At Fripp Pt. they have planted it generally in two rows out of three, and often some twenty hills in a row; in one task, in every row they had planted corn, and as thickly as in a regular corn-field. They refuse to pull it up, and say that if a black man is sent to do it they will kill him. So Mr. G. means to pull it up himself.

Wed., May 11, 8½ P.M.

A big mail at last—letters from Lizzie and Ned. No newspapers, and it is said no news, good or bad—a relief after the gloomy rumors. Katy hears that her father is sick, and will go North by this steamer if possible. Mr. Folsom and I are going to-morrow to find out.

St. Helena, May 16, 1864, Monday, 8½ P.M.

A week of accidents—beginning with my fall from the horse on Sunday—some of them quite serious. I carried my last letter to Ruggles' on Thursday morning—Mr. Folsom and I driving up with Concord directly after an early breakfast, in order to find out about the steamer. As nothing definite could be learned there, Mr. F. drove on to Beaufort, taking Charley Ware with him, while I drove back with Charley's horse, Rob Roy. Meanwhile Katy got packed, and was all ready in case Mr. F. should bring back word for her to start at once. The people came up in great numbers to bid her good bye, with offerings of eggs—some 10 or 12 dozen in all. Just as we were thro' dinner Charley and Mr. Folsom came back with word that the Fulton would not sail until Saturday;—which set our minds at ease. They stepped out of the Concord wagon and began to take the things out, when Concord thought she had been out long enough, and started for the stable first on a walk, then a slow trot, then a fast one, and as Toby rushed out from Dick's house with a stick in his hand to stop her, she steered to the left and dashed the wagon against the harness-house and ran off with the front wheels, leaving on the ground a confused pile of matches, and the remains of a dozen of Porter,[279] four bottles being intact. This was the second time, we learned, that she had practiced with the front wheels; for while they were going thro' the Oaks field in the morning, a jolt in the road had thrown the carriage off from the transient-bolt. The two gentlemen came forward with their noses in the sand, and Concord went on his way rejoicing.

Mr. Hinckley immediately went to work on the wagon, and succeeded in getting it in good order for our use the next day; but to make all sure, Mr. Folsom mounted Drayton and rode to Pine Grove, whence he brought back Mr. Gannett's Concord wagon and Miss Rice to spend the night. In the morning, too, Harriet drove up to bid Katy good bye. Molly, Miss Rice and I were to accompany her to Hilton Head. Miss Rice and Katy started on Mr. Gannett's wagon with Drayton; Molly and I in ours with Concord; Dick and Taft carried the baggage in a mule-cart, and Mr. Hinckley rode Nelly, to drive back Concord. Concord was pretty gay at starting, and when we got to the end of the avenue, having to wait for the gate to be opened, she got contrary and refused to start. Katy driving Drayton just behind could not stop him, and came very near running into us. Seeing how contrary Concord was, Mr. Hinckley offered to change places with me, which I was very ready to do, because I felt Mary would be much safer with him than with me. It turned out that this change was a most fortunate one, and probably saved us from a terrible accident. Mr. Hinckley is one of the very best specimens of a New England mechanic, a reader, a thinker, a thorough blacksmith, a competent carpenter, a good farmer, and a perfect master of horses. It is a real pleasure to see him drive this caracoling little mare, who rises on her hind legs at everything that frets her, and at the barking of a dog dances to vie with Taglioni.[280] He sits as coolly as if he were reading a newspaper, and makes her do as he likes.

At Ruggles' Mr. Tomlinson joined us, on horseback, and we rode along quietly till we came to the Ladies' Island bridge. Mr. T. and I were behind, the wagons having crossed the bridge, when all at once we saw Drayton dashing ahead through a gate that is about an eighth of a mile beyond the bridge. The bridge rises so that we could see nothing between. We put our horses to their fastest, and when we came to the top of the bridge, there lay Katy motionless in the road a few rods from us. I am so unobservant of ladies' dresses that I was not certain at first who it was, altho' I was pretty sure it wasn't Mary. Immediately Mary came running towards us from the opposite direction, so I saw she was safe. She reached Katy first, and soon Mr. T. and I were there, and Thomas— who had jumped out of the wagon—held our horses. She was senseless, with a great gash in the side of her nose, which had bled profusely. Just even with the gate, at the right, is Mr. Eustis' overseer-house, occupied by Mr. Nichols his superintendent, (from Kingston), Mr. Wild,[281] who helps him keep store, and Mr. Holt,[282] a middle-aged man formerly a superintendent, but without any special business now. I ran there and got a pail of water, and by the time I had got back Katy showed signs of life. Meantime the mule-cart had come up, and we took out the baggage and laid Katy in, Mary getting in first and taking her head in her lap. Then we mounted Dick on Nelly to ride after Mr. Hinckley and Miss Rice and see what had become of them, while we carried Katy to the house and laid her on the bed. Mr. Tomlinson then rode off to send the doctor, and shortly after I walked along, but soon met Mr. H. and Miss R. riding quietly with Concord.

It seems there was great carelessness somewhere in harnessing Drayton without any breeching—Mr. F.'s wagon has hold-backs, but Mr. G.'s requires breeching, and there was not unnaturally a little confusion in them.[283] This was the reason Katy could not stop him at the first gate. And in going down the steep declivity of the bridge, the wagon ran upon his heels, starting him into a full run. Katy, who is very timid in a wagon, sprang out, with the result I have described. Mr. H., who was ahead, at first tried to keep so; but Drayton is so much swifter, that he found the only safety was in hauling Concord up suddenly by the side of the road, and letting Drayton pass. It is a wonder how he accomplished this, for the road is on a causey barely wide enough for two carriages to pass. He did it, however; Concord stood stock still for a moment, when Mary slipped out behind, and Drayton passed by at full run, dashed at the gate, which opens in the middle like all gates here, and in the other direction,—flung it open by his force, and tore along the road, Mr. Hinckley after him as fast as Concord would go—constantly losing ground however. The next gate is a mile and a half off, and when Miss Rice saw it she decided not to risk it, but climbed out behind, and dropped senseless in the road, only coming to herself when Mr. H. came up. Drayton, meanwhile, finding that the gate opened against him, stopped and was easily caught. It was found that Miss Rice was badly jarred, her nerves all unstrung, and her ankle somewhat sprained, so she lay upon another bed, and Mary took care of both. Dick drove Drayton home, and Mr. H. rode Concord, leaving me with Nelly and the wagon.

I staid there some hours, in which time we had several callers and had dinner. I occupied myself with a pile of Tribunes, and we were made glad by news brought by Lt. Rhodes of a victory by Grant[284]—God grant it may be true. In the course of the afternoon Mr. Gannett drove up and carried off Miss Rice, and after Mr. Folsom and Harriet came up with Drayton—Harriet staid over night and I went back with Mr. F. Mr. G. and Miss R. had been caught in a shower, and we found them at our house, also Charley Ware, spending the night. The next morning Mr. F. and I started back to bring Katy home. He had had hold-backs put on the thills, but they were not far enough forward for such a huge horse, and the carriage ran on his heels again. He sprang forward, but Mr. F. drew him back, and I thought he had checked him. Just then, however, the rein slipped out of his left hand—which is still weak—and Drayton took another leap, and began to kick and run. I don't believe in jumping out under such circumstances, but I didn't mean to be carried by the house, and had made up my mind if the horse ran to climb over the seat into the back part of the buggy, and then drop out if I wanted to. So I undertook to step over the seat, but having my lap full of bundles was as it were entangled and lost my footing. Seeing that I was going, I jumped, and landed safely beyond the wheels, only I found when I got up that my elbow was out of joint, either having fallen on it, or the wheel having passed over it. Meantime Mr. F. had thrown the horse down, and we soon had him free of the wagon, after which I walked up to the house, where Mr. Nichols immediately pulled my arm in place. Mr. Folsom then went on to Beaufort, and soon Mary, Harriet and Katy set out for home, with Nelly in the wagon—in which a mattress was laid. My arm wasn't very painful—Mr.

Nichols bent it out straight and tied a splint to it—and I spent the time in reading until Mr. Folsom came back, when he carried me to Blithewood (nearly to
the Ferry) to see Dr. Wakefield.[285] We met him on the road, and he said my arm
was all right, threw away the splint, and told me to keep it bent. Then we started
for home. Drayton had been so completely demoralized by his two frights that
it wasn't safe to drive him across the bridge—we took him out, and drew the
wagon over. We got home safely, picking up a lot of newspapers at Ruggles'—
from father, Lizzie, Ned and Prentiss. The list of accidents was completed the
next day by Concord breaking the whiffletree; but to-day she went famously.

Tuesday eve., 8½ P.M.

My arm is getting along nicely, and I use it freely. It is still somewhat swollen
and stiff, but free from pain. Katy is improving, but she has a severe pain in the
back of her head. Miss Rice is nearly well. If Katy is able to go in the Arago next
Sunday, Mary will go with her. As there is so much to be done, and Katy likes
to hear reading, I have given the scholars a vacation this week, only inviting
the adults to come, as I did not wish them to lose any lessons. Messrs. Folsom,
Gannett and Hinckley went to Beaufort to-day, to a meeting to choose delegates to the Baltimore Convention.[286] 32 were chosen, among them 4 colored
men, Robert Smalls[287] and Prince Rivers being two of them. I suppose they will
be admitted to seats in the convention, without votes—certainly I shouldn't
expect them to be allowed to vote.

This is the first hymn we heard down here—that Sunday at Coffin's Point—
("I believe not"—written in pencil).[288]

                              fin   *Dal signo al fine*
Happy morning (*bis*) Gwine rise from de dead, happy morning.
(Glorious)   Weep no more Marta, Weep no more Mary. Jesus rise etc.
(Pleasant) (Sunday)

They often sing it "'Twas a happy" etc. or "What a" etc. I didn't forget Harriet's birthday yesterday, but had to leave my writing unfinished.

Thursday eve.

A mail by the Arago,—papers from Prentiss. Katy is better, but not well enough
to return by the Arago Sunday, so she and Mary will stay till the next steamer.
We are enjoying peas, new potatoes, and oceans of blackberries. Strawberries
and roses about gone.

St. Helena, Thursday, May 26, 1864, 8½ P.M.

Rufus Winsor brought the mail to-night—letters from Lizzie, Lucy and Joseph—papers seldom come till the second day. We have a paper of the 18th with all encouraging news; there must be later advices which we haven't received yet. We have had reports from the rebel pickets that Sherman and Grant are successful (the latter having taken Johnston) and that Butler has been taken prisoner with 70,000 men. The two army corps which Grant has reported to have captured turn out to be one division—it was the very next day (the Friday that Katy was hurt) that we heard it. There has been great pounding Charleston way, and Limus bro't word from Hilton Head the other day that Sumter was taken, but I don't think it at all likely, and the news hasn't been confirmed. But there is great moving about of troops here. Large forces have gone from Beaufort, and yesterday Mary, who was at Coffin's, saw 7 steamers enter the sound, bound some say for the Combahee, while others say it is a feint and the objective point is Bluffton (back of Hilton Head). I heard some guns this morning in the direction of the Combahee.[289] The rebels made a raid on Morgan Island Friday night, and carried off twelve negroes. Morgan Island is one of Mr. Philbrick's plantations, in St. Helena Id., in full sight from Coffin's Point—under Mr. Well's care. The party was led by the young Fripps (some of the old owners of the island) and they seized upon everything eatable and wearable—some shoes they pounced upon as if they were gold. They told the people here they were earning 40 cents a day, while their old mistress was starving—they'd like to catch the man that paid them 40 cts. a day—they'd like to catch Wells. As long as the Kingfisher lay in the sound, Capt. Dutch kept the rebels pretty busy with constant reconnaissances and raids; but the Dai–Ching, which has taken its place, is a slow concern, and lets things alone. Capt. Dutch, we understand, has gone on this expedition (he's a Worcester man, by the way).

Our weather has kept comfortable for the most part. Sunday and Monday were very hot, Monday 95° on our piazza in the shade. We have peas nearly every day—we should have them in the greatest profusion if the birds hadn't destroyed them,—and have had string beans twice. My tomatoes are in blossom, and so are cucumbers. The pomegranates are flowering pretty well, large orange blossoms like the trumpet vine, and we have discovered some delicate white clusters of flowers on the olive trees. The orange trees have leaved out, and at Pine Grove they had a few blossoms—we have had none. Katy's wounds got along well, but she had such a terrible headache that on Friday I rode up to Blithewood, on Nelly, to see Dr. Wakefield. Blithewood is a rather pleasant place on the river just opposite Beaufort, and I had a pleasant ride—dining there and riding back with Mr. Nichols as far as his house. The doctor looked at my arm and pronounced it doing well. He prescribed for Katy, and she immediately began to mend, and heard her classes one or two days this week, and would now be quite well except that a large sty is gathering on her sore eye. I use my arm quite freely,—took quite a row to-day—but it isn't yet entirely limber or strong.

Saturday I spent chiefly in making blackberry wine, and as I had no press I found it a tiresome and dirty job. I only made a small quantity, but at Coffin's they have done it on a large scale—44 quarts of berries were brought in on one day. Sunday we staid at home. Frank Winsor rode along and stopped a while on his way to church, and then to dinner on his way home. Mr. Jackson also called here, and about the middle of the day Harriet came along with Miss Towne and Miss Murray—the teachers at the church. They are two of the oldest and best-known teachers here, and Miss Towne is a very superior person, from Philadelphia. I was very glad to become acquainted with them, and still more that Miss Towne will go North in this steamer with Molly and Katy. In the evening we went to "praise," at which Glasgow preached, the St. Simon's man whom I talked with on the Hamilton Fripp place. There is very little to write about now.

The people are at work hoeing and hauling their cotton—the former being to hoe up the weeds, the latter to haul up the earth into good shape. They will do this twice more. At the same time they thin it out, leaving three or four plants in a hill; bye and bye they will thin again, leaving one or two in a hill, and that will be a job requiring care and skill—this thinning can be done by children. Hauling and hoeing together are reckoned a day's work (a task) and paid at the same rate as listing. Thinning an acre is a day's work. So Robin's four acres make twenty days work, which he finished in nine days, with some help from Ishmael and Ellen. It has been decided as a matter of policy to raise the wages, and pay 50 cents a task for listing, and other things in proportion.[290] When Mr. Gannett announced the fact to his people, John Major spoke up— "Not enough, Mr. Gannett,"—and it seemed that nothing would satisfy them, short of a dollar a task, which is preposterous. I wouldn't have raised the wages at all. They declare that the corn shan't come up, but I believe it is the intention to stop payments until the corn in the cotton is pulled up.

Saturday, 8½ P.M.

Yesterday morning after school I rode on Drayton to Mr. Ruggles', to get Katy's pass, which had been left there by accident. I found Harriet and Mr. Soule at the house on my return—the first time Mr. S. has taken a meal with us. We had asked the Hope children to come over this afternoon, to take leave of Katy and

Mary; and they came rather late, but in good numbers. Mr. Alden, who has the Frogmoor school-farm, has a school now at Hope Place—I told them I should be glad to have them come here, but as I should be alone now they would get better schooling from him. So we got them all with our children on the upper piazza and had them sing nearly an hour to us. They were in the best of humor, and sang very nicely. Patty and Chloe were the leaders for the most part, but part of the time Robert, and once when Patty forgot how to "turn" an odd piece (Whar John Norton)[291] Ellen took it up with her sweet, timid voice, hiding her head all the time behind Flora's back. There were several that were entirely new to us, and one or two that we only knew imperfectly. Here is one that is very striking especially when sung in the open air by a number.[292]

I can't stan' de fire (three times) while Jordan da roll so swif'
    dear sister   O lord   tiddy Dolly
                                        (Queeny) etc.

When the singing was thro', Katy presented the children all with little books and combs, of which she had a store, and they went on their way rejoicing. Tonight we went down to the quarters, to take leave of the people. They were all very cordial and seemed really sorry to part with Mary and Katy. We haven't seen nearly so much of them as we expected and wished this winter, for various reasons, principally because there has been considerable small-pox here—or what they call small-pox. It has been very mild indeed, nobody being danger-ously sick except Rinah (Robin's wife), who was weakly otherwise. On some plantations, as the Oaks and Hopes, it has been very severe, and several have died. It is now over—there are still one or two cases at Mulberry Hill—but we go now thro' the quarters here without any apprehension. A fleet of children followed us about from cabin to cabin, and when we shook hands with the inmates, they all wanted to shake hands again. It is quite a drawback to the sat-isfaction at their greetings, that so many of them beg articles of clothing—not all, by any means, but enough to make it unpleasant.

    Abby, (Isaac's wife), a merry, laughing woman, made quite a call this morn-ing, sitting on the floor and talking, and occasionally begging for a frock, or my slippers. One day I had kept Mylie and Venus after school, and they were bellowing at a tremendous rate, when Abby came up, thinking it might be her young one. I explained matters to her—"Am' you put 'em to res'" said she with a hearty laugh, referring to Mylie's position on a bench. "Putting to rest" seems to be a general term for a severe punishment, and they often advise standing refractory children on a bench, where they will fall down and hurt themselves. I was talking of Venus to her uncle Bristol, who has charge of her. "He de bad-des' little gal from yere to Neurope" said he decidedly "ought to put him on a bar'l, an' den he fall asleep and fall down an' hurt heself, an' dat make him more sensibble." This word "sensibble," and "hab sense" are favorite expressions of the people—"I neber shum since I hab sense" (that is, since I was old enough to know).

One day Mylie and Tom were having a row, and Mary asking what was the matter—"Tom cuss me ma'am." It seems Tom was upbraiding her for not "telling him morning," her excuse being that "Tom too mannish." It is very amusing to have Tom come on an errand. He presents himself at the door, takes off his cap, turns back to you, and in a hoarse, gasping voice "Miss Mary, ma (Phoebe) say mus' gib em pepper for soup ma-a-m" the closing title of respect completely swallowing up the rest of the sentence. I have spoken of the abbreviation "Co'" and lately I have several times heard "Si" and "Bro"—"Si' Rachel," "Bro" Paris. One is constantly surprised at the extent to which they clip and abbreviate: "lee for "little." Two curious instances of their use of special terms is with reference to the distribution of our mail, which is always a most important occasion— Charley Ware, Rufus Winsor, or whoever it is, riding up to the door and taking out a huge bundle of letters, and as we stand about on the steps, announcing the names and tossing the letters to the owners, or dropping them back into a bag to be carried further. "Dey draw letter," or "Mas' Charley sheerin' out letter" is the popular description of the operation.

Sunday, 2 P.M.

This morning after Bible Class we had a concert—they sang us several that were certainly new to us, and very pretty. Afterwards Mary showed them our photograph album, which pleased them very much. Bristol said he "nebber could draw" his picture, because he laughed so, and he "spec it mus' hurt bery much to sit still so long." Miss Rice is here spending the day—Mr. Jackson has just come in from church. Two or three women, Dido, Emma and Doll sang the "Lonesome Valley"[293] (which is in the Continental) in a very rich contralto voice, the others basing her. There were a number of children, and I enjoyed having them join in the singing, but Billy objected, on the ground that they "strain" him.

St. Helena, Wednesday, June 1, 1864, 2½ P.M.

I have been under the weather for five days—a little touch of dysentery,—but I feel quite well now, and I think I shall have school again to-morrow. It was a great disappointment to me not to go to Hilton Head with Molly and Katy. Mr. Folsom was as kind as could be, knowing Katy's timidity with his horses, he went Sunday evening to Fripp Point and got two steady animals of Mr.

Gannett's and his pole, and early the next morning Mr. Hinckley was up fitting the pole to the Concord wagon, and they went off in fine style with Mr. F. as driver and Thomas as tiger. The boat from Beaufort was to touch at Land's End, so they went there and from thence to the Head, sailing about 10½. They found a number of acquaintances on the boat[294]—Miss Towne, Miss Forten, Miss Kendall, Mr. Williams, Mr. Dennett and Judge Cooley, so I fancy they must have had an agreeable voyage; and the weather has been perfect these three days—real June weather. And I all this time shut up in the house. Yesterday I spent wholly on the sofa, not eating a morsel, reading the Schoenberg-Cotta Chronicle,[295] which I enjoyed very much. To-day I have eaten three moderate meals, and think I am all right.

The men came to get their pay to-night, and there was great talking and scolding. Mr. Folsom's manner is admirable with them—the best I ever saw, firm, but kind, and imperturbably good-humored, while they are very unreasonable and freakish. I believe I wrote that it had been decided to raise the wages to 50 cts a task for listing, and so in proportion. But this depended on their cleaning out all the corn and melons that are planted among the cotton. Only four men on this place—Moses, Taft, Jimmy and Robin—came with clean ground, and all the others were paid at the rate of 40 cts. This made quite a storm, and Frank, Billy and Paris refused to receive their money. I believe however they all took it at last. Then Paris was talking I think for an hour with him, all sorts of rigmarole that somebody had been telling him—how that these Lawrence [blank space] can be bought at the North for 10 cts (they are sold to them for 30 cts) and other equally absurd stuff. Mr. F. told him this man told lies, and asked who he was, but Paris couldn't or wouldn't tell, and accused Mr. F. of telling him he lies. Presently, as I was passing, Billy grumbled out something which got me to talking. I told him they ought to be ashamed, when they knew Mr. Folsom so well, who had been here more than a year and never deceived them, to believe the first fellow that comes round telling lies in preference to him; also that I thought them as well paid a set of laborers as there was in the world. He said he had been hoeing and hauling 17 tasks, for which he got $6.30 only. Well, how many hours did it take? But that he wouldn't tell.

Pretty soon Paris, Isaac and Mr. Hinckley joined us, but with all our questioning Billy would never give a straight forward answer how long it took him to do a task, or how many tasks he could do in a day. Nor would any of the others. Pretty soon we got upon the subject of planting corn and melons in the cotton land. I asked what right they had to plant corn in land where they were only hired to work cotton—land that belonged to Mr. Philbrick. "Man! don't talk 'bout Mr. Philbrick lan'. Mr. Philbrick no right to de lan'." I answered that they knew nothing about it; Mr. P. bought the land and paid for it, and all the houses on it; and that when he hired them to work his cotton, if they planted anything else with the cotton, it was the same as cheating. "You eber know me cheat?" says Paris. "NO You hurt my feelin' to say I cheat." Well, I told him, I had no idea that he meant to cheat, but he didn't understand about things when he planted it; but he must know now that it was cheating. At last he went in to get the money that he had refused to take before, and it turned out that he received $16, having worked 17 days. We laughed at him well, but still couldn't get him to say how long it took to do a task, till finally Mr. Hinckley agreed that he would go out some day and do a task with him and see which would do it quickest. He told Billy he thought he must have made a pretty good bargain, or he would be willing to tell how long it took to do his 17 tasks.

Charley Ware spent last night here on his way from Beaufort. He brought four rumors, of which we could believe as many as we chose—that Sherman had advanced, that he had been beaten, that Lee had surrendered, and that Grant had retreated. I believe the first and none of the others.

Friday 3d, 8 P.M.

Mr. Jackson brought the mail tonight with news of Grant's "on to Richmond." I had a letter from Mr. Philbrick, and a pile of N.Y. Posts from Lucy—very acceptable. I feel perfectly well now—had school yesterday and today, but am still easily tired. Everybody is indignant at the mismanagement of the recent expedition. It was up the Ashapoo, not the Combahee, and was under Gen. Birney.[296] Two of the gun-boats went 15 miles beyond the place where they were to land, and waked up a battery, and of course news of their coming was immediately telegraphed. So Birney gave it up and came back. Then the Boston got aground and the Lewis wouldn't help her, and altho' the tide would have got her off in a few minutes, and at any rate a tug was coming which would have pulled her off, the general was scared and ordered her to be set a-fire. There were about a hundred horses on board—splendid horses of the 1st Mass. Cavalry, worth $200 apiece—and altho' they might have been got upon another boat, they were left to burn. This Gen. Birney commands a colored brigade, and came down here with the notion that everybody was persecuting the negroes. He was put in command of the port of Beaufort for a while, and immediately began to interfere in land and wage matters, knowing nothing about them.

Some of Mr. Dennett's negroes went to him to accuse Mr. Dennett of taking horses, cows, etc. from them. The general made it a point to believe everything that the negroes said, without question, so at once rode out to Mr. D's plantation—called him out—"By what right, Sir, do you hold these planta-tions?" (which Mr. D. bought at auction), and proceeded to order him to restore their property to these poor people. On further examination, he found he was wholly wrong. This seems to be the style of the man. Capt. Hooper went to explain some matter to him, and he was highly indignant at these "impertinent captains." Mr. Judd was talking with him, and happened to observe that he thought government had been very liberal towards the negroes—"What business have you, Sir, to think anything about it?" This indiscriminate and sentimental approval of everything the negroes do, and the habit of thinking that they must have everything done for them, is working immense harm here. In the first place, it is creating a feeling of antagonism between the races,—there is actually a strong antipathy on the part of a good many unthinking whites, on account of the pretensions put forth on behalf of the blacks, and the species of arrogance that it fosters in them—not considering that the fault is not so much in the poor negroes themselves as in their so-called friends. (Really one begins to understand what is meant by the expression "nigger worshiper").

In the next place, besides this arrogance, there are other evil effects on the people themselves. This peculiar, transitory situation of theirs—half dependent, half independent—is becoming too narrow for them, and they are learning habits of independence a great deal faster, at any rate, than there is any notion of at the North. Perhaps the lies that are told them and the absurd notions that are put in their heads assist the process of becoming independent, but it is a sad pity that this object would be reached by poisoning their minds against their real friends. By the way, Billy, Paris, Isaac and Bristol have all decided to take out their corn and melons, and Mr. F. thinks all will do so. In what I wrote above, I omitted to speak of the bad effect it has had to grant favors to some that could not be granted to all. The people of some plantations have given them this year the use of twenty acres apiece of land from which they ought to clear $100 an acre (for as much as is put in cotton, say four or five acres). Naturally Mr. Philbrick's people and others that don't have this favor are discontented, and instead of looking upon it as a peculiar privilege of these others, think they themselves suffer a hardship.

The following song is a very sweet one, and particularly striking when taken in connection with the habit of going out in the wilderness to seek religion.[297]

I wait upon de Lord,—I wait upon de Lord my God (*bis*)
                   who take away de sin ob de worl'.
You want to see Jesus—You want to see Jesus, Go in de wilderness
   (Base) Go in de wilderness (*ter*).   To wait upon thy God.

Go seek my Jesus come back	O half-done seeker	O come back
O weeping Mary member	" " Christian	Say aint you a

Coffin's Point, Sunday, June 5, 1864, 11½ P.M.

I rode down here last night on Concord, who is the easiest-trotting horse I ever rode. I didn't often get her into a canter, but she didn't need it. She has got used to gates now, and makes at them with her usual impatience and impetuosity—actually shoving one open with her head before I could get my hand to it, and never regarding the interests of my legs in plunging thro' afterwards. I got here in time to escape a heavy shower in which Miss Rice insisted on returning home. Harriet was having her sewing-school on the piazza when I arrived, and when it was over she had the children sing—some pieces among others which they do not know at Capt. John's. One of them is to a tune almost like "And are ye sure the news is true?" "I saw de beam in my sister eye—Can't saw de beam in mine—I better let my sister be, An' keep my own eye clean.—I had a mighty battle like Jacob an' de angel, In der ole time of ole, Lord I nebber 'tend to let 'em go, Tell Jesus bless my soul."[298]

Another one is very pretty[299]

John, John, of the holy order, sitting on the Golden Road (*ter* [three times])
To see the promised land.—I weep, I mourn, why do you move so slow?
        I'm waiting for some guardian angel, gone along befo'.
Mary and Marta, feed my lambs, feed my lambs, feed my lambs.
  "   "   "   "   "   "   sitting on de golden order.

Songs often differ on different plantations, or are peculiar to them, and the "Graveyard" they sang last night, I hardly recognized, it was so different from the way our people sing it.

As I was showing the young men some little thing in their writing, Paris asked with considerable discouragement whether they could ever know all these things. I told him yes, and told him about Fred Douglass, who, I said, I supposed at his age didn't know so much as he does, and who now writes books and is a great speaker. He was very much interested. I showed them how to write money the other day, and he has got a little blank book and is learning to keep a cash account. He got his receipts all down right, and I explained how to write down his payments on the opposite page. But the next day he came to show me his book, and had got them written down under the receipts.

Monday, June 6, 8 P.M.

Towards night yesterday we mounted our horses and rode on the beach a few rods, then turned to the right and entered a beautiful wood road, with splendid magnolias and live-oaks on all sides. The magnolias are rather past their prime, but I had been shut up so long that I had had no chance of seeing them before. The handsomest was one that stood by itself in an open field. The blossoms are snow-white and very fragrant and as large as a large tea-cup. After winding thro' the woods sometime and crossing a cornfield, we came to the beach again, and rode some distance upon it. I then went with Harriet down to the quarters —she to visit a sick child, I to see a shout, which I found did not differ from ours, except in the tunes they sang. In the evening we had singing, in which we missed Mary. This morning I started early, in company with Mr. Soule and Rufus Winsor, who were on their way to Beaufort. A very small school to-day, the people thinking that I was sick. When it was time for the morning school I heard a sort of singing in the yard, and looking out saw Linnie, Mylie, Minnie and others standing by the fence around the circle in front of the house and singing or rather chanting loud and with animation, shaking sticks and hands towards some object in the garden. When I went out they scud away, but soon gathered about me again, and pointed out a green lizard on a tree, puffing out the red pouch under his neck now and again. Then Linnie began to chant— "Lizard, lizard, mammy tell you spread blanket—do, lizard, spread blanket!"

The "Rock of Jubilee" is one they shouted to at Coffin's—the chorus has a noble effect a little way off, as I heard it last night.[300]

Rock o' Jubilee four corner ob de worl'—O Lord, de Rock o' Jubilee (*bis*)
Base
De Rock o' Jubilee poor Bristol boy
   "   "   "   "   to mercy door
   "   "   "   "   den I rock 'em all about.   (Better put lower [pitch])

Thursday, 9th, 12 P.M.

92 on the piazza. I am surprised that I have suffered so little from the heat so far. Keeping in doors thro' the heat of the day, there hasn't been any day that I have felt the heat more than I often do at the North. The nights are sometimes close, still I sleep soundly thro' them, especially with my mosquito-curtains. I have moved into Katy's old room, and taken her bed, on which curtains were rigged while she was sick. Mr. Folsom has moved up into my former room. School has been very unsatisfactory this week—some days not more than half a dozen scholars. It may be that they haven't got over the irregularity of the past three weeks; but if it is really because they are tired and need a vacation, I shall be inclined to leave sooner than I had intended—except for a few like Paris who will certainly stick thro', and some others whom I want to bring to a certain point, so that they can begin fair in the Fall.

Phoebe has begun to use the Yankee baker to-day, as the stove in the kitchen was so hot. I couldn't give her much information about the way to use it, so she went to experimenting, and told me with much satisfaction that when she had got the water boiling on top, then she set the saucepan inside and it "studdy bile." Mr. Folsom has rigged up a hand mill for grinding corn (like a large coffee-mill) in the gin house, so now we can have corn meal and hominy without hunting Dick, who is not strong enough to use the mill at the quarters. Bristol (Cherry Hill), one of Mary's special scholars, was lamenting her absence the other day—"When I yedde he gwine way, I feel jez' like pain in my head all day."

Monday, 7 A.M.

A cold rain storm, keeping me at Mr. Gannett's all night. Friday was the hottest day of the season,—95½, with copious showers in the afternoon. The yucca is in full blossoms, a tall palm-like plant, armed with hard sharp lance-shaped leaves all along the trunk, called Portuguese bayonet. At the top a splendid spike of white flowers. I saw yesterday some flowers much like the passion flower. Mr. Gannett bro't mail Saturday—letters—and yesterday Charley bro't the papers, a large pile from Lucy, most acceptable. I asked Minnie the other day why she didn't come to school—"My stomach been a da hab me, sir." I don't know that I ever mentioned the curious word "enty" for "is it so?" I tell Jimmy that is the way we do things at the North. "Enty, sir?" "Robert, you haven't written this very well." "Enty, sir?" Did I ever mention "day clean" for "day-break"? There is a man on Port Royal Island called "After Dark," because he is so black you can't see him "for day-clean." I heard Clara the other day say that she and Toby grew up "sic-a [like a] brudder and sister."

Monday, eve., June 13, 8 P.M.

I expected the mail to be sent along to-day, but it was not, so I will add a half-sheet. Mr. Folsom will carry the letters along to-morrow.

Mr. Gannett spent the day, Thursday, in pulling up corn among the cotton. He didn't pull up the whole, but left a moderate amount here and there; only as the people would not pull it up themselves, he determined to have it done. Some of them were very much enraged, and one man—Tony—armed himself with a club and carving-knife and went out to the field, brandishing them, and swearing that he would have his blood. But he never went near Mr. G. in the field, and in the afternoon was as meek as Moses.[301] Mr. G. finished eight acres that day, but has been busy on other things since. Mr. Folsom's people have mostly cleared their land, but John at Mulberry Hill, who has nine acres of cotton, has planted from thirty to forty watermelon vines in every task, making over a thousand vines. If he doesn't remove them, Mr. F. means to have him before the Plantation Commission. The Plantation Commission is a sort of court, appointed from time to time from among the superintendents, to examine cases as they come up. They met three times lately to try two Fripp Point men for riding Mr. Gannett's and Charley Ware's horses without leave. The horses were ridden very hard, and Mr. G.'s seriously injured. But the testimony was so conflicting that they could not come to any conclusion, and dismissed the case, altho' they felt morally certain that the men were guilty. There is a great unwillingness among the people to testify against each other, or do anything to incur each other's ill will, so no Fripp Pt. people would testify against the men, and the Coffin's Pt. and Fripp Pt. testimonies were just opposite to each other.

Mr. Folsom says there is much more manliness and courage at Port Royal Id., where he used to be, than here; the people have had a harder and rougher time of it, while here everything has been easy and plain sailing. Once there was a raid by the rebels on Barnwell's Id., and half a dozen colored men, with a white corporal, went over. They were fired on from the bushes and instantly charged into the bushes, but found the enemy too strong, and were all either killed or taken prisoner. These were not soldiers, but plantation hands, armed with muskets. It was only after long urging that they succeeded in getting guns to arm the people with. It seems to me that one of the very wisest things would have been to make these men into a militia at once—accustom them to arms and to the idea that they had something to do for their own defense. I don't doubt the result would have been more volunteers in the army than they actually get conscripts. We have a couple of pretty little kittens from Mr. Ruggles'; a tortoise shell and a brindled.

St. Helena, Friday, June 17, 1864, 9 P.M.

It has been a cold, dull week, beginning with a cold storm on Sunday; three evenings we had fires. The school has been a good deal better this week, especially the afternoon school. I have got my first class—Ishmael, Ellen, Thomas, Sammy, Sandy and Flora—thro' the multiplication table. Sandy and Flora are far from perfect, but the other four can say nearly the whole (as far as twelve) straight along; while Ishmael very rarely misses in skipping about. I am now beginning with the others, whom Katy carried to some distance in the tables. I find the first class which she heard, reads very well; Ellen is best, and Ishmael next. I don't undertake now to have any regularity in classes; I hear them as they come along, and let them go. The best writers of that class can form and join letters quite well—simple words of three or four letters. I have had them write on slates, unruled, so as to train their eyes, but now I mean to put them into writing books. The men, those who read to Katy and to me, continue to come, but Mary's scholars have dropped off entirely. I don't often give them any lessons but reading and copies. Paris, Dennis, Billy, Henry and Wake write a very clear and legible hand: Bristol, Robert, Tony, Taffy, Toby and Dick are not so good, still fair. I explained to them about writing money the other day, and Paris has got a small blank book and is learning to keep accounts. He can add and subtract correctly, and multiply with help. Some of the others can add and subtract. The morning school has been especially irregular lately, and have not made much progress. Still some, as Adam, Minnie, Gibb and Reddington, who didn't know their letters, are now stumbling along thro' the primer. I thought I would make this resumé of the condition of the school, as it is so long since I have said much about it, and it is now nearly closed.

Night before last, Capt. Soule[302] of the 55th (son of Mr. S.) appeared with two non-commissioned officers and one private, on an expedition after vegetables, as the 54th and 55th are beginning to suffer from scurvy. We had moved the large bed from the room Mr. Folsom used to occupy into Mr. Hinckley's room, and put our provision safe into Mr. F.'s room, so as to put it out of the way of Henry's dog. So we put two of them in that bed, one in the spare bed, and Capt. S. slept with Mr. F. We found them pleasant and intelligent fellows, very light, and I suppose all runaways. Serg't. Lee of the 54th, is from S.C.; Serg't Trotter of the 55th from Miss., and the private from Virginia.[303] [Allen's diary entry of June 15, 1864, noted that "3 sergeants spent night (Trotter, Lee & George)."] To-day Capt. S. and the private drank tea with us on their way back, and bought all the potatoes and onions that were brought in. We made up a pile of weekly newspapers etc., and gave them two jars of canned blackberries. "Henry Esmond"[304] I gave to the Capt., and Pet Marjorie, the copy that Lizzie sent to us, I sent to Capt. Frank Goodwin[305] of the 55th, an old friend of the Lamberts. I am going to Beaufort to-morrow to draw rations if it is pleasant.

Sunday, June 19th, Coffin's Point, 12 P.M.

It rained furiously yesterday morning, so that I didn't go to Beaufort, but staid at home and read and wrote. In the afternoon I rode down here on Concord, to spend Sunday. This last week has been as cold as April, and the fleas, which don't love hot weather, have been very rampant. The sand-flies, which tormented us a month ago, have entirely disappeared now, and the mosquitoes are not by any means very bad as yet.

When I first came down, I wrote in my journal my first crude impressions, and now having been here nearly eight months,[306] I will record my final impressions, by way of comparison. My means of observation have been very limited—only a few plantations—but so far as they go, they have been satisfactory. In the first place, it seems evident that a slave population has been turned into a free peasantry very rapidly and completely. The community is entirely self-supporting and prosperous, and has advanced in the path of independence much more rapidly and further than is generally supposed at the North. I think they have outgrown the admirable system (admirable for a temporary one) which has been in operation here, and that another year it will be much better—probably unavoidable, at any rate—to give up this transitional, quasi-dependent relation, and establish things on a more permanent basis, and on the principle of rendering labor wholly independent of capital. Probably by another year the homesteads, at least, will be secured to all the people. Peasantry is the proper word to apply to these people in their present condition. Their industry is independent, and they are wholly free, but still morally dependent and very ignorant and degraded. It will be a delicate question how fast and in what way to raise them from the condition of peasants to full citizenship, and some of the tendencies and influences at work are not of a healthy and promising character. There is too much sentimentality and theorizing at head-quarters, and a desire to push things, which will make it hard to secure steady and conservative progress.

I am very sorry that I have not been able to visit any schools. We had made a plan to visit Mr. Sumner's but never could have the use of horses when it was convenient to go; perhaps I can manage yet to get to the school at the church, under the care of the two Miss Murrays—Miss Towne being now in the North. From what I can learn, I judge that these two schools go far ahead of any at this end of the island, and would rank fairly with northern schools. By another year, I hope that a good school system will be in operation all over these islands, for this is what we are chiefly to expect progress from. Of the moral condition of the people, I have very little means of judging. It seems to me that the family relations are well and faithfully observed, so far as I have seen. There is very strong family feeling, altho' comparatively little neighborliness. On our place there is very little thieving, but on some places a great deal. Lying is quite prevalent, but I think that the children are tolerably free from both these vices. I have never detected more falsehood than in a northern school of the same size; but then it must be said that there is less temptation, because my school is so short and irregular. I lament that it has not been in my power to give moral lessons to any extent to the children. If I should be here again, I should make a strong effort to have school much more regular and systematic than has been possible this year. It will be a serious time when the military restraints are removed from the islands. There is a strong passion for strong drink, which at present they cannot indulge, and there will be then great danger of reaction. At present there is a great deal of vice in the neighborhood of Hilton Head and Beaufort, so that perhaps the removal of the demoralizing influences of camps will balance the evils that they prevent.

As far as I have carried my scholars, I do not think that there is any inferiority to white children. Ishmael could compete with most boys of his age in the multiplication table, and considering the amount of schooling, I think they have made as much progress as whites. One thing has been constantly deepening in my thoughts—the horrible crime it would be to reduce these people back to slavery, and the awful wickedness and unnaturalness of slavery itself. This one thing is worth coming down here for, if nothing else; to be able to tell the defenders of slavery that their argument on the inability of blacks to take care of themselves is a lie. For these people are the very lowest of the blacks, and if they succeed with free labor the question is settled. This is an experimentum crucis [critical experiment]. I have written several times of the sort of ingratitude and suspiciousness that one sees very painfully. It isn't at all unnatural. Their treatment, except by their superintendents, hasn't been such as to win their confidence, but rather to destroy it; and I suppose there is no doubt that the higher virtues come with civilization, and that barbarism means cruelty, selfishness and falseness. And yet, while there is all this lack of acknowledgement of what has been done for them, the better qualities often peep out in very gratifying form. The people at Pine Grove, who have given Mr. Gannett so much trouble, refused to take any pay for the vegetables and chickens that they brought to Capt. Soule, seeing that they were for the soldiers. And the presents of eggs, baskets, ground-nuts etc. showed a very kind and grateful feeling towards us. My intercourse with the people has been wholly agreeable—except for the brief episode of the rumors of our talking about them, a few weeks ago—and I shall leave them with a great deal of regret.

A good many people are afraid that the freedmen will be subject to extortion and abuse when military protection is removed, and there are indications that there are capitalists who have bought plantations here with no notion but to squeeze all they can out of the people. Still, I do not think there is any serious danger on this score. The people have shown that they can protect themselves pretty successfully, and especially their great guarantee will be the scarcity of labor. I don't believe it will be possible for a good many years—not until the freedmen are educated into their new position—to reduce wages materially. Probably white labor will come here, in competition with them, but I think it will do them good. Their habits of work are so shiftless and their processes so uneconomical that it will do them a great deal of good to be obliged to compete with more skillful laborers; and nothing short of this will teach them, for they are fully possessed with the notion that they understand all about working the crops here, and that nobody can teach them anything about it. I think Mr.

Hinckley's being here and working with them is accomplishing inestimable good in the way of example, but after all competition is going to do the great work. There is one plantation on Hilton Head Id., worked entirely by white laborers; but I don't know how successfully.

In one thing matters are working much better here than I feared. I thought the land question had been so mismanaged that there would be very little cotton raised except by private owners. If there had been the present state of things last year, no doubt this would have been the result, and it is a gratifying proof of the progress made that the people are planting cotton very extensively and cultivating it well, on the tracts they occupy. Probably more cotton is planted this year than last; whether the crop will be greater can't be prophesied yet. Gen. Foster[307] has ordered that all able-bodied white residents shall drill once a week, but I shall go North so soon that I suppose I shall be excused. I think it is strange that this has never been done before, and still more that the colored men have never been formed into a regular militia. This would have been feasible a year or two ago, and would have done immense good. There could have been an efficient militia, which would have answered for the defense of the islands, and which would no doubt have furnished a good many volunteers; and all the abuses and follies of the draft would have been avoided.

9 P.M.

Mr. Frank Winsor has been up to Capt. John's to-day, and expected to find mail, but came back without any. We took a ride to-day on the beach and in the woods—Mr. Soule, Rufus Winsor, Miss Rice and I, while Harriet and Mr. Gannett went in a Concord wagon.

Tuesday 3½ P.M.

Our mail came yesterday in great style,—a Concord wagon drawn by four horses, with Ruggles, Welles[308] etc. By the way, Mr. Welles' wagon has been smashed twice, and Mr. Gannett's once since our chapter of accidents. I gave Bristol some of the senna syrup the other day, much to his delight. "Man!" said he "dis yere too sweet for physic—dis taste too good for cure pain." Dick when he took it, also eulogized it—"Dis aint nasty, Miss Mary"—

Evening

The people have just finished their second hoeing and hauling of cotton, and are listing their "slip" ground—that is, land to plant slips for a second crop of sweet potatoes. The first crop, which comes on, I believe in July, wouldn't last

round to give them seed in the spring. This is one of the best shouting and rowing tunes.[309]

I know member, know Lord. I know I yedde de bell da ring. (*bis*)
                    I want to go to meetin' (*bis*)
                    (Base) Bell da ring.
                    I want to go to 'ciety (Lecter [?])
                    I can't get   "   "
                    De\ church mos' ober.
                    I shout for de heaven bell (meetin' etc)
Say de road so stormy (boggy)
    "   "   Heaven 'nough for me one
Brudder hain't you a member?

First the introduction is sung and the shouting begins with the regular
tune. The words have no regular order, and are sung first to the tune on the first
staff, and then the other.

St. Helena, Sunday, June 26, 1864, 6 P.M.

I went to Beaufort yesterday to draw rations. Dick was going in the tumble-
down, which belongs to him, and which he has painted a brilliant cerulean
hue, with Nelly; so I rode on Concord, and had him bring the rations. It was
a very hot day, but I went by the early boat, and so had the cool of the day. In
the Indian Hill field I fell in with Mr. Hayward,[310] who has charge of that and
the Pope Place, and rode the rest of the way with him. He is a very pleasant
fellow from Vermont, and I judge manages very well. He has 120 acres of cotton, looking very finely, and he says he hasn't had the slightest trouble with
hands. A little beyond Mr. Nichols', we were passing over a little gully, when
a dog rushed out from a hole in the hedge, and began to bark furiously and
bite Concord's heels. She hates dogs, and being exasperated struck from her
shoulder (hind shoulder) in the most scientific manner, breaking the dog's foot,
as Mr. Hayward informed me. I was too busy on my own account to see what
became of the dog, and only have an indistinct recollection of his yelping while
I was dealing with the horse—on whose neck I found myself sitting. Why I
went back into the saddle rather than over his head into the road, I can't say; I
was well enough satisfied with the fact, without trying to analyze it. I got thro'
all my business in time for the noon boat back; but Dick didn't, and staid till the
3½ boat. I had a fearfully hot ride home, and was very tired; however an air-bath
and a water-bath and a nap set me up, and I am alright to-day.

Miss Rice and Mr. and Mrs. Harrison called in the afternoon, and Miss Rice waited for the rations to take her share—indulging in derisive and disparaging remarks on the orderly appearance of a house which had been under male management for four weeks. We draw fresh meat now as part of our rations, and Dick brought home ten pounds; but it was beginning to spoil by the time he got it home. However, we got one good dinner out of it today, and I think shall have another to-morrow. Rinah made her appearance to-day, in company with Flora, but as usual ran under the house as soon as I went to the door. Soon however, she reappeared and stationing herself with her back towards me, and hanging her head upon her breast commenced a conversation of which I understood a few words. I gave each of them a gingerbread cake, and pretty soon they were out on the creek in a dugout, Flora paddling vigorously, and both singing "I am hunting for a city."[311] They sent "huddy" to Miss Mary and Miss Katy, "all two." This afternoon there was a funeral—Doll, a forlorn, scrofulous creature—and Mr. Hinckley and I went to the grove where the burying ground is. The services were conducted by Liab and Aleck—from Fripp Point, Tony from T. B. Fripp, and others. They didn't sing any of their own songs—all church hymns, prayers and exhortations.

Tuesday, June 28, 8 P.M.

Mail to-day—no letter from Molly, but one from Lizzie, and lots of papers. And what makes it worse, the steamer is to sail on Thursday, so there is no chance of my getting Molly's letter before this goes. Yesterday was the hottest day of the season—97—but Mr. Hinckley was at work all day shingling the Cherry Hill house, and stands the heat as well as a native. Towards night Frank Winsor drove up in a sulky on his way to Beaufort, and spent the night. We went to bed early, and before I got asleep I heard wheels driving up, so putting my head out of the window found it was Mr. Gannett and Miss Rice, who were expecting the mail, and also expecting—by virtue of a long-continued firing of guns at Beaufort about sunset—to hear either that Richmond was taken or the island invaded. I went to bed again, but lay tossing about in the sultry air, when there was a galloping of horses into the yard. Mr. Folsom had been away since Saturday night, and now came back with Mr. Stetson and Mr. Sumner—the latter has been North for his health (went with Molly) and has just returned in the Fulton. Mr. Folsom and Stetson went to Beaufort to-day, returning to dinner.

My adult school doesn't amount to much now; they have just finished the last hoeing of the corn, and are about to give the cotton its last working; and the middle of the day is so hot that they stay at home then and work in the afternoon. Morris, by the way, earned the other day $1.50—hoeing any acre $1, hauling one task .25 and thinning two tasks .25. He is one of the best men on the place, but this shows what a man can do—and these jobs are low paid, because they are paid 1½ cents a pound on the stone cotton, besides a cent for picking. The children keep pretty steady to school, however, and my numbers have been materially enlarged lately by "Ma' B. Fripp chil'n"—that is, children from T.B. Fripp. Mrs. Harrison is going North and has given up school, so they came to see if I would teach them. I have 17 of them—George, Alice, Flora, Betsy, Maria, William, Molly, Doe (Zoe?), Richard, January, Rose, Phoebe, Eve, Larry, Morris, Jacob and Jim. Edward came this morning to me and complained— "Dem Ma' B-b-b-B Fripp chil'n f-f-f-fin' one w-w-w-we book." (meaning, not a small book, but "one of our books").

Phoebe's son Waberlee (Rabelais or Wavorley), who is in the 2d. S.C. reg.[312] is at home on furlough. Phoebe has been very constant in going to Beaufort to see him, but always unsuccessfully until a week or two ago, when she went on Saturday and found him. I think the team must have been a stunning turn-out—Phoebe's old blind mule in a tip cart, with Phoebe and Grace (his wife), and Adam for charioteer.

The cotton is beginning to blossom; figs ought to be ripe, but they are stolen as fast as they turn—I don't know that I blame the children, as the trees have been public property for two years. They will begin soon to plant "cow-peas"—a kind of bean used for fodder. Then towards the end of July they begin to "strip blades,"—strip off the corn leaves and dry them for fodder; this is the only substitute for hay. They are paid by the hundred-weight. Then in August and September comes cutting marsh grass for manure, and stacking it where it will rot. The children are going about now and plundering all the mocking-bird's nests of the young birds, which they sell in Beaufort for .50 apiece. It is too bad, but there is no way of preventing it.

St. Helena, Sunday, July 3, 1864, 9½ A.M.

Probably my last letter from here, as I have decided to go North by the Arago next Saturday, if I can get a pass. We are beginning to have the real scorching weather of summer at last. Yesterday it was 90° at 8½ and 5½, and for two or three hours stood at 98°. That was on the piazza—in this room it didn't go above 94 or 5. Still, I haven't suffered at all from the heat, keep a good appetite and wrote steadily all yesterday forenoon. About sunset I took a nice row with Mr. Hinckley to steer. The school this week has been pretty good, altho' the men have hardly come at all, except Paris, Tony, Taffy and Henry. These have been about the steadiest scholars, and show very decided improvement since school began. School is in a pretty good condition to leave now, and I think most of the scholars are so well advanced that they can start fairly in the fall. A few however, have taken a great start quite lately, even since Mary went, and I am sorry not to give them another month, so as to get them to a "sticking point." Minnie, who seemed to be just the most hopeless case—not having more than half a dozen letters in March after I had been tugging her thro' the alphabet, first in a class and then alone, and a month ago looking vacantly at the letters and gasping them out (half the time wrong) in an almost inaudible whine without seeming to care in the least whether she got them right, and unable to do anything unless I pointed each letter out to her, (and not much then)—now stands erect with a book in her hands, and reads clearly, and generally promptly and correctly, words of two letters. She has even gone ahead of Venus, who at one time was very promising. Adam too has improved very much. Edward and Mylie I am quite proud of. Neither of them knew all the letters at the beginning of the school, and now Edward has outstripped all the other morning scholars, and reads fluently simple words of two syllables, while Mylie ranks second after him (Abraham being between). I am ashamed, on the other hand, for Lizzie, who could read easy words when I came, and can't do any more now—she reads with Mylie, but no better. She has been very constant, but very inattentive.

There are some queer blunders which I suppose children always make. [The words] No and on and [the words] was and saw are almost always interchanged. Some scholars when they see [the word] the will read and. I wish I could see marked improvement in the neatness and cleanliness of the children—perhaps it has been so gradual that we haven't observed it, but they do come to school very dirty, both in dress and person. I think the older children and the adults have improved however since we have been here, but it must be confessed that the little children are most attractive when they come in nothing but a tunic. I begin to sympathize with—Mr. Stiggins,[313] was it, who sent moral pocket-handkerchiefs to the negro children in the West Indies? Their clothes are sometimes ingeniously ragged. This week Minnie appeared one day in a tunic, the next day in full dress with a hideous bonnet decked with long green ribbons, the next day in tunic again, and the next she had a dirty red kerchief twisted round her head for a turban. Hetty, who has longish, nearly straight hair, standing up all round her head, "like quills upon the fretful porcupine," had it pressed down the other day with a net strung with black beads an inch or so apart. Ellen, I am sorry to say, is very unneat in her dress, but little Sue the other day looked like an African princess with a neat green gown—short (they usually, the youngest children, have them trailing on the ground)—and a rich green and red turban. The Cherry Hill children are all of them, and always, well dressed.

The other night I was waked up about midnight by singing, and going to the window found that it proceeded from Dick's house—very sweet and pleasant, tunes that were entirely new to me. It seems that after praise, Dick had invited the people to come up and have a supper, Waverly, his brother-in-law, being there that night. So after supper they had singing. But it is very funny what hours they keep. Dick will sometimes get up, in the middle of the night, and go out and cut wood, or read a chapter in the testament, or slaughter his pigs for the market, and then go to bed again. Another peculiarity of the people is their fondness for fire, even in this hot weather. I think even now, and certainly all thro' the Spring, whenever they were at work in the fields they would have a little smouldering fire near them. Mr. Folsom says he believes if a colony of negroes was dropped on a desert island, the ground would spontaneously form into ridges and alleys, and there would be seen the remains of a fire. I suppose it is a natural instinct of an inferior race in a malarious region—a fire is no doubt the best protection against miasma.

Our household gets along after a fashion. We have a theory that whenever either of us wants anything, he is to go to Phoebe and order it. But in point of fact, I do pretty much all the ordering, and we get along as we can. Phoebe's theories of the boundaries between her duties and Thomas' are very edifying. She is to bail the water, he to draw the tea; she cooks the dinner, and there her responsibility ends. He is to find it and bring it in, and she seldom vouchsafes to instruct him. He goes and gropes in the safe, and fetches out what he finds. Yesterday he didn't happen to find the meat, (some cold beef), and had to be sent for it after we sat down.

Robert has been teaching me a number of songs; weary is the common word for tired.

Me no weary yet, O me etc. Satan tell me to my face[314]
          O me no weary yet.

In de mornin when I rise,—tell my Jesus huddy O (*bis*).[315]
"Huddy" is "how do," the common word for greeting.

As I sit here writing (it is now one o-clock) we can hear the very dull and distant sound of guns. An expedition went off somewhere day before yesterday —General Saxton went with it, whether to command or not, I can't say. It sounds in the direction of Pocotaligo [South Carolina]. 96° on the piazza 89° in here.

8 P.M.

85° in this room. I have just returned from a drive with Mr. Hinckley—Concord in the Concord wagon. It has been the coolest part of the day, as we made a breeze in going. We went first to Hope Place—the road is now lined with the most luxuriant summer growth, but there are still the pools of standing water by the side, and with all its exceeding beauty, it looks very unhealthy. The quarters are, however, on a sandy elevation right on the creek, and it must be healthy when once there. The scholars seemed glad to see me, and bro't me sixteen eggs. They sent "huddy over and over again to Miss Mary and Miss Katy." We only staid a few minutes, and then drove along to Frogmoor—I had never been to the house before, and Mr. H. had never been along this road at all. It is a pleasant place, and we drove thro' the quarters. We spoke with Mr. Alden, met Mr. Sumner at the gate, and Mr. Hunn directly outside. From here we went straight across to Saxtonville, a new freedmen's village on the Frogmoor plantation. This is a very large plantation, and besides a school farm of 160 acres, there has been this village laid out, and there is still enough land left to be occupied by the people. The remainder of this plantation, and all of Woodland and Hopes are intended to be held eventually by the colored people, and this year, owing to the confusion in which everything was thrown, they are left simply for the freedmen to occupy and use as they please, each man cultivates what he pleases and as much as he pleases. A good deal of cotton has been put in, and on Hope place it looks quite well (we only saw a little however). On Woodland, we saw none, as the road passes entirely thro' woods, but on Frogmoor, with hardly an exception, it looked wretchedly. The whole plantation has a neglected, shiftless look, and does not speak much in favor of the new system. However, the cotton cultivated by the people on their own account on T.B. Fripp and Hamilton Fripp, looks better. Saxtonville is a long, straight street, with forty six cabins built along it by twos, each having, I believe, four acres of land, which are let to the refugees and others at low rent. They are generally neat, and the land looks well taken care of generally. Passing thro' the street, we struck into a beautiful wood road, which presently brought us out near the signal station. Arrived at home, we found Mr. Gannett, Miss Rice and Mr. Jackson, who had come on horseback, and soon went. It is remarkable that the skies here have so little beauty—I never have seen a sunset that we should call fine at the North.

Tuesday, July 5, 8 A.M.

Yesterday set in with intense fierceness of heat—96° at 10, two degrees hotter than Saturday, and went up to 99° in the course of the day. We didn't feel much like going out, but thought we wouldn't miss the celebration at the church, so about tea, Mr. Hinckley and I started off with Concord in the buggy. When we came to the "Corner," we saw a great throng of children in the yard, waiting for the time for forming the procession. We drove along to the church, tied our horse, and talked for a while with Harry McMillen,[316] who owns a small plantation on Ladies' Island, where he plants this year 65 acres of cotton, employing

21 hands. He is one of the best specimens of the freedmen. Then we went to the stand and got seats, finding there Messrs. Tomlinson, Alden, Sumner Stetson, Gannett, Charley Ware and others, Mrs. Walker, Mrs. Stone, Miss Rice etc. I there learned that the steamer was in—not the Arago, but the Carnac,[317]—and that if we go this week, I must probably go Thursday. Mr. Folsom and Mr. Tomlinson have gone to Beaufort to-day, and will make inquiries.

After waiting a while, the procession hove in sight, marshaled by Mr. Wells on horseback and Mr. Nichols, and the Misses Murray walking by the side of their scholars. They had banners and flags, and came up singing the John Brown song. The exercises were interspersed with singing—Mr. Wells has been drilling them for two or three weeks. First a freedman, Robert Lessington, quite an old man, made a prayer, then Mr. French made an address—Mr. Tomlinson presided. Mr. French has really a rare faculty of speaking to the people, and I suppose if he is—as is alleged—unscrupulous and Jesuitical in his methods, he really desires the welfare of the freedmen, and is interested in them. I have certainly heard no one who compares with him in addressing them. He closed by reading Whittier's boatmen's song. I should have doubted their appreciating it, but he read it so well that it took right hold of them. They laughed and nodded approval with a thorough look of appreciation and enjoyment—Jimmy's jelly black face was radiant with delight, and his white teeth glistened, and whenever the chorus was read, he fairly bent double with his mirth. The second verse told best, particularly the lines "We sell the cow, e sell de pig, but nebber chile we seld." The third verse was a little above them. After Mr. French, Mr. Newcomb,[318] superintendent of the New York school teachers, made a short and prosy speech, also Horn,[319] an Edisto man, spoke, the one that ran Mr. Folsom's steam-engine a while last winter. Before him, the people sang some of their own songs, "Roll Jordan,"[320] "One more ribber to cross,"[321] "Tallest tree,"[322] "Wrestle Jacob,"[323] "Travel on, O weary soul,"[324] "Lonesome valley,"[325] "I can't stay behind my Lord,"[326] which last rolled up splendidly from that great multitude,—they sang it with more zest than any, I think. It is a favorite shouting tune, and their heads and arms at once began to move in time with the music; we were much entertained with seeing one old woman, nicely dressed, with a yellow scarf round her neck, and a white spotted turban, leaning on another woman's shoulder and wagging her head and swaying her body to the music, while she sang, and her thoughts no doubt carried her back to the days when she was a young "member" and used to shout with the best of them.

The exercises were short and successful, and then word was given that bread and molasses and water would be provided for all at a booth opposite, but they must go one at a time, the children first. But there were such numbers that we soon saw that there was great scrabbling and confusion, so Mr. Gannett and I, and soon after others, ran to help marshal them. It was about as hard work as I ever did—we were busy for over an hour, trying to regulate the swaying crowd, and we did succeed in establishing some order, but this part of the order of exercises was on the whole a failure. Then a tremendous shower came up, and we took refuge in the church, after which we proceeded to Mr. Tomlinson's room (at Mr. Ruggle's), where a bountiful repast awaited us.

Thursday, July 7, 3 P.M.

We have had pleasant, cool weather since the fourth,—87° now on our piazza. Yesterday morning Mr. Hinckley and I went in the Concord wagon, first to Cherry Hill, where the new house begins to look very well. It is small, but very pretty. Then to Pine Grove, where we staid some time. The cotton on the "preempted" or occupied land, on the McTureous and Hamilton Fripp plantations, was almost without exception small and miserable in condition. Mr. Gannett's and Mr. Harrison's look very well indeed. We saw at Pine Grove almost the handsomest flowering shrub I ever saw—the crape myrtle. It is a good deal like the pink hawthorn. This morning I went to the quarters and saw most of the women, and this afternoon the men and the children have been coming to bid me good bye. They are very anxious to buy my old clothes, and as an accommodation to them, I let them have several articles, for enough to enable me to buy new—that is, establishing a price enough below that of the new to make the difference between old and new. Some articles I gave away, to Dick, Thomas, old Isaac and old May. Old Isaac is very sick with dysentery, and I think it is very doubtful whether he will get well. His wife—a nice-looking woman from the Marion Chaplin place—is there, taking care of him. I was amused with an abbreviation this afternoon—a characteristic one—Ellen tossing a cap to Edward, with "Here, lee bro'" (little brother).

I undertook to give the scholars each a little present; and to the morning scholars gave one of those cards which Mother prepared. To the men, I gave little articles of mine—Paris a thermometer, Bristol a pencil, Robert a knife, Tony a pocket book etc.—the boys fish-hooks and the girls books and needles. The other day Miss Rice called for me and we went to the church, to visit Miss Murray's school, which I have wished to do for a long time. Miss Towne is away, and the two Miss Murrays have charge of the school. Two sets of scholars in one room, and that, a high echoing church,—especially as their theories are opposed to compulsion—make a great deal of noise. But their proficiency is very good. Three school-houses came down in the last schooner, to be put up for their use opposite the church—this was thought preferable to one large building. Mr. Sumner came in last night, and bro't word that our troops had suffered a disastrous repulse at Fort Johnson.[327] I hope it is exaggerated, but I fear that we cannot expect any confirmation of the report the other day that Beauregard was captured with 15,000 men.

Hilton Head, Friday, 11½ A.M.

I came down here this morning expecting to go North by the Carnac; but found that the Carnac went to New Orleans to-morrow. So I am sitting in Mr. Severance's office to-night. When I shall go North is entirely uncertain. As I miss it this week, I may not try it again until August. Two mails this week (Carnac and Star of the South)[328] but nothing for me. It is understood that things are looking very well at James Island—a couple of companies were captured, but there has been no disaster, and some solid success. A hot day, but with a pleasant breeze from the sea.

Steamer Dudley Buck, Tuesday, July 12, 1864, 10¼ A.M.

Off after all, on a smallish propeller, and have had a very favorable voyage so far, I left home early Friday morning, on Concord, Dick carrying my baggage with Tamar. I went by the Seaside road, which was familiar ground as far as Edgar Fripp's, where I saw a little good cotton. Beyond this comes a string of small plantations,—Ann Fripp, Henry McTureous, Frank Pritchard, Sandiford Place and Jane Pritchard—none of them of any account—and then the Dr. Jenkins place, once owned by Dr. Lawrence of Boston. A good plantation, and a large, showy house, with fine garden. Stetson is superintendent, and I stopped here and got a little breakfast, then rode on to Land's End, where I had to wait a couple of hours for the boat [to Hilton Head]. Finding that the Carnac had gone to New Orleans, I gave up the idea of going North this week, so went round to the hospital to see if I could be of any service there. I soon found Mrs. Russell of New Bedford, head-nurse, who said that they had none of the wounded in the last engagements,—some had been carried to Beaufort, and some left at Morris Island, where she believed they were well cared for. I drank a cup of tea and ate a saucer of blueberries with her, and then we went back and spent the evening and night with Mr. Severance.

The next morning I went to the Quartermaster's office, and learned that this steamer was going, so as I hated to go back, and there seemed nothing to do in the hospital line, I secured a passage. Hilton Head is the hottest place I was ever in. Nothing but sand, which reflects the rays of the sun fiercely, so that altho' there is always a breeze, you feel as if you were in an oven. But the first night in the Dudley Buck was intolerable—very quiet, hot and sultry, with no ventilation. I could hardly sleep in my stateroom and should have carried my mattress on deck, except that it was well covered with returning soldiers, and it would have been hardly possible to find a place without encroaching on some of them. As I have the advantages of a first cabin passage, I thought I ought to put up with its disadvantages.

There are very few cabin passengers—Mr. Gregg,[329] the chaplain of the 7th U.S. colored going home sick, but improved vastly by the voyage, a kindly, earnest, elderly man, with a habit of preaching; Mr. Roundy[330] of Boston, and an agent of the Christian Commission, is a pleasant, sensible man, of no broad culture, I should think, but quite liberal—I have lent him Renan's Life of Jesus,[331] he being out of reading—2d Lieut. Bradish[332] of the 55th, a lively, good natured little coxcomb, who by virtue of seniority is military commander on board (that is, would be if there were any need—he jokes about it occasionally), who has a pet green lizard which he carries round on his shoulder, tied by a red string, and who spits tobacco juice incessantly on the deck; two or three others that I tell "good morning,"—pleasant fellows, but I don't know much of them. There are a great many soldiers, some discharged, some on furlough, and some on their way to their regiments. Two stalwart, bearded fellows of the 13th Indiana, (Lemuel [Samuel] Bassett's reg't—one from his company);[333] a sick German from Wittenberg, whom I gave some of my cordial, and pleased by telling him that I, spent a night in his native town; a stout, jolly red bearded carpenter from Bucks Co. Penn., rather a superior sort of man, I fancy; and lots more whom I have seen less of. There is a little flaxen-headed boy,—he doesn't look more than 15—of the 41st N.Y., who seems to keep aloof from all the rest; I have never seen him speaking to any, and I tried to get into conversation with him, but could get nothing but monosyllables out of him.

The men are very quiet and well behaved,—there is very little profanity, and indeed very little talking of any kind; they spread their blankets on the deck, and sleep most of the time. Tired of their campaigns, I suppose, and thinking of home. There has been very little to entertain us—we passed two gunboats on Sunday, one of which spoke to us. Yesterday morning at 11 we came up to Cape Lookout light, and in the early evening passed Hatteras, by an inner channel which very few dare to try, but which saved us a couple of hours. Our captain[334] is a long, hearty, red-bearded Yankee, who knows what he is about, puts on no airs—I like him. We live very well—with no show, but with a good deal of real comfort. Excellent bread, meat well cooked and plenty of canned or dried fruit. There are a dozen or more young mocking birds on board, and some of them are beginning to sing.

Off Barnegat Lighthouse

Wednesday, 15th, 1½ P.M.

Not so good time as I expected—head winds after this morning. We shall hardly land tonight, I am afraid. The German is better—doing very well. One of the Indianians had an attack of dysentery yesterday, but is doing pretty well today. We passed the Narrows after I had gone to bed, and came to the dock at Jersey City at about 10½. I landed the next morning.

Allen landed the morning of July 14, 1864. He telegraphed Molly; then he conducted business in the city and took the 5 P.M. train from New York to Boston via Stonington, Connecticut. He reached Boston at 6 A.M. on July 15 and went out to West Newton.

Professor William Allen, University of Wisconsin

William Allen and Family at Home

Charleston Journal

———— ∞∞∞ ————

William Allen and Gertrude Allen,[1] his seventeen-year-old niece, sailed from New York with a group of teachers at 11 A.M. on April 7, 1865, aboard the Creole. They reached Hilton Head at 11 A.M. on April 11. He sent Misses Lakeman[2] and Baker[3] to the "plantation" there. He met Messrs. Dodge and Pillsbury and spent the night with Dodge. The ladies spent the night with Miss Lillie. They sailed for Charleston aboard the Golden Gate at 12 P.M. on April 12, reaching there at 1:30 A.M. on April 13, and went first to 4 Glebe Street. After breakfast, Allen went to see Messrs. Blake and Redpath. He took up residence at 47 Warren Street, and that afternoon he had tea with Redpath at Mrs. Peters's. Allen had arrived in Charleston in time for the celebration at Fort Sumter, which was held the next day, April 14, although he chose not to attend. Ironically, Lincoln was shot on the day of the celebration in Charleston.

Charleston, April 14, 1865

Here we are at last, fairly established in the "Teachers' Home"—whose house, do you think, but Chancellor Dunkin's,[4] father's [Harvard] classmate! A queer freak of fortune. It is a great palace of a house, with a fine garden behind it, bushels of roses, a splendid magnolia tree, and the promise of abundant figs. A little creek—an arm of the Ashley river,—makes up to within two or three rods of the house, its banks lined with some graceful waving shrub, loaded with tufts of grayish blossoms.[5] I have the Chancellor's library for my room, & my window looks out upon the garden and the creek. 47 Warren St, if anybody has a map of Charleston.[6] On the whole, I could not be more pleasantly situated & I fancy I shall find my work satisfactory. Mr. Redpath[7] told me at once that he was in quest of just such a person—the care of the schools was too much with his other work. We have been too busy about other things to get my duties and relations fairly marked out, and for a day or two the schools have a holiday.

Today is the great celebration at Fort Sumter;[8] but tickets were very hard to get, and some of the others cared more about going than I did—I never care much for celebrations and crowds—so I am staying at home. The city is jubilant today—at least, we who give a time to its sentiment—over the great news of Lee's surrender,[9] brought down by the Oceanus.[10]

I think Gertrude may be well satisfied with her introduction to the life of a Gideonite, as there never was a jaunt more tiresome and perplexing than ours was until we were fairly landed in this pleasant haven. The ladies were all seasick most of the way down, as the Creole[11] was very crank [liable to lurch] and rolled exceedingly. I myself however had a very pleasant trip. At Hilton Head we left Mr. Lowe[12] in charge of the ladies and their baggage, while Mr. Stebbins[13] and I sallied out to see what chance there was of getting to Charleston. Two of our teachers were to be left at the Head [Hilton Head], so I looked up Mr. Dodge,[14] the Superintendent & asked him to call for them. We couldn't learn of any chance for Charleston, & as our baggage must be got off the Creole, Mr. Severence,[15] the Collector, told me I might get it stored in his basement. That was a great good fortune,—we got a government team, & hurried our baggage away, & by the time it was safely locked up in the basement, the Creole was out in the middle of the stream.

Next, where to spend the night. The hotels were all full, & no private boarding houses could be found—everything chock full. At last, however, we contrived to quarter the ladies on a Miss Lillie,[16] who keeps school there, & who gave them floor & sofa accommodations, while Mr. Lowe, Stebbins & myself were provided with a luxurious counter in a store, where we slept soundly until the store was opened, all too early in the morning. Then we hung round the quarter master's office until we learned that the Golden Gate[17] was going to start at 12, so the other two started off for the ladies, while I with great exertions contrived to get together a team & two darkies & convey our trunks to the dock. It made two loads, and our hearts were cheered just as the first load was starting, by a "man on horseback" who rode up & assured us that unless we hurried the boat would be off. That was about 11, & I remained waiting for the team to return, expecting every minute to see the boat start off with my shawl, over-coat & keys (which I had given Stebbins in case the baggage must be examined). However, it was a good half hour before starting after I arrived there with the second load; I am sorry to say that in the hurry & bustle; one of Miss Chase's[18] trunks slipped thro' our hands, & has not yet turned up. I have written to Alfred Purdie[19] at the Head to look it up. I was very glad to meet on the Golden Gate several St. Helen-ites—Ruggles & his sister, Wells, Williams (the Gen. Sup't), Miss Towne, the Miss Murrays[20] &c., & I had a good time in talking about the Island & its ways. I thought our troubles were now well over, but they had only begun. The Golden Gate is a crazy old craft, unfit for the open sea, & her engine is so worn out that the engineer never left it for a moment but stood watching it as carefully as if it had been the delicate works of a watch.

The wind was pretty fresh, & knocked us about a good deal, & it was a very serious question when the sun set whether the wind would rise or go down. I don't believe the boat could have lived in a very rough sea. Of course we had to go very slowly—the trip is usually made in five or six hours, & we were nearly fourteen. Then the boat was very much crowded, the ladies were some of them terribly sick, & we had neglected (or rather hadn't had time) to bring provisions with us, except a very little. Add to this that the captain[21] had never been at Charleston but once, and had no charts, so that he had to guess his way. Luckily he was a capable, cautious fellow, and when he had fairly lost his way, determined at any rate that he wouldn't run us on any shoals. So when he sounded & found only 4½ fathoms, he headed the boat round, & ran out to sea for an hour. We were all surprised at the way in which we kept turning about, with the rising moon now on the right & now on the left, & some of the passengers were much frightened. The captain didn't let on that he was at all puzzled, & kept his own counsel in spite of all remonstrances and suggestions, but when at last he spied a pilot boat, & got a pilot on board, he confirmed that he hadn't known where he was for over an hour. I assure you we all felt much relieved when the pilot came on board, & enjoyed the rest of the sail very much. It was now midnight, & with a perfectly clear sky, & bright moon. So we stood up the harbor, & came to the dock at about half past one.

We had made the acquaintance of a Mr. Evans on board, [School] Superintendent of James & John's Islands; & he said he had no doubt we could get in at his boarding house, which would be much cheaper than a hotel. So I went up with the ladies, while Mr. Lowe & Stebbins staid to look after the baggage. The reason I went was because I was the one to report to Mr. Redpath as early as possible & get lodgings for the ladies. So immediately after breakfast I set out. Mr. Evans didn't know where to find Mr. Redpath, but he carried me to the house where Mr. Tomlinson[22] rooms, who used to be Gen. Sup't of St. Helena, & is now Gen. Sup't of Freedmen for the whole of Gen. Saxton's[23] department. As I sat waiting for him to come down, who should come in but Mr. Folsom.[24] He is here waiting to go to Georgetown, to take charge of the plantations there. Then Mr. Tomlinson came in, & then Mr. Blake,[25] who has the care of distributing stores to the needy. He directed me where I should find Mr. Redpath, & I immediately set off for the place. Knowing that Lowe & Stebbins were kicking their heels impatiently on the Atlantic Dock, waiting for me to come for the baggage, I hurried Mr. R. as much as I could, but he was delayed here &

interrupted there, & it was a good eleven o'clock before we got to the dock—
he on a mule, I on a horse. As we went along Meeting St., we met the passengers coming up from another boat, & while he stopped to speak to Henry
Wilson,[26]—I don't know which was most surprised, Monroe Mason[27] or I, to
meet the other in Charleston. I think however he was most taken aback to find
me mounted on horse-back.

The rest of the day was employed in moving in, making arrangements
about rooms, board &c., & we were all glad to get to bed early. Our household
is but just started, and hasn't begun to draw rations yet. Until we do, which will
be we hope tomorrow, we are to board at Mrs. Peters'[28] in the next street, where
Mr. Redpath, Mr. Newcomb[29] & several others are boarding. There is enough
furniture in the house for us to get along for a while without buying much. I
have an old couch for a bed, & shall let Gerty have my bed-tick.

It is a very pleasant city, with trees along the streets & great solid looking houses, environed with gardens, & tasteful churches & public buildings.
Much of the city is in ruins, but I haven't seen much of "Shelltown" yet—the
lower part, where Gillmore's[30] missiles came—altho' even as high up as where
we are we see here & there great ugly holes in the walls. Just above Shelltown,
however, is a dismal wash of ruins, where the fire swept over from river to river
in 1861. It stands like the walls of Pompeii. The Unitarian church is precisely on
the edge of this district. It is, I own, with a little compunction that I set up my
bed and trunks in Chancellor Dunkin's library, & one is inclined to look with
a sort of sympathetic pity on this genial and cultivated aristocracy now in exile
at Cheraw & elsewhere. "A nice old gentleman, Sir" said my negro cartman
yesterday of Mr. Dunkin, & for a moment it seemed a hard fate. Then when he
told me his own story,—how he was born free in West Chester Co. Pennsylvania; brought down here as a servant when he was twelve years old, and then
when his master ran away without paying his debts, leaving him to be thrown
in prison for six months, & then sold as a slave for five hundred and eighty dollars; it didn't seem as if even Chancellor Dunkin and Mrs. Gilman[31] need ask
for much sympathy in misfortunes which are only the natural retribution of this
system.

I shan't write any regular journal, but when I have the materials, & feel like
it, will write occasionally a general letter like this, to be sent round. It is a lovely,
cool day. As I sit and write, I hear the mocking-bird, the fife-bird, and the cardinal grosbeak. The fife-bird is peculiarly associated with the White Hills, its
summer habitat, where Mary[32] and I used to listen to it with so much pleasure
on our journey there.

Direct   Care of James Redpath Esq.

Allen did not record all happenings in his journal. Some events, presumably of less interest to his audience of family and friends, he reserved for his diary. According to his diary, he attended a procession of children on the Citadel Green on April 15, 1865. On April 16, he went to the Unitarian Church to hear Beecher;[33] Major Saunders[34] came to dinner, and that afternoon, he went to the Zion Church to hear Garrison.[35] Then, on April 17, he went to the wharf to see Garrison off.

Charleston, Tuesday, Apr. 18, 1865

I am fairly installed in my work—or rather fairly at work, for there is no regular introduction to my position, & indeed no regular position at all as yet. Mr. Redpath is a curious compound. He is an energetic, hard-headed man, with good common-sense ideas about schools, and altho' very positive, perfectly ready to listen to suggestions and adopt them. At the same time, while he has a good deal of organizing & executive ability, he is very deficient in administrative capacity, if I may make that distinction. He forms a good plan, and drives it through, but there is very apt to be a gap somewhere between his conceptions and their execution. Unfortunately, he likes to direct the details, a thing which he doesn't do well; so that he is constantly interfering in the work of his subordinates, and of course, doing it without any system, mars more than he makes. I find a good deal of satisfaction in talking about the school system with him, but I more than doubt whether he will be a satisfactory person to work with, or rather under. He said promptly that he needed my help very much, but I soon found that he hadn't a very distinct idea what he wanted me for, and that if I left it to him my time would be frittered away in unsystematic and unimportant details. So I suggested to him this morning that I should go about and visit all the schools and examine their condition & the capacity of the teachers. He at once acquiesced, & I spent most of the forenoon in the St. Philip's Street School, getting about half thro' it. This school has about 1000 scholars, under Mr. Morse as Principal. There are three departments, or floors, under Miss Buttrick (of Concord), Miss Webb (of Charleston), and Mrs. Morse—the last named however is not well, & Miss Chase, who came down with me, has taken her place temporarily.[36] Gertrude is in her department. Miss Webb has white children, & is considered the best of the indigenous teachers. Her room, however, is noisy, & it sounds queerly to hear her scream out "I say there, if you make that noise again, I'll strap ye." Mr. Redpath's scatter-brained way of managing was well exemplified yesterday in Miss Chase's case. He came in while we were at breakfast, & after telling the other new teachers where he should like to have them go, said to Miss C. that she might go to the Orphan Asylum—

& then walked off. Miss C. was aghast—she didn't know where the Asylum was, nor what she was to do there. However, she went down with the other ladies to Mrs. Hawkes'[37] school in order to go with her to the Asylum. So after dinner down they went—away down to the lower part of the city—& found an empty house—neither occupants nor furniture. I suppose he hadn't succeeded in getting the establishment under weigh, but neglected to inform the ladies that they wouldn't be needed. This appears to be his way—he is always getting at loose ends with the teachers, & yet he is so sound in his views, & so earnest, that they seem to respect and like him. He has one serious fault, of being—I won't say dictatorial, for he is very reasonable and approachable—but he gives directions in a preemptory manner, without consulting beforehand. So I fancy that the position of assistant will be a little difficult—that he won't be disposed to give me a definite sphere & definite powers, or that if he does it, he will be disposed to interfere in it; and for this reason I don't anticipate that I shall care to continue in this relation any longer than till summer. The schools close, I understand, the 15th of July.

We have a pleasant New England household consisting of three gentlemen & nine ladies. The other gentlemen are Mr. Littlefield, a man taller than I, seemingly good solid sort of person; & Mr. Fletcher, from Harvard, a small, young man, a good deal of a talker & a little of a butt in a good-humored way.[38] He has never been away from home before, & he takes all privations & inconveniences in a comically serious way. The rations are disgusting to him, his school-house (better than any I had at Helena) he thinks intolerable, & except for his innate good-humor & his love of flowers & music, I think he would be quite unhappy. Of the ladies, Miss Breck & Miss Green are the most matronly, & assume the management of the household as a sort of matter of course (I do the financial part). Miss Breck is short & lively, Miss Green tall & dark.[39] Miss Southworth (formerly from Northboro') is a pleasant fair haired person, & seems efficient. Miss Chamberlin (Dover, N.H.) is a cultivated, lady-like person, as is also Miss Garland, her comrade, the belle of the household—lively, blonde, & quick-witted—rather fond of shoulderstraps.[40] Of our party, Miss Chase (Exeter) is most of a lady, & I rather think an excellent teacher. Miss White, her comrade, is also tall & good-looking, & I should think would do well. Miss Sargent is short & plain—she does not strike me as very efficient,—yet she is quite bright & intelligent, & may do well.[41] Gertrude & I make the twelve. We have made arrangements with one of the old house-servants—Francis Carrier[42]—to cook for us, he taking our rations & charging us $4.50 a month apiece for extras. I think we shall thus get better living & at less cost than if we undertook to carry it on for ourselves. He feeds us very well, & I hadn't expected to do for less than $ 5. a month. Washing is extra—.60 a dozen for Gertrude & me. In the course of this week I hope to get round to most of the schools—there are eight in all, with about 90 teachers, & 3500 scholars, besides four night-schools, one of which Mr. Fletcher & I started last night.

Wednesday, Apr. 19, 8 p.m.

We received the terrible news today of Mr. Lincoln's assassination, and it has thrown a gloom over the city—for if any rejoice, it must be in secret. A German, who said he ought to have been killed long ago, would have been torn in pieces by the colored people, if he hadn't been rescued by the guard; and more than one have been carried to the prison today for unguarded language. There is fear expressed everywhere, lest there should be some movement on the part of the rebels here; but I apprehend nothing, for of course our authorities will redouble their vigilance, and I think the first effect of the deed will be a reaction of sternness & severity on rebels & rebel sympathizers. A meeting had been called for today at the Unitarian Church, & Mr. Fletcher & I went round. There were about fifteen present, & Dr. Moultrie[43] was chosen to preside. Then Mr. Lowe presented some excellent resolutions, which were seconded by Dr. Mackey[44] (the eminent Unionist) & the meeting adjourned until Friday. It was a very interesting occasion, & I was much struck with the self-command which Dr. Moultrie exhibited. He has been, I suppose, a thorough Secessionist, & it must have been very hard to him to receive, put, and declare passed these strongly loyal resolutions. But he has no doubt decided that any further resistance would only be wickedly needless bloodshed. He is quite old, and was no doubt one of the aristocracy of the place, & it was really melancholy to see him walking sadly away alone, after the meeting was over—and I fancy his shabby clothes tell the story of the result of the rebellion. I was told today of several cases of very old and wealthy persons—Miss Pinckney, over 90, Mrs. Pettigru, &c.—who are now living on the pittance of rice given them by the government.[45] I do not know whether the French Revolution worked a more sweeping ruin of the aristocracy, than that which these proud Carolina families have suffered.

I am told today that it is expected that Mr. Redpath will be appointed Sup't of Schools for the department, with me as Sup't for Charleston. This would give me a definite work and sphere, & would I think be a satisfactory position. This more extended field would be well adapted to Mr. R., who works best on a large scale in a general way, and in pioneer work. He fights the battle of liberalism very intensely & well, & if he has the right sort of persons to attend to details will be—I won't say the best possible, but probably the best attainable person for this position.

Friday morning—

This must be mailed this forenoon. I have written these two general letters, &
shall write others from time to time, but not regularly. I shall write individual
letters chiefly.

*According to his diary, Allen met with Dr. James Kendall Hosmer[46] on April 19, 1865.
(He would meet Hosmer later at Antioch College in Yellow Springs, Ohio, where
they both taught during the 1865–66 school year.) Nicholas Blaisdell[47] called in the
afternoon of April 19.*

Charleston, April 20, 1865

Thursday is the day for rations to be distributed—white & black, I believe,
altho' I have seen none but colored people in the crowd that throngs Hayne St.
all day long. I asked one old man, who said he had just come from the plantation, whether he came with others—"No," he said "Me one and God,—in the
night like a weasel."

*Allen met Lieutenant Colonel Charles Barnard Fox[48] on April 20, 1865. On April
23, he attended a memorial service for President Lincoln, at the Unitarian Church.
Afterwards, he, Captain Soule, and a group of the women teachers, including his
niece Gertrude, visited Magnolia Cemetery. Certain Messrs. Bailey and Randall
called that evening. Captain Pratt[49] and Lieutenant John W. Pollock came to tea on
April 24, then, Colonial Rue Pugh Hutchins called in the evening. On April 26, he
went with a Mr. Compton to look for school houses. In the afternoon, he went to the
Atlantic Dock with a Mr. Macullar. On April 27, he went to see a Mr. Frazier about
church. That evening, Captain Pratt and Adjutant Rice[50] called.*

April 28

Mr. Barrow,[51] a leading Unitarian, who has the charge of giving out tickets for
rations in one of the wards, was giving us some instances of the depth of pov-
erty to which these people are reduced. One old man, who had been a leading
citizen here, brother of a member of Congress, & who is now living in a large
house on the Battery, came to him and asked for a rice-ticket, saying that all he
and his wife had to live on was a silver quarter of a dollar and a 12½ cent piece.
The wife of a wealthy sea-captain had been round that day, almost starved, and
begged him for some assistance. Gov. Aiken,[52] he says, the nicest man I believe
in South Carolina, is living on his wife's jewels. His lands are in the rebel lines,

his slaves are free, his city property is unsalable,—for the present confusion no title can be given[53]—and many others are in just this condition, with no money but confederate, which now of course is utterly worthless. Add to this that they are called on now to pay the arrears of four years' taxes on real estate—a harsh thing, it seems to me—and Mr. Barrow says that Gov. Aiken will have to let two thirds of his houses go to pay the taxes on the other third.

April 29

We saw today the companion piece to the misery Mr. Barrow told me of. We spent this afternoon—Misses Chase, White, Green, Sargent, & Garland, Gertrude & I—on the man of war John Adams; & they carried us over to James Island (Fort Johnson), near where we saw a colony of negroes recently brought here—now half-naked creatures, torn away from their homes & living in wretched huts here, with barely enough to keep them alive. There is no one to blame here. Mr. Pillsbury[54] & Tomlinson are working most energetically to provide for the multitudes who are thrown on their hands. It won't do to let them stay in the city and breed pestilence, and they throng into our lines faster than decent accommodations can be provided for them. It is only an illustration of the way in which the desolation of war has swept over all classes—highest & lowest—and retribution for the national crime has been visited on the innocent as well as the guilty.

Allen records in his diary that certain Messrs. Bailey, Burdette, and McVea and a Dr. Coomb came back from James Island with his party on April 29, 1865.

Apr. 30

I find in Charleston what I have found nowhere else in the South—a class of negroes fit to make citizens of. They are well educated, well dressed, intelligent, of good manners; own property, have built themselves some substantial churches, which they support themselves, and are public spirited & ambitious. Some were free and some were slaves; but they are, I think, mostly of mixed blood. The mulattoes are, I think, generally the best of the native teachers in our schools; & the best single class which I have seen is one of girls of 16 or so—of all shades—taught by a colored young lady, Miss Weston.[55] The first magnolia blossom today.

On April 30, 1865, Allen went with a Mr. Corcoran to "Cardozer's [Cardozo]"[56] for the first of many meetings he had with him. That evening, he went to a Mr. Coryell's home for a singing. Allen attended a prominent Decoration Day (Memorial Day) ceremony at the Washington Race Course on May 1.[57] *He returned from that event with a Mr. Brown. In the evening of May 2, a number of visitors, including Colonel James Chaplin Beecher,*[58] *came to see Allen. In the evening of May 3, General Alfred Stedman Hartwell*[59] *and a Mr. James called on Allen. On May 4, Allen went to see a Mr. Baker,*[60]*and that evening certain Messrs. Bailey and McVey [McVea?] and a Dr. Cre called. On May 5, he visited a Mr. Lewis. Colonel and Mrs. Amiel J. Willard*[61] *called the evening of May 6.*

May 7

The first very hot day. We are luxuriating in blackberries now, which are however not yet so fine as we had last year. We have had a good many visitors this week. Capt. Soule[62] of the 55th, son of Mr. Soule of St. Helena, has been here two or three times; today his regiment has gone to Orangeburg as a sort of internal police. Capt. Goodwin of the same reg't,[63] but detached, on Gen. Potter's staff, was here one evening, & gave me an account of a very important expedition he has lately been on to Sumter—this the very richest part of the state, & a part not before touched by the war. He found a beautiful country, elegant residences & very cultivated people, who did not run away, but who are still intense rebels. Nothing was touched but public property, which was destroyed in great amount, & they brought away 10,000 negroes with them. Not having transportation for quite all, he (Capt. G.) formed the plan of sending the able-bodied men down by themselves in a body. He gave arms to a sufficient number, as protection, & charged them straitly that anyone who should commit any outrage should be shot, & sent them off—not without some misgivings. Arrived at Georgetown, however,—or rather when he followed the track of these men, he found they had gone through with great order & propriety.

Gen. Sherman's army went in a very different style from Potter's, & its track can be known by the broad belt of desolation it left behind it. The stories told of that redoubtable body remind me of the great historic armies, & yet I have never heard of one case of any personal outrage or injury. Such stories as a squad of them strolling into Gen. Saxton's house at Beaufort & eating his dinner, may or may not be true, but show the character which is ascribed to them. Gen. Hartwell I heard say the other day that he couldn't afford to let his men burn houses—it was too demoralizing; & I am very glad he is to be in command at Orangeburg, as he is a gentleman & a man of broad views. He is a graduate of West Newton [English and Classical School] & of Harvard (class of '58 I believe), & called here the other evening, saying he felt as if he was acquainted with me, from having known Nat & James so well.[64]

Our district commander, Gen. Hatch,[65] is a coarse-natured man, but I am inclined to think of very judicious views as regards the colored people. He has just issued an order for all planters to make contracts for labor with their former slaves, subject to military approval; recommending the share system. Mr. Redpath has been getting up a colored "Home Guard" in which I reluctantly consented to be a first lieutenant; & the other day Gen. Hatch called the officers together, & talked to us about our duties and, the influence we were to try to exert upon the colored people. His views were very sensible, & I think he is disposed to a just & judicious policy. I am sorry to say that the influence brought to bear upon the negroes hasn't been altogether the best. They have been encouraged to make their entrance into freedom too much of a triumph & exaltation—to think more of their new rights than of the duties they bring with them.

There has been too much time spent in celebrations and processions. Mr. Redpath has had much to do with this. You talk with him, and his views are very sound and judicious—but put him into the midst of the people, & he boils over with enthusiasm, & thinks of nothing but the excitement of the moment. Well, we must never expect to find perfect instruments for any human work, but it seems too bad that we should find so few calm common-sense minds—so few except unpractical enthusiasts like Gen. Saxton & Mr. Redpath or pro-slavery men like many of the officers. (Mr. Redpath is only unpractical, however, in this way; for doing anything he is admirable.) Luckily Gen. Saxton has a very fine set of superintendents, instructed by their Port Royal experience—Tomlinson, Gannett, Folsom, Alden,[66] Pillsbury &c.—& there is a class of officers, like Hartwell, Goodwin, Soule &c., who are being trained in a splendid school, & who will be eventually among our best men to depend upon in these matters. There is no doubt that if a young man escapes the moral perils of a soldiers' life, it gives him a knowledge of men and a practical cast of mind which is hard to get any other how.

Mr. Redpath showed me the other day a curious paper—a memorial presented by some of the free colored people of Charleston to the Confederate government, offering their services, and speaking of themselves as discarded from the best families of South Carolina. He says this class (from which our best native teachers, Miss Weston & others) were unwilling at first to come into the school arrangement with the mass of the blacks, but wished to be by themselves. Many of them were slave-holders, & very harsh ones at that. They form an excellent parallel to the aristocratic plebeians in the early Roman republic.

The more I hear, the more I am convinced that there is no materials here to make a loyal government out of, except the mechanics & the colored people.

I called at Dr. Mackey's the other evening, & he said "Any loyal public meeting now would only mislead the North." Military rule must be kept up until by emigration, by natural legislation on the suffrage, & by the healing power of time, there is gradually built up a loyal community large enough to be established with power.

Allen went to see a Captain Hewcy about a house on May 8, 1865. He sang, as he often did, in the evening, and certain Messrs. Burnell and Curry called.

Charleston, Tuesday, May 9, 1865, 9 P.M.

I had my Normal Class[67] this afternoon, for the third time. I have this twice a week, and I think it is the pleasantest and most useful part of my time. I found, on going the rounds of the schools, that the southern-born teachers—about 70 in number—were so destitute of anything like good methods, that I have made a plan to invite them to a class twice a week, & I find the plan working very well. There were 34 present today—the largest number I have had. I spend half an hour in giving them ideas of discipline, then ask them to bring up any points that have occurred to them; then we pass to methods of teaching, in which I have an advanced class, which I generally get one of the teachers to take, while I attend to the mass. Mrs. Hawkes, Principal of the "Normal School," will assist me regularly, or alternate with me, when she gets time.

There are three large schools—the Normal, the St. Philip's Street (Mr. Morse) and the Morris Street (Mrs. Pillsbury);[68] of these the Normal contains the highest colored classes, the St. Philip's the highest white. The Normal School (only so called on account of the building in which it is kept) is perhaps the best worth visiting of all. Mrs. Hawkes (from Manchester, N.H.) is an untiring, and admirable person; and Misses Green and Garland are principals of the departments under her. Next in importance to these is the Ashley Street school, under Miss Chamberlin, where Gertrude teaches. This is entirely girls, and Miss C. makes it a model school, by her firm, gentle & lady-like discipline. There are six other schools, of less importance, and about 4000 pupils. We hope to get the High School building next week, & shall probably give it to Miss Chase.

Except in my Normal Class, I don't feel as if I were doing much good. There is no need of two superintendents, & altho' Mr. Redpath gives a good deal of his time to other things, so that he can't possibly give the minute attention to the schools which they need, he still retains their management in his hands, leaving me with a queer and embarrassing sphere of powers. He wishes me to act entirely independently, & so I do—giving directions just as if he doesn't exist. Only every little while he will put in his oar and just tip over everything that I have been doing. So we hitch along—very friendly, & I like him much, but with little satisfaction. Pretty soon he is going to Savannah (for a short time) & then I shall have full swing.

On May 10, 1865, Allen met a Mr. McGill[69] of Savannah at the St. Philip Street School on May 12. In the evening of May 13, he and Gertrude called on Miss Octavia C. Page.[70]

May 14

We had a meeting on Thursday, that I think will be historical.[71] It was called by some of the "leading citizens," in order to prepare the way for reconstruction. They appointed a committee of themselves to draft resolutions; the only Union men on the committee were Mr. Barrow, & a young lawyer named Tharin,[72] who was once publically whipped for his Unionism. I was delayed by business, & only learned by hearsay of the opening scenes at the meeting. It seems a few colored people went in & took seats by themselves, but were turned out by the guard, the meeting cheering vociferously. Just then Mr. Redpath came up & met them coming out, very much excited & asking him "Mr. Redpath are we going to stand this." "Wait here" said he, & hastened off to find Col. Gurney, the Post commander.[73] Not finding him, he returned thro' the Hall, & asked the commander of the guard if he knew that Col. Gurney had told the colored men [they] had a right to attend the meeting. Back stood the bayonets, & in streamed the black men, cheering. Up then jumped Col. Lynah[74] (the chairman—well described by our colored men as "a broken-down aristocracy") & declared the meeting adjourned. Then Macbeth,[75] the mayor of the city, & a red-hot secessionist from the start, made a speech, laying his hand on his heart & declaring that he was a Union man, & that owing to the disturbance the meeting would stand adjourned. The officer of the guard at this mounted the platform & said that there had been no disturbance & would be none; he was there to keep order & should do it. It was at this moment that I arrived—meeting the Irishmen pouring out of the hall, swearing about the "d— niggers."

After the officer, Col. Lynah pronounced the meeting adjourned, & they began to go away. A few however hung around uneasily, & I happened to be standing by Mr. Edw. Mackey[76] who said earnestly "We Unionists must organize now—where's Tharin?" Tharin was on the platform, & after a few hasty words between them, he came forward, & asked the Union men to remain and take some action in this crisis. Putting it to vote whether the meeting should reorganize, there had been such an exodus of the secessionists that it was carried decidedly in the affirmative. At the "contrary-minded," "No!" shouted Col.

Seymour,[77] adding in a lower tone "and much good may it do you, d— you!" Tharin then proposed that Mr. Barrow & Mr. Edw. Mackey should be a committee to wait upon Col. Lynah & invite him to resume the chair. This was a master-stroke, for when the committee announced that he declined, it was equivalent to giving up the contest. Henceforth this clique, Lynah, Macbeth, Seymour, &c., will stand as Winthrop does in Boston.[78]

On Lynah's declining, Mr. Barrow was appointed to the chair & Mr. Mackey Secretary, when Mr. Tharin read a long preamble followed by some short, biting resolutions, aimed against "the oligarchy which has brought desolation & ruin upon the state," & urging that there should be no reconstruction until it can be done in the interest of the non-slaveholding class—that the members of the oligarchy should be allowed to come in humbly in the wake of the movement, but not to take any lead in it. Then resolutions were passed unanimously by about two dozen white Charlestonians—besides northerners & negroes. Gen. Hatch has not permitted the publication of the report, but it will no doubt come out in some northern papers. It seems to me that this meeting will rank as an historical event—that it marks the assumption of power by the class of genuine loyalists. Dr. Mackey's good sense, firmness, & calm eloquence are missed here. Tharin is a young man, bitter & perhaps self-seeking. Mr. Barrow is timid, & is only kept up to the scratch by Mr. Stebbins' influence. I dined there today, & had a long discussion with him, & between us I think he will come out right—he certainly will when Dr. Mackey gets back.

I called the other day on Mr. Proctor, brother of Cousin Lydia, & have met him twice since in the street.[79] I had a long talk with him the other day, about negro-equality, which is also Mr. Barrow's bugbear. Both of them think it will come to blood-shed, & I tell them that thinking so is one way to bring it about—that if things are left to their natural workings they will settle themselves. In my Normal Class, for instance, I notice that the white & colored teachers in many instances sit together, lean on each other's shoulders &c. This would not have been so two months ago. Mr. Redpath is often injudicious in pushing the colored people forward & jarring against the feelings of the whites unnecessarily; & much mischief is done by a noisy fellow named Hurley,[80] who talks to them in a very inflammatory style.

I have been talking with Mrs. Hawkes this afternoon, who was yesterday in James Island, & says the people are suffering terribly; but food is now coming in from Beaufort.

Allen called on Captain Grace[81] at the Arsenal on May 15, 1865. He visited schools with Redpath and his wife[82] on May 16, and Mr. Burnell called again in the evening.

May 17

In the enclosed map, I have given the situation of all our schools, and also of the High School Building, which we hope to have under our control soon. The number of colored scholars has fallen off lately, by reason of sickness and of the large emigration to the islands. New white children come in every day, however, and we ought to have increased accommodations. We are living in a very healthy & cool part of town. There is always a breeze from Ashley River & Bennett's Mill pond blowing in at my window, and I never know how hot it is until I go out. My manner of life is as follows. I go out at nine o'clock to our office at the Morris St. school-house, to attend to any business there may be. From 10 to 1 I am visiting schools, arranging about books, teachers &c.

Mr. Redpath gives me full control now over all the internal arrangements of the schools. In the afternoon I have an hour or two to myself, and at 4½ there is the Normal Class. Monday & Thursday is the regular Normal Class, or methods of teaching & discipline; Wednesday, I have a class in Reading; and Tuesday & Friday Mr. Stebbins has one in Geography. These are for the southern teachers; then for those who wish to fit themselves for teaching, we have just started a Normal School under Mrs. Morse—it is an experiment as yet, & may not succeed. But the best Normal instruction is the daily routine of teaching under the eyes of our skillful northern principals. The poorest teachers have now been nearly all sifted out, & those who are left (about 50 white and 25 colored) are improving rapidly, & will make good teachers in time. About twenty five of them are very constant at the Normal Class.

On May 19, 1865, Allen met Bishop Payne and Colonel Hallowell.[83] In the evening, he and Gertrude went to the home of Mrs. Morse, where he played cribbage with Colonel Hutchins and others.

May 21

It is very gratifying to see how the association of white & colored teachers together in school & in the Normal Class is gradually destroying the prejudices. When the schools were first opened, Mr. Redpath tells me they wouldn't associate at all—now I see them leaning on each other's shoulders, & sitting side by side. But it is curious that the prejudices had two grades, & the mulattoes were at first as exclusive as the whites—Miss Weston, who has the best colored class, refused at first to have any blacks in it. This school system is a great opening wedge, & Mr. Redpath deserves great credit for it. The work that has been accomplished in only three months in organization, discipline & instruction is really astonishing, & is going to do more to break down prejudice than anything else. And gradually public sentiment is changing. Mr. R. was telling me the other day of an interesting case—a young lady who at first wished to have a situation in a school, & needed it, but wasn't willing to teach colored children, & couldn't take the oath, as she told him with tears in her eyes. What induced her to go to hear [William Lloyd] Garrison,[84] I don't know; but when he finished she declared that she was converted, & was willing to take a colored class. So we shall employ her when we have a vacancy. Mrs. Morse has 8 scholars already in her Normal School: four white & four colored.

I don't know that I mentioned calling to see Mr. Proctor, brother of Cousin Lydia. He is quite old and nearly blind. He was shelled out of his house in Wentworth St., & lives with a relative very near me. His furniture was sent up to Columbia, where it was burnt—the loss by that fire seems to have been very great, so many people had sent their property there to be out of harm's way. Of three sons in the rebel army, one died last Fall, in our hospital; one was at home on sick furlough when the city was occupied; & the third has just returned from Johnston's army. They told the story of Mrs. Black, a relative of Mr. Proctor, which I suppose is like hundreds of others. Mrs. Black[85] with her children & her husband's sister was at Columbia; & she wishing to send the children to her friends in Boston, the sister and children joined Sherman's army & followed to Wilmington. The army cut thro' the country like a ship thro' the waves—the water closing in at once behind, & so for weeks nothing was heard from them. Meantime the sister engaged passage on the Gen. Lyon,[86] & word came here to that effect, & Mr. Proctor wrote by a private hand to the mother that all had perished. But word has just come that they were prevented by sickness from going on the Lyon, & that all the family—except one sickly child who died on the march—had arrived in Boston, in the clothing in which they left Columbia—not having had a change in all these weeks.

The destitution here is on the increase. Capt. Pratt, the Provost Marshal, tells me that 200,000 bushels of rice have been distributed in these three months—but the supply is nearly exhausted, & he doesn't know where more is to come from. Mr. Stebbins attends the funeral this afternoon of a child that died of sheer starvation, and others he knows that are following. One very worthy family where he visits—the mother & daughter have between them enough clothing for one to go out decently in the streets. And in all the shops are nice articles—dress patterns &c.—bought perhaps before the war, & now brought in & sold to buy bread. On the islands along the coast which have been settled with negroes from the country, there is terrible suffering—but now they think they have means provided to feed them. If it were not for the blackberries, they must have starved.

At Mr. Redpath's urgent request, I consented to take the first lieutenancy in Co. C. of the Colored Home Guard. Being brought thus in contact with a large body of intelligent men, I decided to turn it to account in a direction which I had been thinking of before—& have invited them to attend a course of lectures on the Government of the United States, which I shall try to make simple & practical. Mr. Barrow and some others are getting up a Union League, and he asks me to repeat this course, or something corresponding, before the League. So I am likely to have my hands full.

This song is sung considerably in our schools.

> Nobody knows the trouble I see—Nobody knows but Jesus.
> "   "   " " "   —Glory Hallelu!

> One morning I was a-walking down—O yes Lord!
> I saw some berry a-hanging down—O yes Lord!

> I pick de berry an' I suck de juice
> Jes' as sweet as honey in de honey-comb

> John saw de mystery—
> De angel a-walking on de sea—

> I carry de mastyr to Pilate hand
> I find no guilty in de man

> Sometime I'm up—sometime I'm down—
> Sometime I almost to de ground

> What make de mastyr pray so bold?
> He got salvation in he soul.

> Altho' you hear me pray so bold,
> I'se troubles and trials here below.

> What make old Satan hate me so?
> 'Cause he had me once and let me go.

> If you want to see old Satan run,
> Just fire off de gospel gun.

In the evening of May 21, 1865, Allen went with some of the lady teachers and Captain Emerson and Captain White[87] to see the rebel ram.[88] He talked with Mr. Carrier in the evening of May 22.

Charleston, May 24, 1865

I was at Mr. Barrow's last night & met there a Mrs. Trainor [Traynor],[89] who did a great deal for our prisoners during the war. One man—who had escaped by hanging in the water under a wharf by his hands from eleven o'clock until day-break, and who took the yellow fever after the exposure—she nursed thro' his sickness, only one person besides herself knowing that he was in the house, and then got him safely into our lines. Her mother was well off—had $10,000 in confederate money—all gone now, & they are reduced to beggary. The old mother walked two miles yesterday and back to get her rations. There were three ladies there, & it was very interesting to hear them talk over their recollections of the bombardment, and of their selling off one possession after another—watches &c.—to keep themselves alive. I was told of one German, who helped off a great many of our prisoners.[90] One night he got 11 off to our fleet, & agreed with them that a gun should be fired for every one that arrived safely. So in the night the city was aroused by eleven heavy guns—and nobody knew what it meant but this old German.

There is no question that our prisoners were treated barbarously here, altho' less so than at Andersonville.[91] I have visited the race-course,[92] the great open field where they were kept night and day, in all weathers and at all seasons, with no shelter. They had enough to eat, I believe, such as it was, but I think an insufficiency of water; and when they died, which they did in great numbers, the dead of each day were buried by themselves, with little numbered stakes to mark them. I suppose there was a register kept of the numbers, but it may be lost. No man was allowed to give them anything, nor any negro; but the women—Irish women—would fight their way up to them (for the guards wouldn't treat women as they would men) and give them something to eat & drink, and wash their heads and necks. And the negroes would throw bread &c. to them as they were marched thro' the streets, which they would catch at and devour like dogs—this was the men who were brought from Andersonville. As for the brutality of the guards in driving them like cattle thro' the streets—the stories are almost incredible.[93]

Allen experienced health problems between May 24 and June 4, 1865. Gertrude came down with a fever during this time as well. In the evening of May 27, Colonel Willard, Mr. Redpath, and Colonel Hallowell called. Allen, along with Mr. Stebbins, Mr. Fletcher, and Miss Green, visited John C. Calhoun's grave on May 28. Captains Pratt (Provost Marshal) and Emerson[94] called in the evening of May 29. In the afternoon of May 30, Allen visited Judge Cooley.[95] *Allen noted in his diary that June 1 was National Fast Day (held in memory of President Lincoln). Mr. Whitton called on him that day. Allen and Gertrude went to get ice cream in the afternoon of June 3. He later noted, for the first time, that Gertrude was sick.*

June 4, Sunday

It is a hot and unhealthy season, and everybody says we must close schools by the first of July. I shall very likely remain myself a while longer, altho' I don't now see any special reason why I should. I know there will be a good deal to do at the North, in the way of making arrangements for the Fall, altho' it is not certain that I shall return here.

Charleston has undergone a great change since we came here. Then nobody was to be seen in the streets—no goods to speak of in the stores—it was a gloomy, deserted city. Now the streets are crowded, and with a better class of people—graybacks swarm—I think there must be more rebel than Union soldiers in the city. The shops too on King Street present a gay and attractive appearance. Business is reviving and with it I hope the destitution in the city will be lessened. I am told however that the suffering is on the increase, and it must be so with those who have no business, and who had at first only a little property on which to live. That is gone, and there is nothing for them now but charity or starvation.

Almost every day some girl of this class comes to me and asks for a situation as teacher, with such a story of destitution as cannot help moving my sympathies, even when I can do nothing—for we have no vacancies, and you wouldn't believe the want of qualifications in these applicants. I have been having the Southern teachers examined, and giving certificates of two grades—the first, as qualified to teach all the common branches; the second, to those who are thorough through Long Division, with a little knowledge of Geography. In six schools, with 38 teachers, I have found one qualified for the first grade, and perhaps ten for the second; and this I think will be about the average. I do not know whether I mentioned the Normal School that we have established, under Mrs. Morse. She has nearly 40 scholars, about 10 of them white; and we shall probably make arrangements for Normal instruction for these and the present teachers to be kept up thro' the vacation. We have made arrangements to send Mr. Littlefield to open a school at Orangeburg, and Mr. Fletcher at Summerville, with a view to operations in the Fall; but Mr. L. is not well enough, & I am not sure we can spare Mr. F., as we have lost several teachers; so we may put it off until Fall.

I hear reports of various visits from the interior of the state. In some places slavery is existing in its fullest form—indeed, with extra severity, owing to the uneasiness of the negroes. In self-defense or rather defense of the system they often shoot them down with very little provocation. But wherever they are near any of our troops, especially if the officers are of the right stamp, the planters come in with more or less willingness and make contracts with their hands, giving them generously half of the crops, besides supporting them thro' the season. This I think very reasonable, or rather liberal. There are some other places which are abandoned by the masters, and carried on by the people on their own account. According to their own statements, they have in large crops, which are doing well. In some such instances the owners have come back, taken the oath, and then made a contract for half the crop—it seems unjust to the negroes, but of course everything depends on the final action of government about the lands. In still other districts there is almost anarchy, with bands of guerrillas shooting down negroes and overawing the community. Near Georgetown matters were in a very bad condition, until at last the negroes organized to retaliate—caught the ring-leader, took him into the woods and shot him. Since then there has been peace, and the region is comparatively safe.

Doctor Hawkes visited Allen in the company of Dr. Marcy[96] during the afternoon of June 4, 1865. Allen visited the Ashley Street and Normal Schools on June 5 with Folsom, a Mr. Ritchie, and Captain James Morris Walton.[97] On June 6, Gertrude became worse, and she moved down to Allen's room, where she could be more comfortable. He sat with her most of the day on June 8. As her conditioned worsened, he called in Dr. De Saussure[98] to see her on June 9. Allen wrote in his diary on June 10, "Gertrude died at 5½. Wrote to Prentiss & carried letter to steamer. With Stebbins to make arrangements for funeral. In aft. To Dr. D's. Funeral at 5." That night, he spent the night at Mrs. Parker's (Mrs. Peters's?). On June 12, he noted that a Miss Dean came to dinner. That evening he went to Roper Hospital, where he met Dr. Briggs.[99] Later, a Captain Perry and a Lieutenant Barber called.

Charleston, June 17, 1865

I have written so fully of Gertrude's sickness and death, that I need not say anything more now.[100] It came upon us with terrible suddenness—we never thought of danger until Thursday fore noon, and Saturday morning at 5½ she passed away. Monday morning Mr. Fletcher & Miss Chamberlin trimmed the Ashley Street school-house with black, and Mr. Redpath went over—I myself was detained until later—and called the scholars together to say a word to them. But he had scarcely begun, when they—her scholars—burst into such sobbing and weeping that he could say nothing. Their grief was more eloquent, he told me, than anything he could say; and they were so overcome that there was nothing to do but dismiss school. One girl, Minda Robertson, cried so long

& so bitterly that she completely exhausted herself, and fainted away.[101] And a few days later, when Miss Chamberlin asked them to sing "Nobody knows the trouble I see," Minda asked to be let go out—she said "Miss Allen was so fond of that song, that she couldn't stay in the room while it was sung."

I listened to a very interesting conversation the other day between some ladies belonging to the very highest aristocracy, & a planter from the country, who had just come down to take the oath. They talked with perfect freedom before me; I do not know whether they knew or not I was a Yankee. At any rate, there was very little that was unpleasant in their tone. They talked with great good humor of their privations and hardships. The gentleman had been visiting a family of their relatives, & was describing the various menial occupations in which he found them engaged—one was cutting wood, one washing hominy at the well, &c. And I fancy that these children of luxury, who have never known before what it was to tie their own shoe-strings, are enjoying themselves with a zest in their new avocations. They expressed a good deal of disappointment at the way in which their servants—to whom they were so much attached—had deserted them, and a good deal of fear that there would be trouble from the laziness of the negroes, & the extravagant expectations they had been led to entertain. The Yankees will have their hands full—was their idea, and that they themselves had nothing to do but stand by & look on. One of the ladies spoke of "the colored people." "Do you call 'em colored people?" said he, "I always call 'em niggers; I always have called 'em niggers, & I always shall." On the whole I doubt whether these people don't enjoy themselves quite as well now as they ever did. There is however a great difference in different neighborhoods, as to the amount of destitution, & the promise for the future. Gen. Hartwell says that about Orangeburg the crops promise very badly, & that the wealthy planters are looking calmly forward to actual starvation. At present everything they have to live on is rice & hominy—nothing else, not even salt—and water to drink. If the crops do turn out a failure, we must prepare for immense & wholesale charity in the Fall.

Sunday, June 18

Friday there was a meeting to bid good-bye to Mr. Redpath, and a queer time they had. After the meeting was organized, a colored man named Dickerson[102] —the most prominent speaker among them—got up and moved some resolutions "that the thanks of the colored people be presented to Mr. James Redpath, for his untiring labors in their behalf, and the good advice he has given them,—to be civil and respectful, especially to the rebels, and the schools he has organized &c. &c." The object, I suppose, was to let it be understood that Mr. R. had always used his influence to make the colored people orderly &

mannerly, as is the case; but this bungling resolution excited violent opposition and indignation—as if Mr. Redpath would encourage them to be "respectable" to rebels. Finally, as nobody cared what resolutions were passed—wanting to hear Mr. R. speak,—they were declared passed; and after the meeting was over, Mr. Pillsbury, Mr. Morse & Dr. Hawkes got together & wrote a new set, which were printed in the next day's paper!

Then Mr. R. made his speech, and I am sorry to say the part of Hamlet was left out. It was a golden opportunity to impress on these people that they must not entertain too unreasonable expectations with regard to land & suffrage—that they must earn them, before they had them. This I know is Mr. R.'s opinion, but when he gets on the stand, he forgets all his conservatism & on this occasion he spoke of nothing but to praise them for loyalty, desire to learn &c.,—all very well, but not the thing needed just then. There is one thing about Mr. R.,—I think he has not the faculty of reading character, & the set of colored men who have been brought to the surface & made much of, are, I think, a conceited & empty-headed set. This Dickerson has considerable "orational lore" as he calls it, being graceful and fluent; but is shallow & untrustworthy. They have started a Library—the Redpath Institute—which has fallen entirely into the hands of such men; & Mr. R. is conscious of the failure & is very desirous that Stebbins & I should go in & give the thing a new turn. So we are looking up some better men, & I think we shall contrive to reorganize the society. There are really enough sensible, intelligent, sober-minded men, who can be relied upon. The Union League is in equally bad hands. It was organized by a fellow named Hurley from Charleston—a noisy, unscrupulous demagogue—& is having a bad influence on the colored people, & Mr. R. urges very strongly that Stebbins, Morse & the rest of us shall go in & counteract these influences.

A "Memorandum" in Allen's 1865 diary contains his transcription of the following resolution:

Resolved

That the thanks of the loyal people of Charleston, S.C., is hereby tendered to Mr. James Redpath, for his untiring devotion to the elevation of the Freedmen, & the good advice he has given them, to be always civil & respectful, and most especial to the rebels. And when we could not afford to them kindness, it would be better to pass them bye, when he was assured, that they manifest ill will toward him, he would only say, as the Xn [Christian] was taught, Forgive them they know not what they do. Their conduct & its success has run them mad, such Xn forbearance, is our opinion, make him the greatest morilist of this age &c.

Resolution drawn up by John C. Chavis, Charleston, S.C.[103]

In the morning of June 18, 1865, Allen talked with Mr. and Mrs. Parker.[104] In the afternoon of June 19, he went to see a black barber named Quash in whom he had confidence because he was respected by the "colored people."

June 21

Mr. Alfred Dunkin[105] (son of the Judge), has just got home from the North. He was tax-collector, & was taken prisoner. Mr. Carrier says he always was a Union man, & before the war never would own a slave. His first words to him were "Well Francis, all this foolishness is over, and now we'll start afresh and begin things over again." From what Mr. C. tells me—and others—I think there were more quiet Unionists of this stamp than we generally suppose—men who bent with the storm, but who now are sincerely anxious for peace & Union. I had a long talk the other evening with Mrs. Clausen,[106] one of the colored teachers; a middle-aged woman. It was at Mrs. Hawkes', who had invited in all the teachers of her school, four colored and about eight white, & there they spent the evening together without the slightest appearance of constraint or exclusiveness. Mrs. C. says that the middle classes are in their hearts—delighted at the overthrow of the aristocracy; but they have been so completely overawed by them that they do not even yet dare to realize the change. I can see this in Mr. Barrow's case, who only comes up by very slow degrees to understand the new order of things. According to Mrs. C. the Rhetts were a sort of ruling family. Barnwell Rhett,[107] (class of '49) editor of the Mercury, and Alfred,[108] (my classmate) were the bullies of secession, and everybody was afraid of them. It was Alfred who shot young Calhoun[109] in a duel, just at the beginning of the war, in a quarrel about rank. Calhoun did not wish to fight until the war was over, but was badgered into it; and by killing him Rhett obtained promotion to his place as colonel. Mrs. C. told me of one man—who was well off—but who is now employed by his own former slave as a groom.

The suffering continues to increase, and Stebbins is hard at work relieving it. I called with him yesterday to see a Mrs. Oxley, who is living in a wretched hovel with her paralytic daughter.[110] The house was struck with a shell, as nearly all have been, and as we went on the piazza, torn all to pieces, we could see a great pool of standing water under it. Mrs. O. and her daughter between them have enough clothes for one to go out upon the street decently clad. Stebbins asked her if she had such & such things. No pepper no tea or coffee—a leetle salt—Mrs. Little[111] sent her some sugar, but that was about gone—Mr. Barrow sent her some candles, but they were used up—mustard she hadn't tasted for four years &c. &c. I am going to carry her round some mosquito netting, of which I have more than I need.

A Mr. Ainsworth called on Allen on June 19, 1865. In the evening of June 20, Stebbins, Weston, Beaird,[112] a Mr. Spencer, and a Mr. Morrison called on him. On June 21, Lieutenant Haviland called.[113]

June 22

I was at tea last night at Mr. Barrow's, & had quite a talk with him. He says in his ward—in which he is at the head of the committee for giving ration tickets—there are reported 60 colored, and 381 whites who need assistance. There are eight wards, and out of them all I think his has the largest proportion of needy colored. The proportion is less, however, for this reason—that able-bodied colored people are reported not to him to receive aid, but to the Provost Marshal to be carried over to the islands, where they can get work.

Allen met a Mr. Bailies on June 22, 1865. On June 25, Mr. Randall came to dinner, and Stebbins and Miss Prescott[114] called.

Charleston, June 27, 1865

We are having splendid weather—hot in the sun, but very comfortable in my room as I sit writing in my shirt-sleeves. Stebbins and I have been overhauling the "Redpath Institute," to see if we can straighten things out, which I fear we can't do. It has no pecuniary basis, has a debt of some $200, with no income, & is entirely ruled by a conceited, obstinate fellow named Chavis.[115] The fact is it was a premature movement. The negroes are not in a condition yet to support anything that requires a constant outlay, & I am afraid that Mr. Redpath in starting it did not count the cost. Then they have been so dissatisfied with Chavis' management that one by one most of the members have dropped off, leaving only four now. The constitution is a curiosity, and was devised by Chavis in the most thoroughly oligarchical spirit that I have ever seen. It restricts the members to 12, who are the sole proprietors of all the property—the shares being $5. each; forbids any member to sell his share to any outsider, and has the officers chosen for an unlimited time. So we talked with Chavis & told him that the thing, in order to succeed, must be carefully organized, on a democratic basis. But he, while agreeing to some suggestions, was so bent on keeping the power as at present in his own hands, that we finally gave up that the thing must fall thro'. We had, however, consulted with some other better men, and interested them in starting anew next Fall. Quash,[116] the barber, seems to be the most generally respected of all the colored people here. He is full black—his father was a native African—but he is a man who has read a good deal, knows some Latin, and speaks very correctly and sensibly. He is coming up to talk with me about getting himself educated.

When Mr. Redpath left, he left the management of the schools in my hands, as Assistant Superintendent. I thought it was proper that I should call on Gen. [heretofore Colonel] Gurney, commanding the post to have my position recognized. I expected a cool reception, for I knew he and Mr. Redpath were at sword's points. And true enough, he was very bitter upon Mr. R., whose course he thinks has done a great deal of harm. I, for my part, could not but agree with him in many points, but still defended Mr. R, where I thought he had done well. I could not deny, however, that Mr. R. has been very much out of the way in not reporting to the Gen'l before going North—the Gen'l was justly angry at this breach of discipline, & said that he intended removing Mr. R. from his position as Sup't of Education in Charleston (his appointment from Gen. Saxton is merely for colored schools). My appointment from him (Mr. R.) he could not recognize (it seems Mr. R. never reported my appointment to Head Quarters, as he should); still, he should be glad to have me act under his own appointment for the rest of the term. So my present title is not Assistant, but Acting Sup't of Ed. Gurney is not a strong man. His views are in the main judicious, but I fancy he is easily manipulated by the citizens.

Gannett and Stetson[117] have been here a couple of days, leaving Sunday; & I had a nice time with them. Gannett told me a good deal about Savannah, where I judge the colored people had found better leaders than here; & are in a more healthy condition. He finds fewer really loyal persons there than I here—either because there are fewer, or because he is thrown into a different set from me. It isn't that he sets a higher standard, for his expression was that by loyalty he meant simply a preference for the United States government. He found very little of that in Savannah, but I am sure there is some here. I fancy that the colonies on the islands are in a much better condition there than those here. They started early enough to get their crops begun in season; while here they have come straggling along all thro' the spring and summer. Then there are some very capable negroes who have the lead there, & they have some very successful municipal governments on their various islands. The island (Skidaway) has a black governor.[118]

In the evening of June 27, 1865, Allen talked with Mr. Burnell. On June 30, E. Whitton called on Allen before school. He met Captain Montell later that day, and the Reverend Toomer Porter called.[119] He met a Mr. Griffin at the Pillsburys' on July 1. He took the 7 A.M. train to Orangeburg on July 2 and dined later that day with Miss Lee and Captain Walton.

Columbia, July 5, 1865

The fourth of July at Columbia, as an honored guest at a colored celebration, and after a journey as quiet and safe as in the heart of Massachusetts—isn't this a wonder for the year of our Lord 1865? I left Charleston Sunday morning in the cars, not having been able to get thro' my business in time to leave Saturday. I had as companions three rebel officers, on their way home from Fort Delaware,[120] and I talked with them most of the way. Two of them belonged to the clan of small planters, & nothing could be more satisfactory than the friendliness with which they accepted the new order of things, and expected the regeneration of South Carolina from it. "I've found out" said one "that this war was got up by the rich men who wanted to keep their niggers—but the poor men have had to do the fighting." The third belonged to the aristocratic family of Mazyck,[121] (Mazeék) and I had a long and full discussion of him with him of slavery, state rights &c. He acknowledged that both were things of the past—"I've taken the oath to support the constitution under your construction, and now I am bound to fight to put down secession—but I believe in it as much as ever." Finally, after a long discussion on the future of the colored race—as to which he took a gloomy view (that they wouldn't work, but must perish) I said "Well, we all desire the same thing, the return of peace & prosperity & the success of free labor." "Peace" said he "has come, and prosperity will come—but not for them."

I had likewise in Charleston a long talk with an Episcopal clergyman, Rev. Toomer Porter—a strong secessionist—and the ground he took was, if sincere, all that one could wish. "We went into this thing sincerely and earnestly; we have fought well; we have failed, and been thoroughly beaten; and now we take the oath in good faith, and mean to live as loyal subjects of the United States. We believe our doctrine of State-rights the true one—but that has been decided against us. Providence has seen fit to abolish slavery—contrary to our wishes and convictions—and now we wish for the best welfare of our former slaves, & hope that free labor will succeed—altho' we fear not."

We reached Orangeburg at about 2, and as soon as I could I went to see Gen. Hartwell, who had promised to make arrangements to send us here, with Miss Lee, one of our teachers (from Templeton) who came up the day before, wishing to visit her former teacher, Miss Campbell.[122] Mr. Jenks also, a connection of the Pillsbury's, & a very good fellow, we met there, & invited to accompany us.[123] The General gave us an ambulance, with a picked driver, & a pair of strong mules, and ordered it to report at 5. By the mistake of the wagon-master, however, we got a pair of most wretched, broken-down horses, & instead of coming to the hotel, the ambulance went to the General's head-quarters, where I found it at 6, after we had waited long & impatiently. So we lost the best hour of the day, and we toiled over the worst sandy road I ever saw until 5, making in that time about 24 miles, when we stopped at a little house to which the General had directed us, occupied by a preacher named Cupp, a refugee from Virginia. Mr. C. was away, but his wife we found a pleasant, lady-like person; and we enjoyed the place much. It is a poor country to start with, and Sherman had stripped it of everything—Mrs C. could provide us nothing but dry corn-bread & coffee. However, she stewed some peaches, & cut up some tomatoes, & onions in vinegar, & we did very well. They left the Valley of Virginia last Fall, lived with four years of constant warfare, & came here just in time for Sherman.[124] As we sat on the piazza in the cool of the evening, the 56th New York reg't came straggling by, on their way to Newberry, & encamped near us. Some two or three dozen of them came in the yard for water, or to try to buy something, & it was very gratifying to see how perfectly respectful & orderly they were—supposing us, of course, to be rebels. There was not the slightest indiscretion.

Mixed in with them were rebel soldiers, on their way home from prison, & the next morning on the road to Columbia, it was a chance, when we overtook a squad whether it would be gray backs or bluecoats. Both indifferently gave us a friendly nod as we passed. I do not know that there is any fact in the history of the war more striking than this, that now within three weeks of its close we should be quietly driving thro' the heart of South Carolina, the road sprinkled with soldiers of both armies, walking friendly in the same direction. We went up some long, sandy, toilsome hills, and came into a broad plain, when at about 9:00 sat under a huge live-oak & devoured a monstrous watermelon & some fine peaches. The scenery is generally very monotonous, but there is hardly anything that would show that you were not in New England except the mocking bird, the passion-flower, & the live-oak & the sweet-gum tree. The sun beats down with fearful heat, but in the shade you feel the heat no more than in the North. And the fine, dry healthy air made me feel like myself, as I have not done in Charleston for a month.

Crossing the Congaree on a rude ferry, (the rebels burned the bridge) and climbing up a steep hill, we were in Columbia, beautifully situated on a long ridge, commanding a very pleasant view. Its main street is like a New England village, broad, lined with trees and plain white houses. The farther part of the town, and I suppose the finest houses, are all in ruins. Mr. Jenks had a letter to a leasing colored man, and he took us at once to the hall when they had got thro' their celebration—got up & managed entirely by colored people, with the reading of the declaration, 2 speeches by men of their own number.

The procession had already gone to the grove, where we followed, & found a fine collation—turkeys, roast pig, chicken pie, cake, apples, peaches & nectarines. And after the collation, Jenks made a short speech, then Gen. Van Wyck (who is the well-known congressman) made then an excellent address, Col. Haughton, commanding the post said a few words, & some of the colored men replied.[125] All the good hotels in Columbia were burned, & we could get no decent accommodations at the poor one that is left, so one of the colored men, named Taylor (whom nobody at the North suspect of being colored) has given us a very comfortable room in his house, where he gives us abundance of fruit milk & fresh butter.[126] Miss Lee is staying with her friends.

Allen met a number of freedmen at a Mr. Pickett's in the afternoon of July 5, 1865, then he and Miss Lee called on Miss Campbell, her former teacher.

July 6

There was a meeting of the colored people yesterday afternoon, at a private house, called to confer with me about school matters; & I had a very satisfactory talk with them. Today I have visited four private schools, kept in private houses, and ranging from 10 to 35 scholars. I have had the most satisfaction from these people of any freedmen I have met. They seem more practical & harmonious than those in Charleston, & to understand their new relation very well. One or two incidents I have been told that contradict some of the arguments of slavery. They say that numbers who were sold away from their families years ago are now coming back. One man who has been away 30 years is here now looking after his wife. If there is any argument for slavery, it is in the certainty a man has of being taken care of when he is old. But today I saw an old woman who, when she became superannuated was sold at auction by a wealthy family for $5. to an Irishman; & he finding it a bad bargain, sold her to the colored members of the Presbyterian church, who have supported her now for five or six years. Also they have supported for 10 years an old man who was turned off by his master & told he was free, when he became past work.[127]

Rather an entertaining thing it was yesterday at a collation they gave us after the talking was through with, to hear these people telling stories about the ignorance of some of the planters. I was called on for a toast, & gave "Freedom & Education, which must always go together." Jenks gave "Equal rights to all men." I went to see Col. Haughton this morning, but found he was not interested in school matters, notwithstanding Gen. Hartwell had given me a letter of introduction, referring to this as the object of my visit. We shall return tomorrow, after a very agreeable & satisfactory visit.

Allen visited Columbia schools with a Mr. Williams on July 6, 1865. In the afternoon, a Mr. Carroll and a Mr. Fitz Simmons (Fitzsimmons?) called, and later a Mr. Cobb called. He visited the State House on July 7. Afterward, Mr. Pickett and certain Messrs. Edwards, Nash, and Black called. Allen took a stage at 4 P.M. for Orangeburg. At Orangeburg on July 8, Allen met Major Gouraud and Mr. Legare.[128]

Orangeburg, July 9

I shall stay here a day in order to learn from Capt. Soule & Maj. Montague about the details of the contract system here.[129]

Charleston, Monday, July 10, 1865

I came down from Orangeburg today in company with Gen. Hartwell & Mr. Trenholm—rebel Secretary of the Treasury—& had a long & very satisfactory conversation with Mr. T.[130] He confirms my previous impression as to the good faith in which the people of the state submit to the national power, and admit that State Rights & Slavery are both dead. As to reconstruction, he feels in no haste, & is perfectly willing that a military rule should be continued a while longer, only insisting that when the time comes they should have full self-government, which he assured me it would be both their desire & their interest to exercise justly—the people of the state he felt sure would avoid all class legislation. I ask him especially whether there would not be danger of that, the legislation being all in the hands of the employers (for I purposefully avoided the subject of negro-suffrage) and he said of course we must take the risk, but he thought practically there was no danger—indeed, there was so great a disposition to conciliate the negroes, that the danger was of too favorable legislation.[131]

I myself am satisfied of two things—that these people have submitted in good faith, & that they are in good faith trying to make the contract system work. They have not enough confidence in its success, & they all agree that freedom is going to be the destruction of the blacks. In this respect Mr. Trenholm is more hopeful than most of them, & says merely that they will suffer more than any other class, but he thinks they will eventually come out right. As to slavery, altho' he believed it a divinely ordained institution, he not only acquiesces in its overthrow, but would oppose any attempt to revive or prolong it. He had for years never expected any other termination of the question—"it was a religious faith with us, and it was the same with you; and it could not be settled except by the sword." And now it is settled once for all.

As to the conduct of the negroes, he says "they have behaved extraordinarily well under the circumstances"—he does not believe that an equal number of whites, freed so suddenly and surrounded with such temptations, would be so temperate & orderly. He himself was the first person in his neighborhood who came forward & made a contract—he has a large plantation near Columbia, & owned 700 slaves—& his example, I learn, was a great help to our commanders there. He confirms the common statements of the shortness of the crop this year—he has about 700 acres of corn, in place of 1300; but the corn is looking very finely. One statement he made that quite surprised me—that the bulk of the cotton crop was made up, not by the large planters, of 1000 bales, but by the small farmers, bringing into the market 3 or 4 bales each. The tendency since the war has been, he says, to turn from planting to farming, and he thinks that they have lived so comfortably & contentedly this way, that the tendency will continue.

He spoke too of the democratic (altho' he didn't use that word)—these small farmers, who have never used slaves, being able now to hire hands, & bring with them very much more quality, sitting at the same table &c., like our northern farmers. For there is great restlessness & disposition to wander, among the freedmen, & he related an instance of a planter in Edgefield district, who had a splendid crop—the negroes had been working under a contract, & the crop was now finished, hardly anything to be done but harvest it—& one night every negro disappeared from the place, leaving the entire crop to him. They had probably heard stories of the land given to freedmen here on the islands, & so had set out to get their share. I asked him whether the greatest difficulty in the way of reconstruction would not be the entire lack of local municipalities thro' the state, & explained briefly our New England system, in which he seemed interested; & said there was nothing like it here—only Commissioners of Cross Roads & Patrol Guards for each District, appointed by the Governor. Mr. Trenholm, by the way (pr. Tren'um) is universally respected and beloved for his charity, and took the office of Sec. of Treas. when he knew the confederacy was to fail, solely that he might if possible perform the impossible, & save something of their possessions to the poor people.

My special object in going into the country was—next to looking into school matters—to examine into the contract system, & I spent a day with Capt. Soule, former Chairman, & Maj. Montague, present Chairman of the Board of Free Labor,—talking also with Lts. Alvord & Trotter, members of the board (the latter colored of the 55th Mass.) upon the subject.[132] This board was appointed by Gen. Hartwell, & sits at Orangeburg, his Hd Qrs., having a branch also at Columbia; & they have made it their business to go about to all the plantations, explaining the new order of things, & insisting upon both parties agreeing to contracts—they leave it to the parties themselves to make the contracts, only rejecting them if unjust to either party. All agree that the blacks as a whole are trying to make the experiment work. Lt. Trotter estimates at a third those who came into it cheerfully & readily—the others being more or less reluctant, & disposed to resist at first—and this third is composed of the most intelligent and cultivated blacks.

I fancy that Mr. Trenholm is too sanguine as to the cheerful acquiescence of the blacks as a whole; he is no doubt correct as to the best ones, those with whom he comes in contact, but these brutal, ignorant fellows, who cannot read or write, are still sullen & bitter. In order to see to the enforcement of contracts, & the preservation of order, small squads of men, under non commissioned officers, are posted at different points (about 10 in all) to exercise police duty. These are mostly of the 55th Mass., & 102nd colored, & they agree with the white officers that the blacks are generally acting honorably. And it is a very significant fact, that not only Lt. Trotter, but these colored corporals & sergeants, have been invited to dinner, & treated courteously & hospitably by the blacks. It seems to be agreed, too, that there is more trouble now in holding the blacks than the whites to their contracts. But outside of our military occupation, which does not yet extend beyond Newberry, there is a real state of anarchy—neither civil nor military government, & I think in many cases a real reign of terror.

With all the favorable symptoms, there is the fearful danger which has become real at Charleston during my absence. Gen. Hartwell feels that he has done a good work in his district in soothing the heated passions on both sides, but he says it would not take much to kindle just such a bloody strife there; & when Hurley (who I think I have written of, as a noisy, intemperate demagogue) went to Orangeburg on his way to Columbia last week, Hartwell summarily ordered him back to Charleston, whence he proceeded North, breathing vengeance. I am not able to ascertain the real origin of these riots. Both parties were no doubt to blame, & each accuses the other of beginning them.[133]

Allen went to see General W. T. Bennett, the new Post Commander, on July 12, 1865.[134]

14th

I can't visit the islands [St. Helena, etc.] without delaying more than I like, & Savannah is unhealthy & besides I couldn't see what I want there, so I think I shall go by the Arago next Thursday.

On July 16, 1865, Mr. Jaques[135] came to dine with Allen, and Messrs. Roswell T. Logan, Edmund Welson, and Southerners came to tea.[136] On July 17, he bought "stereograms"—presumably of the South—to show people back home. He visited James and Johns Islands[137] in a steam flat with Mr. Tomlinson and Captain Walton on July 18. He met Misses Ellen Kempton and Elmira Stanton[138] at Mr. Pillsbury's on July 19, and he attended a Colored Fair[139] that afternoon. He made a trip to Mt. Pleasant, South Carolina, outside Charleston on July 20, where he visited a school. He finished an article to the Nation *on July 21. In the afternoon, he called on a Miss Lariscy and Mr. Carrier. In the afternoon of July 22, Allen called on Mrs. Traynor,[140] but she was not in. He sailed for New York at 5:30* P.M. *aboard the* Granada.[141]

Epilogue

After leaving Charleston, William Allen took a position for the 1865–66 school year as a professor of ancient languages at Antioch College in Yellow Springs, Ohio. He decided not to return there the following year due to administrative strife; instead, he accepted a teaching position for the 1866–67 school year at Eaglewood Military Academy in Perth Amboy, New Jersey. While there, he began work on *Slave Songs of the United States*. In the fall of 1867, he was called to a professorship of ancient languages (and, later, history) at the University of Wisconsin at Madison.[1]

Allen married Margaret Loring Andrews of Newburyport, Massachusetts, on June 30, 1868.[2] He lived the life of a college professor at the University of Wisconsin the remainder of his days. The Allens had three sons—Andrews, William Ware, and Philip Loring—and they raised Katharine, who followed in her father's footsteps at the University of Wisconsin.[3] He usually went East during the summer, spending July and August among friends in Boston. He visited the recently founded Yellowstone National Park in the summer of 1884, and he toured England and southern Europe from April to August 1885. He died December 9, 1889, after a short respiratory illness.

Although Allen never returned to the South after leaving Charleston, he maintained his interest in the language and music of the freedmen. In 1867, he, his cousin Charley Ware, and Lucy Garrison[4] undertook a project to publish a collection of the slave songs they had heard in the South. The three contributed songs and compiled and edited songs from other contributors. Lucy's husband, Wendell Garrison,[5] assisted in readying the volume for publication. The project resulted in the 136-song anthology *Slave Songs of the United States*, the first collection of African American spirituals. The work was not a commercial success, but it contained musical treasures that might otherwise have been lost. It preserved such well-known songs as "Nobody Knows the Trouble I See," "Michael Row the Boat Ashore," and "The Good Old Way," known from the movie *O Brother, Where Art Thou?* as "Down to the River to Pray." The story of the publication of *Slave Songs* is chronicled by Dena Epstein in *Sinful Tunes and Spirituals.*[6]

Except for *Slave Songs,* none of Allen's writings after 1865, with the minor exception of a review of Joel Chandler Harris's *Uncle Remus,*[7] were based on his sojourn in the South. At first glance, a letter by Allen in the July 10, 1866, issue of the Boston *Daily Advertiser* appears to stem from his Southern experience, but a closer reading reveals that he was replying to an earlier article in the *Advertiser* about the Homestead Act of 1866.[8]

Allen was a prolific writer of essays and reviews. A 943-item catalog of Allen's published writings is included in the memorial volume his colleagues published after his death.[9] In a memoir, David Frankenburger summed up the man as a teacher: "He had a profound learning, great ability in classification and arrangement of facts and principles, a rare power of exact statement, a simple sincerity that stooped to no pretence, and a love of truth that inspired to lofty endeavor. He was a natural teacher, born with a "joyous readiness in communicating his acquisitions." But it was especially as a teacher of history that he excelled. "No historical fact is of any value," he said, "except so far as it helps us to understand human nature and the working of historic forces."[10]

Frankenburger quoted Wendell Garrison, who, as an editor of the *Nation,* knew Allen well for his political writings: "His historical studies, though by inheritance congenial to his mind, were pursued with other aims than intellectual amusement, and led up to principles of private conduct and maxims of government. I do not think our literary men, as a class, are divorced from politics in the nobler sense; but it is somewhat uncommon for them to give public expression to their political ideas, and engage editorially in current debate through the press. It is not everyone, indeed, who can command the different styles needed for the two kinds of writing, excessive cultivation of either of which tends to unfit a man for the other. Professor Allen was not, perhaps, equally at home in both; but he practiced both at will and successfully. His interest in national affairs never abated; he was a dispassionate observer and true independent."[11]

The scholarly qualities of objectivity and independence were present in Allen throughout his life. His writings provide unique insights into South Carolina and its people in the midst of a revolutionary transition from slavery to freedom.[12]

Appendix A

Freedmen's Aid Organizations

There were four principle freedmen's aid organizations active on the South Carolina Sea Islands during the war:[1]

New England Freedmen's Aid Society (NEFAS), based in Boston
National Freedman's Relief Association (NFRA), based in New York City
Port Royal Relief Committee (PRRC), based in Philadelphia
American Missionary Association (AMA), based in New York

Except for the American Missionary Association, these organizations had their genesis in the Port Royal Experiment launched by Treasury Secretary Salmon P Chase in early 1862. Following the capture of the Sea Islands in November 1861, Chase fell heir to the task of determining what to do with property (land, real estate, cotton, and slaves) abandoned by the former owners. As part of this initiative, he dispatched Edward Pierce, a Boston attorney, to the islands to survey the condition of the nearly ten thousand freedmen there. Pierce had prior experience working with contraband slaves at Fortress Monroe, Virginia, which recommended him for the job. He left for the islands on January 13, 1862, and about a week later Chase also dispatched the Reverend Mansfield French to assist Pierce. French was a personal friend of Chase, and he had been a prominent evangelist in Ohio when Chase was governor of the state. French and Pierce came to an agreement that, on their return, Pierce would elicit support in Boston for a plan to assist the freedmen, while French would do the same in New York City.

Pierce's report of February 3, 1862, became the blueprint for the Port Royal Experiment approved by Chase. A primary aim of Pierce's plan was to demonstrate that the freedmen could compete in a free labor market. By so doing, the experiment was to point the way to lift former slaves from slavery to emancipation. This provision of the plan was to be fulfilled by plantation superintendents, who would oversee efforts to restore agriculture, especially cotton production, on the islands. However, an unofficial part of the plan involved sending teachers and ministers to the islands to minister to the educational and religious needs of the freedmen. Pierce asked Chase for the government's permission to send selected teachers to the South, while leaving their salaries to private benevolent organizations. For his part, French asked Chase for transportation for missionaries selected by his association to be sent to the South, but for no other funding.

The New England Freedmen's Aid Society had its beginnings when a group calling itself the Educational Commission for Freedmen met in Boston on February 4, 1862, with the aim of seeing to the educational needs of the blacks at Port Royal. It was this organization that sponsored the Boston Gideonites. Some twenty months later, Allen came south under the auspices of the renamed organization.

The National Freedman's Relief Association had its beginnings when Reverend French returned to New York from the Sea Islands after meeting with Pierce. He organized a public drive to attend to the physical and religious needs of the freedmen at Port Royal. The NFRA sponsored the New York City Gideonites.

The first boatload of Gideonites sailed from New York City aboard the *Atlantic* on March 2, 1862. Collectively, these people and those who came after them became known as Gideon's Band, or Gideonites, after Gideon's band of three hundred soldiers in the Bible.[2] The number of original Gideonites varies from fifty-three to sixty-four, depending on how they are counted. Gideonite Susan Walker listed fifty-three participants in her diary but qualified the list as "persons approved by Mr. Pierce."[3] There were others, however, who came through other avenues, bringing the total to sixty-four. Of this number, thirty-three represented Boston, twenty-eight represented New York City, and three represented either Washington, D.C., or Philadelphia. Twelve of the sixty-four were women; fourteen people, thirteen men and a woman, were superintendents, while the rest were teachers or missionaries.

The third principal organization, the Port Royal Relief Committee, was organized under the leadership of the prominent abolitionist James Miller McKim in Philadelphia on March 5, 1862, three days after the *Atlantic* sailed. The purpose of the PRRC was to see to the physical and educational needs of the Port Royal freedmen. The first PRRC teachers sailed for the Sea Islands aboard the sailing steamer *Oriental* on April 9, 1862.[4]

The American Missionary Association was founded in Albany, New York, in 1846 with the mission to educate blacks and to promote racial equality and Christian values. The AMA sponsored the Reverend French's first trip to Port Royal, but it did not begin its own independent aid efforts until about a year later after the other three organizations.

The New England Freedmen's Aid Society, the National Freedman's Relief Association, and the Port Royal Relief Committee signed articles of agreement on March 20, 1862, but philosophically they were far apart. Religiously, the Boston group tended to be Unitarians and Congregationalists, and the Philadelphia group was composed mainly of Quakers, while the New York City group consisted mostly of evangelical Baptists and Methodists. NEFAS and NFRA members, especially, were often antagonistic toward one another. PRRC members identified with NEFAS members more closely than with NFRA members, while evangelical AMA members were more compatible with NFRA members.

Like Allen, most NEFAS teachers were Unitarians. The educational and religious philosophy of these men and women, in contrast to that of evangelicals, was expressed in a statement by the Unitarian preacher Reverend O. B. Frothingham, who served as the NEFAS corresponding secretary:

It is asked, "Is a teacher less prepared to instruct the people in letters, because to the learning of the schools, and the wisdom of men, he adds divine teaching, and the Word of God?" We answer frankly, yes, if the two classes are mingled together, or if the teaching of divinity and the Word of God crowd out, take precedence of, limit, define, or color the instruction of letters, or the wisdom of men. Rationalists and Unitarians, who reject the scheme of salvation, whose religion is chiefly ethical, who preach the interests of this life, intellectual culture, domestic virtue, social kindness, the priceless worth of the simply human relations, may mingle such religion as they have with education, because education is their religion. But evangelical men, who are supremely interested in the salvation of souls, cannot confound them with secular interests without encountering the dangers of compromising both, not in the regards of the people only, but in their own elements.[5]

Appendix B

Black St. Helena Residents

Name	Age/Position	Plantation/Relation
Abby (Jenkins)	Adult	From John Fripp Place Isaac Jenkins's wife
Young Abby	Student	Unknown
Abraham	Student	From John Fripp Place Limus and Clara's son Adam's and Young Margaret's brother Playmate of Dick's son Tom
Adaline	Student	Unknown
Adam	Student	From John Fripp Place Limus and Clara's son Abraham's and Young Margaret's brother
Aleck (Fripp Point)	Adult Preacher	From Fripp Point
Aleck (John Fripp)	Adult	From John Fripp Place
Alice	Former student of Mrs. Harrison	From T. B. Fripp Place
Amaritta	Adult	From Coffin Point Elderly husband and four children

Name	Age/Position	Plantation/Relation
Ann (short for Anacusa)	Adult Allens' washwoman	From John Fripp Place Justina's, Wakazeer's, and Waverly's sister Phoebe's daughter Dick's wife Tom's, Selina's, and Archy's mother
Archy	Child	From John Fripp Place Dick and Ann's son Tom's and Selina's brother About 4 years old in 1864
Aunt Jenny	Elderly adult	Old woman known by the title "Sarah McKee, the Belle of Beaufort, the gold-wearer"
Becca (dialect for Rebecca)	Student?	Unknown
Bella	Adult student	From Mulberry Hill Lucretia Scott's daughter Paul Scott's stepdaughter Hacless's sister Little Paul's stepsister Ned's wife
Benjy	Student	From Hope Place
Betsy (Mulberry Hill)	Adult student	From Mulberry Hill
Betsy (T. B. Fripp)	Former student of Mrs. Harrison	From T. B. Fripp Place
Betty	Student	From Hope Place
Billy Field, formerly Bowman	Young-adult student	From John Fripp Place Lucy and Jimmy's son Bristol's, Robert's, and Molsy's brother Justina's husband
Bristol (Cherry Hill)	Adult	From Cherry Hill Rinah's (Hope Place) and Venus's uncle

Name	Age/Position	Plantation/Relation
Bristol Singleton	Young-adult student	From John Fripp Place Lucy and Jimmy's son Billy's, Robert's, and Molsy's brother Venus's uncle
Butcher	Adult Foreman at Cherry Hill	From Cherry Hill Lame
Celia	Student	From Hope Place Young Lucy's sister
Charlotte	Student	From John Fripp Place
Chloe	Adult student	From Mulberry Hill

Clara	Adult	From John Fripp Place
		Maria's (Mulberry Hill)
		Dick's, Will's, and
		   Tamar's sister
		Grew up with Toby
		   "sic-a" (like a) sister
		Limus's wife
		Adam's, Abraham's,
		   and Young Margaret's
		   mother

Clarissa	Adult	From Hope Place Queen's and Benjy's mother
Cuffee	Student	From John Fripp Place Dido's nephew Mother dead Gibb's and Frank's brother
Dan	Adult River pilot	From Fripp Point
Daniel	Adult Carriage driver	From Coffin Point First black adult Allen met
Old Deborah	Elderly adult	From Cherry Hill Young Jimmy's grandmother

Name	Age/Position	Plantation/Relation
Young Demas	Young boy Gate opener or tiger	From Coffin Point First black child Allen met
Demus	Young-adult student	Unknown
Dennis	Adult student	From John Fripp Place Margaret's husband
Dick	Adult student Allen's servant and handyman Nelly's (horse) groom	From John Fripp Place Maria's (Mulberry Hill) son Will's, Tamar's, and Clara's brother Ann's husband Tom's, Archy's, and Selina's father
Dido	Adult	From John Fripp Place William's wife
Dinah	Adult	From Cherry Hill Linda's mother
Doe or Zoe	Former student of Mrs. Harrison	From T. B. Fripp Place
Doll	Adult	Funeral held June 26, 1864
Dolly (Hope Place)	Student	From Hope Place Rinah's sister
Dolly (Mulberry Hill)	Adult student	From Mulberry Hill
Edward	Student	From John Fripp Place Robin's son Ishmael's and Ellen's brother
Eliza	Adult	From John Fripp Place Peg and Sandy's daughter Taffy's sister Married, but Allen did not reveal to whom
Elisabeth	Student	From Mulberry Hill Quash and Rosina's daughter Polly's, Minna (Mulberry Hill)'s, and John's sister

Name	Age/Position	Plantation/Relation
Ellen	Student	From John Fripp Place Robin and Rinah's daughter, about 12 Ishmael's and Little Sue's sister
Emma	Student	From John Fripp Place
Eve	Former student of Mrs. Harrison	From T. B. Fripp Place
Flora (John Fripp)	Student	From John Fripp Place Taft's daughter Possibly Sarah's sister
Flora (T. B. Fripp)	Former student of Mrs. Harrison	From T. B. Fripp Place
Frank (John Fripp)	Adult	From John Fripp Place Laura's and Mary's father and "quite old"
Young Frank (John Fripp)	Student	From John Fripp Place Cuffy's and Gibb's brother Abraham's friend
Gabriel Wig	Young-adult student	From John Fripp Place Moses the Foreman's son
George	Former student of Mrs. Harrison	From T. B. Fripp Place
Gibb	Student	From John Fripp Place Cuffee's and Frank's brother Taft's nephew
Gilead	Student	From Cherry Hill Elder Henry's and Mary's nephew
Glasgow	Adult Preacher	From St. Simon's Island Preempted land on Hamilton Fripp Place
Grace	Adult	From John Fripp Place Waverly's wife Old Phoebe's daughter-in-law

Name	Age/Position	Plantation/Relation
Hacless (dialect for Hercules)	Adult student	From Mulberry Hill Lucretia Scott's son Paul Scott's stepson Bella's brother Little Paul's stepbrother
Old Hannah	Adult	From T. B. Fripp Place Married Frank February 11, 1864 Had 15 children, 6 of whom were living
Hannah	Student	From Hope Place
Harry	Student	From Hope Place
Elder Henry (Cherry Hill)	Adult student Sometimes cook	From Cherry Hill Mulatto Mary's husband Gilead's uncle and father figure
Henry (Coffin Point)	Adult	From Coffin Point Bid in auction against Titus
Henry (John Fripp Place)	Young-adult student	From John Fripp Place Allen guessed he was Paris's brother, which may or may not have been the case Married Jane November 29, 1863
Hetty	Student	From John Fripp Place Father sold to New Orleans Molsy's daughter by a husband sold away Moses Burbian's stepdaughter Judy's older sister Young Sandy's half sister Mylie's stepsister

Name	Age/Position	Plantation/Relation

Old Isaac	Aged adult	From John Fripp Place
		Dependent on nephews
		  Robin and Moses
		Old Moses's brother
		His wife was from the
		  Marion Chaplin Place

Old Isaac's unnamed wife	Adult	From Marion Chaplin Place
Little Isaac	Adult	From John Fripp Place Either Isaac Jenkins's or Old Isaac's nephew
Isaac Jenkins	Adult student	From John Fripp Place Moses the Foreman's son Abby's husband
Issac (Toddler)	Child	From John Fripp Place About 2 years old

Ishmael	Student	From John Fripp Place
		Robin and Rinah's son,
		  about 12
		Ellen's and Little Sue's
		  brother
		Sammy's playmate

Jacob	Former student of Mrs. Harrison	From T. B. Fripp Place
"Ragged" James	Student	From Hope Place
Jane	Student	From John Fripp Place Peg's granddaughter Married Young Henry November 29, 1863
January	Former student of Mrs. Harrison	From T. B. Fripp Place
Jeffrey	Adult	From Mulberry Hill Formerly from Woodlands
Jim (T. B. Fripp)	Former student of Mrs. Harrison	From T. B. Fripp Place

Name	Age/Position	Plantation/Relation
Jimmy	Adult Cattle driver	From John Fripp Place William's brother Lucy's husband Billy's, Bristol's, Robert's, and Molsy's father

Young Jimmy or Jim
  (Cherry Hill)
	Young adult
	Ne'er-do-well field hand
		From Cherry Hill
		Old Deborah's great-
		  grandson

Joan	Adult	From John Fripp Place
		Peg's and Taft's sister
		Moses the Foreman's wife
		Tony's, London's, Paris's,
		   Gabriel's, Robin's, and
		   Young Moses's mother

John (John Fripp)	Adult	From John Fripp Place Carpenter Mulatto Lucy's brother-in-law Thomas's father

John (Mulberry Hill)	Student	From Mulberry Hill
		Quash and Rosina's son
		Polly's, Elisabeth's, and
		   Minna's (Mulberry Hill),
		   brother

Young "Sober" John	Student	From Mulberry Hill
John from the mainland	Adult	Middle-aged refugee from the mainland

Judy	Student	From John Fripp Place
		Father sold to New Orleans
		Molsy's daughter by a
		  husband sold away
		Moses Burbian's
		  stepdaughter
		Hetty's younger sister
		Young Sandy's half sister
		Mylie's stepsister

Name	Age/Position	Plantation/Relation
Justina (Field) Bowman	Adult	From John Fripp Place Phoebe's daughter Ann's, Wakazeer's, and Waverly's sister Billy's wife
Larry	Former student of Mrs. Harrison	From T. B. Fripp Place
Laura Simmons	Young-adult student	From John Fripp Place Married Paris Simmons November 29, 1863 Frank's daughter Mary's sister
Lauretta	Student	Unknown
Liab	Adult Preacher	From Fripp Point
Libby	Student	From Hope Place Nat's sister

Limus (John Fripp)	Elderly adult	From John Fripp Place
		Exempted because of
		   infirmity from cutting
		   marsh grass by Captain
		   Fripp
		Clara's husband
		Adam's, Abraham's, and
		   Young Margaret's father
		50+ years old

Limus (Pine Grove)	Adult
	Entrepreneur
	   Ran Pine Grove–
	   Hilton Head
	   boat trade
		From Pine Grove (William
		   Fripp Place)

Linda	Student	From Cherry Hill Dinah's daughter About 15 years old
Linnie	Student	Unknown
Little Sue	Child	From John Fripp Place Robin and Rinah's daughter Ishmael's and Ellen's younger sister

Name	Age/Position	Plantation/Relation
Lizzie	Student	Unknown
London Simmons	Young-adult student	From John Fripp Place Moses the Foreman's son
Lucretia (Scott)	Adult	From Mulberry Hill Lucy's and Rosina's sister Paul Scott's wife Hacless's, Bella's, and Little Paul's mother Deserted by former husband, who lived on Lady's Island with another woman
Young Lucretia (Hope Place)	Student	From Hope Place Died unexpectedly January 13, 1864, after a cold New Year's Day boat excursion
Lucy	Adult	From John Fripp Place "Leading lady" at John Fripp Place Jimmy's wife Billy's, Bristol's, Robert's, and Molsy's mother
Young Lucy (Hope Place)	Student	From Hope Place Celia's sister
Young Lucy (Mulberry Hill)	Adult student	From Mulberry Hill
Margaret	Adult	From John Fripp Place Dennis's wife
Young Margaret	Student	From John Fripp Place Limus and Clara's daughter Abraham's and Adam's sister About 12 years old
Maria (Mulberry Hill)	Adult	From Mulberry Hill Will's, Tamar's, Clara's, and Dick's mother
Maria (T. B. Fripp)	Former student of Mrs. Harrison	From T. B. Fripp Place
Mary Ann	Student	Unknown

Name	Age/Position	Plantation/Relation
Old Mary	Elderly adult	From Cherry Hill
Mary (Cherry Hill)	Adult	From Cherry Hill Henry's wife Gilead's aunt and mother figure
Mary (John Fripp)	Adult	From John Fripp Place Frank's daughter Laura's sister
Old May	Elderly adult man	From Cherry Hill Abused and broken during slavery but managed to cultivate three acres of cotton with his wife in 1863
Menia	Student	From Cherry Hill
Minda	Adult Substitute washwoman for Ann	From Cherry Hill Tony's wife Reddington's grandmother
Minna (John Fripp)	Student	From John Fripp Place
Minna (Mulberry Hill)	Student	From Mulberry Hill Quash and Rosina's daughter Polly's, Elisabeth's, and John's sister
Minnie	Student	From John Fripp Place
Molly	Former student of Mrs. Harrison	From T. B. Fripp Place
Molsy (Burbian)	Adult student	From John Fripp Place Jimmy and Lucy's daughter Billy's, Bristol's, and Robert's sister Former husband sold to New Orleans Moses Burbian's wife Hetty's, Judy's, and Young Sandy's mother Mylie's stepmother

Name	Age/Position	Plantation/Relation
Morris (Cherry Hill)	Adult	From Cherry Hill Given young Jimmy's gin Good worker
Morris (T. B. Fripp)	Former student of Mrs. Harrison	From T. B. Fripp Place
Old Moses	Aged adult	Very elderly Deemed feeble "secesh time" but made a living working under the occupation Possibly Moses the Foreman's father Old Isaac's brother
Moses the Foreman	Adult Foreman of John Fripp Place	From John Fripp Place Joan's husband Tony's, London's, Paris's, Gabriel's, Robin's, and Young Moses's father
Young Moses Burbian	Adult	From John Fripp Place Moses the Foreman's son Old Isaac's nephew Molsy's husband Mylie's and Young Sandy's father Hetty's and Judy's stepfather
Mylie	Student	From John Fripp Place Moses Burbian's daughter by a wife then dead Molsey's stepdaughter Judy's and Hetty's stepsister Young Sandy's half sister
Nat	Student	From Hope Place Libby's brother
Ned	Adult student	From Mulberry Hill Formerly from Woodlands
Nelia (dialect for Cornelia)	Student?	Unknown
Nero (Edisto)	Adult Mechanic who repaired the steam gin at John Fripp Place	Refugee from Edisto Island

Name	Age/Position	Plantation/Relation
Old unnamed woman	Elderly adult	From John Fripp Place Allen learned she was crazy
Old woman's daughter	Young adult? Disabled	From John Fripp Place Covered with sores
Old woman with yellow scarf	Elderly adult	Unknown Allen thought she was probably a good shouter in her youth
Old Paris Gregley	Adult student Foreman at Mulberry Hill	From Mulberry Hill 50+ years old
Young Paris Simmons	Young-adult student	From John Fripp Place Moses the Foreman's son Laura's husband
Patty	Student	From Hope Place
Paul Scott	Adult	From Mulberry Hill Lucretia Scott's husband Hacless's and Bella's stepfather Little Paul's father
Little Paul	Adult	From Mulberry Hill Paul and Lucretia Scott's son Hacless's and Bella's stepbrother
Peg	Adult	From John Fripp Place Joan's and Taft's sister Sandy's wife Eliza's and Taffy's mother Jane's grandmother
Peter	Student	From John Fripp Place Moses and Molsy Burbian's son
Old Phoebe	Adult Allens' cook	From John Fripp Place Ann's, Justina's, Wakazeer's, and Waverly's mother
Phoebe (T. B. Fripp)	Former student of Mrs. Harrison	From T. B. Fripp Place

Name	Age/Position	Plantation/Relation
"Pickaninny," unnamed	Child	From John Fripp Place Brought to class by Mylie

Polly	Adult	From Mulberry Hill
		Quash and Rosina's
		   daughter
		Will's wife
		Elisabeth's, Minna's
		   (Mulberry Hill), and
		   John's elder sister

Quash Fortune	Adult	From Mulberry Hill
		Rosina's husband
		Polly's, Elisabeth's, Minna's
		   (Mulberry Hill), and
		   John's father
		Allen mentioned "Quash's
		   funeral" in his diary entry
		   of June 8, 1864

Queen	Student	From Hope Place
Quintus	Adult	From Coffin Point
Reddington	Student	From Cherry Hill Tony and Minda's grandson
Reuben	Adult	From T. J. Fripp Place
Richard	Former student of Mrs. Harrison	From T. B. Fripp Place
Rinah (Rivers)	Adult	From John Fripp Place Joan's daughter by a previous husband Robin's wife
Young Rinah (Hope Place)	Student	From Hope Place Venus's sister Bristol's (Cherry Hill) niece
Robert Lessington	Adult Religious leader	Freedman, quite old
Robert Middleton	Young-adult student	From John Fripp Place Lucy and Jimmy's son Billy's, Bristol's, and Molsy's brother

Name	Age/Position	Plantation/Relation
Robin Rivers	Student	From John Fripp Place Old Isaac's nephew Moses the Foreman's son Ishmael's, Ellen's, and Edward's father
Rodwell	Adult Mule cart driver	From Coffin Point
Rose	Former student of Mrs. Harrison	From T. B. Fripp Place
Rose (Coffin Point)	Young adult? Harriet Ware's "girl"	From Coffin Point
Rose (Hope Place)	Student	From Hope Place
Rosina (Fortune)	Adult	From Mulberry Hill Lucy's sister Quash's wife Polly's, Elisabeth's, Minna's (Mulberry Hill), and John's mother
Rullus	Unknown, "Co," referred to by Gibb	Probably John Fripp Place
Sammy	Student	From John Fripp Place Toby's son Ishmael's playmate
Sandy	Adult Carpenter	From John Fripp Place Peg's husband Eliza's and Taffy's father
Young Sandy	Student	From John Fripp Place Moses and Molsy Burbian's son Hetty's, Judy's, and Mylie's half brother About 14 years old
Sarah	Student	John Fripp Place? Possibly Flora's (John Fripp) sister

Name	Age/Position	Plantation/Relation
Selina (or Seline)	Child	From John Fripp Place Dick and Ann's little daughter Tom's and Archy's sister About 2 years old
Taffy	Young-adult student	From John Fripp Place Peg and Sandy's son Eliza's brother
Taft	Adult	From John Fripp Place Joan's and Peg's brother Tyra's husband Flora's father and (possibly) Sarah's father Gibb's uncle
Tamar	Student	From Mulberry Hill Maria's daughter Will's, Clara's, and Dick's sister
Thomas	Student Helped out at the Allens' when Dick was disabled	From John Fripp Place John's (John Fripp) son
Old Tim	Adult Local black teacher	Held school in the summer of 1863 Allen knew of him by reputation only
Titus	Adult	Bid in auction against Henry (Coffin Point)
Toby	Adult scholar	From John Fripp Place Grew up with Clara "sic-a" (like a) brother Sammy's father
Toddler, unnamed	Child	From John Fripp Place Hung onto Emma and Charlotte during class
Toddler Isaac	Child	From John Fripp Place Isaac Jenkins's nephew About 2 years old

Name	Age/Position	Plantation/Relation
Tom	Student	From John Fripp Place Dick's son Archy's and Selina's brother About 12 Abraham's playmate
Tommy	Student	From John Fripp Place
Tony (Cherry Hill)	Adult	From Cherry Hill Minda's husband Reddington's grandfather
Tony (John Fripp)	Young-adult student	From John Fripp Place Moses the Foreman's son
Tony (T. B. Fripp)	Adult Preacher	From T. B. Fripp Place
Tyra	Aged adult Too old for strenuous work	From John Fripp Place Taft's wife Flora's mother and (possibly) Sarah's mother Gibb's aunt
Venus	Student	From Hope Place Young Rinah's sister Bristol's (Cherry Hill) niece
Wakazeer	Adult	From John Fripp Place Phoebe's son Ann's, Justina's, and Waverly's brother
Wake	Young-adult student	Unknown
Waverly (Waberlee, Rabelais, or Wavorley)	Adult 34th USCT Regiment, formerly 2nd S.C. Volunteers	From John Fripp Place Old Phoebe's son Ann's brother Dick's brother-in-law
Will	Adult	From Mulberry Hill Maria's son Tamar's, Clara's, and Dick's brother Polly's husband
William (John Fripp)	Adult Carpenter	From John Fripp Place Jimmy's brother Dido's husband

Name	Age/Position	Plantation/Relation
William (T. B. Fripp)	Former student of Mrs. Harrison	From T. B. Fripp Place
Woman in the Long Pasture	Adult	From Coffin Point
Wyna (dialect for Lavinia or Melvina)	Student	From Hope Place

Appendix C

St. Helena Outsiders

Acronym	Organization	Headquarters
ABMU	American Baptist Missionary Union	Boston
AMA	American Missionary Association	New York
NEFAS	New England Freedmen's Aid Society	Boston
NFRA	National Freedman's Relief Association	New York City
PRRC	Port Royal Relief Committee	Philadelphia
USCT	United States Colored Troops	

Appendix C (*continued*)

Name	Origin	Position	Miscellaneous
Austin Adams?	Dubuque, Iowa?	Associate of Judge Dennis Cooley	Possibly Judge Cooley's partner in the firm of Cooley, Blatchley, and Adams ·
John A. Alden	Unknown	Superintendent at Dr. Pope Place and Indian Hill succeeding Mr. Phillips	Replaced Phillips at Dr. Pope Place and Indian Hill
William Henry Alden	Westville, Conn.	Superintendent at Frogmore, Woodlands, and Hope Place	
Mary (Molly) Allen	West Newton, Mass.	NEFAS teacher	Allen's wife / Caty Noyes's cousin
Lieutenant J. Wesley Benjamin	New York?	157th New York Regiment, stationed at Folly Island	Wounded at Gettysburg / Allen's tablemate on the *Arago*
Lieutenant A. H. Bradish	Boston, Mass.	55th Massachusetts Regiment	*Dudley Buck* passenger
Reverend Dr. William Henry Brisbane	Madison, Wis., originally from Beaufort County, S.C	S.C. tax commissioner / Baptist minister / Former slaveholder turned abolitionist	Allen received a report from Gannett and Winsor about Brisbane and Judge Smith's antics at the land sale February 18, 1864
Mr. Carter or Mr. Clark (typist error)	Unknown	S.C. Tax Commission agent	The typescript journal calls him both "Carter" and "Clark," but Allen's diary of March 4, 1864, noted "Carter"

Name	Origin	Position	Miscellaneous
Judge Dennis N. Cooley	Dubuque, Iowa "a Westerner" per an April 1864 letter by Harriet Ware	S.C. tax commissioner who replaced Judge Smith	Returned North on the boat with Mary and Caty May 30, 1864
Mr. Davis	Unknown	Assistant chaplain, 54th Massachusetts Regiment?	Not listed in the roster of the 54th Massachusetts
Jules S. DeLacroix	Newburyport, Mass.	Superintendent at Dr. Lawrence Place	Acquaintance of Mary and Caty
Napoleon C. Dennett	Worcester, Mass.	Superintendent of Port Royal Plantations	Returned North on the boat with Mary and Caty May 30, 1864 Contributor to *Slave Songs*
Captain John C. Dutch	Worcester, Mass.	Acting master, USS *Kingfisher*	Highly regarded for holding Confederate incursions in check
Mr. Dyer E. P. Dyer or C. Edward Dyer	Hingham, Mass., or Dorchester, Mass.	Teacher at the Corner and Mary Jenkins Place NEFAS teacher	Employed by Philbrick
Lieutenant Colonel John Johnson Elwell	Orwell, Ohio	Chief quartermaster, Department of the South	Delivered long, vacuous speech at the meeting at the church on January 17, 1864
Frederick A. Eustis	Milton, Mass.	Original Gideonite Heir to Eustis Place on Lady's Island	

Appendix C (*continued*)

Name	Origin	Position	Miscellaneous
Charles Follen Folsom	Jamaica Plain, Mass.	Superintendent at the John Fripp Place, Cherry Hill, and Mulberry Hill	Employed by Philbrick Allens' housemate at the Big House Close friend of Gannett and Miss Rice
Charlotte Forten	Philadelphia, Pa.	PRRC teacher	"Mulatto" Prompted John G. Whittier to write the St. Helena Hymn for the Philadelphia School (Towne/Murray school) Returned North on the boat with Mary and Caty May 30, 1864 Contributed to *Slave Songs*
Reverend Mansfield French	New York, N.Y., formerly of Ohio	Original Gideonite NFRA leader	Allen had reservations about French's honesty and the wisdom of his counsel to the freedmen
Captain Henry A. Gadsden	Unknown	Captain, USS *Arago*	Allen thought him a snob
William Channing Gannett	Boston, Mass.	Original Gideonite Superintendent at Pine Grove and Fripp Point	Employed by Philbrick Close friends with Folsom, and Miss Rice
Corporal Gustus George	Virginia	55th Massachusetts Regiment	Allen guessed he was a "runaway" slave
James Gregg	Maryland	Regimental chaplain, 7th USCT Regiment	Presbyterian minister *Dudley Buck* passenger

Name	Origin	Position	Miscellaneous
Dr. James P. Greves (Spelled "Graves" in Allen's journal and diary)	New York, N.Y.	Original Gideonite	Accompanied Judge Cooley and Mr. Adams to see Allen Delivered doctor's letter and package of maple syrup from Beaufort to Allen
William Ware Hall	Providence, R.I.	NEFAS teacher at Coffin Point	Employed by Philbrick Friend of Harriet and Charley Ware
Mr. Hammond	Unknown	Superintendent, Parris Island, S.C.	Testified before the 1863 Freedmen's Inquiry Commission about predations on the freedmen by Union troops
Captain Harding	Unksnown	Captain, *Dudley Buck*	Allen described him as a "long, hearty, red-bearded Yankee sea captain"
Mr. Harrison	Unknown	Superintendent at T. B. Fripp Place (Cedar Grove), Episcopal minister	Mentioned by last name only in Charlotte Forten's journal and in Elizabeth Ware Pearson's *Letters from Port Royal*
Mrs. Harrison	Unknown	Teacher at T. B. Fripp Place	Harrison's wife
Mrs. Harrison's sister	Unknown	May have assisted Mrs. Harrison	
Dr. Ferdinand Vandeveer Hayden	Westfield, Mass.	Chief Medical Officer at Beaufort	Pulled Allen's broken tooth
Mr. Hayward	Vermont	Superintendent at Pope Place and Indian Hill	Allen judged him to be a competent superintendent

Appendix C (*continued*)

Name	Origin	Position	Miscellaneous
Edward Hinckley	Cape Cod, Mass.	Jack-of-all-trades	Mrs. Edward Hinckley was secretary of the West Newton, Mass., branch of the New England Freedmen's Aid Society
Theodore Holt	New York	Original Gideonite sent to Port Royal in March 1862	Unemployed former superintendent at Eustis Place Lived with Nichols and Wild in the overseer's house on the Eustis Place
Captain Edward W. Hooper	Boston, Mass.	Original Gideonite Aide to General Saxton	Head of the Freedmen's Bureau under General Saxton
Mr. Horn	Edisto Island, S.C.	Operated Folsom's steam engine	Freedman employed by Folsom the previous winter
John Hunn	Camden, Del.	PRRC agent Philadelphia St. Helena's Society per Allen	Ran store for PRRA on the Edgar Fripp (Seaside) Place
Anne E. Jenkins Hunn	Camden, Del.	Helped Hunn keep store	Hunn's wife
Elizabeth Hunn	Camden, Del.	Helped Hunn keep store	Hunn's daughter
Dr. Hunting	Unknown	Local physician	Attended to Folsom after hunting accident
Mrs. Hunting	Unknown	Unknown	Dr. Hunting's wife
Sergeant Ide	Saratoga County, N.Y.	Jailor at the Oaks Plantation	
Frederick Jackson	Boston	Gannett's assistant Arrived on the ship with Mary Walker et al.	Nephew of prominent abolitionist Francis Jackson

Name	Origin	Position	Miscellaneous
Henry G. Judd	Unknown	NFRA leader General superintendent, Port Royal Island	Favored Judge Smith over Reverend Brisbane in the land sales debates
Miss Kellogg Sarah Louise Kellogg Martha Louise Kellogg	Avon, Conn. Elizabeth, N.J.	Teacher at Oliver Fripp Place AMA teacher NFRA teacher	Arthur Sumner's assistant
Miss Kendall Mary E. Kendall?	Plymouth, Mass.	Secretary, Plymouth, Mass., branch of the NEFAS	Acquaintance of Mary and Caty, who returned North May 30, 1864, with them, Laura Towne, and Charlotte Forten
Dr. Francis William Lawrence	Boston (Cambridge), Mass.	Owner of Dr. Jenkins Place near Land's End	
Lucilla Train Lawrence	Framingham, Mass.	Unknown	Dr. Lawrence's wife
Sergeant Arthur B. Lee	Boston, Mass. (originally from S.C.)	Commissary sergeant, 54th Massachusetts Regiment	Allen guessed he was a "runaway" slave
Reverend Charles Lowe	Somerville, Mass.	NEFAS Educational Commission official	Member of the NEFAS Committee on Teachers Acquaintance of Folsom
Reverend James D. Lynch	Baltimore, Md.	Mulatto Methodist Episcopal missionary Preacher at St. Helena Village	Allen thought him too wordy

246

Appendix C (*continued*)

Name	Origin	Position	Miscellaneous
John Major	Port Royal Islands	Leader of Fripp Point freedmen and spokesman on wages and land sales at Judge Smith's hearing and on other occasions	Did not work for Philbrick Judge Smith dismissed his contentions as unfounded and exaggerated but privately advised Philbrick to raise wages
Reverend C. S. Martindale	Cleveland, Ohio	AMA representative	Formerly with American Bible Society in Ohio Allen's tablemate on the *Arago*
Harry McMillen	Beaufort, S.C.	Owner of a small plantation on Lady's Island	Former slave, who worked on a plantation in Beaufort for nearly 40 years Testified before the Freedmen's Inquiry Commission in June 1863
George Shattuck Morison	Milton, Mass.	Superintendent along with Clifford Waters at T. B. Chaplin Place near Land's End	Harvard class of 1863 along with Waters
Ellen Murray	Newport, R.I.	PRRC teacher	Lifelong teacher on St. Helena Island
Harriet Murray	Newport, R.I.	PRRC teacher	Ellen Murray's sister and teaching assistant
George Newcomb	New York, N.Y.	NFRA superintendent of schools	Associate of Mansfield French
John G. Nichols	Kingston, Mass.	Superintendent at Eustis Place	

Name	Origin	Position	Miscellaneous
Catherine P. (Caty) Noyes (Allen spelled her name Katy)	Boston, Mass.	NEFAS teacher	Indentified as "Miss R. P. Noyes" in Second Annual NEFAS Report Mary Allen's cousin and housemate at the Big House
Reverend Solomon Peck, D.D.	Roxbury, Mass.	ABMU missionary Preceded Gideonites to Port Royal	Founder of churches, including the Brick Church, on the Port Royal Islands Sarah Peck's husband *Arago* passenger
Sarah Elizabeth Reeve Peck	Roxbury, Mass.	NFRA teacher	Reverend Solomon Peck's wife *Arago* passenger
Elizabeth H. Peck	Roxbury, Mass.	Original Gideonite NFRA teacher	Reverend Peck's daughter *Arago* passenger
Sarah C. Peck	Roxbury, Mass.	NFRA teacher	Reverend Peck's daughter *Arago* passenger
Edward S. Philbrick	Brookline, Mass.	Original Gideonite Port Royal Plantation owner	Allen's employer Owned 11 plantations totaling 6,795 acres and leased two additional plantations from the government
Reverend William S. Phillips	Unknown	AMA representative Former superintendent at Dr. Pope Place and Indian Hill replaced by John Alden	Allen wrote that Phillips had a bad reputation among both whites and blacks on St. Helena Died February 12, 1864
Mr. Pickens	Unknown	Speculator in mules and carts	
Mr. Reed	Unknown	S.C. Tax Commission agent in charge of horse sales	

Appendix C (*continued*)

Name	Origin	Position	Miscellaneous
Mary E. Rice	Cambridgeport, Mass.	Teacher at Fripps Point and Pine Grove	Employed by Philbrick Gannett's housekeeper
		Recommended by John Ware, Charles Ware's uncle	Close friend of Gannett and Folsom
Miss S. E. Richardson	Providence, R.I.	NEFAS teacher	Thorpe's niece
Prince Rivers	Edgefield District, S.C.	Sergeant, 33rd USCT Regiment, formerly 1st S.C. Volunteers	Allen received good reports about Rivers and his dealings with the freedmen
Captain Zina H. Robinson	Bath, Maine	9th Maine Regiment	Allen's tablemate on the *Arago*
Lieutenant Rhodes	Unknown	Unknown unit, probably stationed at Beaufort or Land's End	Perhaps General Saxton's aide replacing Captain Hooper
Charles A. Roundy	Boston, Mass.	Christian Commission agent	Allen found him "pleasant and sensible" *Dudley Buck* passenger
T. Edwin Ruggles	Milton, Mass.	Original Gideonite, superintendent at the Corner Plantation (J. B. Fripp Place)	Employed by Philbrick Ruggles's home was on the Reverend Robert Fuller Place, of which he was superintendent in 1862–63
Mrs. Russell	New Bedford, Mass.	Head Nurse, Hilton Head Island military hospital	
General Rufus B. Saxton	Greenfield, Mass.	Military Governor of South Carolina and the Department of the South	Allen generally admired Saxton, but he had reservations about some of his policies regarding the freedmen

Name	Origin	Position	Miscellaneous
Matilda G. Thompson Saxton	Philadelphia, Pa.	Unknown	General Saxton's wife
Captain Samuel Willard Saxton	Greenfield, Mass.	Aide to General Saxton	General Saxton's brother
Captain John Scott	Unknown	Unknown, probably military	Gannett's friend and one of Folsom's hunting party
Theodoric C. (T. C.) Severance	Cleveland, Ohio	Assistant Treasury agent, collector of the Port of Hilton Head	Husband of Caroline M. Seymour Severance and father of Seymour Severance
James Seymour Severance	Boston, Mass.	NEFAS teacher	Allen's friend
Judge Abram D. Smith	Milwaukee, Wis.	S.C. tax commissioner	Allen criticized the S.C. Tax Commission in general and its commissioners, including Smith, in particular
Judge Austin Smith	Westfield, Chautauqua County, N.Y.	Special agent, U.S. Treasury	Held hearing on land sales squabbles April 21, 1864, which Allen attended
Richard Soule, Jr.	Brookline, Mass.	Original Gideonite Philbrick's agent	Philbrick's uncle
Captain Charles Carroll Soule	Brookline, Mass.	55th Massachusetts Regiment	Son of Richard Soule, Mr. Philbrick's agent and uncle
Edward G. Stetson	Lexington, Mass. Allen cites New Bedford as Stetson's home	Superintendent Dr. Jenkins Place on the north end of Lady's Island	

Appendix C (*continued*)

Name	Origin	Position	Miscellaneous
Lieutenant Henry Atkins Stone	Newburyport, Mass.	33rd USCT Regiment, formerly 1st S.C. Volunteers Formerly of the 8th Maine Regiment	In charge of constructing the signal station on St. Helena
Matilda Anna Sracey Stone	Newburyport, Mass.	Unknown	Lieutenant Henry A. Stone's wife
Lieutenant Colonel James D. Strong	New York	33rd USCT Regiment, formerly 1st S.C. Volunteers, stationed at Beaufort	Colonel Thomas Wentworth Higginson's regiment
Reverend Silas Franklin Strout	Androscoggin, Maine	Regimental chaplain, 9th Maine Regiment	
Arthur Sumner	Cambridge, Mass.	NEFAS teacher at Oliver Fripp Place	Assisted by Miss Kellogg
Mr. Thorndyke	Unknown	Commissary agent or owner in Beaufort	
David Franklin Thorpe	Providence, R.I.	Original Gideonite, superintendent at T.J. Fripp Place	Graduate of Brown University
Reuben Tomlinson	Philadelphia, Pa.	General superintendent of St. Helena and Lady's Islands Plantations	
Laura Matilda Towne	Shoemakertown, Pa.	PRRC teacher	Lifelong teacher on St. Helena Island

Name	Origin	Position	Miscellaneous
Sergeant James Monroe Trotter	Cincinnati, Ohio (originally from Mississippi)	55th Massachusetts Regiment	First black promoted to the officer ranks
Dr. Adoniram Judson Wakefield	Boston, Mass.	Original Gideonite NEFAS-sponsored physician	Known and trusted among the Gideonites
Mary Walker	Cambridge, Mass., originally from North Carolina	Ware's "colored" housekeeper	Fugitive slave Formerly lived with the Ware family in Mass. Stayed at Coffin Point during the summer 1864
Charles Pickard Ware	Milton, Mass.	Superintendent at Coffin Point, Justice of the Peace	Employed by Philbrick Allen's first cousin Harriet Ware's brother
Harriet H. Ware	Milton, Mass.	NEFAS teacher	Allen's first cousin Charles Ware's sister
Mr. Warren	Concord, Mass.	Unknown	Acquaintance of Folsom
Clifford Crowninshield Waters	Salem, Mass.		Superintendent along with George S. Morison at T. B. Chaplin Place near Land's End Harvard class of 1863 along with Morison
George M. Wells	Providence, R.I.	Superintendent at Mary Jenkins Place	Employed by Philbrick He and Samuel D. Phillips wrote official letters in 1862 about a panic among the blacks when soldiers conscripted men for the army
Mrs. George M. Wells	Providence, R.I.?	NEFAS teacher	Possibly Mary L. Wells, West Hartford, Conn.
Eliza J. Wells	Unknown	NFRA teacher at Cuthbert's Point on Lady's Island	Employed by Philbrick
Dr. W. H. Westcott	Rochester, N.H.	Acting assistant surgeon, USS *Kingfisher*	

Appendix C (*continued*)

Name	Origin	Position	Miscellaneous
Mr. Wild	Unknown	Eustis Place storekeeper	Unknown
Charles Williams	Unknown	Government superintendent at Oliver Fripp Place, Justice of the Peace	Returned North on the boat with Mary and Caty May 30, 1864
Rufus Hathaway Winsor	Brookline, Mass.	Philbrick's Clerk	Allen mentioned that Winsor was the one "hurt so badly at Mrs. Fay's"
Frank Gordon Winsor	Brookline, Mass.	Training as an assistant at Pine Grove	Rufus Winsor's brother
Lieutenant Ephraim Albert Wood	Wellesley, Mass.	55th Massachusetts Regiment	Former pupil at West Newton School, where Allen was a principal
Major "So-and-so"	Unknown	Unknown unit	Delivered bombastic but brief "spread-eagle" speech at the meeting at the church January 17, 1864
"Man from the main"	Mainland S.C.	Worker	Appeared to be white
Dudley Buck Army Private 1	Unknown	13th Indiana Regiment	From Samuel Bassett's regiment
Dudley Buck Army Private 2	Unknown	13th Indiana Regiment	From Samuel Bassett's regiment
Dudley Buck German passenger	Wittenberg, Germany	Unknown	
Dudley Buck passenger	Bucks County, Pa.	Carpenter	Described by Allen as "jolly red-bearded"
Dudley Buck "Flaxen-headed boy"	New York?	41st New York Regiment	Very quiet and young, Allen thought him no more than 15 years old

Appendix D

William Allen's St. Helena Reading List

Allen cited sources marked by * in his article "The Freedmen and Free Labor in the South."

    d = diary

    j = journal

Appendix D (*continued*)

Date First Mentioned	Publication/Title	Author	Comments
November 6, 1863 j	*Des idées napoléoniennes*	Napoleon III, author	Work by Louis-Napoléon to transform Bonapartism into a political ideology
November 6, 1863 j	*The New Gospel of Peace According to St. Benjamin*	Richard Grant White, author	Satire of the Civil War written in biblical language
November 6, 1863 j	*Romola*	George Eliot, author	1862–63 serialized novel
December 2, 1863 j	Boston *Commonwealth**	James M. Stone, publisher	Weekly newspaper Allen cited a letter from Dr. Howe to Hon. T. D. Eliot in the January 8, 1864, issue of the *Commonwealth*
December 2, 1863 j	*Philip van Artevelde*	Sir Henry Taylor, author	1834 tragic play
December 13, 1863 j	*Levana or the Doctrine of Education*	Jean Paul Richter, author	1807 work on humanist theories of education
December 13, 1863 j	Various newspapers*	Various	Assorted newspapers sent by Allen's brothers and sisters Allen named ten papers To those may be added the *New York Times* and the *New York Semiweekly Post*, which he cited in the May *Christian Examiner*
January 1, 1864 d	Littell's *Living Age*	Eliakim Littell, editor	Weekly literary magazine comprising selections from British and American newspapers and magazines
January 1, 1864 d	*The Ordeal of Free Labor in the British West Indies**	William G. Sewell, author	1861 book

Date First Mentioned	Publication/Title	Author	Comments
January 2, 1864 d	*The Results of Emancipation**	Augustin Cochin, author Mary Louise Booth, translator	1862 translation of an 1861 book written in French
January 2, 1864 d	*Dix ans d'impérialisme*	George William Frederick Villiers, author	1863 book
January 2, 1864 d	*Tale of Two Cities*	Charles Dickens, author	1859 novel
January 4, 1864 d	*Considérations sur les causes de la grandeur des Romains et de leur décadence (Considerations on the Causes of the Grandeur and Decadence of the Romans)*	Charles-Louis de Secondat, baron de La Brède et de Montesquieu, author	1734 book Montesquieu published many works that Allen may have read Given his interest in Roman history, however, *Grandeur and Decadence* is the work he most likely was reading
January 5, 1864 d	"Lenore"	Gottfried August Bürger, author	1774 poem
January 9, 1864 d	"Cooper Union Speech"*	Wendell Phillips, author	December 22, 1863, speech delivered at the Cooper Union in New York City
January 9, 1864 d	*Christian Examiner**	Thomas B. Fox and Joseph Henry Allen, editors	Bimonthly religious review advocating Unitarianism Allen read the *Examiner* regularly
January 10, 1864 j	*Boston Daily Advertiser**	Nathan Hale, editor (until his death, in 1863)	Daily newspaper with a Republican perspective Allen cited a letter from "E. A.," which appeared in the January 4 issue of the *Advertiser*

Appendix D (*continued*)

Date First Mentioned	Publication/Title	Author	Comments
January 10, 1864 j	*Congregationalist*	Reverend H. M. Dexter, editor	Newspaper with a Christian perspective
January 10, 1864 j	*New York Evening Post*	William Cullen Bryant, editor	Daily newspaper
January 10, 1864 j	*Army and Navy Journal and Gazette of the Regular and Volunteer Forces*	Francis Pharcellus Church and William Conant Church, publishers	Weekly newspaper specializing in war news
January 10, 1864 j	*Atlantic Monthly*	James Russell Lowell, editor	Literary and cultural monthly. Charlotte Forten's "Life on the Sea Islands" was printed in the May 1864 issue
January 10, 1864 j	*Independent*	Henry Ward Beecher, editor, Theodore Tilton, assistant editor	Congregationalist weekly newspaper
January 10, 1864 j	*National Anti-Slavery Standard*	Oliver Johnson, editor	Weekly antislavery newspaper published in New York
January 10, 1864 j	*Philadelphia Inquirer*	William W. Harding, owner	Daily newspaper
January 10, 1864 j	*Slavery in South Carolina and the Ex-Slaves or the Port Royal Mission*	Austa M. French, author	1862 book. Allen thought Mrs. French's book ridiculous
January 10, 1864 d	*The Life of Jesus*	Joseph Ernest Renan, author Charles E. Wilbour, translator	1863 translation of book

Date First Mentioned	Publication/Title	Author	Comments
January 18, 1864 d	"Arthur Schopenhauer," *Christian Examiner*	Author unknown	Article about Arthur Schopenhauer, German philosopher known for his pessimistic outlook
January 20, 1864 j	*New York Weekly Tribune**	Horace Greeley, editor and publisher	Weekly newspaper advocating immediate abolition and radical Republicanism Allen may have learned of General Banks's January 1864 call for elections in Louisiana and Arkansas through the *Tribune*
January 22, 1864 d	"Weiss's Life of Theodore Parker," *Christian Examiner*	Author unknown	Review of the 1864 book *Life and Correspondence of Theodore Parker* by John Weiss
January 28, 1864 d	*Propositions Concerning Protection and Free Trade*	Willard Phillips, author	1850 book
January 29, 1864 d	*Austin Elliot*	Henry Kingsley, author	1863 novel
January 31, 1864 d	*Preliminary Report Touching the Condition and Management of Emancipated Refugees**	Freedmen's Inquiry Commission	1863 report of a special commission that investigated complaints from freedmen
January 31, 1864 d	*First Annual Report of the Educational Commission for Freedmen**	Educational Commission for Freedmen	1863 report of the Boston Educational Commission, later, the New England Freedmen's Aid Society
January 31, 1864 d	*Journal of a Residence on a Georgian Plantation*	Frances Anne (Fanny) Kemble, author	1863 book

Appendix D (*continued*)

Date First Mentioned	Publication/Title	Author	Comments
February 5, 1864 j	*History of the Romans under the Empire*	Charles Merivale, author	1850 book
February 9, 1864 d	*Mrs. Lirriper's Lodgings*	Charles Dickens, author	1863 short story
February 11, 1864 d	*Cricket on the Hearth*	Charles Dickens, author	1845 novella
February 17, 1864 d	*Notes on the Rebel Invasion of Maryland and Pennsylvania and the Battle of Gettysburg, July 1st, 2nd and 3rd, 1863*	Michael Jacobs, author	1864 booklet
February 17, 1864 d	"The Battle of Gettysburg and the Campaign in Pennsylvania," *Blackwood's Edinburgh Magazine*	Author unknown, William Blackwood and Sons, publisher	Article on Gettysburg in Blackwood's monthly magazine, published in Edinburgh, Scotland
February 18, 1864 d	*Galignani's Messenger*	John Anthony and William Galignani, publishers	Daily English-language newspaper published in France
February 18, 1864 j	*Pet Marjorie: A Story of Child Life Fifty Years Ago*	H. B. Farnie, author	1858 booklet
February 27, 1864 d	*Report of the Condition of the Freedmen of the Mississippi**	James E. Yeatman, author	1863 report published by the Western Sanitary Commission

Date First Mentioned	Publication/Title	Author	Comments
February 27, 1864 d	*Suggestions of a Plan of Organization for Free Labor, and the Leasings of Plantation along the Mississippi River*[*]	James E. Yeatman, author	1864 plan published by the Western Sanitary Commission The plan was appended to Yeatman's report already cited
February 29, 1864 d	*Report of Maj. Gen. William S. Rosecrans, U.S. Army, Commanding the Army of the Cumberland*	General William S. Rosecrans, author	1863 official Army report
March 2, 1864 d	*The Whip, Hoe and Sword*[*]	George Hughes Hepworth, author	1863 book about slavery and Union operations in the Department of the Gulf under General Banks Allen found only one important observation in Hepworth's book
March ?, 1864	Louisiana Labor System, Department of the Gulf General Order No. 23[*]	General Nathaniel P. Banks, author	Order promulgated on February 3, 1864 Allen may have read the order in a newspaper
March ?, 1864	"Dr. Howe's Report on the Colored Refugees in Canada," *Friends' Review*[*]	Samuel Rhoads, editor	Quaker journal Allen cited the February 27, 1864, issue
March ?, 1864	*Considerations on Representative Government*[*]	John Stuart Mill, author	1861 book

Appendix D (continued)

Date First Mentioned	Publication/Title	Author	Comments
March ?, 1864	New York Evening Post, Semi-Weekly Edition*	Edward Philbrick, author	Philbrick's article appeared in the March 8, 1864, issue of the Post, which Allen probably received about March 15
Allen appears to have finished researching his essay for the May Christian Examiner by about mid-March.			
March 12, 1864 d	"Exports and Imports" (Allen's quotation marks)	Author unknown	Probably an article from one of the periodicals Allen read, based on his use of quotation marks
March 12, 1864 d	Campaigns of 1862 and 1863	Emil Schalk, author	1863 book
March 14, 1864 j	Continental Monthly	John F. Trow, publisher	Magazine dedicated to literature and national policy
March 16, 1864 j	Tribune Almanac and Political Register	Horace Greeley, editor and publisher	Annual almanac published by the New York Tribune
March 20, 1864 d	"Compensation"	Ralph Waldo Emerson, author	1841 essay Allen had a long-standing interest in transcendentalism
March 26, 1864 d	Acc't of Brothers Grimm	Author unknown	Unknown
March 28, 1864 d	Römische Geschichte (Roman History)	Theodor Mommsen, author	1854–56 book in three volumes
March 28, 1864 d	On Picket Duty and Other Tales	Louisa May Alcott, author	1864 book

Date First Mentioned	Publication/Title	Author	Comments
April 6, 1864 d	On Liberty	John Stuart Mill, author	1859 book based on an 1854 essay Allen read from Mill's work repeatedly during April and May
April 11, 1864 j	Strafford	Robert Browning	1837 play Browning's first play
April 15, 1864 j	Vanity Fair	William Makepeace Thackeray, author	1847–48 novel
April 15, 1864 d	General Butler in New Orleans	James Parton, author	1863 book
April 27, 1864 d	The Newcomes: Memoirs of a Most Respectable Family	William Makepeace Thackeray, author	1853–55 serial novel
May 4, 1864 d	The Cotton Kingdom	Frederick Law Olmsted	1861 two-volume book Allen cited Olmsted in his essay "The War Policy, and the Future of the South," Christian Examiner 73 (November 1862), 435–454
May 31, 1864 d	Chronicles of the Schönberg–Cotta Family	Elizabeth Rundle Charles	1862 book about Martin Luther
June 5, 1864 d	The Bothie of Tober-na-Vuolich	Arthur Hugh Clough, author	1848 narrative poem
June 6, 1864 d	Cicero's Brutus or History	Marcus Tullius Cicero	46 B.C. history of Roman oratory
June 12, 1864 d	Colombe's Birthday	Robert Browning, author	1844 play

Appendix D (*continued*)

Date First Mentioned	Publication/Title	Author	Comments
June 13, 1864 d	*Constitutional History of England*	Thomas Erskine May, author	1863 two-volume book
June 18, 1864 d	*Strafford—Sordello*	Robert Browning, author	1837 play and 1840 epic poem printed together
June 26, 1864 d	"Flight of the Duchess"	Robert Browning, author	1845 poem
July 3, 1864 d	"Drama of Exile"	Elizabeth Barrett Barrett	1845 poem
July 11, 1864 d	*Nathan der Weise*	Gotthold Ephraim Lessing, author	1779 play
July 13, 1864 d	*Zaïre (The Tragedy of Zara)*	Voltaire, author	1732 play

Appendix E

Charleston Contacts

Appendix E (*continued*)

Name	Origin	Position	Miscellaneous
Mr. Ainsworth	Unknown	Unknown	
Mr. Albee	Unknown	Department principal of the Morris Street School	
William H. Alden	Westville, Conn.	NEFAS teacher, plantation superintendent	Superintendent of Frogmore, Woodlands, and Hope Place when Allen was on St. Helena
Gertrude E. Allen	West Newton, Mass.	NEFAS teacher at the Ashley Street School	Allen's niece, daughter of Thomas Prentiss Allen Died on June 10, 1865
First Lieutenant Henry Hobart Alvord	Bay City, Mich.	102nd USCT Regiment Board of Labor member at Orangeburg, S.C.	
Mr. Bailey	Unknown	Unknown	
Mr. Bailies	Unknown	Unknown	
Mr. Baker	Unknown	Unknown	Possibly William A. Baker, who contributed to *Slave Songs*
Mary F. Baker	Hopkinton, Mass.	NEFAS teacher	Allen left her at Hilton Head
Lieutenant Barber	Unknown	Unknown	
James Barrow	Charleston, S.C.	Unitarian leader	Spoke at the April 23, 1865, memorial service for President Lincoln Secretary of the April 19, 1865, Unitarian meeting
E. P. Beaird or E. F. Beaird	Charleston, S.C.	Teacher Upholsterer	Both men are listed as Charleston residents in the 1870s

Name	Origin	Position	Miscellaneous
Henry Ward Beecher	Brooklyn, N.Y.	Congregational minister and abolitionist	In Charleston to attend the April 14, 1865, celebration at Fort Sumter
Colonel James Chaplin Beecher	Boston, Mass.	35th USCT Regiment	Half brother of Henry Ward Beecher and Harriet Beecher Stowe
Brevet Brigadier General W.T. Bennett	Detroit, Mich.	102nd USCT Regiment	Followed General Gurney as post commander at Charleston
Nicholas Blaisdell	Boston, Mass.	NEFAS teacher	
Mr. Black	Unknown	Unknown	
James P. Blake	New Haven, Conn.	Yale class of 1862 NEFAS agent	In charge of distributing stores in Charleston Drowned on Edisto Island Christmas Day 1865
Elizabeth P. Breck	Northampton, Mass.	NEFAS teacher, department principal at the Morris Street School	
Dr. Charles Edward Briggs	Pembroke, Mass.	Surgeon, 54th Massachusetts Regiment	
Mr. Brown	Unknown	Unknown	
Mr. Burdette	Unknown	Unknown	
Mr. Burnell	Unknown	Unknown	
Harriet Buttrick	Concord, Mass.	NEFAS teacher at the St. Philip Street School	
Miss Campbell	Springfield, Mass.?	Private school mistress	Miss Lee's former teacher
Thomas W. Cardozo	Charleston, S.C.	Cofounder of the Avery Institute	Allen met with Cardozo or visited his schools on ten occasions

Appendix E (*continued*)

Name	Origin	Position	Miscellaneous
Francis Carrier	Charleston, S.C.	Cook at Allen's boarding house	Former house servant of Chancellor Dunkin
Mr. Carroll	Unknown	Unknown	
Melissa Chamberlin	Dover, N.H.	NEFAS teacher, principal of the Ashley Street School	Gertrude Allen's mentor
Luella J. Chase	Exeter, N.H.	NEFAS teacher at the St. Philip Street School	
John C. Chavis	Charleston, S.C.	Unknown	Ardent supporter of James Redpath, whom Allen found obstinate
Mrs. C. W. Clausen (black)	Charleston, S.C.	"Indigenous" teacher in Dr. Hawkes's Normal School	Made observations about Southern class distinctions
Mr. Cobb	Unknown	Unknown	
Mr. Compton	Unknown	Unknown	
Judge Dennis N. Cooley	Dubuque, Iowa	Appointed to settle titles in Charleston after the war	Allen met Cooley on St. Helena, when he was a S.C. tax commissioner
Dr. Coomb	Unknown	Unknown	
Mr. Corcoran	Unknown	Unknown	
Mr. Coryell	Unknown	Unknown	
Mary E. Cupp	Middletown, Va.	Kept way station between Orangeburg and Columbia, S.C.	The Cupps fled Virginia after the Battle of Cedar Creek

Name	Origin	Position	Miscellaneous
Mr. Curry	Unknown	Unknown	
Miss Dean	Unknown	Unknown	
Mr. Dickerson (black)	Charleston, S.C.	Unknown	Made a motion for a resolution thanking James Redpath for his service
James George Dodge	Boston, Mass.	Superintendent of Freedmen on Hilton Head	Over freedmen on government plantations
Alfred Huger Dunkin	Charleston, S.C.	Unionist, tax collector before the war, recently released from a Confederate prison	Son of Chancellor Dunkin Allen was living in the chancellor's home
Mr. Edwards	Unknown	Unknown	
Captain Edward Bulkeley Emerson	Pittsfield, Mass.	54th Massachusetts Regiment	
Mr. Evans	Unknown	Superintendent of schools on James and Johns Islands	
Charly Fitzsimmons?	Charleston, S.C.	Unknown	"Engineer"
Harrison T. Fletcher	Harvard, Mass.	NEFAS teacher, principal of the King Street School	
Charles Follen Folsom	Jamaica Plain, Mass.	Plantation superintendent	Superintendent of John Fripp Place, Mulberry Hill, and Cherry Hill when Allen was on St. Helena
Lieutenant Colonel Charles Barnard Fox	Boston, Mass.	55th Massachusetts Regiment	
Mr. Frazier	Unknown	Unknown	

Appendix E (*continued*)

Name	Origin	Position	Miscellaneous
William Channing Gannett	Boston, Mass.	Original Gideonite, plantation superintendent	Superintendent of Fripp Point and Pine Grove when Allen was on St. Helena
Elizabeth H. Garland	Dover, N.H.	NEFAS teacher, department principal at the Normal School	
William Lloyd Garrison	Boston, Mass.	Abolitionist	Founder of the antislavery newspaper *Liberator* In Charleston to attend the April 14, 1865, celebration at Fort Sumter
Captain Frank Goodwin	Boston, Mass.	55th Massachusetts Regiment	Allen knew of Goodwin as a friend of the Lamberts
Major George Edward Gouraud	New York, N.Y.	55th Massachusetts Regiment	Medal of Honor recipient for gallantry at the Battle of Honey Hill, S.C.
Captain James William Grace	New Bedford, Mass.	54th Massachusetts Regiment	
Mary C. Green	Boston, Mass.	NEFAS teacher, department principal at the Normal School	
Mr. Griffin	Unknown	Unknown	
Colonel (later General) William Gurney	New York, N.Y.	Charleston post commander	
Colonel Edward Needles Hallowell	Philadelphia, Pa.	Commander, 54th Massachusetts Regiment	Succeeded Colonel Robert Gould Shaw

Name	Origin	Position	Miscellaneous
Brigadier General Alfred Stedman Hartwell	South Natick, Mass.	Commanded a brigade, which included the 54th and 55th Massachusetts and the 102nd USCT Regiments Reassigned to Orangeburg, S.C., on May 1, 1865	Hartwell's brigade saw action around Charleston at the end of the war His black regiments headed the column that marched into Charleston when it fell, in February 1865
General John Porter Hatch	Oswego, N.Y.	Military commander of Charleston, February–August 1865	Allen found him coarse natured
Colonel Nathaniel Haughton	Washington Township, Ohio	Commander, 25th Ohio Volunteer Regiment	
Dr. Esther Hill Hawkes	Manchester, N.H., later Lynn, Mass.	Medical doctor, NEFAS teacher, principal of the Normal School	Came with Dr. Marcy on June 4, 1865, to visit Gertrude Allen when she lay ill
Captain Hewcy	Unknown	Unknown	
Reverend James Kendall Hosmer, D.D.	Deerfield, Mass.	Educator, historian, and writer	Color bearer of the 52nd Massachusetts Regiment Allen and Hosmer both taught at Antioch College in 1865–66 Contributed to *Slave Songs*
Mr. Hunter	Unknown	Principal of the Chalmers Street School	
Timothy Hurley	Boston (Charlestown), Mass.	Publisher of the *South Carolina Leader and Missionary Record*	Allen found him an obnoxious demagogue

Appendix E (*continued*)

Name	Origin	Position	Miscellaneous
Lieutenant Colonel Rue Pugh Hutchins	Ohio	94th Ohio Regiment	
Mr. James	Unknown	Unknown	
Richard E. Jaques?	Charleston, S.C.	Confederate Army private	Wrote series of letters to sweetheart L. A. Syme during the siege of Charleston
A. S. Jenks?	Philadelphia, Pa.	Unknown	Later, controller of the Philadelphia school system Contributed to *Slave Songs*
Ellen S. Kempton	New Bedford, Mass.	NEFAS teacher	
Captain Ketcham	Unknown	Master of the *Golden Gate*	Seriously injured by an accidental shotgun blast to his arm on August 5, 1865
Sarah E. Lakeman	Salem, Mass.	NEFAS teacher	Allen left her at Hilton Head
Miss Lariscy	Unknown	Unknown	
Thomas Berwick Legare	Orangeburg, S.C.	Unknown	Allen met Legare on July 8, 1865, on his return trip from Columbia, S.C.
Ellen M. Lee	Templeton, Mass.	NEFAS teacher	
Mr. Lewis	Unknown	Unknown	
Sarah P. Lillie	Hopedale, Mass.	NEFAS teacher on Hilton Head	
Mrs. Little	Charleston, S.C.	Charlestonian	Sent destitute Mrs. Oxley some sugar

Name	Origin	Position	Miscellaneous
J. Sherman Littlefield	East Stoughton, Mass.	NEFAS teacher, principal of the Meeting Street School	
Roswell T. Logan	Charleston, S.C.	Associate editor, *Charleston Daily News*	*Charleston Daily News* began publishing on August 14, 1865 Logan was Allen's "Mr. O." in "Feeling of the South Carolinians"
Reverend Charles Lowe	Somerville, Mass.	Unitarian minister and NEFAS official	Delivered a celebrated sermon on the death of President Lincoln on April 23, 1865, at the Archdale Street Unitarian Church
Colonel James Lynah	Charleston, S.C.	Confederate Charlestonian	67 years old when war began
Charles Macbeth	Charleston, S.C.	Mayor of Charleston	Surrendered the city to Colonel A. G. Bennett, 21th USCT Regiment
Dr. Albert G. Mackey	Charleston, S.C.	Mason and Unionist Charlestonian	
Edward Mackey	Charleston, S.C.	Unknown	Related to Dr. Mackey
Dr. Henry O. Marcy	Boston, Mass.	Regimental surgeon, 35th USCT Regiment	
Monroe (or Munroe) Mason	Milford, Mass.	Unknown	Allen may have known Mason from his school days at the Roxbury Latin School
First Lieutenant Edmund Mazyck	Charleston, S.C.	Provisional Confederate Army	Recently returned from imprisonment at Fort Delaware

Appendix E (*continued*)

Name	Origin	Position	Miscellaneous
Mr. McGill	Savannah, Ga.	Unknown	
Mr. McVea	Unknown	Unknown	
Major Calvin S. Montague	Kalamazoo, Mich.	102nd USCT Regiment Board of Labor chairman at Orangeburg, S.C.	Allen met with Montague, Lieutenants Alvord and Trotter, and Captain Soule to discuss contract administration
Captain F. M. Montell	New York	Naval captain	Later, Freedmen's Bureau agent in Berkeley County, S.C.
Mr. Morrison	Unknown	Unknown	
Arthur T. Morse	Bradford, N.H.	NEFAS teacher, principal of the St. Philip Street School	
Louisa A. Morse	Bradford, N.H.	NEFAS teacher at the St. Philip Street School	Arthur Morse's wife
Dr. James Moultrie	Charleston, S.C.	President of the Archdale Street Unitarian Church	
Ellen Murray	Newport, R.I.	PRRC teacher	Taught at the Penn Center School on St. Helena until her death, in 1908 Contributed to *Slave Songs*
Harriet Murray	Newport, R.I.	PRRC teacher	Ellen's sister
Mr. Nash	Unknown	Unknown	

Name	Origin	Position	Miscellaneous
George Newcomb	Unknown	NFRA superintendent of schools	
Mrs. Oxley	Charleston, S.C.	Destitute elderly Charlestonian	
Miss Oxley	Charleston, S.C.	Invalid	Mrs. Oxley's paralytic daughter
Octavia C. Page	Watertown, Mass.	NEFAS teacher	
Thomas Parker?	Charleston, S.C.	Unknown	Margaret Parker's husband
Margaret Parker?	Charleston, S.C.	Unknown	Thomas Parker's wife
Bishop Daniel Alexander Payne	Wilberforce, Ohio	President of Wilberforce College; Bishop of the A.M.E. Church	In Charleston to reorganize the church there
Captain Perry	Unknown	Unknown	
Caroline Peters	Charleston, S.C.	Boarding house keeper, where Messrs. Redpath and Newcomb lived	
Mr. Pickett	Unknown	Unknown	
Gilbert Pillsbury	Hamilton, Mass.	NEFAS official, commissioner of freedmen at Hilton Head, then Charleston	Later, mayor of Charleston
Ann Frances Ray Pillsbury	Ludlow, Mass.	NEFAS teacher, principal of the Morris Street School	Wife of Gilbert Pillsbury

Appendix E (*continued*)

Name	Origin	Position	Miscellaneous
Reverend Doctor Anthony Toomer Porter	Charleston, S.C.	Charleston Episcopal minister / Founder of the Porter-Gaud School	Ardent secessionist
Captain Joseph T. Pratt	Philadelphia, Pa.	32nd USCT Regiment / Provost marshal of Charleston	
Lieutenant John W. Pollock	Pa.	32nd USCT Regiment	
Sarah F. Prescott	Boston, Mass.	NEFAS teacher	
William Proctor	Charleston, S.C.	Elderly Charlestonian	Brother of Allen's cousin Lydia / Resided at 33 Wentworth Street
Alfred Purdie	Unknown	Government agent?	
Quash (black barber)	Charleston, S.C.	Barber	Respected by blacks in Charleston
Mr. Randall	Unknown	Unknown	
James Redpath	Kalamazoo, Mich.	Superintendent of Charleston Public Schools	Journalist and antislavery activist / Later, assisted Jefferson and Varina Davis in preparing memoirs
Mary Cotton Redpath	Wolfeboro, N.H.	One of the originators of the Memorial Day at the Race Course in Charleston on May 1, 1865	James Redpath's wife / Allen wrote, "With Mrs Redpath &c. to Race Course" in his diary on May 1, 1865

Name	Origin	Position	Miscellaneous
Lieutenant Marshall N. Rice	Massachusetts	35th USCT Regiment	Rice served as an adjutant in Charleston
Mr. Ritchie	Unknown	Unknown	
Miss Robbins	Unknown	Principal of the St. Michael's School	
Minda Robertson	Charleston, S.C.	Ashley Street School pupil	Became distraught over Gertrude's death
Thomas Edwin Ruggles	Milton, Mass.	Original Gideonite	Yale graduate and farmer, superintendent of the Corner Farm when Allen was on St. Helena Contributed to *Slave Songs*
Amanda S. Ruggles	Milton, Mass.	NEFAS teacher on St. Helena	T. Edwin Ruggles's sister
Letitia Sargent	Gloucester, Mass.	NEFAS teacher	
Major Thomas Jefferson Saunders	Davenport, Iowa	Paymaster under General William T. Sherman	Medical doctor by training
Dr. Louis McPherson de Saussure	Charleston, S.C.	Charleston physician	Brought in to see Gertrude Allen as she lay dying
Theodoric C. Severance	Cleveland, Ohio	Assistant Treasury agent, collector of the port of Hilton Head Abolitionist	Husband of abolitionist and suffragette Caroline Seymour Severance
Colonel Robert W. Seymour	Charleston, S.C.	Long-time Charleston lawyer	
Captain Charles Carroll Soule	Brookline, Mass.	55th Massachusetts Regiment	Allen first met Soule on St. Helena

Appendix E (*continued*)

Name	Origin	Position	Miscellaneous
Lucy M. Southworth	North Brookfield, Mass.	NEFAS teacher, department principal at the Morris Street School	
Mr. Spencer	Unknown	Unknown	
Elmira B. Stanton	Lowell, Mass.	NEFAS teacher	
Reverend Calvin Stebbins	Boston, Mass.	Minister at the Archdale Street Unitarian Church	Recent graduate of Harvard Divinity School Short-lived tenure at Archdale Street Church
Edward Gray Stetson	Lexington, Mass.	Plantation superintendent	Superintendent of Dr. Jenkins Place when Allen was on St. Helena
Mr. Taylor (black)	Columbia, S.C.	Unknown	Allen stayed in Taylor's home near Columbia, S.C., on July 5, 1865
Robert Seymour Tharin	Charleston, S.C.	Unionist Charlestonian	
Reuben Tomlinson	Philadelphia, Pa.	Superintendent of freedmen at Charleston	General superintendent of St. Helena and Lady' Islands when Allen was on St. Helena Contributed to *Slave Songs*
Laura Matilda Towne	Shoemakertown, Pa.	PRRC teacher	Taught at the Penn Center School on St. Helena until her death in 1901 Contributed to *Slave Songs*
Maria Traynor	Charleston, S.C.	Charlestonian	Assisted Union prisoners of war at Andersonville, Ga., and Charleston, S.C.

Name	Origin	Position	Miscellaneous
George Alfred Trenholm	Charleston, S.C.	Confederate secretary of the Treasury	Allen had an extended interview with Trenholm on the train from Orangeburg to Charleston
Second Lieutenant James Monroe Trotter	Cincinnati, Ohio	55th Massachusetts Regiment Board of Labor member at Orangeburg, S.C.	First black promoted to the officer ranks Allen met Trotter as a sergeant on St. Helena
Captain James Morris Walton	Pittsfield, Mass.	Judge advocate, 54th Massachusetts Regiment	Prosecuted Edward W. Andrews and others in court-martial proceedings in Orangeburg, S.C., that began July 3, 1865
Louisa Webb or Jennie Webb	Charleston, S.C.	"Indigenous" teacher at the St. Philip Street School	Both women listed as teachers in the *Freedmen's Record,* vol. 1
Edmund Welson (or Wilson)	Anderson District, S.C.	Planter	Allen's "planter from the Anderson District" in "Feeling of the South Carolinians"
George M. Wells	Providence, R.I.	Original Gideonite, plantation superintendent	Superintendent at the Mary Jenkins Place when Allen was on St. Helena
Mr. Weston	Unknown	Principal of the Tradd Street School	
Joanna J. Weston or Maria F. Weston	Charleston, S.C.	"Indigenous" teacher	Both women listed as teachers in the *Freedmen's Record,* vol. 1
Captain Josiah C. White	Unknown	35th USCT Regiment	
Almira P. White	Exeter, N.H.	NEFAS teacher, possibly at the St. Philip Street School	

Appendix E (*continued*)

Name	Origin	Position	Miscellaneous
David E. Whitton	Wolfeboro, N.H.	NEFAS teacher, principal of the Wentworth Street School	
Lieutenant Colonel Amiel J. Willard	Albany, N.Y.	35th USCT Regiment	Later, justice of the South Carolina Supreme Court
Mrs. Amiel J. Willard	Unknown	Unknown	A. J. Willard's wife
Charles Williams	Unknown	Government superintendent at Oliver Fripp Place, justice of the peace	Superintendent at the Oliver Fripp Place when Allen was on St. Helena
Mr. Williams	Unknown	Unknown	
Henry Wilson	Natick, Mass.	U.S. senator from Massachusetts, former governor of the state, later, U.S. vice president under Grant	Radical Republican Arrived in Charleston on the *Oceanus* for the April 14, 1865, celebration at Fort Sumter
Brigadier General Charles Henry van Wyck	Bloomington, N.Y.	Congressman from New York	Later, U.S. senator from Nebraska
Two unnamed Confederate officers	Vicinity of Orangeburg, S.C.?	Unknown	Returning from Fort Delaware imprisonment

Notes

Preface

1. See Michael D. Coker, *The Battle of Port Royal* (Charleston: The History Press, 2009).

2. William Francis Allen, Charles Pickard Ware, and Lucy McKim Garrison, eds., *Slave Songs of the United States* (New York: A. Simpson, 1867).

3. James Robert Hester, "Slave Songs of Augusta," B.A. thesis, Augusta State University, 2010.

4. Dena J. Epstein, *Sinful Tunes and Spirituals: Black Folk Music to the Civil War* (Urbana: University of Illinois Press, 2003). Willie Lee Rose, *Rehearsal for Reconstruction: The Port Royal Experiment* (Athens: University of Georgia Press, 1964). Gerald Robbins, "William F. Allen: Classical Scholar among the Slaves," *History of Education Quarterly* 5 (December 1965), 211–23.

5. Eric Foner, *Reconstruction: America's Unfinished Revolution* (New York: Harper and Row, 1988).

6. Allen's scholastic life was summarized by his brother Joseph: "William Francis Allen graduated at Harvard College in 1851; was a private teacher in the family of Mrs. Waller, New York, for three years; spent two years in Europe; was an Associate Principal of the West Newton English and Classical School from 1856 to 1863; was for two years in the employ of the Freedmen's Aid and Western Sanitary Commission; the conductor of the classical department of Antioch College, O., and at Eaglewood, N.J., and is now Professor of Ancient Languages and History in Wisconsin University, Madison, Wis." Joseph Allen, *Genealogical Sketches of the Allen Family of Medfield* (Boston: Nichols and Noyes, 1869), 23.

A Note on the Transcriptions and Sources

1. William F. Allen Family Papers, Wisconsin Historical Society, Mss 384, Box 1, Folders 8–9; Box 2, Folders 2 and 6; and Microfilm 33. The collection does not contain Allen's diary for October–December 1863—if he kept one during that time. His St. Helena diary begins on January 1, 1864. The terms "journal" and "diary" in the WHS collection are reversed as Allen used them. Here, they are in keeping with Allen's usage; thus, "diary" in the WHS collection is termed "journal" here and vice versa.

2. Allen's designations generally but not always coincided with the key provided here. For example, he referred to the "McTureous Place," but he did not distinguish between the Martha and the James McTureous Places. For more on the former owners of the plantations, see Guion Griffis Johnson, *A Social History of the Sea Islands: With Special Reference to St. Helena Island, South Carolina* (Chapel Hill: University of North Carolina Press, 1930).

Introduction

1. Dr. Thomas Low Nichols, *Forty Years of American Life* (London: John Maxwell and Company, 1864).

2. Ralph Waldo Emerson, "Nature," a 1836 essay that laid the foundation for transcendentalism.

3. For a short memoir of Allen, see David B. Frankenburger, Reuben G. Thwaites, Frederick J. Turner, and Joseph H. Crocker, eds., *Essays and Monographs by William Francis Allen* (Boston: Geo. H. Ellis, 1890). For an extended biography, especially of Allen's academic career, see Owen Philip Stearns, "William Francis Allen: Wisconsin's First Historian," master's thesis, University of Wisconsin, 1955.

4. Something of Allen's early years can be gleaned from a passage his mother wrote in 1832: "My days have been, so far, quiet for me since last week; for the older children went to school the week after Thanksgiving, and the little ones began to go last week to an Infant School. I am left entirely alone except William, who is, in himself, a host." Elizabeth W. Allen, *Memorial of Joseph and Lucy Clark Allen* (Boston: George H. Ellis, 1891), 83.

5. Roxbury Latin School, Roxbury, Mass., was a boys' school founded in 1645 by the Reverend John Eliot. See Jeremiah Evarts Greene, *Roxbury Latin School: An Outline of Its History* (Worcester, Mass.: Charles Hamilton, 1887).

6. Martha Brooks (or Brookes) Waller, New York City, 18th Ward, had five children, according to the 1850 federal census: Fernando, age 12; Frank, age 10; Anna, age 8; Edwin (Elwyn), age 5; and Emma, age 2. Frank became an artist of modest reputation, and Elwyn became a noted chemist. Mrs. Waller lived with or next door to her father, Joshua Brooks; her mother, Martha; and her sister, Sophia. Mrs. Waller's husband, Joseph Fernando Waller, is listed in the 1857 *New York City Directory*, but he may not have lived with her and the children because she appears to have been the head of the household in the 1850 and 1860 censuses, and he is not listed with the family.

7. Ralph Waldo Emerson, "The American Scholar," speech delivered August 31, 1837, to the Harvard Phi Beta Kappa Society, explaining a true American scholar's relationship to nature. Oliver Wendell Holmes Sr. called the speech "the declaration of independence of American intellectual life." Susan Cheever, *American Bloomsbury: Louisa May Alcott, Ralph Waldo Emerson, Margaret Fuller, Nathaniel Hawthorne, and Henry David Thoreau: Their Lives, Their Loves, Their Work* (New York: Simon and Schuster, 2006), 34.

8. Theodore Parker, Lexington, Mass., transcendentalist, abolitionist, and reformist minister of the Unitarian Church. Parker was one of the "Secret Six" who funded John Brown's raid on the arsenal at Harpers Ferry, Virginia.

9. William Henry Channing, *My Symphony* (New York: Barse and Hopkins, 1900).

10. Arnold Hermann Ludwig Heeren (d. 1842), professor of history at the University of Göttingen. Heeren brought economics, social considerations, and politics into the study of ancient history. The *Encyclopedia Britannica* (11th edition, 1911) describes him as a "pioneer of the economic interpretation of history."

11. Nathaniel Topliff Allen, West Newton, Mass.

12. Mary Tileston Lambert, West Newton, Mass., daughter of the Reveremd Henry Lambert and Catherine Brown Porter.

13. Stearns, "William Francis Allen: Wisconsin's First Historian," 41–42.

14. St. Helena journal, January 31, 1864. Stearns wrote about Allen's brush with the draft: "How he contrived to substitute teaching duty for the New England Freedmen's Aid Society in lieu of military service, the records fail to indicate. There is a strong possibility . . . that

he was acquainted with Edward Atkinson, Octavius B. Frothingham, Thomas Wentworth Higginson, and Edward S. Philbrick, vice-president of the New England Aid Society. In any event, he was hired by Philbrick in the summer of 1863, and was then given an official teaching appointment by the [Boston] Educational Commission." Stearns, "William Francis Allen: Wisconsin's First Historian," 55–56.

15. In order to close the Southern ports of Charleston and Savannah, the North selected Port Royal harbor as a base of naval operations. Accordingly, a flotilla under the command of Commodore Samuel Francis DuPont with twelve thousand soldiers under General Thomas West Sherman was sent to secure the harbor and the adjacent islands. The islands fell in breathtakingly short fashion after a sea battle between the inept Southern shore batteries and DuPont's gunships on November 7, 1861. The white inhabitants fled the islands before Sherman's invasion, leaving behind about ten thousand slaves in their haste.

16. For an overview of the Port Royal Experiment, see Willie Lee Rose, *Rehearsal for Reconstruction: The Port Royal Experiment* (Athens: University of Georgia Press, 1964).

17. See Appendix A for a discussion of the principal freedmen's aid organizations active at Port Royal during the war.

18. "Original" Gideonites were those who came to the South on the *Atlantic* in March 1862.

19. Catherine Porter Noyes, Boston, Mass. Allen spelled her name "Katy," but she spelled it "Caty." For her St. Helena diary, see Catherine Porter Noyes Papers, Schlesinger Library, Radcliffe Institute, Harvard University. Miss Noyes taught on St. Helena Island until 1866, and she taught at Beaufort with Elizabeth Hyde Botume in 1869.

20. Charles Pickard Ware and Harriet Ware, Milton, Mass., were brother and sister. Emma Forbes Ware, ed., *Ware Genealogy* (Boston: Charles H. Pope, 1901).

21. William Francis Allen, Charles Pickard Ware, and Lucy McKim Garrison, eds., *Slave Songs of the United States* (New York: A. Simpson, 1867).

22. Besides being vice president of the New England Freedmen's Aid Society, Philbrick headed a consortium of fifteen investors, which owned eleven plantations and leased two others on the Sea Islands.

23. See Appendix B for a list of St. Helena inhabitants Allen came to know.

24. Much of Philbrick's thinking can be gathered from his letters. See Elizabeth Ware Pearson, ed., *Letters from Port Royal Written at the Time of the Civil War* (Boston: W. B. Clarke Company, 1906).

25. St. Helena journal, November 10, 1863, and February 21, 1864.

26. See Appendix C for a list of outsiders with whom Allen came into contact.

27. Henry George Spaulding, "Under the Palmetto," *Continental Monthly* 4, no. 2 (August 1863), 188–203. What Allen described here was not a spiritual or a shout, as related by Spaulding, but an example of "lining out a hymn" or "Dr. Watts singing" (in this case to the tune of Old Hundredth). For an explanation of lining out hymns, see William T. Dargan, *Lining Out the Word* (Berkeley: University of California Press, 2006). For a musical transcription of a lined-out hymn ("Amazing Grace" to the tune "Pisgah"), see George Pullen Jackson, *White and Negro Spirituals* (Locust Valley, N.Y.: J. J. Augustin, 1943), back fly leaf.

28. St. Helena journal, November 28, 1863. Hooper was aide-de-camp to General Rufus Saxton, military governor the Department of the South. Hooper was a fertile source of information for Allen about the freedmen and especially about official matters affecting them. A few of Hooper's letters are included in a Harvard collection. See Edward William Hooper Papers, 1862–1866 (Miss. Am 1727), Houghton Library, Harvard University, Cambridge, Mass.

29. St. Helena journal, November 22, 1863. Allen used his knowledge of black dialect years later in reviewing Joel Chandler Harris's *Uncle Remus*. See W. F. Allen, "Southern Negro Folk-Lore," *Dial* 1, no. 9 (January 1881), 183–85.

30. For more on the conscription of Port Royal freedmen and their resistance to it, see Gerald Robbins, "The Sea Island Experiment 1861–1865," master's thesis, University of Wisconsin, 1959, 36–77. See also Bennie J. McRea Jr., Curtis M. Miller, and Cheryl Trowbridge-Miller, *Nineteenth Century Freedom Fighters: The 1st South Carolina Volunteers* (Charleston: Arcadia, 2006). For more on the Port Royal land sales, see Robbins, "The Sea Island Experiment 1861–1865," 78–116. See also Willie Lee Rose, "'Squatter Rights' or 'Charitable Purposes'" and "'The Righteous Rail against Us,'" in Rose, *Rehearsal for Reconstruction*, 272–319.

31. Frankenburger et al., *Essays and Monographs by William Francis Allen*, 10–11.

32. See Appendix D for a list of Allen's St. Helena reading materials.

33. William Grant Sewell, *The Ordeal of Free Labor in the British West Indies* (New York: Harper and Brothers, 1861). William Francis Allen, "The Freedmen and Free Labor in the South," *Christian Examiner* 76 (May 1864), 344–74.

34. St. Helena journal, June 1 and 3, 1864.

35. St. Helena journal, June 19, 1864.

36. Frankenburger et al., *Essays and Monographs by William Francis Allen*, 8.

37. William Greenleaf Eliot, St. Louis, Mo., commissioner of the Western Sanitary Commission, cofounder, with Commission president James Erwin Yeatman, of Washington University in St. Louis. The Commission was a private agency charged with caring for sick and wounded soldiers. Founded by abolitionists, it saw to the needs of the freedmen and war refugees as well.

38. Stearns, "William Francis Allen: Wisconsin's First Historian," 59. For a description of conditions at Helena, see Rhonda M. Kohl, "'This Godforsaken Town': Death and Disease at Helena, Arkansas, 1862–63," *Civil War History* 50, no. 2 (June 2004).

39. Colonel John Eaton Jr., Sutton, N.H., General Superintendent of Freedmen, Department of the Tennessee and State of Arkansas.

40. Allen, "Free Labor in Louisiana," *Christian Examiner* 78 (May 1865), 383–99.

41. Hannah E. Stevenson, Boston, Mass., secretary, NEFAS Committee on Teachers.

42. Gertrude E. Allen, West Newton, Mass., daughter of Thomas Prentiss Allen. She died on June 10, 1865, of "the fever of the climate" after a few days' illness.

43. The August 1865 "CASH ACCOUNT" page of Allen's diary contains this entry: "Mr. Lambert (nurse)." This appears to be a reminder to repay his father-in-law for the cost of a nurse.

44. Charleston journal, April 19, 1865.

45. James Redpath, Kalamazoo, Mich., journalist and antislavery activist, superintendent of Charleston public schools by military appointment in February 1865. For more on Redpath, see John R. McKivigan, *Forgotten Firebrand: James Redpath and the Making of Nineteenth-Century America* (Ithaca, N.Y.: Cornell University Press, 2008).

46. Stearns, "William Francis Allen: Wisconsin's First Historian," 64–67.

47. See Appendix E for a list of people with whom Allen came in contact during his stay in Charleston.

48. Allen traveled by train from Charleston to Orangeburg, then overland from Orangeburg to Columbia, following the approximate route of Interstate 26 today. The Charleston-to-Orangeburg line was part of the South Carolina Railroad, originally, the Charleston and Hamburg Railroad.

49. Charleston journal, July 5, 1865.

50. Allen, "My dear sister," August 7, 1865, William F. Allen Family Papers, Box 1, Folder 3, Wisconsin Historical Society. Allen speculated about where he might be assigned if he returned to the South, and he expressed a preference for Charleston because he was "already acquainted there."

51. Charleston journal, July 10, 1865.

52. William Francis Allen, "A Trip in South Carolina," *Nation* 1, no. 4 (July 27, 1865), 106–7. Allen's letters were written on July 6 from Columbia, on July 9 from Orangeburg, and on July 12 from Charleston.

53. Allen, "State of Things in South Carolina," *Nation* 1, no. 6 (August 10, 1865), 172–73.

54. Allen, "Feeling of the South Carolinians," *Nation* 1, no. 8 (August 24, 1865), 238–39.

55. Allen, "South Carolina, One of the United States," *Christian Examiner* 79 (September 1865), 226–51.

56. Allen, "The Southern Whites," *Nation* 1, no. 11 (September 14, 1865), 331–32.

57. Allen, "The Basis of Suffrage," *Nation* 1, no. 12 (September 21, 1865), 362–64. Dr. Francis Lieber, a German-American jurist and political philosopher, was a professor of history and political economy at South Carolina College (now the University of South Carolina) from 1835 to 1856. He authored *Instructions for the Government of United States Armies in the Field* (General Order 100, 1863) governing the wartime conduct of U.S. troops. Charles Sumner, of Boston, Mass., was a U.S. senator from Massachusetts. He was almost killed by Congressman Preston Brooks of South Carolina on the floor of the Senate in 1856 after he delivered an antislavery speech titled "The Crime against Kansas." Major General Robert Cumming Schenck, of Dayton, Ohio, was a congressman from Ohio. President Lincoln appointed Schenk to the rank of general at the outset of the war. He commanded troops in major engagements, including both Battles of Bull Run. Interestingly, the Fourteenth Amendment, Section 2, established a provision similar to that advanced by Lieber, Sumner, and Schenck, and the Fifteenth Amendment, Section 1, established a provision like that contained in Phillips's proposal.

58. Allen, "The Negro Dialect," *Nation* 1, no. 24 (December 14, 1865), 744–45.

59. For an overview of the *Christian Examiner,* see Frank Luther Mott, "The Christian Disciple and the Christian Examiner," *New England Quarterly* 1, no. 2 (April 1928), 197–207.

60. Allen, "The War Policy, and the Future of the South," *Christian Examiner* 73 (November 1862), 435–54. Allen, "Democracy on Trial," *Christian Examiner* 74 (March 1863), 262–94. Robert Gascoyne-Cecil, "Democracy on Its Trial," *Quarterly Review* 110, no. 219 (July 1861), 247–88. Stearns, "William Francis Allen: Wisconsin's First Historian," 49–55.

61. Allen, "The Freedmen and Free Labor in the South," *Christian Examiner* 76 (May 1864), 344–74.

62. John Stuart Mill, "The Criteria for a Good Form of Government," ch. 2 of *Considerations on Representative Government* (London: Parker, Son, and Bourn, 1861).

63. Latin, *prædium*, a farm or estate. Prædial servitude was a feudal system of agrarian tenancy approximating slavery. The tenants' work was done sloppily.

64. Wendell Phillips, "Cooper Union Speech," delivered at the Cooper Union for the Advancement of Science and Art, New York, on December 22, 1863.

65. Congress established the Bureau of Refugees, Freedmen, and Abandoned Lands in March 1865. Freedmen's Inquiry Commission, *Preliminary Report Touching on the Condition and Management of Emancipated Refugees: Made to the Secretary of War* (New York: John F. Trow, 1863).

66. James E. Yeatman, *Suggestions of a Plan of Organization for Free Labor, and the Leasing of Plantations along the Mississippi River* (St. Louis: Western Sanitary Commission, 1863).

67. Sewell, *The Ordeal of Free Labor in the British West Indies.*

68. Allen, "The Freedmen and Free Labor in the South," 373–74.

69. Allen, "Free Labor in Louisiana," 383–99.

70. Colonel John Eaton, *Report of the General Superintendent of Freedmen, Department of the Tennessee and State of Arkansas for 1864* (Memphis: Published by Permission, 1865).

71. General Nathaniel P. Banks, "Louisiana Labor System," Department of the Gulf General Order No. 23, February 8, 1864. Wendell Phillips, "Speech before the Massachusetts Antislavery Society," *Antislavery Standard*, February 11, 1865.

72. Allen, "Free Labor in Louisiana," 393–94.

73. Edward S. Philbrick, "Letter in Response to Question about Wages for Laborers, April 16, 1864," *Second Annual Report of the New England Freedmen's Aid Society* (Boston: NEFAS Publishing Office, 1864).

74. Allen, "Free Labor in Louisiana," 396.

75. Smalls and Rivers were active in the Beaufort area while Allen was on St. Helena. He was especially impressed by a speech Rivers made at the land sale on February 21, 1864. And he noted on May 17 that both men were elected as delegates to the Republican National Convention, which was to be held in Baltimore on June 7–8, 1864.

76. Allen, "South Carolina, One of the United States," 226–51.

77. Orestes Augustus Brownson, *The American Republic: Its Constitution, Tendencies, and Destiny* (New York: P. O'Shea, 1865).

78. Henry Ward Beecher, "Universal Suffrage," and Wendell Phillips, "The Lesson of President Lincoln's Death," *Universal Suffrage, and Complete Equality in Citizenship, the Safeguards of Democratic Institutions* (Boston: Geo. C. Rand and Avery, 1865), 5–11 and 14–16.

79. Allen, "South Carolina, One of the United States," 251.

80. Thomas Prentiss Allen was Allen's brother. George Ellis Allen was Allen's cousin and associate principal of the West Newton English and Classical School.

81. Dena J. Epstein, *Sinful Tunes and Spirituals: Black Folk Music to the Civil War* (Urbana: University of Illinois Press, 2003), 308.

82. Frankenburger et al., *Essays and Monographs*, 16.

83. Ibid., 13.

84. Stearns, "William Francis Allen: Wisconsin's First Historian," 74.

85. Ray Allen Billington, *Frederick Jackson Turner: Historian, Scholar, Teacher* (New York: Oxford University Press, 1973), 31. (Interestingly, the inside front cover of the Google Books online copy of *Slave Songs* is labeled "from the books of Ray A Billington."). Turner (1861–1932) was professor of history at the University of Wisconsin until 1910; he then taught at Harvard. He was known for his "Frontier Thesis" and for his "Sectional Hypothesis," which profoundly influenced the study of America history throughout much of the twentieth century. Billington traced Turner's interest in history directly to Allen, when he noted that "As a junior in the fall of 1882 . . . he [Turner] discovered a new interest that made the classics seem dull and archaic. He found history, through a remarkable teacher named William Francis Allen. From the time he entered Professor Allen's class, Fred was a lost soul, so absorbed with this exciting field of learning that all other studies seemed unimportant. He often testified in later life that no other person so greatly influenced his future. 'Allen,' he wrote in 1920, 'has always looked over my shoulder and stirred my historical conscience.'" This was only a slight exaggeration. That wise and good man shaped his young student into a first-rate historian, equipped him with the tools of the trade, broadened his perspectives, and kindled the enthusiasms that sustained him for the rest of his life." Billington, *Frederick Jackson Turner: Historian, Scholar, Teacher*, 25.

St. Helena Journal

1. U.S. Mail Steamship Company vessel, burned at Dog-Tooth Bend on the Mississippi River on February 6, 1865.

2. Atlantic mariners' couplet, whose origin is lost in antiquity.

3. The Russian Atlantic and Pacific fleets wintered at New York and San Francisco, respectively, during 1863. Their movement to the United States is thought to have served two purposes: to deter Britain or France from entering the U.S. Civil War on the Confederate side and to avoid the Russian Navy being bottled up in vulnerable home ports should Britain or France intervene in the Polish Insurrection of 1863.

4. The Reveremd Joseph Allen, D.D., Northborough, Mass., Allen's father. Reverend Allen was the longtime minister of the Northborough Unitarian Church. (Allen himself was a lifelong Unitarian.)

5. No information about Chaplain Davis was found in the rosters of black regiments or elsewhere. Samuel Harrison was the chaplain of the famous 54th Massachusetts. Perhaps Davis was an assistant under Harrison.

6. James Seymour Severance, Concord, Mass., son of abolitionists T. C. and Caroline Seymour Severance.

7. Edward S. Philbrick, Brookline, Mass., original Gideonite. Philbrick headed a consortium that purchased eleven plantations in the March 1863 land sales. These plantations included Coffin Point, Fripp Point, Pine Grove, Cherry Hill, John Fripp Place, Mulberry Hill, Corner Farm, and the Mary Jenkins Place, all on St. Helena Island, and Cuthbert's Point on Lady's Island.

8. Thomas Edwin Ruggles, Milton, Mass., original Gideonite, superintendent of the Corner Farm.

9. Charles Follen Folsom, Jamaica Plain, Mass., superintendent of the John Fripp Place, Mulberry Hill, and Cherry Hill.

10. General Alfred Howe Terry, commander, Morris Island, S.C., Division of General Quincy Adams Gillmore's X Corps.

11. Allen's wife Mary (Molly) Tileston Lambert Allen. Catherine P. (Caty) Noyes, Boston, Mass., Mary Allen's cousin. Allen spelled her name "Katy." He referred to her as "Miss Noyes" in his March 19, 1864, diary entry. The *Second Annual Report of the New England Freedmen's Aid Society* lists her erroneously as Miss R. P. Noyes.

12. The Reverend C. S. Martindale, American Missionary Association (AMA), formerly with the American Bible Society in Ohio.

13. Captain Zina H. Robinson, Bath, Maine, 9th Maine Regiment.

14. Lieutenant J. Wesley Benjamin, Cortland, N.Y., 157th New York Regiment, had been wounded at Gettysburg. The 157th New York was stationed on Folly Island, S.C., from August 1863 until February 1864.

15. Sarah Elizabeth Reeve Peck, Roxbury, Mass., wife of the Reverend Solomon Peck. Elizabeth H. Peck, original Gideonite, and Sarah E. Peck, Nation Freedman's Relief Association (NFRA) teachers. The Reverend Solomon Peck, D.D., Roxbury, Mass., American Baptist Missionary Union missionary. Peck preceded the Gideonites to Port Royal, having begun a school in Beaufort in January 1862.

16. *Des idées napoléoniennes* (Napoleonic ideas), 1839 book about Napoleon I written by Napoleon III.

17. Richard Grant White, *The New Gospel of Peace According to St. Benjamin* (New York: Sinclair Tousey, 1863).

18. *Romola*, 1862–63 serialized novel by George Eliot.

19. *Adam Bede*, 1859 novel by George Eliot.

20. This must have been the 54th. The 57th Massachusetts (white) was not mustered in until five months later.

21. Captain Henry A. Gadsden, commander, USS *Arago*.

22. Captain Samuel Willard Saxton, Greenfield, Mass., assistant aide-de-camp to General Rufus B. Saxton, military governor of South Carolina and the Department of the South. Captain Saxton was General Saxton's brother.

23. USS *Wabash*, U.S. Navy steam screw frigate launched in 1855.

24. Battery Gregg and Battery (Fort) Wagner were Confederate battlements guarding the upper third of Morris Island. A Union attack on these battlements in July 1863 failed, with heavy losses. The 54th Massachusetts, a black regiment, suffered especially heavy casualties, including its commander, Colonel Robert Gould Shaw. The batteries finally fell into Union hands in September 1863.

25. Lieutenant Colonel James D. Strong, New York, 33rd USCT Regiment, formerly 1st South Carolina Volunteers.

26. Colonel Thomas Wentworth Higginson, commander, 1st South Carolina Volunteers. Higginson was one of the "Secret Six" who funded John Brown's raid on the arsenal at Harpers Ferry, Virginia. For an account of Higginson's service with the 1st SCV, see Thomas Wentworth Higginson, *Army Life in a Black Regiment* (Boston: Fields, Osgood and Co., 1870), and Susie King Taylor, *Reminiscences of My Life in Camp with the 33D United States Colored Troops, Late 1st South Carolina Volunteers* (Boston: Susie King Taylor, 1902).

27. The British steamship *Peterhof* was seized by the U.S. cruiser *Vanderbilt* on February 25, 1863. For more on the seizure of the *Peterhof*, see E. Delafield Smith et al., *The British Steam-Ship "Peterhof," A Report of Her Seizure by the United States Cruiser "Vanderbilt"* (New York: L. H. Biglow, 1863).

28. Method of measuring a ship's progress through the water.

29. The Reverend Silas Franklin Strout, Androscoggin County, Maine, chaplain, 9th Maine Regiment.

30. Dyer was the teacher at the Corner Farm and Mary Jenkins Place. He was either E. P. Dyer, Hingham, Mass., or C. Edward Dyer, Dorchester, Mass., both of whom were New England Freedmen's Aid Society (NEFAS) teachers and original Gideonites.

31. Rufus Hathaway Winsor, Brookline, Mass., Philbrick's clerk.

32. Captain Edward W. Hooper, Boston, Mass., original Gideonite, aide-de-camp to General Saxton.

33. Ellen Murray and her sister Harriet of Newport, R.I., were Port Royal Relief Committee (PRRC) teachers. (Their mother, Mrs. F. Murray, lived with them.) Ellen cofounded the Penn School with Laura Towne.

34. Ellen Murray and Laura Towne opened a school at The Oaks Plantation, which they moved to the Brick Church in September 1862.

35. Coffin Point Plantation.

36. Superintendent Hammond protested against the treatment of the freedmen by the 178th New York, "Les Enfants Perdus," Regiment in February 1863. See Willie Lee Rose, *Rehearsal for Reconstruction: The Port Royal Experiment* (Athens: University of Georgia Press, 1964), 240, and Rupert Sargent Holland, ed., *Letters and Diary of Laura M. Towne Written from the Sea Islands of South Carolina 1862–1884* (Cambridge, Mass.: Riverside Press, 1912), 102–3.

37. William Channing Gannett, Boston, Mass., original Gideonite, superintendent of Fripp Point and Pine Grove.

38. Dashboard: a barrier at the front of a horse-drawn carriage to protect the driver from matter thrown up by the wheels and the horses' hooves.

39. Allen's "casina" was Dahoon holly or Cassena (*Ilex cassine*). His "mocking-bird flower" is unknown by that name to professional botanists Richard Porcher of Charleston and Joe Marcus of the Lady Bird Johnson Wildflower Center, Austin, Tex. On the basis of Allen's description, however, it was probably Bushy Bluestem (*Andropogon glomeratus*), which grows in the United States from Florida to New England.

40. Ruggles's home was on the road between St. Helena and Lady's Island on the Rev. Robert Fuller Place, near the Corner Farm, where he was superintendent.

41. Harriet Ware, Milton, Mass., original Gideonite, Charley Ware's sister, and Allen's first cousin.

42. William Ware Hall, Providence, R.I., teacher at Coffin Point. Charles Williams, government superintendent of the Oliver Fripp Place.

43. Richard Soule Jr., Brookline, Mass., original Gideonite, Edward Philbrick's uncle. Lieutenant Ephraim A. Wood, 55th Massachusetts Regiment.

44. Charles Pickard Ware, Milton, Mass., superintendent at Coffin Point, Harriet Ware's brother and Allen's first cousin.

45. The house Allen described still stands at Coffin Point under the National Registry of Historic Places designation of Coffin Point Plantation.

46. Probably Chinaberry trees. Allen also called them "Asia-berry trees," saying they were like the "ailanthus."

47. Allen shared later impressions after about four months and again after almost eight months among the people. See St. Helena journal entries for February 21 and June 19, 1864.

48. Sea Island cotton (*Gossypium barbadense*) was cultivated for its fine, long-staple fibers.

49. Benny, or sesame, seed was introduced by African slaves. Benny represents the African word *bene*.

50. Mary E. Rice, Cambridgeport, Mass., teacher at Fripp Point and Pine Grove. She, Gannett, and Folsom were close friends.

51. Allen noted many of the plantations on St. Helena Island and the difficulty of keeping their names straight (December 4, 1864, journal entry). He often associated plantations with their owners, and at least once he wrote of the character of the owners (December 19, 1863, journal entry). Altogether, there were about two hundred plantations on the Sea Islands, fifty of which were on St. Helena.

52. Allen omitted the Corner Farm, which we can state by process of elimination is where Ruggles was superintendent.

53. Allen had a long-standing interest in problems posed by land transfers and the implementation of a free labor system in the South. He published articles on free labor in the May 1864 and May 1865 issues of the *Christian Examiner.*

54. John Ware, M.D., Boston, Mass., Charley Ware's uncle.

55. Slave quarters. See Elizabeth Ware Pearson, ed., *Letters from Port Royal Written at the Time of the Civil War* (Boston: W. B. Clarke Company, 1906), 18, 77.

56. Harrison, superintendent of the T. B. Fripp Place, is also mentioned by last name only in *The Journals of Charlotte Forten Grimké* and in Pearson's *Letters from Port Royal.*

57. "Old Hundredth", known widely as the tune to "Praise God from Whom All Blessings Flow."

58. The practice Allen heard was "lining out" or "Dr. Watts singing." Allen was to hear this practice often. See December 13, 1863, journal entry for example.

59. This note may reveal something of the marriage dynamic between Allen and Mary.

60. See May 17, 1864, journal entry in which Allen identifies this song as "Happy Morning," *Slave Songs* No. 13. A parenthetical pencil entry there, "I think not.," may have been made by Mary Allen, indicating that she did not think the song was "Happy Morning."

61. Frogmore Plantation.

62. The Reverend William S. Phillips, AMA missionary. Allen said of him, "[He] is a man whom nobody speaks well of." Phillips died on February 12, 1864, according to a February 15, 1864, letter from William McClue to the Reverend S. S. Joclyn of the AMA. American Missionary Association, H5284.

63. Northern term for the Confederacy. See Junius Henri Browns, *Four Years in Secessia: Adventures within and beyond the Union Lines* (Hartford, Conn.: O. D. Case, 1865).

64. Sweet potatoes: the slips were small shoots or twigs cut for planting or grafting.

65. U.S. Mail Steamship Company vessel, sister of the *Arago.*

66. Allen's "vermifuge" was wormwood (*Artemisia absinthium*), used as a herbal agent to purge intestinal worms. His "burrs" were probably common cockleburs (*Xanthium strumarium*).

67. Nathaniel Langdon Frothingham, Boston, Mass., Unitarian minister and writer of sermons, hymns, and poetry.

68. The Reverend Theodore Parker, Lexington, Mass., transcendentalist, abolitionist, and Unitarian reformer.

69. Adams Express Company was a freight company founded in 1854, with roots going back to 1839.

70. For a discussion of "creolization" of the coastal black dialect, see Charles Joyner, *Down by the Riverside* (Urbana: University of Illinois Press, 1984).

71. Plate 1 from Stephan Michelspracher's *Spiegel der Kunst und Natur* (Mirror of Art and Nature), published in Augsburg in 1615.

72. George M. Wells, Providence, R.I., original Gideonite, superintendent of the Mary Jenkins Place. George H. Hull, Chelsea, Mass., superintendent of Cuthbert's Point, Lady's Island.

73. New England Freedmen's Aid Society, originally the Boston Educational Commission.

74. Philbrick's consortium owned eleven plantations, and it leased two others from the government. For an account of contentions over land on the Sea Islands during the war, see Ira Berlin et al., eds., *Freedom: A Documentary History of Emancipation 1861–1867,* Series I, Volume III: *The Wartime Genesis of Free Labor: The Lower South* (Cambridge: University of Cambridge Press, 1990), 102–13.

75. Eliza J. Wells, NFRA teacher at Cuthbert's Point on Lady's Island.

76. The possessions of the former owners, including land, animals, and household goods, were to be sold for taxes in February and March 1864. See March 5, 1864, journal entry for example.

77. The Reverend Charles Lowe, Somerville, Mass., Unitarian minister and NEFAS official.

78. Allen recorded the weddings of Henry and Jane and Paris and Laura in his November 29, 1863, journal entry, saying that he was mistaken about Jane having been married in his entry here. He does not indicate later whether Henry was Paris's brother.

79. The kind of attachment the freedmen of St. Helena Island felt for their homes is examined in depth in Erskine Clarke, *Dwelling Place: A Plantation Epic* (New Haven: Yale University Press, 2005).

80. John Hunn, Camden, Del., Quaker abolitionist and Underground Railroad supporter.

81. Mr. Valentine is unidentified. He may have been a maintenance man at the West Newton English and Classical School or, perhaps, a handyman Allen knew.

82. Harvard award named after Benjamin Count Rumford.

83. George Shattuck Morison, Milton, Mass., co-superintendent with Clifford Waters at T. B. Chaplin Place.

84. Victorian parlor game.

85. Port Royal Relief Committee (PRRC).

86. Play on the words "office seeker" coined by the nineteenth-century humorist Robert Henry Newell.

87. Anne E. Jenkins Hunn, Camden, Del.

88. Elizabeth Hunn, Camden, Del.

89. Joseph Henry Allen, Jamaica Plain, Mass., Allen's brother.

90. Allen may have heard the distant rumble of the shelling of Charleston and Fort Sumter by long-range guns on Morris Island. The shelling continued intermittently between August 17 and December 31, 1863. See Stephen R. Wise, *Gate of Hell: Campaign for Charleston Harbor, 1863* (Columbia: University of South Carolina Press, 1994).

91. The *Commonwealth*, weekly newspaper published in Boston.

92. *Philip van Artevelde*, 1834 tragic play by Sir Henry Taylor.

93. *Sistine Madonna* and *Madonna della seggiola*, c. 1512–1514 paintings by Raphael.

94. Perhaps *The Immaculate Conception*, c. 1618–1619 painting by Diego Velásquez.

95. Annie Lambert, perhaps Mary's cousin. See January 30, 1864, journal entry.

96. David Franklin Thorpe, Providence, R.I., original Gideonite, superintendent of T. J. Fripp Place. Miss S. E. Richardson, Providence, R.I.

97. William Henry Alden, Westville, Conn., superintendent of Frogmore, Woodlands, and Hope Place.

98. A "place to stand" from Archimedes's explanation of the principle of leverage.

99. Francis Everett Barnard, Dorchester, Mass., first "martyr" of the Gideonite Band.

100. Samuel D. Phillips, Boston, Mass., original Gideonite. Phillips was a nephew of the abolitionist Wendell Phillips.

101. John A. Alden, superintendent of Dr. Pope Place and Indian Hill. Alden became the Freedmen's Bureau superintendent of Edisto Island in 1865. He may have been related to William H. Alden, who was appointed to Edisto Island by the New England Freedmen's Aid Society on his recommendation.

102. The Indian Hill Site is on the National Register of Historic Places.

103. John G. Nichols, Kingston, Mass. Frederick A. Eustis, Milton, Mass., original Gideonite, heir to the Eustis Place on Lady's Island.

104. Reuben Tomlinson, Philadelphia, Pa., general superintendent of St. Helena and Lady's Islands.

105. Lieutenant Henry Atkins Stone, Newburyport, Mass., 33rd USCT Regiment, formerly of the 8th Maine Regiment. Louisa Parsons Stone Hopkins, New Bedford, Mass.

106. Dr. Ferdinand Vandeveer Hayden, Westfield, Mass., chief medical officer at Beaufort.

107. Nonsensical English fairy tale, "The Old Woman and Her Pig," in which one event after another delays an old woman on her way home from buying a pig until one event triggers the chain of events in reverse, and she arrives at home on time after all.

108. Mr. Thorndyke is unidentified; whether he was an agent or the owner of the commissary is uncertain.

109. Poem by James Montgomery originally titled "The Stranger and His Friend." New York minister George Coles set the poem to music, and the resulting hymn was adopted by

some churches, eventually becoming a favorite of Joseph Smith, the founder of the Latter Day Saints.

110. Sculpture by William Wetmore Story.

111. Thomas Prentiss Allen, Allen's brother.

112. Lucy Clarke Allen, Allen's sister.

113. *Levana oder Erziehungslehre* (*Levana or the Doctrine of Education*), 1807 book about humanist theories of education by Jean Paul, formerly Johann Paul Friedrich Richter.

114. Hymn by William Cowper set to a 1735 tune by William Tans'ur. See November 15, 1863, journal entry. Once again, Allen was treated to the practice of "lining out" a hymn.

115. Plantation managers G. M. Wells and Samuel D. Phillips wrote letters in May 1862 to Edward L. Pierce, Treasury Department agent in charge of the Port Royal Experiment, about clumsy attempts to recruit blacks.

116. Young boy who rode along to open and close gates.

117. Laura Matilda Towne, Shoemakertown, Pa., PRRC teacher, cofounder with Ellen Murray of the Penn School.

118. Joseph D. Eddings, St. Helena Island, S.C.

119. Jules S. DeLacroix, Newburyport, Mass.

120. Dr. Francis William Lawrence, Cambridge, Mass. Lucilla Train Lawrence, Framingham, Mass. The Honorable Charles Russell Train, Framingham, Mass.

121. "The Lonesome Valley," *Slave Songs* No. 7.

122. Henry George Spaulding, "Under the Palmetto," *Continental Monthly* 4, no. 2 (August 1863), 188–203.

123. "Praise, Member," *Slave Songs* No. 5.

124. Topsy from Harriet Beecher Stowe's *Uncle Tom's Cabin*.

125. Spaulding, "Under the Palmetto."

126. "I Can't Stay Behind," *Slave Songs* No. 8.

127. "Pray All De Member," *Slave Songs* No. 47.

128. "Bell Da Ring," *Slave Songs* No. 46.

129. "Shall I Die?," *Slave Songs* No. 52.

130. "Pray All De Member," *Slave Songs* No. 47.

131. James H. Palmer, Deerfield, Mass., NEFAS teacher.

132. Sarah Rebecca Bassett, Nantucket, Mass., pupil at the West Newton School, where Allen was associate principal.

133. Mary Ware Allen, Allen's sister.

134. "Praise, Member," *Slave Songs* No. 5.

135. Allen began his diary on this day.

136. Medicine patented in 1845.

137. Emancipation Proclamation, January 1, 1863.

138. *Mary Benton,* steamer built at Goodspeed's Yard, Haddam, Conn., in 1850.

139. Laura Towne described the day as "piercing cold."

140. 1859 novel by Charles Dickens.

141. Moting is the process of removing motes (specks of dirt and debris) from ginned cotton.

142. Elizabeth Waterhouse Allen, Allen's sister.

143. Edward Augustus Holyoke Allen, Allen's brother.

144. "Adeste Fidelis."

145. *Christian Examiner,* bimonthly religious review advocating Unitarianism and peace. See Frank Luther Mott, "The Christian Disciple and the Christian Examiner," *New England Quarterly* 1, no. 2 (April 1928), 197–207.

146. Lucy Clarke Ware, Allen's mother.

147. *Boston Daily Advertiser,* daily news with a Republican perspective.

148. *Congregationalist and Boston Recorder,* Christian perspective on news of the day.

149. *New York Evening Post,* daily newspaper.

150. *Army and Navy Journal and Gazette of the Regular and Volunteer Forces,* weekly newspaper specializing in war news published in New York.

151. *Littell's Living Age,* weekly literary magazine with selections from British and American newspapers.

152. *Atlantic Monthly,* literary and cultural magazine published in Boston.

153. *Independent,* Congregationalist weekly newspaper published in New York.

154. *National Anti-Slavery Standard,* weekly newspaper published in New York.

155. *Philadelphia Inquirer,* daily newspaper.

156. Edward Gray Stetson, Lexington, Mass., later superintendent of Dr. Jenkins Place near Land's End on St. Helena. His brother was Thomas Meriam Stetson. Apparently, Stetson succeeded Delacroix as the superintendent of Dr. Jenkins Place. See December 20, 1863, and July 12, 1864, journal entries.

157. Other than their last name, no information was found on the Harrisons or on Mrs. Harrison's sister.

158. The Reveremd Dr. William Henry Brisbane, Baptist minister and former slaveholder turned abolitionist. Judge Abram D. Smith, Milwaukee, Wis. Dr. William E. Wording, Castine, Maine.

159. Henry G. Judd, general superintendent, Port Royal Island, NFRA leader.

160. The Reverend Augustine Root, Lakeville, Mass., AMA missionary and plantation superintendent.

161. The Reverend Mansfield French, New York, N.Y., original Gideonite, NFRA leader.

162. *Slavery in South Carolina and the Ex-Slaves or The Port Royal Mission,* 1862 book by Austa French.

163. Clifford Crowninshield Waters, Salem, Mass., co-superintendent of T. B. Chaplin Place.

164. Josiah Milton Fairfield, Boston, Mass.

165. Arthur Sumner, Cambridge, Mass.

166. The Reverend William James Potter, New Bedford, Mass.

167. Nehemiah Adams, D.D., *A South-Side View of Slavery,* 1854.

168. William Henry Trescott, Barnwell's Island, S.C.

169. Sir William Howard Russell, *My Diary North and South,* 1863.

170. Lieutenant Colonel William H. Reynolds, 1st Rhode Island Artillery.

171. William Sprague IV, governor of Rhode Island (1860–1863).

172. General Isaac Ingalls Stevens, former governor of Washington Territory, originally from Massachusetts.

173. "Shall I Die?," *Slave Songs* No. 52.

174. "My Body Rock 'Long Fever," *Slave Songs* No. 45.

175. The Reverend James D. Lynch, Baltimore, Md., Methodist Episcopal Church missionary. Lynch worked in the Augusta, Ga., area after the war, as evidenced by a July 25, 1865, letter from Freedmen's Bureau agent Captain J. E. Bryant to the NFRA. AMA 19393. www .drbronsontours.com/bronsonrevjameslynchintrotoaugustajuly251865.html.

176. "Jehovah, Hallelujah," *Slave Songs* No. 2.

177. Lieutenant Colonel John Johnson Elwell, chief quartermaster, Department of the South.

178. *New York Weekly Tribune,* newspaper advocating immediate abolition and radical Republicanism, edited by Horace Greeley.

179. Captain Scott is unidentified. He may have been a military officer.

180. Dr. Hunting was a physician on St. Helena. He was mentioned several times by Allen and by Laura Towne in her diaries and letters, but no other information was found about him.

181. Albert Gallatin Browne, Salem, Mass., U.S. Treasury Department agent.

182. Smallwood is unidentified.

183. "Jehovah, Hallelujah," *Slave Songs* No. 2.

184. Matilda Anna Sracey Stone, wife of Lieutenant Henry A. Stone, Newburyport, Mass.

185. Coarse woolen fabric.

186. Frances Anne (Fanny) Kemble, *Journal of a Residence on a Georgian Plantation in 1838–1839* (London, 1863).

187. *History of the Romans under the Empire,* 1850 book by Charles Merivale.

188. According to his diary, Allen began writing an essay on the freedmen on February 5, 1864.

189. Hiram P. Barney, New York, N.Y., collector for the Port of New York City.

190. Salmon Portland Chase, Cincinnati, Ohio, U.S. Treasury secretary.

191. Deceiver.

192. "Michael Row the Boat Ashore," *Slave Songs* No. 31.

193. "Archangel, Open the Door," *Slave Songs* No. 44.

194. "The Graveyard," *Slave Songs* No. 21.

195. "I Hear from Heaven Today," *Slave Songs* No. 3.

196. Catherine Brown Porter Lambert, Northborough, Mass., Allen's mother-in-law.

197. *Pet Marjorie: A Story of Child Life Fifty Years Ago,* 1858 booklet by H. B. Farnie.

198. From an 1853 children's book, *A Kiss for a Blow and Other Tales,* by Henry Clarke Wright.

199. The land sale began February 18, 1864.

200. Sergeant Prince R. Rivers, Beaufort, S.C., 33rd USCT Regiment, formerly 1st South Carolina Volunteers. Rivers is mentioned in numerous contexts during the Civil War and Reconstruction. Allen identifies him (*Slave Songs of the United States,* xviii) as the man J. Miller McKim questioned about the origin of spirituals. He went on to become a general in the militia and a state legislator. He was Intendant of Hamburg, S.C., during the Hamburg Massacre, in 1876. For more on Rivers, see Isabel Vandervelde, *Aiken County: The Only South Carolina County Founded during Reconstruction* (Spartanburg, S.C.: Art Studio Press, 1999).

201. For an account of the Mutual Aid Society and other black self-help initiatives, see Martin Abbott, "Freedom's Cry: Negroes and Their Meetings in South Carolina, 1865–1869," *Phylon Quarterly* 20, no. 3 (Fall 1959), 263–72.

202. These sentiments represent Allen's evolving impressions of slaves and slavery. See November 10, 1863, and June 19, 1864, journal entries.

203. Unsuccessful Department of the South expedition into Florida in February 1864.

204. "I Can't Stay Behind," *Slave Songs* No. 8.

205. "Archangel, Open the Door," *Slave Songs* No. 44.

206. General Truman Seymour, commander, Department of the South, District of Florida under General Gillmore.

207. Eugenia Sophia Teulon Allen, Allen's sister-in-law.

208. William Eustis, Natchez, Miss.

209. Reed and Carter are unidentified, as is Pickens.

210. Clark is an apparent error. Allen refers to this agent as Carter in his March 4, 1864, diary entry.

211. Napoleon C. Dennett, Worcester, Mass., superintendent of plantations at Port Royal.

212. Dr. W. H. Westcott, Rochester, N.H., acting assistant surgeon, USS *Kingfisher.*

213. Mrs. George M. Wells (possibly Mary L. Wells), West Hartford, Conn., NEFAS teacher.

214. "Hold Your Light," *Slave Songs* No. 12.

215. "Wrestle Jacob," *Slave Songs* No. 6.

216. Theodoric C. (T. C.) Severance, Cleveland, Ohio, assistant Treasury agent and collector for the Port of Hilton Head. Severance was an abolitionist and the husband of the abolitionist and suffragette Caroline M. Seymour Severance.

217. "Pray All De Member," *Slave Songs* No. 47.

218. Either Sarah Louise Kellogg, Elizabeth, N.J., NFRA teacher, or Martha Louise Kellogg, Avon, Conn., AMA teacher. Laura Towne mentioned "Louise Kellog" in her diary on January 1, 1863, which could refer to either of these ladies. Sarah was assigned to Beaufort and Martha to Hilton Head, so the weight of the evidence points to the former.

219. Charlotte Forten (later Grimké), Philadelphia, Pa., PRRC teacher. (Forten's future husband was Francis Grimké, the mixed-race nephew of the abolitionist Grimké sisters, Sarah and Angelina. The Grimké sisters were born into a prominent slaveholding family in South Carolina, but they became staunch, outspoken opponents of slavery because of cruelties toward slaves that they witnessed.)

220. Term for an unmanageable horse, from the 1862 novel *John Brent* by Theodore Winthrop.

221. "Michael Michael Row the Boat Ashore," *Slave Songs* No. 31.

222. "Hold Your Light," *Slave Songs* No. 12.

223. "The Graveyard," *Slave Songs* No. 21.

224. "Sail, O Believer," *Slave Songs* No. 32.

225. "I Want To Go Home," *Slave Songs* No. 61.

226. In Roman mythology, female devotees of Bacchus.

227. "Heaven Bell A-Ring," *Slave Songs* No. 27.

228. "Archangel, Open the Door," *Slave Songs* No. 44.

229. "I Can't Stay Behind," *Slave Songs* No. 8.

230. "Shall I Die?," *Slave Songs* No. 52.

231. "Turn, Sinner, Turn O!," *Slave Songs* No. 48.

232. "My Body Rock 'Long Fever," *Slave Songs* No. 45.

233. "Roll, Jordan, Roll," *Slave Songs* No. 1.

234. Brigadier General Thomas Fenwick Drayton of the Confederate Army. Generals Ames and Stevenson are unidentified.

235. "Busy Bee" is probably Isaac Watts's "How Doth the Little Busy Bee." "Little Children" is unidentified.

236. Beethoven's Symphony No. 6 in F Major, Op. 68.

237. James A. McCrea, AMA missionary.

238. "Blow Your Trumpet, Gabriel," *Slave Songs* No. 4.

239. William Robert Ware, Cambridge, Mass., Allen's cousin and Charley and Harriet Ware's brother.

240. Henry Lambert, Northborough, Mass., Allen's father-in-law.

241. Probably the Reverend Edward Brooks Hall, Providence, R.I., Allen's uncle.

242. The "great storm" was a Nor'easter that struck the Atlantic coast on April 4–5, 1864. Lieutenant Colonel Theodore Lyman, General George Gordon Meade's aide-de-camp, wrote of the storm, "Rain all night and today worse than ever, a perfect type of a north-easter; cold & windy & wet. Took a ride, when it let up a little, and saw the Blue Ridge covered with snow. Muddy Run was running full with red water, and the Hazel River had swept away its bridge, though the pontoons at Welfords [ford] held fast." David W. Lowe, ed., *Meade's Army* (Kent, Ohio: Kent State University Press, 2007), 119.

243. "Happy Morning," *Slave Songs* No. 13.

244. Unidentified spiritual.

245. "Turn, Sinner, Turn O!," *Slave Songs* No. 48.

246. Jane M. Lynch, Baltimore, Md., NFRA teacher.

247. Elizabeth Howard, NFRA teacher.

248. "Shall I Die?," *Slave Songs* No. 52.

249. "My Body Rock 'Long Fever," *Slave Songs* No. 45.

250. "I Can't Stay Behind," *Slave Songs* No. 8.

251. The two long shafts on a horse-drawn carriage to which the horse is fastened.

252. Edward Hinckley, Cape Cod, Mass. See August 27, 1864, diary entry, where Allen refers to him as "Edw. Hinckley." Allen noted that Hinckley came down on the schooner. Frank Winsor, Mary Walker, and Mr. Jackson (see notes 252, 253, and 254) probably arrived at the same time.

253. Frank Gordon Winsor, Brookline, Mass.

254. Mary Walker, Cambridge, Mass., fugitive slave originally from North Carolina. For more on Mary Walker, see Sydney Nathans, *To Free a Family: The Journey of Mary Walker* (Cambridge, Mass.: Harvard University Press, 2012), 199–216. Mrs. Walker lived for a time in the home of Ann Ware Winsor, Harriet and Charley Ware's sister. She came to Coffin Point to allow Harriet to return home at the behest of their older sister, Elizabeth Ware.

255. Frederick Jackson, Boston, Mass., nephew of the prominent abolitionist Francis Jackson. The younger Jackson purchased Pine Grove from Edward Philbrick in early 1865.

256. Allen's uncle and aunt Ellis and Lucy Lane Allen celebrated their golden wedding anniversary on April 11, 1864.

257. Allen's family practiced homeopathic medicine. See March 23, 1864, journal entry. An 1883 book of home cures listed the following: "A good iron tonic, an excellent remedy, and one that is always at hand, can be made by taking a handful of clean iron nails, putting them into a bottle, adding two quarts of cider, and shaking well; in a few hours the cider will turn dark or black; dose, a tablespoon before eating and retiring." Moore Russell Fletcher, "Retarded Menstruation—Chlorosis," *Our Home Doctor* (Boston: Fletcher, 1883), 238.

258. *Strafford*, 1837 play by Robert Browning, his first.

259. James E. Yeatman, *Report of the Condition of the Freedmen of the Mississippi* (St. Louis: Western Sanitary Commission, 1863), and Yeatman, *Suggestions of a Plan of Organization for Free Labor, and the Leasing of Plantations along the Mississippi River* (St. Louis: Western Sanitary Commission, 1864).

260. John Stuart Mill, *On Liberty* (London: John W. Parker, 1859), based on Mill's 1854 essay.

261. *Galignani's Messenger*, English-language newspaper published in France by John Anthony and William Galignani.

262. *Vanity Fair*, 1847–48 novel by William Makepeace Thackeray. Possibly, but less likely, the humorous weekly magazine *Vanity Fair* published 1859–63 in New York.

263. "Hunting for a City," *Slave Songs* No. 24.

264. "The White Marble Stone," *Slave Songs* No. 54.

265. Dr. James P. Greves (pronounced Graves), New York, N.Y., original Gideonite.

266. Trumpet vine.

267. Judge Dennis N. Cooley, Dubuque, Iowa, South Carolina tax commissioner, replaced Judge Smith. He is referred to as "a Westerner" in an April 1864 letter by Harriet Ware.

268. Mr. Adams, according to Allen's April 22, 1864, diary entry. Possibly Austin Adams, Dubuque, Iowa, law partner of Judge Cooley in the firm of Cooley, Blatchley, and Adams.

269. Judge Austin Smith, Westfield, Chautauqua County, N.Y., U.S. Treasury special agent.

270. Other than this mention by Allen, no other information was found about John Major.

271. This hearing at Coffin Point is discussed in Willie Lee Rose, *Rehearsal for Reconstruction*, 312.

272. Either jointgrass (Calamagrostid Canadensis) or witchgrass (Panicum capillare).

273. "I Can't Stand the Fire," *Slave Songs* No. 55.

274. "Hunting for a City," *Slave Songs* No. 24.

275. Matilda G. Thompson Saxton, Philadelphia, Pa.

276. Except rank and last name, no information was found to identify Lieutenant Rhodes. That he accompanied General Saxton to the church may indicate he became the general's aide after Captain Hooper's departure, which Allen noted in his April 17, 1864, journal entry.

277. "My Body Rock 'Long with Fever," *Slave Songs* No. 45.

278. Mr. Warren is unidentified.

279. Heavy, dark-brown ale.

280. Marie Taglioni, Romantic-era Italian/Swedish ballet dancer.

281. Mr. Wild is unidentified.

282. Theodore Holt, Gideonite, said to have been a gardener in New York before becoming a missionary.

283. Allen's "holdbacks" and "breeching" were variant methods of harnessing. The purpose of either was to prevent the vehicle from running up on the draft animal when stopping.

284. Battle of the Wilderness, May 5–7, 1864.

285. Dr. Adoniram Judson Wakefield, Boston, Mass., original Gideonite. Wakefield was located at the Thomas B. Fripp Plantation.

286. Republican National Convention, Baltimore, Md., June 7–8, 1864.

287. Robert Smalls, Charleston, S.C., black wheelman of the steamer *Planter*, who commandeered the ship and escaped with his family from Charleston Harbor May 13, 1862. After the war, he became a politician, and he was elected to the South Carolina state legislature and to the U.S. House of Representatives. His example helped convince President Lincoln to accept African American soldiers into the Union Army. For more about Smalls, see Andrew Billingsley, *Yearning to Breathe Free* (Columbia: University of South Carolina Press, 2007).

288. "Happy Morning," *Slave Songs* No. 13. Apparently someone, probably Mary Allen, did not think this was the song they heard.

289. The Combahee River, which empties into St. Helena Sound near Beaufort.

290. Philbrick raised wages on the private advice of Judge Austin Smith.

291. Unidentified song.

292. "I Can't Stand the Fire," *Slave Songs* No. 55.

293. "The Lonesome Valley," *Slave Songs* No. 7.

294. According to the *New York Times*, the USS *Fulton* arrived in New York from Port Royal on June 3, 1864, and among the passengers were Miss M. Allen, Miss C. P. Noyes, Miss L. Towne, Miss C. L. Forten, Miss J. P. Kendall, J. R. Dennett, and the Honorable D. M. [N.] Cooley. Williams was not listed among the arriving passengers.

295. *Chronicles of the Schönberg-Cotta Family*, 1862 book about Martin Luther by Elizabeth Rundle Charles.

296. Expedition under General William Birney up the Ashepoo River in which the U.S. Transport Steamer *Boston* ran aground and was lost.

297. "Go in the Wilderness," *Slave Songs* No. 19.

298. "I Saw the Beam in My Sister's Eye," *Slave Songs* No. 23.

299. "John, John, of the Holy Order," *Slave Songs* No. 22.

300. "Rock O' Jubilee," *Slave Songs* No. 33.

301. Numbers 12:3.

302. Captain Charles Carroll Soule, Brookline, Mass., 55th Massachusetts Regiment. Allen would meet Soule again in Charleston and at Orangeburg, S.C., where he was assigned to the Board of Labor.

303. The three soldiers Allen met were Sergeant Arthur B. Lee, Sergeant James Monroe Trotter, and Corporal Gustus George. Lee, of Boston, Mass., was a commissary sergeant with the 54th Massachusetts Regiment. Trotter, of Cincinnati, Ohio, and George, of Virginia, belonged to the 55th Massachusetts. Allen would meet Trotter again in July 1865 at Orangeburg, S.C., where (then Lieutenant) Trotter served on the Board of Labor. Trotter was born in 1842 to Mississippi planter Richard S, Trotter and his slave Letitia. When the elder Trotter married in 1854, he sent Letitia, James, and two younger sisters to Cincinnati, Ohio. There, James Trotter attended the Gilmore School for freed slaves, where he studied music. After the war, he moved to Boston, where he worked for the Post Office. Trotter published a book about black music: James M. Trotter, *Music and Some Highly Musical People* (Boston: Lee and Shepard, 1880). President Grover Cleveland appointed him recorder of deeds for Washington, D.C., in 1887; he succeeded Frederick Douglass in that office. The James M. Trotter Convention Center in Columbus, Mississippi, is named in his honor. Trotter's wife, Virginia Isaacs Trotter, was the great-grand-daughter of Mary Hemings, sister of Sally Hemings of Monticello fame. His son, William Monroe Trotter, the prominent newspaper editor and founder of the *Boston Guardian,* was an early civil rights activist.

304. Historical novel by William Makepeace Thackeray.

305. Captain Frank Goodwin, Boston, Mass., 55th Massachusetts Regiment.

306. See November 10, 1863, and February 21, 1864, journal entries for Allen's earlier impressions.

307. General John Gray Foster, commander, Department of the South.

308. Probably George M. Wells, sometimes listed as Welles.

309. "Bell Da Ring," *Slave Songs* No. 46.

310. Mr. Hayward is unidentified.

311. "Hunting for a City," *Slave Songs* No. 24.

312. 34th USCT Regiment, formerly 2nd South Carolina Volunteers.

313. Mr. Stiggins from Charles Dickens's *Pickwick Papers.*

314. "Not Weary Yet," *Slave Songs* No. 16.

315. "Tell My Jesus 'Morning,'" *Slave Songs* No. 20.

316. Harry McMillen, Beaufort, S.C., Lady's Island plantation owner. A former slave, McMillen worked in bondage on a plantation in Beaufort for nearly forty years.

317. U.S. Army vessel.

318. George Newcomb, NFRA superintendent of schools.

319. Mr. Horn is unidentified.

320. "Roll, Jordan, Roll," *Slave Songs* No. 1.

321. "Praise, Member," *Slave Songs* No. 5.

322. "Blow Your Trumpet, Gabriel," *Slave Songs* No. 4.

323. "Wrestle On, Jacob," *Slave Songs* No. 6.

324. "Travel On," *Slave Songs* No. 43.

325. "Lonesome Valley," *Slave Songs* No. 7.

326. "I Can't Stay Behind," *Slave Songs* No. 8.

327. Failed Union amphibious assault on Fort Johnson on James Island, July 3, 1864.

328. Steamships.

329. James Gregg, chaplain, 7th USCT Regiment.

330. Charles A. Roundy, Boston, Mass., member of the Boston Young Men's Christian Association, Christian Commission.

331. *The Life of Jesus,* 1863 translation by Charles E. Wilbour of a book by Joseph Ernest Renan.

332. Lieutenant A. H. Bradish, Boston, Mass., 55th Massachusetts Regiment.

333. Private Samuel P. Bassett, Company K, 13th Indiana Regiment.

334. Captain Harding, Captain of the USS *Dudley Buck.*

Charleston Journal

1. Gertrude E. Allen, West Newton, Mass.

2. Sarah E. Lakeman, Salem, Mass., NEFAS teacher.

3. Mary F. Baker, Hopkinton, Mass., NEFAS teacher.

4. Benjamin Faneuil Dunkin, Boston, Mass., and Charleston, S.C., chancellor of the Equity Court of Appeals and chief justice of the South Carolina Supreme Court, 1865–68.

5. Coming Creek. Virginia sweetspire (*Itea virginica*).

6. Chancellor Dunkin built the house at the corner of Warren and Smith Streets in 1823–24. When Charleston streets were renumbered in 1886, the property was redesignated as 89 Warren Street, its current address.

7. James Redpath, Kalamazoo, Mich., journalist and antislavery activist, appointed superintendent of Charleston public schools by military authorities in February 1865. Years later, as an agent of Belford Publishing, Redpath assisted Jefferson Davis in preparing *A Short History of the Confederate States of America* (New York: Belford Company, 1890), and he assisted Varina Davis in preparing *Jefferson Davis, Ex-President of the Confederate States of America: A Memoir by His Wife* (New York: Belford Company, 1890).

8. The April 14, 1865, flag-raising celebration featured Major General Robert Anderson, who, as a major, had endured thirty-four hours of bombardment by Confederate batteries before surrendering Fort Sumter on April 14, 1861.

9. General Robert E. Lee surrendered at Appomattox Court House on April 9, 1865.

10. The *Oceanus* also conveyed passengers from Charleston to Fort Sumter for the flag-raising celebration.

11. The *Creole* and her sister, the *Yazoo,* were coastal steamers of the New York and Virginia Steamship Company.

12. The Reverend Charles Lowe, Somerville, Mass., Unitarian minister and NEFAS official.

13. The Reverend Calvin Stebbins, Boston, Mass., Unitarian minister and recent graduate of Harvard Divinity School.

14. James George Dodge, Boston, Mass., superintendent of freedmen on government plantations on Hilton Head.

15. T. C. Severance, Cleveland, Ohio, assistant Treasury agent and collector for the Port of Hilton Head.

16. Sarah P. Lillie, Hopedale, Mass., NEFAS teacher on Hilton Head.

17. Steamer *Golden Gate.*

18. Luella J. Chase, Exeter, N.H., NEFAS teacher.

19. Alfred Purdie was possibly a government agent.

20. Thomas Edwin Ruggles, Milton, Mass., superintendent of the Corner Farm, and Amanda S. Ruggles, NEFAS teacher. (Two Ruggles sisters, Eliza and Amanda, came to St. Helena. Eliza died around the time Allen arrived there.) George M. Wells, Providence, R.I., superintendent of the Mary Jenkins Place. Charles Williams, government superintendent of the Oliver Fripp Place. Laura Matilda Towne, Shoemakertown, Pa., PRRC teacher. Ellen and Harriet Murray, Newport, R.I., PRRC teachers.

21. Captain Ketcham, master of the *Golden Gate*. Ketcham was seriously injured by an accidental shotgun blast to his arm on August 5, 1865.

22. Reuben Tomlinson, Philadelphia, Pa., superintendent of freedmen at Charleston, formerly general superintendent of St. Helena and Lady's Islands.

23. General Rufus B. Saxton, military governor of South Carolina and the Department of the South.

24. Charles Follen Folsom, Jamaica Plain, Mass., superintendent of the John Fripp Place, Mulberry Hill, and Cherry Hill when Allen was on St. Helena. He and the Allens shared the John Fripp Big House.

25. James P. Blake, New Haven, Conn., Yale class of 1862, in charge of distributing stores in Charleston. Blake was shortly after named superintendent of freedmen's schools on Edisto Island. He drowned in St. Pierre Creek on the island on December 25, 1865.

26. U.S. senator Henry Wilson arrived in Charleston on the *Oceanus* on April 13, 1865, for the Fort Sumter celebration.

27. Monroe (or Munroe) Mason, Milford, Mass. Possibly Allen knew Mason as a student at the Roxbury Latin School.

28. Caroline Peters, Charleston, S.C. The 1850 census lists George Peters, age 32, Boarding House Keeper and his wife, Caroline, age 32, as residents of St. Philips and St. Michaels Parish, Charleston.

29. George Newcomb, NFRA superintendent of schools.

30. General Quincy Adams Gillmore, commander of federal forces at Charleston during the siege of the city.

31. Caroline Howard Gilman, Southern author. Allen included eight antebellum slave songs from Mrs. Gilman's collection in *Slave Songs*. Hers is the earliest known collection of slave songs.

32. Mary Tileston Lambert Allen died of complications from childbirth on March 23, 1865, a few weeks before Allen came to Charleston. Allen left his daughter Katharine in West Newton, Mass., in the care of Mary's parents.

33. Henry Ward Beecher. Beecher had come to Charleston for the Fort Sumter celebration.

34. Major (Dr.) Thomas Jefferson Saunders, Davenport, Iowa, Army paymaster under General William T. Sherman.

35. William Lloyd Garrison. Garrison had come to Charleston for the Fort Sumter celebration.

36. Arthur T. Morse, Bradford, N.H., NEFAS teacher, principal of the St. Philip Street School. Harriet Buttrick, Concord, Mass., NEFAS teacher. Either Louisa Webb or Jennie Webb, both of whom are listed as teachers in the *Freedmen's Record* 1, no. 9 (September 1865), 139. Louisa A. Morse, Bradford, N.H., NEFAS teacher, Arthur Morse's wife.

37. Dr. Esther Hill Hawkes, Manchester, N.H., later, Lynn, Mass., medical doctor and NEFAS teacher, principal of the Normal School.

38. J. Sherman Littlefield, East Stoughton, Mass., NEFAS teacher, principal of the Meeting Street School. Harrison T. Fletcher, Harvard, Mass., NEFAS teacher, principal of the King Street School.

39. Elizabeth P. Breck, Northampton, Mass., NEFAS teacher, department principal under Mrs. Pillsbury at the Morris Street School. Mary C. Green, Boston, Mass., NEFAS teacher, department principal under Dr. Hawkes at the Normal School. (One Mary A. Green is also listed in the *Freedmen's Record* 1, no. 5 [May 1865], 87.)

40. Lucy M. Southworth, North Brookfield, Mass., NEFAS teacher, department principal under Mrs. Pillsbury at the Morris Street School. Melissa Chamberlin, Dover, N.H., NEFAS teacher, principal of the Ashley Street School. Elizabeth H. Garland, Dover, N.H., NEFAS teacher, department principal under Dr. Hawkes at the Normal School.

41. Almira P. White, Exeter, N.H., NEFAS teacher. Letitia Sargent, Gloucester, Mass., NEFAS teacher.

42. Francis Carrier, Charleston, S.C., former house servant of Chancellor Dunkin.

43. Dr. James Moultrie, Charleston, S.C., president of the Archdale Street Unitarian Church.

44. Dr. Albert G. Mackey, Charleston, S.C., noted Mason and Unionist in Charleston.

45. Harriott Pinckney (b. 1776), daughter of Charles Cotesworth Pinckney of Revolutionary War fame. The 1860 census listed her as a "single lady." Mary Chesnut mentioned Miss Pinckney in her diary entry of April 8, 1861: "Went to see Miss Pinckney, one of the last of the 18th century Pinckneys. She inquired particularly about a portrait of her father, Charles Cotesworth Pinckney, which she said had been sent by him to my husband's grandfather. I gave a good account of it. It hangs in the place of honor in the drawing-room at Mulberry. She wanted to see my husband, for 'his grandfather, my father's friend, was one of the handsomest men of his day.'" Ben Ames Williams, ed., *A Diary from Dixie by Mary Boykin Chesnut* (Cambridge, Mass.: Harvard University Press, 1998), 33–34. Jane Amelia Postell Pettigru, Charleston, S.C., wife of Charleston lawyer James Louis Pettigru. Pettigru famously commented on learning that South Carolina had seceded from the Union, "South Carolina is too small to be a Republic, and too large to be an insane asylum."

46. The Reverend James Kendall Hosmer, D.D., Deerfield, Mass., educator, historian, and writer. Hosmer was the color bearer of the 52nd Massachusetts Regiment. Allen taught with Hosmer at Antioch College in the 1865–66 school year.

47. Nicholas Blaisdell, Boston, Mass., NEFAS teacher.

48. Lieutenant Colonel Charles Barnard Fox, Boston, Mass., 55th Massachusetts Regiment.

49. Captain Joseph T. Pratt, Philadelphia, Pa., 32nd USCT Regiment, provost marshal of Charleston. Lieutenant John W. Pollock, Pa., 32nd USCT Regiment. Lieutenant Colonel Rue Pugh Hutchins, Dayton Ohio, 94th Ohio Regiment.

50. Lieutenant Marshall N. Rice, 35th USCT Regiment Adjutant.

51. James Barrow, Charleston Unitarian leader, spoke at the memorial service for President Lincoln.

52. William Aiken, Charleston, S.C., former governor of South Carolina.

53. Judge Dennis N. Cooley, Dubuque, Iowa, had been brought to Charleston to settle disputed titles. Allen first met Cooley on St. Helena in April 1864.

54. Gilbert Pillsbury, Hamilton, Mass., abolitionist and commissioner of freedmen on Hilton Head, then Charleston when it fell, in February 1865. Pillsbury later became mayor of Charleston.

55. Joanna J. Weston or Maria F. Weston, both of whom are listed as teachers in the *Freedmen's Record* 1, no. 9 (September 1865), 139.

56. Thomas W. Cardozo, cofounder of the Avery Normal Institute. Allen met with Cardozo or visited his schools on ten occasions. He wrote Cardozo a letter dated May 30, 1865, titled "Organization of Charleston Schools," the purpose of which was to "explain our plan of operations with regard to the schools."

57. For an account of that Memorial Day, see Paul A. Shackel, *Memory in Black and White: Race, Commemoration, and Post-bellum Landscape* (Walnut Creek, Calif.: AltaMira Press, 2003), 25.

58. Colonel James Chaplin Beecher, Boston, Mass., 35th USCT Regiment. Beecher was the half brother of Harriet Beecher Stowe.

59. Brigadier General Alfred Stedman Hartwell, South Natick, Mass. Hartwell commanded a brigade, which included the 54th and 55th Massachusetts Regiments and the 102nd USCT Regiment. His command was deployed to Orangeburg, S.C.

60. Mr. Baker is unidentified. Possibly William A. Baker, who was a contributor to *Slave Songs*.

61. Lieutenant Colonel Amiel J. Willard, Albany, N.Y., 35th USCT Regiment. Willard was assigned as a prosecutor to the Office of the Judge Advocate in Charleston. He later sat on the Supreme Court of South Carolina during Reconstruction. Mrs. Willard's particulars are not known.

62. Captain Charles Carroll Soule, Brookline, Mass., 55th Massachusetts Regiment. Soule's regiment was soon reassigned to Orangeburg, S.C., where he served as chairman of the Board of Labor.

63. Captain Frank Goodwin, Boston, Mass., 55th Massachusetts Regiment. Goodwin was an old friend of the Lamberts, Allen's in-laws. Goodwin was on the staff of Brigadier General Edward E. Potter, N.Y., U.S. Volunteers. Potter's command made the last significant raid through South Carolina, in April 1865.

64. Nathaniel Topliff Allen, West Newton, Mass., Allen's cousin, founder and principal of the West Newton English and Classical School. James T. Allen, West Newton, Mass., associate principal of the West Newton School.

65. General John Porter Hatch, Oswego, N.Y., military commander of Charleston from February until August 1865.

66. William Channing Gannett, Boston, Mass., was superintendent of Fripp Point and Pine Grove when Allen was on St. Helena. William H. Alden, Westville, Conn., was superintendent of Frogmore, Woodlands, and Hope Place.

67. Allen's normal class was a class on teaching for teachers.

68. Ann Frances Ray Pillsbury, NEFAS teacher, principal of the Morris Street School, and Gilbert Pillsbury's wife.

69. Mr. McGill, Savannah, Ga., is unidentified.

70. Octavia C. Page, Watertown, Mass., NEFAS teacher.

71. Reconstruction meeting held at Hibernian Hall on May 11, 1865. The Hall, located at 105 Meeting Street, was constructed in 1840.

72. Robert Seymour Tharin, Charleston, S.C., Unionist.

73. Colonel (later General) William Gurney, New York, N.Y., Charleston post commander.

74. Colonel James Lynah, Charleston, S.C., former military man. Lynah was sixty-seven years old when the war began.

75. Charles Macbeth, Charleston, S.C., mayor. Macbeth surrendered the city to Colonel A. G. Bennett, 21st USCT Regiment.

76. Edward Mackey, Charleston, S.C., probably related to Dr. Mackey.

77. Colonel Robert W. Seymour, Charleston, S.C., long-time Charleston lawyer.

78. Allen's quip is an apparent reference to the recognized fact that there was no statue of John Winthrop, famous governor of the Massachusetts Bay Colony, in Boston. In other words, "Lynah, Macbeth, Seymour, &c.," like Winthrop, were nowhere to be found.

79. William Proctor, 33 Wentworth Street, Charleston, S.C., accountant for mercantile firms in Charleston.

80. Timothy Hurley, Boston, Mass., publisher of the *South Carolina Leader and Missionary Record,* a Charleston-based black newspaper.

81. Captain James William Grace, New Bedford, Mass., 54th Massachusetts Regiment. The Charleston Arsenal was an eleven-acre U.S. Army facility erected near the intersection of Ashley Avenue and Mill Street in 1841. It was taken from Confederate control when Charleston fell in February 1865.

82. Mary Cotton Redpath, Wolfeboro, N.H., James Redpath's wife. She was one of the originators of the Memorial Day observance at the Charleston Race Course on May 1, 1865, which Allen attended.

83. Bishop Daniel Alexander Payne, Bishop of the A.M.E. Church and president of Wilberforce College, Wilberforce, Ohio. Bishop Payne was in Charleston in May 1865 to reorganize the A.M.E. Church there. Colonel Edward Needles Hallowell, Philadelphia, Pa., commander of the 54th Massachusetts after the death of Robert Gould Shaw at Fort Wagner.

84. Garrison spoke at the Zion Church in Charleston on April 16, 1865, a meeting that Allen attended.

85. Mrs. Black is unidentified.

86. The screw steamer *General Lyon* (not the side wheeler USS *General Lyon*) burned, with the loss of six hundred lives, on a passage from North Carolina to Norfolk, Virginia, on March 17, 1865.

87. Captain Josiah C. White, 35th USCT Regiment.

88. Ironclad steam ram CSS *Columbia.* Gertrude Allen described the excursion in a May 21, 1865, letter to her parents: "We have just been down to see a rebel ram, or iron-clad uncle says is the name, lying at the wharf on the Cooper river. I believe she was run aground by the rebel pilot and then sunk. She is to go North soon, and we thought of taking passage, but finally concluded it was rather warm weather to perform the voyage in a boiler." (The *Columbia* was indeed soon taken north to Hampton Roads, Virginia, arriving there on May 25, 1865.)

89. Maria Traynor, Charleston, S.C. According to the National Archives collection of Confederate Papers, Mrs. Traynor received at least one Confederate pass during the war. She also received at least two Union passes during the occupation of Charleston: one for herself and three children on January 6, 1865, and another one for herself alone on August 31, 1865. Allen went to see Mrs. Traynor on his last day in Charleston, presumably to discuss her experiences in aiding Union prisoners, but she was not in. See July 22, 1865, diary entry.

90. For instances of Germans helping Union prisoners escape, see Captain Alured Larke and Captain R. H. Day, "Escaped Union Prisoners Of War to the Provost Marshal General of the Department of the South," *Statements of Escaped Union Prisoners, Refugees, & Confederate Deserters,* National Archives, Washington, D.C.

91. Andersonville Prison, also known as Camp Sumter, near Andersonville, Ga.

92. Washington Race Course in Charleston was founded in 1835. It was the site of a prisoner-of-war camp during the closing days of the war. Allen attended the Decoration Day ceremonies there on May 1, 1865.

93. The interest of German and Irish Charlestonians in Union prisoners is explained by noting that many of the prisoners were of German or Irish extraction.

94. Captain Edward Bulkeley Emerson, Pittsfield, Mass., 54th Massachusetts Regiment.

95. Judge Dennis N. Cooley, Dubuque, Iowa. Cooley had been appointed as a South Carolina tax commissioner when Allen was on St. Helena; he was appointed to settle disputed titles in Charleston after the war.

96. Dr. Henry O. Marcy, Boston, Mass., Regimental Surgeon of the 35th USCT Regiment.

97. Captain James Morris Walton, Pittsfield, Mass., judge advocate, 54th Massachusetts Regiment. Walton was in Orangeburg for the court-martial of Edward W. Andrews and others, which began on July 3, 1865. Allen quoted a Union officer, quite possibly Walton, in a letter to *Nation:* "Whoever wishes these people [Southern whites] more severely punished than they already are, must be very fond of revenge." Allen, "State of Things in South Carolina," *Nation* 1, no. 6 (August 10, 1865), 172.

98. Dr. Louis McPherson de Saussure, Charleston, S.C., established Charleston physician.

99. Roper Hospital was named for Colonel Thomas Roper, who in 1829 bequeathed $30,000 to the Medical Society of South Carolina to build a hospital to treat sick and injured people "without regard to complexion, religion, or nation." The hospital began admitting patients on a regular basis in 1856 in time for a succession of yellow fever, cholera, typhoid fever, and smallpox epidemics that ravaged the city. The hospital was seized by the federal government in February 1865. Dr. Charles Edward Briggs, Pembroke, Mass., Surgeon, 54th Massachusetts Regiment.

100. Allen's diary shows that he wrote numerous letters concerning Gertrude in the week following her death.

101. Minda Robertson, Ashley Street School pupil, is unidentified.

102. Mr. Dickerson is unidentified.

103. A handwritten copy of Chavis's resolution, dated June 16, 1865, resides in the South Caroliniana Library at the University of South Carolina in Columbia.

104. Possibly Thomas and Margaret Parker, Charleston, S.C. The 1870 census listed Thomas and Margaret Parker as property owners in Charleston Ward 4, which was adjacent to Ward 6, where Allen resided.

105. Alfred Huger Dunkin, possibly the namesake of the antisecessionist Charleston postmaster Alfred Huger.

106. Mrs. C. W. Clausen, Charleston, S.C., teacher in Dr. Hawkes's Normal School, listed as a teacher in the *Freedmen's Record* 1, no. 9 (September 1865), 139.

107. Robert Barnwell Rhett Jr., Harvard class of 1849, leading secessionist and owner of the *Charleston Mercury.*

108. Alfred Moore Rhett, Harvard class of 1851, brother of Barnwell Rhett.

109. Colonel William Ransom Calhoun, killed in a duel with Lieutenant Colonel Alfred Rhett on September 5, 1862.

110. Mrs. Oxley and daughter are unidentified Charlestonians.

111. Mrs. Little, Charleston, S.C., is unidentified.

112. Possibly either E. P. or E. F. Beaird. Both men were included in Charleston city listings in the 1870s. E. P. was a teacher, and E. F. was an upholsterer.

113. Lieutenant James F. Haviland, New York, N.Y., 127th New York Regiment.

114. Sarah F. Prescott, Boston, Mass., NEFAS teacher.

115. John C. Chavis, ardent supporter of James Redpath.

116. Quash, Charleston, S.C., is an unidentified black barber. Allen had his hair cut on May 25, possibly by Quash.

117. Edward Gray Stetson, Lexington, Mass., superintendent of Dr. Jenkins Place near Land's End when Allen was on St. Helena.

118. The Reverend Ulysses L. Houston, Savannah, Ga., black pastor of First Bryan Baptist Church. Houston became "governor" of about a thousand freedmen on Skidaway Island, on the basis of assumed rights conferred by General Sherman's Field Order 15 (promise of forty acres and a mule).

119. Captain F. M. Montell, New York, U.S. naval officer, later, Freedmen's Bureau agent in Berkeley County, S.C. The Reverend Dr. Anthony Toomer Porter, Charleston, S.C., founder of the Porter-Gaud School in Charleston. Allen quoted Porter in a letter to the *Nation:* "We went into this contest believing we were in the right—we have fought and been beaten—now we submit in thorough good faith, and desire to become loyal citizens of the United States." Allen, "A Trip in South Carolina," *Nation* 1, no. 4 (July 27, 1865), 106.

120. Fort Delaware was a fortress on Pea Patch Island in New Castle County, Del., used as a prison for Confederate soldiers. See Captain John Sterling Swann's contemporary account, *Prison Life at Fort Delaware.*

121. First Lieutenant Edmund Mazyck, Charleston, S.C., Provisional Confederate Army. Mazyck served with distinction as an artillery officer during the defense of Fort Wagner on Morris Island, S.C. He later served with the Army of Northern Virginia. He attended the Medical College of South Carolina after the war, graduating in the class of 1880. His headstone inscription is "Lieutenant Doctor Edmund Mazyck." Allen quoted him in a letter to the *Nation:* "I have taken the oath to support the Constitution . . . and I mean to keep it. I am not convinced that I was wrong, still I am bound now to fight to put down secession." Of the prospects for the freedmen, Allen quoted him as saying, "Peace we have, and prosperity is coming; but not for them." Allen, "A Trip in South Carolina," 106.

122. Ellen M. Lee, Templeton, Mass., NEFAS teacher. Miss Campbell possibly conducted a school near Springfield, Mass., about fifty miles from Templeton. Abiah Root, a close friend of Emily Dickinson, attended the school.

123. A. S. Jenks, Philadelphia, Pa., whom Allen listed as a contributor to *Slave Songs.* Jenks became controller of the Philadelphia school system in 1868.

124. Walter P. and Mary E. Cupp, Middletown, Va. Allen later referred to his experience at the Cupp's : Allen, "A Trip in South Carolina," 106. The Cupps had fled Frederick County, Virginia, after the Battle of Cedar Creek, which was fought near Middletown on October 19, 1864. Cupp's Ford on Cedar Creek and Cupp's Mill are in the vicinity of Middletown.

125. Brigadier General Charles Henry van Wyck, Bloomingburg, N.Y., congressman from New York, later a U.S. senator from Nebraska. Colonel Nathaniel Haughton, Washington Township, Lucas County, Ohio, commander, 25th Ohio Volunteers.

126. Mr. Taylor, Columbia, S.C., colored man in whose home Allen spent the night of July 5, 1865. Allen alluded to Taylor in an essay in the *Christian Examiner.* He related how "He [Taylor] happened to be visiting upon a plantation near Columbia, when General Sherman's army passed through, and says that the 'Yankee soldiers' hung him three times to make him confess where the owner of the plantation had hidden his silver,—which he did not know." Allen, "South Carolina, One of the United States," *Christian Examiner* 79 (September 1865), 234n.

127. Allen recounted these incidents in "The Southern Whites," *Nation* 1, no. 11 (September 14, 1865), 332.

128. Major George Edward Gouraud, New York, N.Y., 55th Massachusetts Regiment. Gouraud won the Medal of Honor at the Battle of Honey Hill, S.C., November 30, 1864. He

gained fame later for introducing Edison recording technology to England in 1888. Thomas Berwick Legare, Orangeburg, S.C.

129. Major Calvin S. Montague, Kalamazoo, Mich., 102nd USCT Regiment, Board of Labor chairman at Orangeburg.

130. George Alfred Trenholm, Charleston, S.C., last Confederate secretary of the Treasury. Allen quoted Trenholm as saying, "The people of South Carolina are too weary and sick at heart to think of politics; all they want is peace." Allen, "The Southern Whites," 331.

131. Allen expounded on his own views on the suffrage (black and white) in "The Basis of Suffrage," *Nation* 1, no. 12 (September 21, 1865), 362–64.

132. See the notice of June 21, 1865, by Captain Soule: *Chairman of the Orangeburg, South Carolina, Commission on Contracts to the Freedmen's Bureau Commissioner, Enclosing a Speech to the Freepeople; and the Commissioner's Reply*. First Lieutenant Henry Hobart Alvord, Bay City, Mich., 102nd USCT Regiment, member of the Board of Labor at Orangeburg. Second Lieutenant James Monroe Trotter, Cincinnati, Ohio, 55th Massachusetts Regiment.

133. For an account of the July 1865 Charleston riots, see Robert J. Zalimas Jr., in John David Smith, ed., *Black Soldiers in Blue* (Chapel Hill: University of North Carolina Press, 2002), 374–80. "A Disturbance in the City: Black and White Soldiers in Postwar Charleston."

134. Brevet Brigadier General W. T. Bennett, Detroit, Mich., 102nd USCT Regiment. Bennett succeeded General Gurney.

135. Possibly Confederate Private Richard E. Jaques, who wrote a series of letters to his sweetheart, L. A. Syme, during the siege of Charleston.

136. Roswell T. Logan, Charleston, S.C., associate editor, the *Charleston Daily News,* and Edmund Welson (Wilson in the 1850 census), Anderson District, S.C. Logan was the anonymous "Mr. O." whom Allen quoted in a letter to the *Nation:*

> [Mr. O.] answered in general terms that . . . the people of the State were fully convinced of the failure of the rebellion, and desired in good faith to return under the government of the Union; and that they were also convinced that slavery was at an end and were ready to do whatever was necessary to try the experiment of free labor. . . . Mr. O. told me that as soon as possible after our occupation he called his house-slaves together, and told them they were free now to get work where they could, and he was free to hire whom he liked; that it was probable it would be better for both parties to make a change, as there would be some embarrassment in keeping together under their new relation; however, that was for them to decide, and they need be in no haste about the decision, as they could stay with him until they made up their minds. . . . Mr. O. looked upon the prospect of free labor more hopefully than most Southerners. He considered it still an experiment, in which large numbers of the negroes would perish, but which would eventually succeed.

From Allen, "Feeling of the South Carolinians," *Nation* 1, no. 8 (August 24, 1865), 237–38.

137. Allen went to Johns and James Islands to assess the progress of black farmers, who were working land without white intervention. He described the results as "highly encouraging." Allen, "State of Things in South Carolina," 172.

138. Ellen S. Kempton, New Bedford, Mass., NEFAS teacher. Elmira B. Stanton, Lowell, Mass., NEFAS teacher.

139. "It was a well conducted affair—managed, I believe, by a ladies' sewing circle, and for the benefit of the poor." Allen, "State of Things in South Carolina," 172.

140. Maria Traynor, Charleston, S.C. Allen related how Mrs. Traynor assisted Union prisoners at the race course prison in Charleston. See May 24, 1865, journal entry.

141. U.S. Mail Steamship Company vessel.

Epilogue

1. Allen's letters and diary from 1867 provide insights into the publication of *Slave Songs of the United States*. See William F. Allen Family Papers, Wisconsin Historical Society, Mss 384, Box 1, Folder 4, and Box 2, Folder 6.

2. Margaret Loring Andrews Allen died March 20, 1924, in Madison, Wis. She is buried with her husband in Forest Hill Cemetery in Madison.

3. Andrews Allen received a B.S. in civil engineering from the University of Wisconsin in 1891. He died on March 21, 1931. His son and grandson presently live in the Minneapolis, Minn., area. William Ware Allen received a B.A. in history from the University of Wisconsin in 1894 and an LL.B. in 1896. He practiced law in Madison, Wis. He died on August 27, 1898. Philip Loring Allen graduated Phi Beta Kappa with a B.L. (Bachelor of Letters) from the University of Wisconsin in 1899. He authored the book *America's Awakening: The Triumph of Righteousness in High Places* (New York: Fleming H. Revell, 1906). The Philip Loring Allen Dissertation Fellowship at the University of Wisconsin is awarded in his honor. He died on May 26, 1908. Katharine Allen graduated Phi Beta Kappa with a B.L. from the University of Wisconsin in 1887, and she went on to become a professor there, retiring as assistant professor of Latin in 1930. She died on August 12, 1940, from injuries suffered in an automobile accident near Whitewater, Wis., forty-five miles southeast of Madison. All of William Allen's children are buried in Forest Hill Cemetery in Madison.

4. Lucy McKim Garrison was the daughter of James Miller McKim, leader of the Philadelphia-based Port Royal Relief Committee. Nineteen-year-old, Lucy accompanied her father on an inspection tour of the islands in June 1862, and she became enthralled with the songs of the slaves. In November 1862, she wrote an historic letter titled "Songs of the Port Royal 'Contrabands'" to *Dwight's Journal of Music*.

5. Wendell Phillips Garrison was an editor of the *Nation*. He was the third son of the abolitionist William Lloyd Garrison and was named after the elder Garrison's colleague Wendell Phillips.

6. Dena J. Epstein, *Sinful Tunes and Spirituals: Black Folk Music to the Civil War* (Urbana: University of Illinois Press 2003), 303–58.

7. W. F. Allen, "Southern Negro Folk-Lore," *Dial* 1, no. 9 (January 1881), 183–85.

8. William Francis Allen, Untitled Letter, Boston *Daily Advertiser* 108, no. 7 (July 10, 1866), 2. This article was given the inferred title "Homesteads for Negroes" in David B. Frankenburger, Reuben G. Thwaites, Frederick J. Turner, and Joseph H. Crocker, eds., *Essays and Monographs by William Francis Allen* (Boston: Geo. H. Ellis, 1890), 372. The article to which Allen replied was Anonymous, "Practical Reconstruction," Boston *Daily Advertiser* 107, no. 149 (June 23, 1866), 2. The Homestead Act of 1866, which passed June 21, 1866, opened 46 million acres of land for public sale in Alabama, Arkansas, Florida, Louisiana, and Mississippi.

9. Frankenburger et al., *Essays and Monographs*, 353–81.

10. Ibid., 13.

11. Ibid., 16.

12. The writings of other Northerners who spent time in Civil War South Carolina are helpful in studying the state at that time. See Henry Noble Sherwood, ed., "Journal of Miss Susan Walker, March 3d to June 6th, 1862," *Quarterly Publication of the Historical and Philosophical Society of Ohio* 7, no. 1 (January–March 1912); Rupert Sargent Holland, ed., *Letters and Diary of Laura M. Towne Written for the Sea Islands of South Carolina 1862–1884* (Cambridge, Mass.: Riverside Press, 1912); Charlotte Forten, "Life on the Sea Islands, Part I," *Atlantic Monthly* 13 (May 1864), 587–96, and Forten, "Life on the Sea Islands, Part II," *Atlantic Monthly* 3 (June 1864), 666–76; Thomas Wentworth Higginson, *Army Life in a Black Regiment*

(Boston: Fields, Osgood and Co., 1870), and Christopher Looby, ed., *The Complete Civil War Journal and Selected Letters of Thomas Wentworth Higginson* (Chicago: University of Chicago Press, 2000); Austa French, *Slavery in South Carolina and the Ex-Slaves; or the Port Royal Mission* (New York: Winchell M. French, 1862); Caroline E. Janney, ed., *The South as It Is: John Richard Dennett* (Tuscaloosa: University of Alabama Press, 2010); Elizabeth Hyde Botume, *First Days amongst the Contrabands* (Boston: Lee and Shepard, 1893); and Elizabeth Ware Pearson, ed., *Letters from Port Royal Written at the Time of the Civil War* (Boston: W. B. Clarke Company, 1906).

Appendix A

1. For a description of the various freedmen's aid organizations and the interrelations among them, see Henry Lee Swint, *The Northern Teacher in the South, 1862–1870* (Nashville: Vanderbilt University Press, 1941).

2. Judges 6–8.

3. Henry Noble Sherwood, "Journal of Miss Susan Walker, March 3d to June 6th, 1862," *Quarterly Publication of the Historical and Philosophical Society of Ohio* 7, no. 1, 47–48.

4. The *Oriental* was shipwrecked off Bodie Island thirty-three miles north of Cape Hatteras in late May 1862.

5. Octavius Brooks Frothingham, "Education and Religion," *Independent*, July 12, 1866.

Selected Bibliography

Allen, William F. Family Papers. Wisconsin Historical Society, MSS 384 and Microfilm 33.

Allen, William Francis. "The War Policy, and the Future of the South." *Christian Examiner* 73 (November 1862), 435–54.

———. "Democracy on Trial." *Christian Examiner* 74 (March 1863), 262–94.

———. "The Freedmen and Free Labor in the South." *Christian Examiner* (May 1864), 344–74.

———. "Free Labor in Louisiana." *Christian Examiner* 78 (May 1865), 383–99.

———. "South Carolina, One of the United States." *Christian Examiner* 79 (September 1865), 226–51.

———. "A Trip in South Carolina." *Nation* 1, no. 4 (July 27, 1865), 106–7.

———. "State of Things in South Carolina." *Nation* 1, no. 6 (August 10, 1865), 172–73.

———. "Feeling of the South Carolinians." *Nation* 1, no. 8 (August 24, 1865), 238–39.

———. "The Southern Whites." *Nation* 1, no. 11 (September 14, 1865), 331–32.

———. "The Basis of Suffrage." *Nation* 1, no. 12 (September 21, 1865), 362–64.

———, "The Negro Dialect." *Nation* 1, no. 24 (December 14, 1865), 744–45.

——— Untitled Letter. Boston *Daily Advertiser* 108, no. 7 (July 10, 1866), 2. Reprinted as "Homesteads for Negroes" in David B. Frankenburger, Reuben G. Thwaites, Frederick J. Turner, and Joseph H. Crocker, eds., *Essays and Monographs by William Francis Allen.* Boston: Geo. H. Ellis, 1890.

———. "Southern Negro Folk-Lore." *Dial* 1, no. 9 (January 1881), 183–85.

———, Charles Pickard Ware, and Lucy McKim Garrison, eds. *Slave Songs of the United States.* New York: A. Simpson, 1867.

Atkinson, Edward. *First Annual Report of the Educational Commission for Freedmen.* Boston: David Clapp, 1863.

———. *Second Annual Report of the New England Freedmen's Aid Society* (Educational Commission). Boston: NEFAS Printing Office, 1864.

Billingsley, Andrew. *Yearning to Breathe Free: Robert Smalls of South Carolina and His Families.* Columbia: University of South Carolina Press, 2007.

Billington, Ray Allen. *Frederick Jackson Turner: Historian, Scholar, Teacher.* New York: Oxford University Press, 1973.

Botume, Elizabeth Hyde. *First Days amongst the Contrabands.* Boston: Lee and Shepard, 1893.

Clarke, Erskine. *Dwelling Place: A Plantation Epic.* New Haven: Yale University Press, 2005.

Coker, Michael D. *The Battle of Port Royal.* Charleston: The History Press, 2009.

Dargan, William T. *Lining Out the Word.* Berkeley: University of California Press, 2006.

Epstein, Dena J., *Sinful Tunes and Spirituals: Black Folk Music to the Civil War.* Urbana: University of Illinois Press, 2003.

Foner, Eric. *Reconstruction: America's Unfinished Revolution.* New York: Harper and Row, 1988.

Forten, Charlotte. "Life on the Sea Islands, Parts I and II." *Atlantic Monthly* 13 (May–June 1864), 587–96, 666–76.

Frankenburger, David B., Reuben G. Thwaites, Frederick J. Turner, and Joseph H. Crocker, eds. *Essays and Monographs by William Francis Allen.* Boston: Geo. H. Ellis, 1890.

French, Austa. *Slavery in South Carolina and the Ex-Slaves; or the Port Royal Mission.* New York: Winchell M. French, 1862.

Higginson, Thomas Wentworth. *Army Life in a Black Regiment.* Boston: Fields, Osgood and Co., 1870.

Holland, Rupert Sargent, ed. *Letters and Diary of Laura M. Towne Written from the Sea Islands of South Carolina 1862–1884.* Cambridge, Mass.: Riverside Press, 1912.

Jackson, George Pullen. *White and Negro Spirituals.* Locust Valley, N.Y.: J. J. Augustin, 1943.

Janney, Caroline E., ed. *The South as It Is: John Richard Dennett.* Tuscaloosa: University of Alabama Press, 2010.

Johnson, Guion Griffis. *A Social History of the Sea Islands: With Special Reference to St. Helena Island, South Carolina.* Chapel Hill: University of North Carolina Press, 1930.

Joyner, Charles. *Down by the Riverside: A South Carolina Slave Community.* Urbana: University of Illinois Press, 1984.

Kimball, M. G., ed. *New England Freedmen's Aid Society Freedmen's Record.* Cambridge, Mass.: John Wilson and Sons, 1865.

Looby, Christopher, ed. *The Complete Civil War Journal and Selected Letters of Thomas Wentworth Higginson.* Chicago: University of Chicago Press, 2000.

McKivigan, John R. *Forgotten Firebrand: James Redpath and the Making of Nineteenth-Century America.* Ithaca, N.Y.: Cornell University Press, 2008.

McRea, Bennie J., Jr., Curtis M. Miller, and Cheryl Trowbridge-Miller. *Nineteenth Century Freedom Fighters: The 1st South Carolina Volunteers.* Charleston: Arcadia, 2006.

Mott, Frank Luther, "The Christian Disciple and the Christian Examiner." *New England Quarterly* 1, no. 2 (April 1928), 197–207.

Nathans, Sydney. *To Free a Family: The Journey of Mary Walker.* Cambridge, Mass.: Harvard University Press, 2012.

Owen, Robert Dale, James McKaye, and Samuel G. Howe. *Preliminary Report Touching the Condition and Management of Emancipated Refugees.* New York: John F. Trow, 1863.

Pearson, Elizabeth Ware, ed. *Letters from Port Royal Written at the Time of the Civil War.* Boston: W. B. Clarke, 1906.

Robbins, Gerald. "The Sea Island Experiment 1861–1865." Master's thesis, University of Wisconsin, 1959.

———. "William F. Allen: Classical Scholar among the Slaves." *History of Education Quarterly* 5 (December 1965), 211–23.

Rose, Willie Lee. *Rehearsal for Reconstruction: The Port Royal Experiment.* Athens: University of Georgia Press, 1964.

Spaulding, Henry George. "Under the Palmetto." *Continental Monthly* 4, no. 2 (August 1863), 188–203.

Sherwood, Henry Noble, ed. "Journal of Miss Susan Walker, March 3d to June 6th, 1862." *Quarterly Publication of the Historical and Philosophical Society of Ohio* 7, no. 1 (January–March 1912).

Stearns, Owen Philip. "William Francis Allen: Wisconsin's First Historian." Master's thesis, University of Wisconsin, 1955.

Swint, Henry Lee. *The Northern Teacher in the South, 1862–1870*. Nashville: Vanderbilt University Press, 1941.

Taylor, Susie King. *Reminiscences of My Life in Camp with the 33D United States Colored Troops, Late 1st South Carolina Volunteers*. Boston: Susie King Taylor, 1902.

Vandervelde, Isabel. *Aiken County: The Only South Carolina County Founded during Reconstruction*. Spartanburg, S.C.: Art Studio Press, 1999.

Williams, Ben Ames, ed. *A Diary from Dixie by Mary Boykin Chesnut*. Cambridge, Mass.: Harvard University Press, 1998.

Williamson, Joel. *After Slavery: The Negro in South Carolina During Reconstruction, 1861–1877*. New York: W. W. Norton, 1975.

Index